RURAL INDIGENOUSNESS

THE IROQUOIS AND THEIR NEIGHBORS

Christopher Vecsey, *Series Editor*

SELECT TITLES IN THE IROQUOIS AND THEIR NEIGHBORS SERIES

Rural Indigenousness

A HISTORY OF IROQUOIAN AND ALGONQUIAN PEOPLES OF THE ADIRONDACKS

Melissa Otis

Syracuse University Press

∞ The paper used in this publication meets the minimum requirements
of the American National Standard for Information Sciences—Permanence
of Paper for Printed Library Materials, ANSI Z39.48-1992.

For a listing of books published and distributed by Syracuse University
Press, visit www.SyracuseUniversityPress.syr.edu.

ISBN: 978-0-8156-3596-3 (hardcover)   978-0-8156-3600-7 (paperback)
978-0-8156-5453-7 (e-book)

Library of Congress Cataloging-in-Publication Data
Names: Otis, Melissa, author.
Title: Rural indigenousness : a history of Iroquoian and Algonquian
    peoples of the Adirondacks / Melissa Otis.
Description: Syracuse, New York : Syracuse University Press, [2018] |
    Series: The Iroquois and Their Neighbors | Includes bibliographical
    references and index.
Identifiers: LCCN 2018040335 (print) | LCCN 2018043462 (ebook) |
    ISBN 9780815654537 (e-book) | ISBN 9780815635963 (hardcover :
    alk. paper) | ISBN 9780815636007 (pbk. : alk. paper)
Subjects: LCSH: Iroquoian Indians—New York (State)—Adirondack
    Mountains—History. | Algonquian Indians—New York (State)—
    Adirondack Mountains—History.
Classification: LCC E99.I69 (ebook) | LCC E99.I69 O85 2018 (print) |
    DDC 974.7/50049755—dc23
LC record available at https://lccn.loc.gov/2018040335

Contents

Illustrations

Acknowledgments

THIS PROJECT took more than seven years to complete (on paper), and I have many people to acknowledge and thank. I could not have accomplished the writing of this book alone. Any mistakes are, of course, my own. In reality, this undertaking encompassed a lifetime, and it helped me to find my way home. Thus, I must first thank my parents for having the good sense to raise my sisters and me in the Adirondacks, a beautiful haven to grow up in. I only wish they were still here to read the completed effort. In addition, I must thank the work itself for reuniting me with family and friends still living in the Adirondacks; they were always in my heart but we had not been physically connected for many years. I also need to acknowledge the influence of Ray Tehanetorens Fadden, whose Six Nations Indian Museum in Onchiota, New York, and his life as an educator sparked a lifelong desire in me to learn about the history of the Indigenous people of New York State and elsewhere. Mr. Fadden inspired me to appreciate the varied and rich culture and history of the Iroquoian, Algonquian, and other Indigenous peoples of North America. Visiting the museum as a young Girl Scout taught me to look beyond the stereotypes, and this lesson remained with me all of my life.

I would next like to express my deep gratitude to Dr. Cecilia Morgan for her professional guidance and valuable support and, above all, her patience as she edited and without judgment guided me back to the world of the historian. I want to also thank Dr. Ruth Sandwell, who provided me guidance and opportunities to network and teach, and Dr. Heidi Bohaker, who gave useful and constructive feedback on my chapters as well as networking and coaching advice. I am also very appreciative of the feedback provided by Dr. Alice Nash of the University of Massachusetts–Amherst, whose comments led to some breakthrough moments. Each of these scholars offered me many ways to think about and consider my work. To all of you, I am very grateful.

I also wish to express my appreciation to Dr. James Rice, Dr. Marge Bruchac, and Dr. Carl Benn for their valuable and useful suggestions and willingness to give their time, which was very much appreciated. A special thanks goes to Dr. Christopher Roy, whose work on the Abenaki and his willingness to share information with me was invaluable. I am grateful to the writing groups that helped me consider my work, including the Toronto Environmental History Group, the Labor History Group, and especially the Indigenous History Writing Group. Their feedback was instrumental and assisted in countless ways.

I would also like to acknowledge the generous financial assistance provided by the University of Toronto's Guaranteed Funding, Doctoral Completion Award, and Research Travel Grant Awards. I want to also recognize the conference funding grants I received, including those from the Graduate Student Association, the University of Toronto, and several professional organizations. Their generosity allowed me to present my work and receive additional feedback. I am especially grateful to the Conference on Iroquois Research, American Society for Ethnohistory, and the Canadian Historical Association/Société historique du Canada. Finally, I want to thank the Social Sciences and Humanities Research Council of Canada for its substantial funding of my postdoctoral fellowship at Carleton University under the sponsorship of Dr. Ruth Phillips. All of this support combined provided me the opportunity to research and finalize this historical narrative.

I am particularly grateful for the assistance given to me by current and former Adirondackers John Kahionhes Fadden of the Six Nations Museum at Onchiota, Martha Lee Owens, the late Clarence Petty, Beverly Locke and her sister Edith Russell, and the late Philip Straight Arrow Joseph for their interest, suggestions, and sharing of stories. A special thanks goes to John Fadden and Phil Joseph for literally spending years with me as I crafted this book, and to their wives, Eva

Thompson Fadden and Wilma Black Joseph, for their hospitality and patience with my interruptions into their daily lives. I hope my work accurately and respectfully expresses everyone's contributions.

I am indebted to and must thank dozens of archivists and local historians for their thoughtful and sometimes daunting assistance with the collection of data. I have to especially acknowledge Bill Zulo, the former historian and curator of the Indian Lake Museum and former Hamilton County historian, for his support and generosity of time. Bill went out of his way to provide me access and put up with my many questions and requests to view material at the Indian Lake Museum, which was often closed when I wanted to visit. Also, my thanks go to the staff of the Adirondack Museum in Blue Mountain Lake, including Jerry Pepper, research library librarian; Laura Rice, director; and Angela Snye, Hallie Bond, and other members of the staff whom I relentlessly pestered and who graciously put up with me. They, too, went out of their way to provide me access to the museum, library archives, and stored material objects.

Because I received so much help from the amazing staff of archives large and small throughout the Adirondacks and elsewhere, I will acknowledge them based on my chronological visits. I cannot thank them enough. This long list includes Raymond W. Smith, Long Lake archivist, now retired; Jennifer Kuba, librarian of the Adirondack History Center Museum; Michele Tucker, curator at the Adirondack Research Room of the Saranac Lake Free Library; the Clinton County Historical Association; Mark McMurray, curator of Special Collections and university archivist at St. Lawrence University; Janet Moore, local history librarian of the Potsdam Library; Emma Remington, director of the Parishville Museum and town historian, as well as her assistant, Joseph McGill; Christopher D. Fox, curator at the Thompson-Pell Research Center at Fort Ticonderoga; Andy Kolovos, archivist and folklorist at the Vermont Folklife Center; Janet Hall, Keene historian; Janet Cross, retired deputy clerk of Essex County and patient teacher of how to conduct research in a county clerk's office; the librarian and archivist at the Keene Valley Library; Prudence Doherty, librarian of Special Collections at the University of Vermont;

the site administrator at the Chimney Point State Historic Site; the archivists at the Vermont State Archives and Records; Paul Carnahan, librarian of the Leahy Library for the Vermont Historical Society; the librarians at the Feinberg Library's Special Collections; the librarians for the Adirondack Collection at the North Country Community College Library; Anne Weaver, Lake Pleasant town historian; Amy Peters, the interim Hamilton County historian; the staff at the Northville Public Library; the late Lynne Billington, Piseco Lake town historian and thoughtful hostess who graciously invited a lone traveler to attend their historical association meeting; the staff of the Hamilton County Clerk's Office; the librarians of the Akwesasne Cultural Center Library, and especially Sue Ellen Herne, the Akwesasne Museum program coordinator, for all of her assistance; the staff of the Wead Library of Malone; Kay Ionataie:was Olan for her thorough research and survey of Native artifacts along the Champlain Valley and for her permission to copy those found on the New York State side; the staff of the New York State Library, Manuscripts and Special Collections, especially Helen E. Weltin; historian Beverly P. Reid and former director Patricia Perez of the Lake Placid Public Library's research room; Gary and Shelly Glebus, Schroon Lake's town historian and his wife, for sharing their hospitality as well as local information; Doris Cohen, for sharing her vast collection and memories of local families; Linda Auclair, director of the Goff Nelson Memorial Library; director Gail Murray and the staff of the Town of Wells Historical Society and Goodsell Museum Research Room for their enthusiastic response to my requests; the staff of the Melvil Dewey Library and Media Center at Jefferson Community College; archivist Doris Lamont and executive director Jamie Purillo at the Saratoga Springs History Museum; City of Saratoga Springs historian, Mary Ann Fitzgerald; the staff of the Saratoga County Historical Society and Brookside Museum; Teri Blasko at the Saratoga Springs Public Library; Jean Woutersz, town of Wilton historian; archivist Erica Wolfe Burke and director Todd DeGarmo at the Center for Folklife, History and Cultural Programs at the Crandall Public Library; John Austin, Warren County historian; Tom Lynch, (retired) records manager of the very impressive

Warren County Clerk's Office—Records Center and Archive; Melitta White, reference librarian for the local history collection at Adirondack Community College; Jane O'Connell, librarian at the Hillview Free Library; the staff of the Washington County Historical Society's Research Library; Richard "Rick" Hill, program director for the Indigenous Knowledge Centre (IKC) at the Six Nations Polytechnic at Six Nations of the Grand River Territory; and the staff at the National Archives of Canada. Finally, I want to express my gratitude to the staff at Syracuse University Press for their assistance with the publication of this book, especially to Alison Maura Shay and to the book's mapmaker, cartographer Joe Stoll of Syracuse University's geography department.

I would like to offer a special thanks to Adirondack family and friends who insisted I stay with them and put up with me during my travels. They fed me in multiple ways for days at a time so I could complete my research. These special people in my life include Harry Otis Gough and Maggie Bartley, Tracy and Joyce Spooner, and Heather Lamb, as well as my sister Kelli, whose "part-way there" stopover and hospitality was welcome on a number of occasions. These were not the only people to open up their homes to me; I also want to thank Paul and Darlene Hooper and Sharyn Hutchins, who fed me from their family's table and offered their welcome during this period. And I thank my brother-in-law, Richard Dixon for loaning me his digital camera. I'm afraid the hundreds of pictures snapped took a toll on its lifespan. If I have forgotten anyone, please accept my apologies—I received so much support it has been difficult to remember everyone. To all of you I express my gratitude.

Finally, I want to thank my immediate family, who have been nothing but supportive of this rather unorthodox journey. To my daughter, Sarah, thank you for being my inspiration to strive to become the best adult me possible. Even now, I am most proud to be known as Sarah's mom. I also want to posthumously acknowledge my parents, Audrey L. MacKenzie and Gregory P. Otis, for their lifelong support and encouragement. Their love of learning and of the arts, combined with an amazing sense of humor and capacity to love have guided me throughout my life. Also, to my sister Kelli who forced me out of my self-imposed cocoon on more than one occasion, thank you for providing some balance in my life. And much appreciation to my mother-in-law, Alice Dixon, and my uncle, James MacKenzie, whose interest and stories provided needed encouragement, especially as the years wore on. Most especially, I need and want to thank and acknowledge the countless forms of support provided by my husband, Gregory P. Dixon. You provided the financial and emotional support I needed to complete this project. I am a lucky woman to have a husband who is always ready for adventure. For all your love and support, I am eternally grateful. I dedicate this book to you.

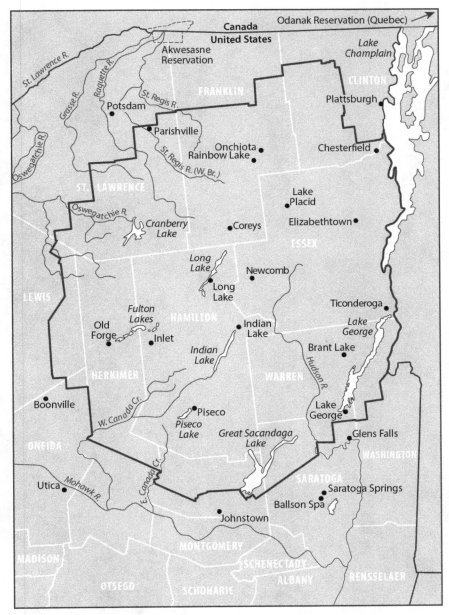

Adirondack region map. Courtesy of Syracuse University Cartography Laboratory.

Rural Indigenousness

Introduction

"Our Collection on Native Americans Is Limited"

REFERENCES CONTAINED in local histories about the relationship of Native Americans to the Adirondacks have changed over time. For example, Martin V. B. Ives's 1899 *Through the Adirondacks in Eighteen Days* claims, "On leaving Saratoga one enters at once, if he travels north, a country where every rock, tree and hill has an aboriginal history."[1] Ten years later, Henry Raymond noted, "There are scarcely any records of the Indian ownership of this vast region and few traces of its occupation."[2] By 1921, Alfred L. Donaldson concluded, "The consensus of authoritative opinion seems to be that the Indians never made any part of what is now the Adirondack Park their permanent home."[3] While these statements appear contradictory, they are typical of the thinking about the history of Indigenous peoples in the Adirondacks, a mountainous area in northeastern New York State. Today the region is a well-known state park, but prior to the twentieth century its ruggedness created a sense of mystery about this place. For the purposes of this book, the park is considered synonymous with the geographic region that sometimes expands its borders.

While nineteenth-century observers were perhaps more sensitive to the Aboriginal presence in the Adirondacks, by the twentieth century

Some of the content from chapters 1 and 2 was previously published in *Environment, Space, Place* 5, no. 2 (2013) under the title "Location of Exchange: Algonquian and Iroquoian Occupation in the Adirondacks Before and After Contact."

this awareness of their presence was becoming increasingly rare. Even recent scholarship suggests the area was unoccupied by humans prior to the arrival of Europeans, aside from its occasional use as a hunting territory. Not only is this lack of a Native presence apparent in the scholarship about the region, but it is often the prevailing perspective of those who live there. I grew up in the eastern part of Adirondacks, and I can vouch for the belief in a lack of history about Indigenous peoples occupying and using this space except as an intangible hunting territory. My research began as a means of questioning the validity of the assumptions about the lack of a history of Native peoples in the Adirondacks. The results uncovered a story waiting to be told.

This book is about making visible the history of Algonquian and Iroquoian peoples who called this region their homeland over the centuries. The sources show that the Adirondacks have been an Indigenous homeland for millennia and that Native people were visible to the Europeans and Euro-Americans who came to the region as early as the seventeenth century and well into the nineteenth, and that it was late nineteenth and twentieth century historians who made them invisible. This book is also a study of how Indigenous culture continued and changed under settler colonialism within this geographic space, which was not much suited to commercial farming. As a result, other occupations emerged into which Native peoples could fit and may have helped lay the groundwork for wilderness tourism in the Adirondacks. Ultimately, the book is a history of the survival of Iroquoian and Algonquian peoples in a nonreservation, rural environment up to the present time.

To understand Indigenous peoples' affiliation with the Adirondacks, one has to expand the geographic reach to include parts of today's upstate New York, New England, and southern Quebec and Ontario as these regions affected who, when, why, and how Iroquoian and Algonquian peoples came there. In countless ways, this is a story about labor as it shifted over time to accommodate changing economic needs; it is also much more. As imperial borders in North America were modified and solidified into national borders by the early nineteenth century, interactions between these Native peoples and the settlers and tourists who came to the Adirondack region created complex and changing notions of identity. Despite their rustic setting, the Adirondacks were (and still are) a complex place for anyone trying to make a living and raise a family there, and the area's story does not easily fit into neat categories.

This book focuses especially on the history of the Mohawk from Akwesasne and on Abenaki with ties to Odanak during the long nineteenth century, an era that encompasses the period after the American Revolution and up to World War I. Along with the Oneida, these are the peoples who most often called this region home and continued to occupy the Adirondacks in changing ways. In particular, this history explores the "St. Regis" (Akwesasne) and "St. Francis" (Odanak) Indians, as they were often called during this period, as these Mohawk and Abenaki peoples were the most involved in the wilderness tourism era of the Adirondacks. This era began on a small scale at the end of the 1830s and ended as the automobile entered the region around 1920. The heyday of wilderness tourism in the area ran from the 1840s to 1910.

Chapters 1 and 2 examine pre- and early-European contact periods and influences. It is in these two chapters that I demonstrate the need to go beyond a stereotypical understanding of hunting territory and instead see this space as a zone of interaction and an Indigenous homeland for the Algonquian and Iroquoian peoples who lived in this area. The Adirondacks were part of the fabric of these peoples' lives as a geographic space of resources and labor, a space that was very familiar to them. At times the region acted as a "zone of refuge" from violence and settler colonialism for neighboring (often Algonquian) peoples from southern New England. Following the American Revolution, a shift occurred in terms of how Iroquoian and Algonquian peoples began to occupy the Adirondacks, and some created a space for themselves in this familiar place and began to live there year round. In order to ensure their economic survival, Mohawk and Abenaki peoples began to take on aspects of rural White society. Most, however, maintained their identity as Native peoples and contact with their communities in Canada and in New York State at

Akwesasne and Oneida. Chapters 3, 4, and 5 focus on the nineteenth century, a time when Aboriginal peoples, as the Donaldson quote in the opening paragraph states, were imagined as disappeared. Instead, my research has found their enduring presence, as they created new occupational roles, including as guides, entrepreneurs, artists, and performers. The reality of settler colonialism forced Algonquian and Iroquoian peoples in the Northeast into new livelihoods that expected them to fit into specific niches such as these. However, these roles also allowed the Mohawk and Abenaki peoples in the Adirondacks to use their traditional skills to earn a living and adapt to a modernizing world, thereby allowing them to continue to use their own knowledge. These adaptions to rural Euro-American ways while preserving and protecting traditions were often a double-edged sword that Iroquoian and Algonquian peoples had to wield in order to survive the period. Chapter 6 briefly brings this history up to date. By providing a study over such a long period, it is my plan to demonstrate both "change *and* continuity as an interconnected whole."[4]

This written account is important for local reasons, but it is also more broadly relevant. For instance, this work examines and complicates the history of landscapes known as hunting territories and forces us to reconceptualize home. Given the diversity of use and occupation by Mohawk, Oneida, Mahican, and Abenaki nations and bands in both pre- and early-European contact periods, it is difficult to truly call the Adirondacks a wilderness within modern definitions of the term. It is also a history of labor and of Indigenous peoples in relation to settler occupation from first contacts to the beginning of the twenty-first century. Further, it complicates our understanding of the role of Indigenous peoples actively involved in tourism. While this industry usually required Native peoples to take on a stereotyped role, this book demonstrates this was not always the case.

In addition, the Adirondacks are a forgotten region of the eastern frontier story. As currently defined, frontiers are considered to be contested spaces where peoples interact with varying responses and results. By the early nineteenth century, the northeastern frontier was thought to be long settled and nonexistent. Similar to the discussions of the Old Northwest in Richard White's seminal *The Middle Ground*, the Adirondacks saw competition between Iroquoian and Abenaki and Euro-American trappers that resulted in violence and cautious cooperation following the American Revolution. This is a period in Adirondack history that has not been much explored by scholars.[5] Although the region was physically a part of New York, the state did not get directly involved in these conflicts. Eventually these Native and non-Native peoples had to work out their differences on their own terms. Chapter 2 contemplates this period and explores its relationship to the start of exchanges between Natives and newcomers as the eighteenth century turned into the nineteenth.

Locally, this work provides a history of Iroquoian and Algonquian peoples in the Adirondacks from prior to European contact until the early twenty-first century. By the time of European contact, this region was clearly acknowledged as Iroquois (especially Mohawk and Oneida) territory and probably had been for centuries. By the middle of the nineteenth century, these and other Indigenous peoples had become a minority population within this rural landscape. It is difficult to know the exact numbers of the full-time Euro-American population of the Adirondacks in the nineteenth and twentieth centuries; trying to determine the Indigenous population is impossible. For one, the boundary lines of New York State's Adirondack Park have expanded over time, making it difficult to get a comparable measure for the region. The park has grown from 3.1 million acres in 1892 to its present-day 5.9 million acres. Further, some towns are within and outside of the park. As well, I—and other scholars of the region—include several border town communities such as Saratoga Springs because they are an integral part of the history but are technically outside the park's "Blue Line." (A blue line was used on the 1892 map to outline the Adirondack Park, and the park's boundaries have been called this ever since). Moreover, numerous individuals and families were (and still are) part-time inhabitants, either as seasonal residents or resource-industry workers who may or may not have been counted.[6]

The census figures for Native peoples are inaccurate at best, as they were often misidentified as "White" or "Colored," and sometimes (perhaps even often) they were not counted at all. For example, as the second chapter describes, a handful of Native communities existed in the Adirondacks into the mid-nineteenth century; however, they were never identified in the census, so it remains unclear who they were and how many lived there. Additionally, many came seasonally to work in resource and tourism occupations, and at the end of the season they returned home. As a result, whether some were counted depended on what month the census was taken. Historian Karl Jacoby's best estimate for the entire population of the Adirondacks in 1880 is between sixteen thousand and thirty thousand, depending on whether one includes border towns. The best I can conclude is that the Indigenous population living in the region during the nineteenth and early twentieth centuries was small and it fluctuated. Nevertheless, based on their contribution to the region's history and given the area's sparse population in general, the Indigenous population could not be insignificant.

The book's overarching argument is that the relationship between Algonquian and Iroquoian peoples and the Adirondacks was one of continuity, homeland, and ultimately survival. Additionally, this text examines and complicates landscapes too often known only as "hunting territories" and forces us to reconceptualize the terms "occupation" and "homeland." I argue that the area acts as a location of exchange for Indigenous peoples who came to the region, often for economic purposes, but also for more complex and cultural ones that changed over time. I define *location of exchange* as a purposeful and occupied place where reciprocal acts occur, creating opportunities for entangled exchanges between people(s) and the land. *Reciprocal acts* can be between humans and the land, so long as there is some kind of exchange—for example, leaving an offering in exchange for mining flint (see chapter 1)—as well as being a result of the land providing a space for reciprocal acts between peoples. This place was, or became, familiar to Iroquoian and Algonquian peoples as they performed new work and considered the location a homeland and occupied it in a variety of ways. In addition to experiencing the Adirondacks as a place of resources and labor, Algonquian peoples in particular migrated into this landscape as a place of refuge during the eighteenth and nineteenth centuries. Eventually they began to work and sometimes intermarry with incoming Euro-American settlers, creating intimate exchanges that helped to negotiate a shared history. Not only did they share relationships, but Mohawk and Abenaki peoples especially became part of the fabric of a distinct Adirondack cultural identity.

While heeding historian James Axtell's caution that scholars not overemphasize Native peoples' influence in shaping an American identity from English colonists,[7] I propose that historians can suggest that European colonists and early American settlers did more than borrow technology from Indigenous peoples to adapt to their environment. Examining a regional history like that of the Adirondacks brings out the "intercultural alliances" created between Natives and newcomers. Such alliances have been described by Cynthia VanZandt, who argues that experimentations with accommodation were significant and helped construct the settler experience. My work demonstrates these influences went past the initial settlement period, after which Native peoples often seem to disappear once the Euro-American population became dominant. As we grow to understand Indigenous culture better and consider it beside the history of initial rural settlement, we begin to see that threads of cultural practices were being negotiated and woven between Natives and settler society and beyond. Unless Native peoples truly were removed from a space at a certain time, thus cutting off their participation in that locale's past, their presence, and contributions belong alongside the dominant culture's history; just as the history of women, African Americans, immigrants, and workers are recognized as having an imprint on North American societies.

Terminology and Definitions

Naming is a complicated issue in the writing of the history of North America (in this book, North America refers to the United States and Canada). For example, Indigenous peoples often called each other by uncomplimentary names that often stuck. Indeed, the name Adirondack is thought to be an Iroquoian word meaning "bark eater," used to denigrate Algonquian peoples for using bark in the winter to survive (at least, that is what local lore says). Naming is also considered to be a colonial practice used by settler societies to take over a space.[8] My choice is to use the name of the individual nation(s) or band(s) when it is appropriate, but even that is problematic. Do I use the name by which the dominant culture has come to know the Indigenous people(s), or the name they call themselves? I considered and even wanted to do the latter; however, I was concerned this use might be confusing to readers who are not familiar with the Indigenous nations' original names. Therefore, I use both names the first time I mention a group but continue with the recognized name throughout so this history is easily understood by all peoples. One exception is Haudenosaunee, which has become better known and used today alongside Iroquois. Haudenosaunee refers specifically to the political and philosophical union of the Iroquois Confederacy, but in recent times it has become an analogous term for the People of the Longhouse. In addition, on a few occasions and where it is obvious, I use Kanienkehaka alongside Mohawk to get readers used to seeing the name they call themselves. The Kanienkehaka play an important part in this history (as do the Abenaki), and I owe them that much. Otherwise, I extend my apologies for privileging the dominant culture yet again. Unfortunately, it is often the non-Native population who needs the most educating about our shared history, and I do not want to create barriers for anyone to learn it.

The use of the name Mahican for the Algonquian people of the upper Hudson River whose territory extended to the southern shores of Lake Champlain and east of Lake George also has its complexities. According to T. J. Brasser, the nation's name for themselves while in New York was Muhheakunneuw (singular) or Muhhekunneyuk (plural), and it is probably the Dutch who gave us Mahican. Although they spoke Algonquian, the Mahican's way of life was more similar to the Iroquois as were many of the Algonquian peoples of the lower Hudson River Valley and southern New England. Now situated in the state of Wisconsin, the nation chose to adopt the name Mohican although they often refer to themselves there as Wampana'kiak, or "Easterners," to reflect where they came from.[9] Since the name

Mohican did not come into use until after they left New York State, I chose to employ Mahican.

The use of Western or western Abenaki has multifaceted issues. They have been known by many names, including band names such as Penacook, Cowasuck, and Missisquoi. The Odanak band council indicates the name Abenaki is a combination "of the terms w8bAn (light) and Aki (land), which mean people in the morning or people of the East" (the 8 represents a nasalized o [n]).[10] "Western Abenaki" was developed by linguists in the late twentieth century to distinguish the people living at Odanak from other Abenaki speakers. Historian Colin Calloway used "western Abenaki" as a way to refer to the Abenaki living in the western portion of Abenaki country. However, recent scholars find that the name Western or western Abenaki obscures more than it clarifies. Even the term Abenaki is problematic and is a convenience to group these bands together as one people.[11] In addition, Odanak was inhabited by "eastern" Abenaki and other Algonquian and Francophone speakers over time. Because the peoples with connections to Odanak have complicated interrelationships and identities, and they are so important to the Native history of the Adirondacks (especially after the American Revolution), from here forward I refer to them as Abenaki. This is the name and spelling the Odanak band council uses in English; moreover, it reduces verbiage and illustrates their complex ethnicity (and there is no other accurate name available).

Sometimes I resort to a version of "Algonquian and Iroquoian peoples" because I need to refer to these two nationalities together, or because there is a lack of clarity in the records about which nation was involved, especially in the pre-European contact and early contact period. I rarely, but occasionally, use St. Regis and St. Francis to reinforce how they were identified by nineteenth-century Euro-Americans. These terms also reflect the cosmopolitan nature of both of these mission villages-turned-reserves, which are culturally Mohawk and Abenaki but are also home to peoples of other Iroquoian and Algonquian nations. As chapter 2 describes, Algonquian peoples from New England and southeastern New York needed places of refuge due to violence and settlement practices by European settlers, and many fled to Odanak in Quebec. Even Iroquoian peoples left their home villages in today's central and western New York to move to French mission communities along the St. Lawrence River. Originally established at Sault-Saint Louis in 1667 by a handful of Oneida, the Jesuit mission village of Kahnawake attracted Mohawk converts by 1673. Later, the mission villages of St. Regis and La Présentation were established nearby in the 1740s. The peoples of La Présentation—a mixture of Onondaga, Cayuga, and Oneida—became known as the Oswegatchie Indians locally (the village was sometimes referred to as La Galette in Canada and was later called Fort Oswegatchie by the English). Many moved to Akwesasne just before the War of 1812; however, some returned to the remains of their homelands in the quickly expanding state of New York. The Iroquois moved to these and other places for religious, economic, political, and social reasons, even though their homelands were intact until 1783. This does not mean the peoples in these mission villages did not travel back to their homelands in today's central and western New York over the years. The records indicate residents of the St. Lawrence River mission villages and their kin in the Mohawk Valley and elsewhere stayed in contact with each other, and the former sometimes even returned to Iroquoia.[12] The seventeenth and eighteenth centuries were difficult and complicated times; "home" was located in many and diverse places.

Another concern is the use of the names Algonquin and Algonquian. Algonquin identifies the Indigenous bands associated with the Ottawa River Valley and the area north of the St. Lawrence River. They were known to use the Adirondacks as a hunting territory prior to contact and during the colonial era. Additionally, many of the Indigenous peoples of eastern Canada, southeastern New York, and all of northern and southern New England were Algonquian peoples who shared a common language root. A number of the Indigenous peoples who came to the Adirondacks prior to the nineteenth century were from New England. With a few exceptions (Abenaki or Mahican, most notably), we do not know what specific nation they were from. As a result, I often use the term Algonquian to refer to unknown groups of traditionally Algonquian peoples. I should also note that I use the term *peoples* (with an "s") when I refer to more than one group. For example, I use "Iroquoian peoples" because I want to emphasize that the confederacy consisted of multiple nations. If I mean one group of people (e.g., the Mohawk), I omit the "s."

I also struggled with how to use, or not use, broader terms such as *Aboriginal, Indigenous, Indian, Native American, American Indian* (when referring to Indigenous peoples from the United States only), and *First Nations* (when referring to Canadian Indigenous peoples only). The last two terms did not lend themselves often to this work, as the Adirondacks truly are a borderlands region. I decided to use the four other terms interchangeably when making broad references, particularly in arguments that apply across Indian nations and also for variety for the reader's benefit. As Trent University's Indigenous Studies doctoral program website used to state: "The terms 'Aboriginal,' 'Indigenous,' 'Native' and 'Indian' will be used interchangeably . . . reflecting the complexities surrounding appropriate terminology and the diverse contexts in which [these] terms are applied." Bowing to their wisdom, I chose to proceed with these multiple names without defining them.[13] I have capitalized all of these identifiers, as I do broad references to other groups of peoples, such as European, Canadian, and American.

Even naming peoples of European heritage is difficult. Generally I refer to colonial peoples as European(s). After the Revolutionary War, I use the designations Euro-American, Euro-Canadian, or Euro–North American. Occasionally, I use the term *settler society* to remind the reader that the Adirondacks, as part of North America, lies within a settler state. Settler colonialism is more than a past event; it is a process and it is still a very present and heightened condition for the Aboriginal peoples in the settler society countries of the United States, Canada, Latin America, Australia, and New Zealand. I also use the terms *newcomers, Anglo-American,* and *White* to replace these designations solely for variety. While I hesitate to use a color to designate a people, "White" is recognized as another way to refer to those of us of European ancestry in North America. As we know, race is a social construct that has been used to categorize humans based on our outward appearances but has no genetic basis. Even using appearance as a means of identification is faulty, given that peoples may blend with their neighbors. This project does recognize racism and examines it in all of the chapters. Concerning issues of culture, this book considers ethnicity, which I define as "a people who voluntarily or involuntarily identify with, or are identified with, a social group with 'common national or cultural traditions.'"[14] I have capitalized the identifier White as I do the names Native and Aboriginal out of respect for all the peoples whose history I narrate.

Euro-American Adirondackers have been, and mostly still are, rural peoples both geographically and culturally. However, they have never fit the stereotype of rural farmer. While the Adirondacks are larger than the six smallest states in the United States, very little of the region's soil is useful for commercial farming. By the 1840s, the region's population was employed in a number of resource-driven industries such as mining, lumbering, and tanning. The labor done by Adirondackers to survive there during the long nineteenth century was a mixture of subsistence farming, hunting, fishing, and gathering, including maple tree sap for syrup production alongside wage work. As this book shows, the lifestyle of White Adirondackers and much of the work they performed were very similar to those of the Indigenous peoples living in and about the region. They were hardworking peoples surviving in a difficult terrain; though this history is not focused on them, they play an integral part. Finally, the term *Native* became an issue in the writing of chapter 3. The research demonstrates that both Aboriginal and Euro-American Adirondackers became known as Native, especially "Native guides," by outsiders. Therefore, to reduce confusion I avoid the term Native to identify Indigenous peoples in chapter 3.

In addition to naming peoples, referring to place became tricky. First, as mentioned earlier in the discussion about population, the boundaries of the Adirondacks have changed over time, especially in terms of the park's borders. Despite the fact that it is the largest park in the continental United States, there are communities that are or have been associated with the area over time which for various reasons exist just outside the park's socially constructed boundary. Places like Saratoga Springs, Ballston Spa, Glens Falls, and Queensbury are featured in Adirondack literature and regional museums, as are "jumping off" communities like Plattsburgh, Canton, Watertown, Booneville, and Utica. Indeed, the first chapter of Frank Graham's political history of the Adirondacks begins with Saratoga Springs and its influence on the development of the Adirondacks.[15] As a result, these cities are included as part of this history, although the first four are more integral than the last five.

Methodology

This book is a social and microhistory narrative of Indigenous and settler society contact in the Adirondacks. Methodologically, this work employs ethnohistory as its foundation. Ethnohistorical research is interdisciplinary and employs a range of sources to locate peoples who are often overlooked in most historical texts. Ethnohistory attempts to tell the story of those who left little or no written records. While it focuses on the long nineteenth century, this Adirondack history also employs French historian Fernand Braudel's concept of *la longue durée* in order to identify change and continuity.[16]

This book is not a narrative about colonization as an event, although it is present as context. Instead, this is a history that looks at the reasons why Algonquian and Iroquoian peoples came to and sometimes stayed in the region. It examines their relationship with the land and later their rural, Euro-American neighbors, as well as affluent tourists. However, this study acknowledges that by the late eighteenth century the Adirondacks became, and still are, the colonized space of an Iroquoian homeland, the Mahican having been driven out by the Mohawk a century earlier. With the exception of chapter 1, this narrative is a history about the contact between the colonized and colonizer, one that explores their relationships over time through work and family entanglements. It accepts the notion that settler colonialism was and still is an active process occurring during this history. This does not mean that White settlers who moved into this and some other regions initiated or deliberately enacted colonizing processes. Larger political and monied forces had usually commenced and achieved this end already through various methods that forced Indian peoples off their homelands and then opened these involuntarily surrendered places up for settlement, often at a profit. This work acknowledges that settler society often assisted in the process of colonialism by moving onto these grudgingly ceded lands and bringing with it the settlers' imported practices. These practices frequently functioned to further alienate Indigenous peoples from their homeland and eventually forced them out. It is important to recognize that this process of settler colonialism, examined in chapter 2, occurred and continues when one tells the history of any place in North America, and the Adirondacks are no exception.

The Adirondacks: Land Sales and Cessions

Recent historical scholarship about the Adirondacks revolves around the region being an unusual public- and private-propertied New York State park. Themes such as wilderness, conservation, and preservation, along with the conflicts they created (and still create), fill the literature. So far as the formation of the Adirondack Park and this work are concerned, neither the park nor the legislation around it had any more adverse effect on Iroquoian and Algonquian peoples than it did on the local, rural population. Unlike other examples of conservation and park creation in both the United States and Canada, Native peoples were not run off or limited in their ability to hunt and fish there any more than their Euro-American neighbors.[17] Whether legal or not, much of the land in the Adirondacks was sold or taken prior to the American Revolution in several large transactions. Transfer of the rest of the region was fraudulently negotiated after the Revolutionary War by New York State and various unauthorized representatives of the Haudenosaunee's Six Nations Confederacy in Ontario and the Seven Nations Confederacy residing mostly in Quebec.

The first known land sale, and one that the Mohawk vehemently contested, was the Kayaderosseras Patent (1703–8), which included Saratoga and some of the southeastern portion of the Adirondacks.

In this case, two Mohawk men named Ter-jen-nin-ho-ge (or Joseph) and De-han-och-rak-has (or Hendrick) sold the land to David Schuyler and Robert Livingston on August 26, 1702 for "divers goods." The Kanienkehaka understood the request for land to be enough for a few farms. When they discovered it was allegedly for seven hundred thousand acres, they complained to Sir William Johnson, who was the British superintendent of Indian Affairs for the northern district from 1756 until he died in 1774. Johnson assisted them in reducing the land grant to twenty-three thousand acres in the 1760s.[18]

Before the Seven Years War, French investors attempted to create seigneuries along Lake Champlain and Lac du Saint Sacrement (now Lake George). However, no genuine attempts to settle these seigneuries were made by French settlers. These seigneuries included those of Sieur Robert (1737), which covered today's towns of Willsboro and Essex; Sieur Pean, encompassing an area along the Chazy River; and Alainville, located between Lakes George and Champlain. These lands were ceded by the French to the English after the Seven Years War. The Mohawk were not involved in these negotiations, and it is doubtful the English paid the Mohawk for this land previously claimed but generally unsettled by the French.

The Royal Proclamation of 1763 decreed that all land sales from Native peoples had to go through the British Crown, which issued royal patents. Shortly before the American Revolution, Irish immigrant William Gilliland attempted to create a baronial manor with tenants out of the old Roberts seigneury. He purchased his tract in 1764 from at least two individuals who already held title to the land through royal patents. Gilliland, however, objected to the fees and never licensed the land under his name. After the American Revolution, New York State legislated that royal patents of land not completely licensed would be ceded to the state.[19]

Better known and more enduring in Adirondack history is the Totten and Crossfield Purchase of 1772. Fronted by New York City shipwrights Joseph Totten and Stephen Crossfield, this purchase was the scheme of up to thirty financiers. The most notable investors in the Totten and Crossfield purchase were the brothers Edward and

Ebenezer (Eben) Jessup. The brothers were well-connected lumbermen with holdings in and around the southern part of the Adirondacks, and they had another forty-thousand-acre tract petition for land in the region pending in their own names. A copy of the April 10, 1771, "Application to the King" by Totten and Crossfield is located in Alfred L. Donaldson's 1921 *A History of the Adirondacks*, which also outlines the territory desired and indicates the investors were seeking the Crown's permission to purchase and vest from the Indians the right and title to these lands. The purchase price was 1,135 pounds (roughly 190,900 in 2017 dollars) to the Mohawk for supposedly eight hundred thousand acres. However, they were actually trying to obtain 1.15 million acres in the southeastern and central Adirondacks resulting in the sale amounting to less than threepence an acre. The deal was brokered by Sir William Johnson. Four Mohawk men agreed to sell the land and claimed they were doing so in the name of the Kanienkehaka nation. The agreement acknowledged the Mohawk were the land's "proprietors." The "Indian Grant to Totten and Crossfield," dated July 15, 1772, was ceremoniously transacted at Johnson Hall. The document lists the Mohawk representatives as "Hendrick alias Tayahansara, Lourance alias Agguragies, Hans alias Canadajaure, and Hans Krine alias Onagoodhoge, Native Indians of the Mohock Castle. . . ." In addition to payments to the Kanienkehaka, the investors made piecemeal payments to the Crown even after the Mohawk accepted payment in order to influence his majesty's decision. In 1773, the group petitioned the King for his decision claiming that "many persons of small means have sold their homes and farms in order to invest in these Indian Lands." The King did not issue the letters of patent for this purchase before the American Revolution broke out. Loyal to the Crown, the Jessup brothers and other investors fled to Canada and served the king, and as a result this land was surrendered to the state.[20]

The rest of the lands in the Adirondacks were ceded after the American Revolution. The region came under the control of the new United States and tentatively the state of New York at the turn of the nineteenth century. The 1783 Treaty of Paris ending the Revolutionary

War between the Americans and the English established a border that gave sovereignty of all lands north of the negotiated boundary to Great Britain and lands in the south to the Americans. England had betrayed their Iroquois (and other Native) allies during these negotiations by omitting them, and the Americans refused to consider them. To compensate the Iroquois, the Crown purchased lands from the Mississauga and offered the Haudenosaunee territory north of Lake Ontario. Followers of Mohawk Pine Tree (War) Chief Joseph Brant moved to what is known today as the Six Nations of the Grand River west of Hamilton, Ontario. Mohawk Pine Tree Chief John Deseronto (or Deserontyon) and his community from Fort Hunter along the Mohawk River settled at the Bay of Quinte on the northeastern side of Lake Ontario. New York State conveniently considered the Kanienkehaka's territory along the Mohawk River abandoned. The state considered the lands of Iroquoia and those Haudenosaunee remaining within their homeland to now be within the boundaries of New York State. New York gave away Cayuga and Onondaga land to local veterans of the American Revolution even before negotiations with the Iroquois began.[21]

The new United States federal government met with representatives of the Six Nations at Fort Stanwix (present-day Rome), where they treated the Haudenosaunee who had not sided with them as conquered people. The Oneida and Tuscarora had been allies of the colonists. American representatives took six non-allied Iroquois chiefs hostage, purportedly to ensure the return of captives and runaway slaves, and they demanded land cessions. Negotiating from a position of weakness and divided, the Iroquois negotiators (who were Pine Tree Chiefs and technically did not have the authority to cede land according to Haudenosaunee law) dealt with issues from the Revolutionary War that were codified under the 1784 Treaty of Fort Stanwix. The Grand Council of Sachems, who had the real authority to decide land issues, subsequently rejected the treaty, but the damage was done.[22]

Separate from the federal government discussions and in an effort to shore up their claim to the territories in today's northern, central, and western New York, the state of New York settled land issues with the Mohawk through a series of negotiations with unauthorized Pine Tree Chiefs Joseph Brant and John Deseronto. Brant also negotiated the sale of 512 acres of his own private property. The Kanienkehaka from Fort Hunter, under John Deseronto, eventually sold their claim "to private buyers." Brant did most of the negotiating for the Mohawk originally from Canajoharie. However, he neglected to consider their hunting territory when he settled the matter, a failure he later regretted. This territory included the Adirondacks. These negotiations ended on March 29, 1797, at Albany with the signing of the Treaty with the Mohawk, 1797.

Complicating these negotiations were declarations by the Caughnawaga, as they were known at the time, or Kahnawake (the latter will be used from this point unless Caughnawaga is used in a direct quote) and other members of the Seven Nations of Canada, who were also making claims on parts of the Adirondacks. The Seven Nations consisted of the Kahnawake, Oswegatchie Onondaga and Cayuga, Lake of Two Mountains Iroquois, Lake of Two Mountains Nippissing, Lake of Two Mountains Algonquin, Huron of Lorette (Wendake), and the Abenaki of St. Francis (Odanak). St. Regis (Akwesasne) replaced Oswegatchie after that community was forced to be abandoned in 1806, and many in that community moved to Akwesasne. The Kahnawake and the state of New York, which denied the Seven Nations claim, met several times and settled the matter on May 31, 1796, for a lump payment of 1,233 pounds (138,458 in 2017 dollars) and an annuity in the amount of 213 pounds (23,918 dollars). At these negotiations, Kahnawake and Akwesasne members represented the Seven Nations, and these two communities seemed to have fared the best, albeit none of them got much. Seven Nations representatives included: Ohnawiio, also known as Good Stream, representing Kahnawake; Oteatohatongwan, also known as Colonel Louis (Lewis) Cook, representing Akwesasne (St. Regis); Teholagwanegen, also known as Thomas Williams, representing Kahnawake; and William Gray, who also served as interpreter. The Seven Nations claimed their territory went as far south as "a creek or run of water between Fort Edward and George, which empties into South Bay, and from thence extending on a direct line to a large meadow or swamp where the Canada Creek, which empties into the Mohawk opposite Fort Hendrick, the Black and Oswegatchee Rivers have their sources." The Kahnawake eventually blamed Brant, who took offense at the implications he and his fellow delegates had fraudulently given away the Seven Nations territory and claimed he had met with them before their agreement was made.[23]

The Oneida were defrauded of the rest of their land in the Adirondacks by the state of New York under the Treaty of Fort Schuyler in 1788. They were under the impression the state was leasing most of their territory to protect the Oneida from incoming settlers, but in reality the state made a land grab to secure its tentative claim to what is today central and western New York. The seizure of this land under the Fort Schuyler treaty also included the western Adirondacks. The treaty allowed the Oneida to continue to fish and hunt in the Adirondack portion of their territory. The continued efforts by the state to whittle away the Oneida's remaining territory forced many to leave the area for places like Wisconsin and Ontario.[24] Encroachment by Euro-American and immigrant settlers was the reason Iroquoian and Algonquian peoples lost their ability to work in and traditionally occupy the Adirondacks long before conservation laws surfaced.

Metaphysically, the region, similar to others, is problematic and conflicted. Historical actors develop complicated, multiple, and layered identities, especially those who face limited opportunities at home based on ethnicity, class, and gender and who therefore choose to migrate for economic purposes.[25] The Aboriginal historical actors in the Adirondacks, especially those that crossed the border between the United States and Canada for economic reasons, were no different. Their identities included female, male, Algonquian-speaking, Iroquoian-speaking, Francophone, Anglophone, Catholic, Protestant, Traditionalist, hunters, basketmakers, bead workers, guides, farmers, performers, entrepreneurs, wage earners, American, Canadian, attached to reserve communities, not attached to reserve communities, mixed ethnicity, full ethnicity, blended families, full-time residents, part-time residents, and visitors. Because of this layering of identities, no two families had the same experience, but they shared a home, no matter how long, in the Adirondacks—a home where older patterns of seasonal use continued long after such patterns had become obsolete in most places in the Northeast.

A Brief Eurocentric History of the Adirondacks to 1920

To set the context for what is to follow, it is important to have a sense of what the typical history of the Adirondacks entails. I have chosen to place this Eurocentric history in the introduction in order not to detract from the history of Iroquoian and Algonquian peoples who are the focus of this book.

The first European accounts of the Adirondacks were recorded by the French; Jacques Cartier sighted the mountains on October 3, 1535, atop Mount Royal in present-day Montréal. Nearly seventy-five years later, Samuel de Champlain traveled with Algonquian and Huron (Ochateguins) peoples down "The Lake Between," which he named after himself. He was told by his Huron (also known as Wendat) and Algonquian allies that the Adirondacks were inhabited by their enemies, the Iroquois. Champlain's commentary indicates settlements on islands and the coast had dispersed due to warring between the Mohawk and the Algonquian and Huron nations. The reference to the Adirondacks states, "I saw on the south, other mountains, no less high than the first, but without snow. The Savages told me that these mountains were thickly settled, and that it was there we were to find their enemies."[26] Champlain and his party went ashore around Ticonderoga or Crown Point and did battle with the Haudenosaunee on July 29, 1609. This is the first written account of a European physically entering the region.

The Dutch were not far behind Champlain; they arrived in Albany around September 19 that same year. Henry Hudson sent a small boat with his mate and four men to explore the Hudson River's northern regions in search of a route to China. On the way, they encountered Indigenous peoples who told them the name of the river was Cohatatea (Iroquois) and Mahaganeghtuc or Shatemuc (Mohegans). They quickly discovered that "this 'River of the Mountains'" was no such passage and returned to the *Half Moon* anchored near Hudson

City (today's Jersey City). The Dutch built forts or trading posts near today's Albany, which was on the territory of the Mahican. The town that grew around Fort Orange was named Beverwyck or "Dorpe Beverswyck" (Beaver District Village), directly alluding to the reason the Dutch were there. The Mahican garnered the position of middleman in the early Dutch fur trade. The Mohawk successfully fought them for this position and drove the Mahican south and east of the Hudson River by 1628.[27]

During the colonial period, the Adirondack Mountains were a natural barrier between European powers. The French were positioned along the St. Lawrence River to the north, the English in the east, and, initially, the Dutch to the south until 1664 (and briefly 1773–74) when the English took over. The French eventually extended their reach into the Adirondacks along the shore of Lake Champlain but were challenged by the English in eighteenth-century wars. The region was officially Mohawk, Oneida, and Mahican hunting territory at the time of contact. The Onondaga, with territory along the eastern shore of Lake Ontario, used some of the northwestern lands. In addition, Abenaki and other Algonquian peoples (and possibly the Huron) were known to use the region, either in cooperation with the Kanienkehaka and Oneida or at their peril. Situated between European imperial powers, the Adirondacks became a military route and sometimes a battleground around the perimeter during the colonial wars of the eighteenth century. Both the French and the English built forts in the region. These fortifications, located on Lake Champlain in Essex County, were at Crown Point (French Fort St. Frédéric and nearby English Fort Crown Point) and Ticonderoga (French Fort Carillon, later the British Fort Ticonderoga). Eighteenth-century battles between Europeans and later between the English and their colonists during the Revolution were fought in the area, especially along Lake Champlain and Lake George. Southern, western, and northern perimeters of the Adirondacks also saw their share of intrigue and battles based on their proximity to the Mohawk River Valley, Lake Ontario, and the St. Lawrence River. This military activity, together with the region's geography and climate, helped to

keep the periphery of the Adirondacks only lightly explored and settled by Europeans. There are no records to indicate the interior was
ever explored, much less settled by Europeans.

With the exception of a few hearty individuals, many of whom
were trappers, Euro-Americans were hesitant to settle in the region
until after the War of 1812. A few of these trappers brought their
families. Part of the reason for this hesitation was the continued reputation of the Mohawk located just to the north at Akwesasne. White
Americans were afraid to settle in the area until the Kanienkehaka
were no longer a threat. The other reason for slow settlement was
that the Adirondacks were mostly unsuitable for farming, and many
who came to the area early left. Once industries such as lumbering,
mining, and especially tanning entered the area, people were able to
earn a wage, which increased the ability of families to survive in the
Adirondacks year round.

New York State commissioned a geological survey in the late
1830s. It was at this time the survey leader Ebenezer Emmons named
the High Peaks region "the Adirondacks" in 1838, purportedly after
a tribe of Indians who had lived there. Another name for the region
was the "Great Northern Wilderness," and residents living in the St.
Lawrence River Valley referred to the area (and still do) as "the South
Woods." Almost simultaneously, the first tourists entered the region.
They were usually well-to-do men, there to admire the sublime landscape or perhaps to treat their tuberculosis. On their heels, anglers and
hunters arrived and spent weeks there away from the city. Both types
of tourists needed the aid of local guides to traverse the region. The
railroad further opened the area and created additional opportunities
to visit and settle. In 1869, Boston minister William Henry Harrison
"Adirondack Murray" Murray published his *Adventures in the Wilderness*, which brought tourists to the area en masse.[28]

Industrial exploitation and mass tourism created a tension that
initiated the call to save the region from these dueling pressures.
Samuel H. Hammond's *Wild Northern Scenes* (1857) wished for a
one-hundred-mile diameter circle to surround the area to preserve
its forests. Henry David Thoreau's 1864 *The Maine Woods* called for

the preservation of wilderness in every state and used the Adirondacks as an example. Verplanck Colvin championed the preservation of the area as early as 1868 while on a land patent assignment to Lake Pleasant, and he continued his campaign until the park was created in 1892. In 1872, during a speech to the Albany Institute, Colvin outlined the damage created by lumbering he had seen while climbing Mt. Seward two years earlier. This speech before an influential group became a report that eventually secured Colvin the appointment of New York State Superintendent of the Adirondack Survey; he held the position until 1900. On the heels of the 1883 legislation that created the Niagara Reservation, "thus setting a precedent for 'buying scenery,'" New York "downstaters" argued for preservation of the Adirondacks to protect the water supply for the Erie Canal and the Hudson River. Adding credence to their argument was a drought in 1883, which affected the Hudson, Mohawk, and Black Rivers, and threats of fire, often created by sparks from trains. On the other hand, there was also a concern about spring flooding carrying debris and earth into New York Harbor by way of the Hudson River, which caused the harbor to silt. As a result, powerful New York City and other industrialists began a campaign to protect this and other New York State rivers with their headwaters in the Adirondacks. A powerful constituency of conservationists, sports enthusiasts, manufacturers, and naturalists crusaded for the preservation of the Adirondacks, a campaign that culminated in the New York Forest Preserve in 1885. It became the state legislated Adirondack Park in 1892. The park's legacy was written into the 1894 New York State Constitution originally under Article 7, Section 7, as a "forever wild" space that can only be undone by a vote from the people of the state of New York.[29]

Conclusion

What follows is the story of the relationship between Indigenous peoples and the Adirondacks, including rural, White Adirondackers and urban tourists, usually from the Northeast. Chapter 1 examines what it might have been like prior to European contact and later Euro-American settlement in the region. It considers why Algonquian and

Iroquoian peoples came here, how they occupied the space, how Europeans and later Euro–North Americans viewed the space, and why today we need to reconsider the complexities of these types of landscapes. It introduces the concept of *location of exchange*, which permeates this book. Chapter 2 studies early relationships and exchanges between especially Mohawk, Oneida, and Abenaki peoples and the newcomers during the late eighteenth and early nineteenth centuries leading up to the wilderness tourism era. It was a violent period that required Native peoples to borrow from traditional leadership strategies in order to live with incoming Whites and reinvent ways to thrive there. It introduces the Algonquian family, perhaps Abenaki, of Sabael Benedict as he negotiated this era.

Chapters 3, 4, and 5 explore the long nineteenth century, a crucial period when Indian peoples supposedly were disappearing, and the relationship between Kanienkehaka, a few Oneida, and, increasingly, Abenaki peoples in the wilderness tourism industry of the Adirondacks. The distance between Odanak and the Adirondacks is much greater than that of the Mohawk of Akwesasne, which are located much closer to the region. As a result the Abenaki had a stronger tendency to settle in the region and leave more records, making their presence during this era notable. The third chapter explores Indigenous peoples' work as guides in the Adirondacks, which culminated in their guiding for tourists, at times literally alongside Euro-American Adirondackers. Exchanges become more peaceful but also complicated, as the case of the family of Abenaki Mitchel Sabattis demonstrates. The chapter also examines the more intimate entanglements between Indigenous and non-Indigenous Adirondackers in work and family contexts, as well as their dealings with urban sportsmen who hired them as guides. The resulting portrait creates a complex understanding of the term "Native," as these outsiders combined the two peoples in order to explain their wilderness vacation. Chapter 3 also suggests that historians who study the history of Indigenous peoples during the nineteenth century and later, especially in the eastern part of North America, need to consider the categories of class and rural status as much as they do ethnicity and gender, as they are all important categories of analysis to understand and untangle these histories.

Turning next to entrepreneurial efforts by Iroquoian and Algonquian Adirondackers, chapter 4 demonstrates that roles for Aboriginal peoples in the tourism industry were not limited to Euro–North American stereotypes of their culture. There is little research on this topic, and this type of work should be considered alongside the more widely studied scholarship that focuses on tourism as a phenomenon that created or imposed stereotypes. Chapter 4 introduces the Oneida and Abenaki family of Emma Camp Mead, whose entrepreneurial skills continued a long history of entrepreneurship among North American Indigenous peoples. The complexity of Aboriginal peoples' exchanges in the tourism industry and with capitalism is depicted through the examples of this and other families.

When stereotypes were employed by the Native artists and performers who either lived in or had connections to the Adirondacks, the records reveal they often performed these stereotypes for complicated reasons. Chapter 5 introduces the Abenaki families of Julius Denis, Annie Fuller, and Margaret Camp Tahamont, examining the complexity of marketing cultural wares, the trope of the "vanishing Indian," and efforts by Native peoples to teach Euro-Americans through performance. This chapter also looks at the issues surrounding mixed heritage: Aboriginal peoples' history of intermarriage with Europeans and later Euro–North Americans contributed to notions of their lack of authenticity and the vanishing of "real" Indians from the area. The fifth chapter reminds us of the value and pitfalls of performance as Abenaki and Mohawk peoples made and sold goods to and performed for non-Native audiences. It also points out the gendered ways in which Native and non-Native peoples connected: non-Native men connected through their Native guides, while non-Native women connected through the handiwork of Native women. This chapter underscores the great need to extend Native peoples' history past the contact period in any North American historical narrative about place or American culture.

Chapter 6 brings the history of Indigenous peoples with ties to the Adirondacks briefly, although only partially, up-to-date through the experiences of the Joseph (Abenaki) and Fadden (Mohawk) families from the late nineteenth to the early twenty-first century. These families reveal the continuity and adaptability of Native peoples in this place. Their experience conveys a continuing sense that the region is still part of Mohawk territory as demonstrated by the 1974 takeover of an abandoned Girl Scout camp at Moss Lake in the western Adirondacks. Following on the heels of more national and international Indigenous civil rights efforts, this act of resurgence in the region makes evident that today's Mohawk continue to consider the Adirondacks as part of their homeland. Together, these recent histories demonstrate that the Adirondacks are still an indigenous space and that Native peoples belong in, and more importantly, throughout the narrative of its history and culture. This chapter introduces and explains the notion of *rural indigenousness* as a framework for considering Indigenous identity in rural spaces.

Finally, the book's conclusion confirms that the history of Aboriginal peoples in North America is still relevant, unfolding, and needs to be remembered in the continuing saga of the continent. Using the Adirondacks as an example, I argue that for too long historical texts and education about North America have contributed to the trope of the vanishing Indian and offer only a shallow version of the continent's complex histories. On the contrary, it is not Native American history that is irrelevant to mainstream history, but it is mainstream education that continues to make them and their history ephemeral.

I

"Just a Hunting Territory?"

The Adirondacks as Indigenous Homeland

THE ADIRONDACKS are a separate part of the Canadian Shield shaped by a bedrock dome and glacial movement. The region contains some of the oldest and youngest rocks exposed on earth, and the mountains continue to rise approximately 2–3 millimeters a year, or nearly one foot per century. The present day "Adirondack Park" is a state-sponsored parkland of nearly six million acres of public and private property, nearly one-third of the territory of the state of New York. The park is equivalent to the size of the states of Vermont or New Hampshire. It is the largest park within the continental United States and is "a 9,000 square-mile oval of highlands, located between Lake Champlain and the Black River Valley." At the time of European contact, the area was covered by a dense forest of conifer and deciduous trees. The terrain is varied depending on location, going from swampy and bog-like ground to the forty-six High Peaks, which are located in the northeastern portion of the region—all but four are over four thousand feet. The tallest mountain in the state, Mount Marcy, is located here and is 5,344 feet.[1] The Adirondacks contain approximately two thousand summits that qualify as mountains that have been described as "compressed and confused." In addition, the landscape contains over thirty thousand miles of waterways, which include three thousand lakes and ponds of various sizes, many of them manmade. There are fourteen major rivers that drain outward in a complex pattern that confuses those unfamiliar with the region.[2] The area's climate is considered harsh, especially in the winter when the snowfall is heavy. This geography and climate explain why Europeans avoided this place and perhaps why they, and Euro-Americans, assumed Native peoples did as well.

Colonial maps were some of the first records to recognize the area as Iroquois hunting territory. As early as 1612, Champlain noted "Yroquois" near both Lake Ontario and Lake Champlain. Lewis Evans's 1755 map provided only a few known landmarks, mostly around Lake Champlain, and labeled the region "Couch [text] sachrage." The text states, "This country by reason of mountains and swamps and drowned lands is impassable and uninhabited." In 1757, the Richard Seal map labeled the area "Antient Country of the Iroquois" and notes in text, "Parts but little known."[3] Guy Johnson's 1771 map of Iroquois territory showed only the southern part of the Adirondacks. He placed the map's compass there along with the following text: "The Boundary of New York not being Closed this part of the Country still belongs to the Mohocks." Thomas Pownall's 1776 map labeled the area "Coux [text] axrâge"; this text was a table of contents for peripheral landmarks. Pownall's map was part of a book that described the region as a hunting ground and stated that the Indigenous peoples called the region "Couxsachrâgé which signifies the Dismal Wilderness or Habitation of Winter." Pownall could not find any information about the region; he suggested the Indians either did not know much about it or were wisely keeping the knowledge to themselves. Text on a map is indicative of Europeans seeing the land as "terra incognita," reflecting how empire was being imagined and invented across a space.[4] So, for more than two hundred years, the Adirondacks were not a place Europeans really went or used. Indeed, they could not even imagine how they could use this landscape.

More recent publications have continued the trend of suggesting the Adirondacks were an uninhabited space. The preface of Jerry Jenkins's 2004 *Adirondack Atlas* claims the region was so inhospitable it was avoided by Native Americans and Europeans. Karl Jacoby's chapters about the area mostly ignore the precolonial era; he suggests that until the nineteenth century, the Adirondacks were "a lightly inhabited border zone." Jacoby explains the region had too short a growing season, was only lightly hunted, and was frequently fought over by Iroquoian and Algonquian nations, all of which kept it from being inhabited.[5] As a result, with a few exceptions—such as the account of Jesuit Isaac Jogues being brought there in the seventeenth century and some sporadic military activity during the seventeenth and eighteenth century around the perimeter—much of the area's pre- to mid-nineteenth-century history has been overlooked.

My research, however, reveals a more complex history of Iroquoian and Algonquian peoples in the Adirondacks during the precolonial era and thereafter. It demonstrates this space was much more than "just a hunting territory," a phrase that allowed, and in some instances still allows, Euro–North Americans to see this landscape and others similar to it as empty and free for exploitation and appropriation. The term *territory* is described as "vague and caught up with notions of ownership, sovereignty and conflicting European and Native values, all of which varied through time." Those landscapes known as hunting territories were often communal and were marked by "a sense of 'shared' or 'contested' space."[6] Indigenous peoples in North America had a deeper relationship with this land than incoming Europeans did. Indigenous peoples take their identity from kinship networks that incorporate entities other than humans, which include, among other things, the land and various geographic features. As a result, humans expect things from the land and conversely the land expects something from the humans who use it. "Acts of reciprocity in this extended community are not solely—perhaps not even *primarily*—for the benefit of humans."[7]

Despite the lack of direct contact with and records about the Adirondacks during this period, histories about the region prior to the American Revolution emphasize there was no permanent occupation by Native peoples. However, the few European documents and early Euro-American settlement histories provide the occasional clue to contradict these general findings and help to demonstrate the Adirondacks were part of annual, seasonal rounds and home to Algonquian and Iroquoian peoples. In addition, Iroquoian oral history and some early writings pertaining to New France that include the area indicate the Adirondacks were shared by Native peoples from time to time through formal, political agreements, and that the area was protected. Altogether, these histories, alongside other sources, including artifacts, demonstrate that precolonial Iroquoian and Algonquian labor in the region was extensive, varied, and required a profound knowledge about the area that sporadic trips could not support. Pieced together, these sources show that the Adirondacks were an Indigenous homeland and have been for centuries.

The notion of "home" is conflicted and contradictory; scholars struggle with the concept to this day. The conception of home for Indigenous peoples, especially for those who conducted seasonal rounds, is even more complicated. Some scholars advocate a need to de-center the concept of what and where home is, especially as we contemplate the idea of home for peoples like the Abenaki, who seasonally moved about for resources and labor. These scholars argue it is human activity that makes home meaningful. Others suggest that Indigenous peoples shifted where they lived in order to eat, but home held the remains of their ancestors and ceremonial material. Even the more village-dwelling Iroquois were similarly attached to places of occupancy and ancestral graves. Social anthropologist Andrew Gray's work is more prescriptive and suggests a "polythetic" consideration of four views with regard to Indigenous peoples' relationship to their environment: political control, use of the land for resources, a spiritual relationship, and a "historical and semantic relationship" with the territory. Cultural and linguistic anthropologist Keith Basso's well-regarded work on the concept of a "sense of place" argues that geographic landscapes are filled with cultural evidence, and the challenge is to translate what the landscape is trying to tell us. Place-making represents the accrued experiences a people have in an area—experiences that are informed by their ideas of place. The crucial question for Basso is not about where or how a place was formed. Instead he asks: what is it made with, what are its qualities, and how has it been constructed?[8] As Basso and these other scholars imply, home is more than how the space is used. There is an emotional tie to it because there is cultural significance there.

This chapter provides examples of how the region's geographical spaces were constructed over time, especially in terms of labor practices and lived experiences that were known, or were possible, prior to colonial encounters. This study uncovers ample support for various forms of labor and precolonial seasonal occupancy in the Adirondacks, year round. Merriam-Webster defines *occupation* as "an activity in which one engages" and in terms of a vocation as "the principal business of one's life."[9] Native peoples were very active in the region engaging in the principal business of their lives, and they used and guarded the area as an important resource and as part of their sovereign territory. By examining how Algonquian and Iroquoian peoples used and related to the land, we can tease out a more fully articulated account of their presence here and demonstrate that the Adirondacks have long been home to Iroquoian and Algonquian peoples and that the region was part of their sociocultural environment. The records reflect at least seasonal precolonial and early contact settlements and that women also came into the region. Iroquoian men may have spent as much, if not more, time here (and in other hunting territories) than they did in their home villages.[10] Perhaps some Algonquian families stayed in the Adirondacks as long as they stayed anywhere as part of their seasonal rounds. In addition, legends and sacred spaces existed in and about this place. People were born, died, and were buried here.

This chapter argues that we need to broaden and complicate our understanding of spaces known as hunting territories, as well as what we consider to be forms of occupation, in order to understand the varied exchanges that occurred in this place and in others like it. A complimentary descriptor that I propose we consider is *location of exchange*. Merriam-Webster defines *location* as "a position or site occupied or available for occupancy or marked by some distinguishing feature" and "a tract of land designated for a purpose." *Exchange* is defined as "the act of giving or taking one thing in return for another" and "reciprocal giving and receiving."[11] A term such as *location of exchange* implies a venue of both activity and residency encompassing a myriad of functions, year round and at different sites throughout the region.

As mentioned in the introduction, I have defined location of exchange as a purposeful and occupied place where reciprocal acts occur, creating opportunities for entangled exchanges between people and the land. Reciprocal acts could be between people and the land, so long as there was some kind of exchange; these acts could also be a result of the land providing a space for reciprocal acts between peoples. I am not suggesting we replace the term "hunting territory" as an identifier of these spaces, since it is a well-established and recognized name for these places. Rather, I am proposing we complicate these spaces for the benefit of most North Americans, and a corresponding term might assist in this endeavor.

By no means does this chapter attempt to be a comprehensive precolonial history of the area. Indeed, the telling of this history may not currently be possible due, especially, to the lack of archaeological work here—historians have not been the only discipline to ignore the region during this period. Archaeology has generally overlooked the Adirondacks for a variety of reasons, including the belief that it was uninhabited, the soil is too acidic and destroys artifacts, and easier choices for fieldwork exist elsewhere. Further, precolonial archaeological evidence is typically found by farmers and road construction crews unearthing them by accident, but both farms and roads are scarce in much of the Adirondacks. In addition, the damming of rivers has created lakes and changed the water levels and environment to make searches more complicated. Thankfully, in the past few years a handful of nearby college and university professors with archaeology and other scientific expertise have begun to take an interest in uncovering the region's precontact past.[12]

Despite the lack of research, evidence of Indigenous occupation has been discovered. For example, an 1890 *New York Times* article described farmers plowing up bones and hatchets in a field near Beaver Lake in the western part of the Adirondacks. "A curious trench is also pointed out on the shore of the lake as having been excavated by the Indians. It has been used as a 'wolf pit,' and is still so called." During the summer of 1987, Mohawk educator and storyteller Kay

Ionataie:was Olan compiled a list of private and public collections of Native artifacts along both shores of Lake Champlain, including relics found in farmers' fields. Road construction in the region has also turned up artifacts, although they are rarely reported. The late Gregory P. Otis, my father and a former project engineer for the State of New York in both Essex and Warren Counties, told me that job sites often unearthed American Indian relics, but the items mostly found their way into the crews' pockets. He recalled that a corn grinding stone was found on a job site in Keene (c. 1970) that was given to the state archive.[13]

Compounding these challenges are the plethora of amateur and scavenger diggings that have destroyed the best known locations. Jess Corey (c. 1819–96), proprietor of the Rustic Lodge built in 1850 over a preexisting, probably Abenaki village, owned a collection of artifacts allegedly in the thousands from his property on the Indian Carry at Coreys in Franklin County. It was reported that if someone admired a piece, he gave it to them. In addition, Adirondack guides often told stories of Native peoples' settlements being unearthed by accident and that "it is highly probable that many of the 'clearings' which the paleface now inhabits were first made by the [Indian] or, perhaps, by a race antedating him."[14]

The era prior to the American Revolution was outside the scope of my original project. However when I began my research, I did not know how much information was available. As a result, I asked and looked for everything an archive had about Native peoples within their local history collection. Many of the nearly two dozen archives I visited, including the Adirondack Museum (recently renamed "Adirondack Experience, The Museum on Blue Mountain Lake," and hereinafter referred to as the Adirondack Experience museum) and the New York State Museum and Archive included some regional information and/or artifacts that covered this period. Regrettably, most of the artifacts were and still are in storage, hidden from public view. Combined, these documents and material culture have much to say, and they need to be introduced for consideration. Ultimately, this chapter demonstrates that the precolonial history of the Adirondacks is one waiting to be fully developed.

Early History of Algonquian and Iroquoian Peoples in the Adirondacks

The Adirondacks have been known to, and named by, Algonquian- and Iroquoian-speaking peoples for centuries. Paleo-Indian sites have been located along "the shores of the waning Champlain Sea" as early as 9000 BCE and thus demonstrate occupation here since at least this period (Paleo-Indians is a term used by archaeologists to describe the ancestors of Native Americans during the period 15000–7000 BCE). The Champlain Sea covered an area over twenty thousand square miles and included the St. Lawrence Lowlands, the Ottawa River Valley, and present-day Lake Champlain. In addition, it completely covered the Adirondacks and other parts of New York and New England. A mixture of sea and glacial water, this sea receded to our present-day understanding of the landscape after the land was released from the weight of the glaciers and rebounded. It is thought this is the time period when *Homo sapiens* first colonized the Western hemisphere. The currently accepted theory suggests that these ancestors followed big game in and out of the region. During at least some of the following archaeologically delineated archaic period (c. 7500 BCE–0 CE), the Adirondacks acted as a frontier-like space separating Algonquian peoples from those of the Maritimes and the Great Lakes, with whom they have linguistic ties (evidence of both have been found in the region). The mountains performed a similar function upon the arrival of Iroquoian peoples who pushed out Algonquian speakers.[15]

The Abenaki called the Adirondacks *Wawobadenik* prior to the arrival of the Iroquois. They may have considered at least the northwestern region around Lake Champlain to be part of their territory. Iroquoian peoples are believed to have arrived, either literally or figuratively through ethnogenesis, somewhere between 1,200 and 4,000 years ago.[16] The Oneida and, in particular, the Mohawk considered the Adirondacks part of their sovereign territory. The time period is still debated as to when Iroquoian peoples arrived in present-day New York

State. Anthropologist Dean Snow argues that a northern Iroquois culture began around the Clemson Island archaeological site in central
Pennsylvania, suggesting an Appalachian origin. He estimates the Iroquois arrived in New York around 900 BCE. Historian Jon Parmenter
and archaeologist William J. Engelbrecht suggest an Iroquois nation
began c. 600 BCE from "multiple ancestral groups and of diverse
contacts" and that the Iroquois League developed around 1600. Six
Nations historian and Tuscarora scholar Richard (Rick) W. Hill Sr.
argues the Iroquois have been in and around central New York for
approximately four thousand years. Mohawk Doug George-Kanentiio
agrees citing oral history of a solar eclipse occurring at the time of the
confederacies' founding on August 31, 1142. I am not in a position
to resolve either of these important date debates, although I do admit
I find the oral history's reference to a known solar eclipse persuasive.
Regardless of the date of their arrival or consolidation creating their
palpable presence in the region, it was cause for conflict with surrounding Algonquian neighbors. For example, the Abenaki claim the Iroquois' arrival cut them off from trading partners and mining resources,
such as flint. The Abenaki and Iroquois fought over the territory, and
Bitawbákw (the lake between) to the Abenaki, or *Caniaderiguarunte*
(the lake that is the gate of the country) to the Iroquois—known today
as Lake Champlain—became their de facto border.[17]

A number of Iroquoian and Algonquian peoples have called the
area home over the centuries. To the Kanienkehaka, or Mohawk, the
area was called *Tso-non-tes-ko-wa*, which simply means "the mountains," or *Tsiiononteskowa*, meaning "big mountains." Another term
was *Ah-di-lohn-dac*, meaning "bark-eater," a reference to porcupines.
Randy Cornelius, an Oneida language archivist with the Oneida
Nation in Wisconsin, told me they called the Adirondack region
latilu-taks, which means "they're eating the trees" and is a reference
to beaver. The Oneida territory in the Adirondacks went from present-
day Utica on the Mohawk River to the St. Lawrence River in a pie
wedge-shaped form. Their territory included present-day Stillwater
Reservoir north and west to Harrisville and then north to Black Lake
and up into the Thousand Islands in the St. Lawrence River. While

this boundary is generally accepted by most scholars, maps, and the Oneida nations in Wisconsin, Ontario, and Oneida, New York, some Traditional Mohawk Nation Council members from Akwesasne claim the Oneida's territory did not reach into the Adirondacks but was limited to the area just north of Rome and west of Old Forge. As with many nations, boundary disputes exist, and the Adirondacks are no exception.[18]

Another Algonquian nation that considered the Adirondacks as part of their country were the Muhheakunnuk or Mahican, whose territory comprised at least the east side of present-day Lake George (which they may have called *Andiatarocte*, "where the lake closes") and probably the southern part of Lake Champlain. The Mohegan people of southern New England also claim to have lived in the area along the shores of Lake Champlain before migrating to the present-day state of Connecticut. They have a legend called "The Tale of Chahnameed," which takes place in their "New York Mohegan Homeland" along Lake Champlain. In addition, the northern Iroquoian-speaking Wendat (Huron) and Algonquin nations north of the St. Lawrence River labored in the area, and the Laurentian Iroquois occupied northern and western parts of the region.[19]

The Adirondacks were part of territorial agreements between Iroquoian, Algonquian, and early European officials. Rick Hill believes the Adirondacks were part of the Iroquoian territorial concept of the "Dish with One Spoon." He explains that the Iroquois consider "all of nature as a Great Dish With One Spoon, [and that this is] a reference to sharing from that dish equally." A number of these territories or "dishes" accrued over time and space as Iroquoian and Algonquian peoples came in contact with one another. During peaceful times, these territories were neutral places and open to all allies to use for subsistence purposes, so long as permission was requested by allies and granted by the Haudenosaunee. Iroquoian history describes the parties' need to use a beaver tail in a common bowl, since knives could be used as weapons. This territorial sharing was codified in the "Dish with One Spoon wampum belt." The concept probably began with the formation of the League of Five Nations (Haudenosaunee), and other nations were added over time, including Europeans.[20] This treaty, documented by the belt, tried to limit warfare by allowing all participants to practice subsistence hunting and resource gathering within the dish's territory. According to Hill, this early agreement was betrayed because of the fur trade, which resulted in the war between the Mohawk and the Indigenous peoples known as the Adirondacks. However, the concept and the belt continued to be utilized. Mohawk elder Tom Sakokweniónkwas Porter describes a treaty and wampum belt between the Iroquois and the Ojibwa in 1763. This may be the same belt Mississauga Missionary, Peter Kahkewaquonaby Jones mentioned in 1840 when he referred to a council meeting between his people and the Iroquois. Jones described the same belt design and added that it was the first treaty between the Ojibwa (also known as Chippewa or, as they call themselves, Anishnaabeg) and the Iroquois "many years ago, when the great council was held at the east end of Lake Ontario." The location of this council is just west of the Adirondacks, thus suggesting that the Anishnaabeg were also aware of the region.[21]

The French adopted the concept of the "Dish with One Spoon" in their negotiations with the Haudenosaunee, and at least two of their late seventeenth-century treaties incorporating the concept are intriguing with regard to the Adirondacks. The peace treaty at Three Rivers, brokered by Samuel de Champlain starting in 1622 and formally agreed to in 1624, culminated in the Mohawk, the "French Indians," and the Mahican promising to allow each other to hunt in their declared territories. Of special interest to the French-allied Indians was the ability to trade with the Dutch for wampum, which the French did not have. The Adirondacks were included as part of these negotiations. The area was described as being rich with game because the conflict between the Iroquois and the Algonquin nations had depressed hunting there. The peace was unofficially broken in July of 1626 and formally in 1627 when the Mahican attempted to gain more control. A later Three Rivers Treaty Council occurred in 1645 when the French and their allied tribes were invited by the Haudenosaunee, through diplomat Kiotseaeton, to "link arms" and create a treaty alliance. As part of their commitment, the Iroquois offered to open their hunting territory so everyone could share out of a common bowl. Kiotseaeton described their hunting territory as well stocked with game and fish, and said that there was no reason to fear going there as they had established trust with each other.[22] It is likely the Three Rivers Treaty Council of 1645 included the Adirondacks as part of the hunting territory the Iroquois were willing to share.

Place of Resources and Labor

During the precolonial era, Iroquoian and Algonquian peoples journeyed to the Adirondacks for extended periods for a number of resource and labor-related purposes, and in exchange they left evidence of their time there. For example, while often using the lakes and rivers for transportation, Native peoples also left a system of foot trails in the region that today are state and local roadways. For instance, there was a north-south Indian trail that went from Saratoga to Canada that New York State Routes 9, 9N, and parts of Route 22 have paved over. Parts of the east-west-directed New York State Route 8 involve the "Piseco Indian Trail," which today connects Morehouseville, Piseco, Oxbow, and Fish Mountain to Wells in Hamilton County. Another central and western region Indian trail that became a highway was the old Albany Trail. It is likely that both water and land trails were used as part of a system to travel to and from favorite hunting and fishing encampments, as well as for military, diplomatic, and trade purposes. Indeed, the Iroquois secured control of the Richelieu River—Lake Champlain—Lake George—Hudson River corridor to the Mohawk River for such purposes. In addition, the archaeological evidence indicates the use of interior water systems.[23]

The Adirondacks were used for seasonal purposes that stretched across the year as Native peoples came to fish in the spring, hunt a variety of game and fowl in the spring, summer, and fall, and trap and hunt in the winter. Animals hunted in the Adirondacks during this time included moose, deer, bears, panthers, lynx, and wolves, while beaver, otter, muskrat, pine marten, and wolverines were trapped.[24] Successful hunters were admired and needed in both Iroquoian and

Algonquian communities. The Iroquois hunted deer year round; each of the Five Nations was known to consume approximately two thousand deer per year. One of their practices was to set fire to grasses in the spring to create meadows to attract deer and other game; this also helped quicken the growth of these grasses as the fire heated the still-cold soil without damaging the roots. The Dutch recorded that the Iroquois also burned "woods, plains, and meadows in the fall of the year." Fire was known to be used around the fringes of the Adirondacks to create meadows to attract game. As a rule, fire was too dangerous in the interior due to the types of trees and the large amount of debris on the ground, which made it easier for fires to burn out of control. For example, eighteenth-century Scandinavian scientist Pehr (Peter) Kalm's *Travels into North America* describes how forests had been set on fire by Native peoples around Crown Point, and as a result the number of fir trees had been decreased in the area. As well, Indians living around Washington County were known to burn land there to attract deer and create an environment to grow berries. In addition, the Iroquois practiced subsistence wildlife management strategies. They used their gardens to attract animals including small game such as squirrel, rabbit, and quail.[25]

Often hunters traveled a great distance and set up camps. Most Iroquoian women remained in the village while the men and boys traveled, but some women accompanied the hunters, and there is at least one record of this occurring in the Adirondacks during the 1640s. Father Isaac Jogues's biographers, Father Francis Xavier Talbot and Father Jerome Lalemant, describe Father Jogues accompanying his Mohawk captors into the Adirondacks in October for hunting purposes. He left along with the women and older men in December carrying a pack of smoked meat, while the younger men remained. It is believed he may have been brought to the Saranac Lake area. The women's principal role on the hunt was to process the meat and hides. Both sexes carried meat back to the village "in pack baskets with the aid of a burden strap passed over the forehead." The strap served both a utilitarian and spiritual purpose, as it was decorated to appease the game in the hope of preventing them from retaliating. The remaining hunters began returning to their communities approximately two weeks before the Pleiades would be overhead, as this positioning of the stars was the sign for the midwinter ceremony to begin in late January or early February. After the ceremonies, hunters reoutfitted for deep snow hunting and trapping.[26]

Abenaki families also celebrated a midwinter festival around February when they were living together in a seasonal village. At other times, bands moved seasonally throughout a family's territory. Abenaki women performed the same work as those Iroquoian women who traveled with hunters. However, the vast majority of Abenaki women and children traveled with their male counterparts and complemented the work being performed by the men. Abenaki male hunters were depended on by their community to provide meat for the family, protein which was combined with women's agricultural and gathering duties. Family units made seasonal rounds for hunting, fishing, trapping, and other enterprises, such as mining and gathering berries and plants for food, dyes, and medicine. They practiced some agriculture, but unlike their southern New England Algonquian relatives and Iroquoian neighbors they did not settle in year-round villages near their fields. Instead, they either left a few people there or came back to their seasonal village to tend their crops. Abenaki communities were based on a gendered division of labor: men warred, hunted, and made houses, canoes, and tools for hunting and military purposes, while women gathered food and medicines, took care of crops (except tobacco), cared for children, and prepared food, skins, and clothing. Their society was patrilineal, with one to several families living together in one bark house. If circumstances warranted, a son-in-law might move in with his wife's family, at least for a while. All the households together made up the tribe. Winter hunting groups were temporary and made up of selected individuals and families. Hunting territories were based around families, and rights to hunt in these territories were extended by the male head of the family, although after the American Revolution leases and deeds for agricultural lands were signed by both men and women. Leadership was based on need and consensus. Usually men filled leadership positions, but sometimes women took on those roles, often at the family level.[27] More about Abenaki social, economic, and political practices are described in chapter 2.

The Iroquois and the Abenaki had similar work and domestic duties, but they used the resources and land in somewhat different ways. The Iroquois placed more emphasis on horticulture than the Abenaki and, as a result, probably had a larger population. Like other peoples who relied on seasonal rounds, the Abenaki purposefully kept their population below what the land could support. They often only hunted in 75 percent of their territory as a conservation practice. While the Abenaki did practice horticulture, they did not depend on it like their Iroquoian neighbors. Because they did not live in them year round, the Abenaki did not have to move their more permanent seasonal villages as often as Iroquoian villages were moved.[28]

Besides hunting and trapping, good fishing opportunities attracted Native peoples to the Adirondacks. As the evidence of numerous camps throughout the region demonstrates, in the spring Iroquoian men and some women, as well as Algonquian families, journeyed to recently thawed rivers and lakes in the area to catch fish. The Granville section of Washington County contained an Abenaki encampment where they were known to fish, hunt, and mine slate for hatchets and arrowheads. In addition, Putnam might have been the location of an old Mahican or Mohawk community. Piseco Lake in Hamilton County was a well-known fishing spot and is believed to be an Aboriginal word meaning "fish lake." The fishing weir in Fish Creek, which connects Saratoga Lake with the Hudson River, was believed to have been built by the Mahican and later used by the Kanienkehaka.[29] Another technique used by Native fishermen was to fish at night with a torch to lure fish to the surface. The artifact found at the bottom of Loon Lake, New York, demonstrates this practice (fig. 1).

Iroquoian and Algonquian peoples also mined in the Adirondacks, both for their own use and for trade. They exploited raw materials in the area, such as quartz crystals for tools, weapons, and decoration; flint and chert fall under this categorization. Jesuit accounts describe the Iroquois leaving tobacco offerings to a race of invisible men who lived at the bottom of Lake Champlain near Ticonderoga.

THIS OLD TORCH, USED AT NIGHT BY INDIANS TO ATTRACT FISH TO WITHIN SPEARING DISTANCE, WAS FOUND AT THE BOTTOM OF LOON LAKE, NOT FAR FROM HERE. 9/7/ 😊, BY TWO SKIN DIVERS—— ROBERT J. BROWN AND WILLIAM H. BROWN, WHO DONATED IT TO THE SIX NATIONS INDIAN MUSEUM.

1. Fishing torch for night fishing found at the bottom of Loon Lake, NY. Photograph by Melissa Otis. Courtesy of and located at Six Nations Indian Museum, Onchiota, NY.

The offering was meant to appease the beings, who lived there at the bottom of the lake and prepared the flint "all cut for the passerby, provided the [Iroquois] pay their respect by giving them tobacco."[30] Washington County local historian Fred Tracy Stiles describes the "Podunk" Indians going to Fort Ann in Washington County to get flint for arrows, spear points, knives, and the heads for tomahawks. Further, both Iroquoian and Algonquian peoples mined quartz crystals, such as Herkimer diamonds, in the Adirondacks. These crystals had specific spiritual properties, as healers and shamans included them in their medicine bundles.[31]

In addition, Native peoples mined for iron ore and lead, at least after contact. Various reports refer to Indians long knowing about lead mines in St. Lawrence County and nearby Franklin County, but they kept the locations secret. During the eighteenth century, the Iroquois left captives on the beach at Whallons Bay on Lake Champlain in Essex County in order to get lead from around Split Rock Mountain. Later, during a more peaceful period, they gifted a local farmer with a piece of lead large enough that the farmer used it as a doorstop. As chapter 2 describes, it was probably Louis Elijah Benedict who showed the Henderson party the large iron mine at Adirondac (Tahwus) in the central Adirondacks during the mid-nineteenth century. In fact, iron ore was so plentiful in the Adirondacks that it impaired compasses from pointing north.[32]

Copper beads and implements have been found in the Adirondacks. Forty-five graves at the Ticonderoga flint site contain copper beads. Nineteenth-century amateur archaeologists David Kellogg and G. H. Perkins suggest copper was brought to the region from elsewhere. Perkins notes that the Champlain Valley was the site of extensive trading and that many stone implements found in America could be found here. *The Adirondack Atlas* does not list copper deposits in its discussion of metals and minerals in the region, which perhaps confirms Kellogg and Perkins's conclusion. We do know that copper was available and mined by Native peoples throughout the East. However, New York State is underrepresented in these studies and needs more research.[33] Assuming copper was not available locally, these finds demonstrate trade occurred in the area, or at least that precolonial trade goods were brought here.

Horticulture was practiced in the region by at least the early contact era and probably before. We know that the Iroquois were practicing a maize agriculture "during the millennium prior to European contact" and the cultivation of maize, beans, squash, sunflowers and tobacco was prevalent in Iroquoia by 1300 CE. Northern flint maize, or *Zea mays indurata*, was grown in Iroquoia by CE 640, Quebec by CE 1150, and south-central Ontario by CE 700–900. The growing of crops was practiced widely across the Northeast, including alongside the Ottawa River and Lake Nipissing, both of which are north of the Adirondacks, and part of the Canadian Shield. The Iroquois moved frequently prior to contact, and they chose settlement locations with enough rainfall, frost-free days, and soil with lime, and often near good fishing. As early as the 1670s, Iroquoian women at Kentaké (or Sault Saint Louis, the community established prior to Kahnawake south of Montreal) began to plant seeds between sheets of birch bark to create seedlings in order to deal with the shorter growing season of the St. Lawrence River Valley. In 1724, the Jesuit priest Joseph François Lafitau recorded that the Kanienkehaka grew only summer crops and that their corn could be planted and harvested within three months, usually from late April or May to August, in the Mohawk Valley.[34] These observations tell us corn could be grown in upstate

New York at that time by the Iroquois in as little as three months under good conditions. The Abenaki in northern New England and southern Quebec also grew corn but less intensively than their Iroquoian neighbors.

While the vast majority of crops for Mohawk and Oneida families were cultivated in the Mohawk Valley by women, children, and older individuals, the number of early pioneer records describing Indian corn fields in the Adirondacks cannot be ignored. While the Adirondacks have a notoriously short growing season, they also have microclimates that extend the season along lakes and river systems, and on at least one uplifted plateau that also enjoys a longer growing season. Local records indicate corn and other crops were planted along the lake valleys, such as those of Lakes George, Champlain, and Saratoga, and even in the center of the region near Piseco Lake, Indian Lake, and the Indian Carry at Coreys. For example, a meadow called Indian Joe Field near Saratoga was noted by pioneering settler Gideon Putnam, who arrived around 1789. Putnam indicated the field had been "cleared and cultivated by the Indians," and it was thought that some of the herbs growing in it were planted by them.[35]

The Iroquois were known to plant on elevations for a phenomenon called the "thermal blets," which lengthens frost-free days. The "Indian Council Grounds" in North Elba was a summer camping grounds located in the High Peaks region just outside Lake Placid (it was thought to be Iroquoian). This spot is an uplifted plateau surrounded by the highest mountains in the region and may explain why corn grew in this place. Locally known as the Plains of Abraham, this space is currently occupied as a farm and has been since the first decades of the nineteenth century.[36]

Furthermore, a group of hunters, often accompanied by women, might plant a crop of corn if they were going to be in the area for more than a few months. The Abenaki and Iroquois often returned to the same seasonal encampments for their work. They apparently lived there long enough at times to plant and, if fortunate, harvest corn for their extended use. As mentioned earlier, gardens were also used to lure game. Dried corn stalks were used for fishing line floats, the husk for lighting fires, and the leaves as a makeshift steamer, all of which were useful for seasonal occupation. In addition, and among other things, the stalks could be made into a medicinal lotion for cuts and bruises and the leaves used as an improvised bandage.[37] In a discussion of how Piseco Lake got its name, John Knox states that "the Indians made Piseco a regular camping ground during their travels in this section of the Adirondacks. . . . Some of the lands adjacent to the lake were cleared by them and the squaws were able to grow corn and other vegetables while the men were out fishing and hunting for the winter's supply."[38]

Moreover, the Abenaki were known to use the Indian Lake region as a summer camp. They cleared the land for gardens by burning a small area around the base of trees. The burning eventually killed the tree, which was collected for firewood. They used the ash from the burning and fish they caught to fertilize their beans, corn, and squash. Since these are the same crops as the Iroquoian "three sisters," it would not be unreasonable to suggest the Iroquois also grew these crops there while they fished and hunted in the region. The Haudenosaunee also similarly cleared fields and used ash and fish for fertilizer.

Another horticultural activity included the tapping of maple trees. Stiles describes Native peoples showing the first pioneers to Washington County how to make maple syrup and even telling them how it was discovered (see chapter 2). In addition, the Iroquois were known to cultivate and sometimes plant nut and fruit producing trees.[39] Indigenous peoples regularly managed nut and fruit trees in the eastern part of the United States before and after European contact. They used a wide range of nuts and fruits for food sources and actively cultivated them through land clearing, importing plants from other locations, and planting. The planting and management of apple orchards was probably an after-contact practice.[40] For example, newcomers commented on an apple orchard around Saratoga Springs that possibly had had some spiritual significance:

Thirteen apple trees are planted on a circular ridge, elevated about a foot above the surface, having a diameter of 24 feet. Immediately inside the ridge is a depression having a breadth some six or eight feet, inside if which . . . is a mound about two feet higher than the place occupied by the trees. On the outside is another depression 10 feet wide. Directly at the north edge of the whole are two old and one young tree with sufficient space between the old trees for an Indian lodge, for which it was undoubtedly designed.[41]

The number thirteen is significant, as both Iroquoian and Algonquian peoples recognize thirteen lunar months in a year. Regardless of whether there was a spiritual significance attached to this orchard or if it was the imaginings of a local reporter, it does demonstrate the adaptability of the Mohawk (or maybe the Mahican) people here and their occupation of this place. It and other horticultural activity together with mining activity further destabilizes assumptions that hunting territories do not represent real proprietorship over the land.

While important, horticulture never totally replaced collecting wild food. It is possible Algonquian and Iroquoian peoples gathered local plants while they were working in the Adirondacks, although it is difficult to say this with certainty or to know which plants were collected other than one used as a dye, as chronicled in Kalm. His *Travels in North America* noted French botanical studies of local plants gathered for food and medicine that were based on information provided by their Indigenous allies. While at Fort Saint-Frédéric at Crown Point in 1749, Kalm commented on the use of the *gallium tinctorium* or *tisauojaune rouge* plant that grew in abundance around the fort. The plant was used by the Native peoples as a dye for porcupine quills, which were used to decorate, and the dye rarely faded. French women adopted the use of the plant to color their cloth.[42]

In addition to the previously mentioned microclimates, the region contains unusual habitats that are and have been home to rare plants. Some unusual landscapes there include bogs, limey outcrops, and arctic and alpine-like environments in the High Peaks. To obtain some of the plants that grow in the High Peaks region, one would have to travel to Labrador, Greenland, and even farther. In the mid-nineteenth century, travel and natural history writer Alfred Street described some unusual plants in Essex County: "On the summits of the highest mountains are many rare plants, some of them only found elsewhere in extreme northern latitudes. The *Arenaria groenlandica* (Greenland sandroot), and *Potentilla tridentata* (white cinquefoil), are only found on the loftiest peaks of these mountains, or of the White Mountains, New Hampshire, while the golden rod of Whiteface and Mount Marcy are found on no other mountains in the State. There are two beautiful specimens of kamaia or laurel found in the marshes."[43]

Today, some of the rare plants growing in these environments include Lapland rosebay, mountain sandwort, and diapensia, as well as sedges (grass with seeds) and uncommon mosses and liverworts. It is known that the latter have been used for medicinal purposes; for example, liverwort is used to treat pulmonary tuberculosis (a disease many traveled to the Adirondacks for a possible cure) and liver issues. Mosses have multiple uses. However, we cannot be sure whether the rare types growing there now existed in the past and if they were medically useful.[44] Without more complex research involving ethnobotanists and other scientific experts, we can only speculate. Nevertheless, as Kalm's writings indicate, Native peoples were aware of and used plants from the region. It seems doubtful that the Iroquois seasonally working in the region ignored useful plants, particularly if they could not get them in their home villages in the Mohawk Valley and if the Adirondacks were the closest place to obtain them. For the Abenaki or other Algonquian peoples, "home" was a relative term. We know they moved seasonally within a specified territory to hunt, trap, fish, and gather plants, nuts, and fruits. Here, too, it is unlikely that those Algonquian peoples who worked in the Adirondacks during their seasonal rounds ignored the useful and unique plants of the area.

In addition to meeting commonplace needs, the Adirondacks were a spiritual place. Young Kanienkehaka men paddled elm bark canoes up the northern reaches of the Hudson River and into the High Peaks for vision quests. Similarly, the Oneida held as sacred an ice cave along the Oswegatchie River. The Oswegatchie served as a boundary line

between the Oneida and the Mohawk in the eastern part of the Adirondacks. Oneida historian Loretta Metoxen notes that the cave's original
importance and location have been lost. There are several known ice
caves in and around this area, including one with a mountain, stream,
and valley named after it. It is also possible the cave was flooded when
the Stillwater Reservoir was created and is now gone.[45]

The Abenakis' spiritual center was the eastern side of Lake Champlain, and thus there are no known Abenaki spiritual places located
in the Adirondacks. However, western bands of Abenaki had a transformer deity called Odzihozo who turned himself into a rock in
today's Burlington Bay, a site that has spiritual meaning and is just
across the lake from the Adirondacks. Today this site is called Rock
Dunder (Abenaki with ties to more eastern parts of northern New
England have a different cultural hero called Gluskap; these different
cultural heroes combined with language differences are some of the
reasons Gordon Day separated these Algonquian-speaking peoples
into Eastern and Western Abenakis).[46]

Despite the dearth of professional archaeological work, plenty
of artifacts have been found throughout the region in hunting and
fishing camps as well as in rock shelters. These artifacts demonstrate
that the region was not an empty landscape and that Iroquoian and
Algonquian peoples lived in the area at least seasonally over extended
periods. While archaeologists acknowledge the great value of studying rock shelters because they were a base of operation and thus provide and protect artifacts, they have not systematically studied hunting
camps, as it is easier to study villages.[47] As a result, historians and
other scholars covering this period have to rely on nonprofessional
records and the very early findings of recent local scholarly efforts.

Far outnumbering the handful of professional archaeology efforts
in the Adirondacks are the numerous amateur finds. Literally thousands of pottery shards, tools, pipes, and other evidence are in the
possession of dozens of local archives and private collections. Pottery
artifacts are especially important finds (fig. 2). Material culture such
as pots are more than illustrative, they are "the recovered medium
through which a range of social actions are negotiated and played

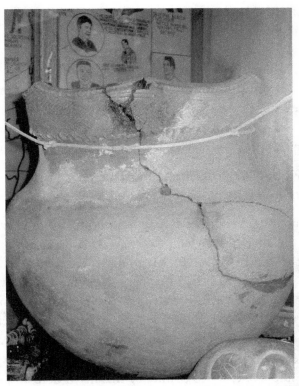

2. Iroquoian vessel found in rock shelter near Silver Lake Mountain, NY. Photograph by Melissa Otis. Courtesy of and located at Six Nations Indian Museum, Onchiota, NY.

out." Pottery styles and decoration are signs of identity and in foreign places signaled peaceful dealings. Iroquoian cooking pots were "symbols of family and hospitality." Further, pipes, tools, and points were made by men and were meant to travel, whereas pottery vessels were made by women and were considered too heavy to transport, so they were usually manufactured and discarded nearby.[48] In addition to shards, intact pots have been found in rock shelters and near lakes, as documented by the vessel in figure 2. Amateur archaeologist Peter Schuyler Miller (1912–74) wrote about the discovery of unbroken pots in the Adirondacks. He described their being "tucked away in a rock shelter—the Indian equivalent of hanging up a coffee-pot beside the lean-to for the boys who will use it next week." He also described how one intact pot found in a shelter on the Cedar River was broken by "playful lumber jacks." Rick Hill points out that Iroquoian people left pottery jars to inform others that area was part of their territory. In this case, they probably left pots at the system of hunting and fishing camps that were part of a supply chain the hunters used to send meat and hides back to their villages in the Mohawk Valley.[49]

Eurocentric and Androcentric Influences on Precolonial History

Given the abundant proof of activity and occupancy in various forms, why does the myth of an empty space with no precolonial history persist in the Adirondacks? Part of the answer may be based on the very regional location of the information. As far as I know, there are no works that suggest this breadth of coverage and no one has gone to each of these archives and pulled the information together. However, I believe it goes deeper than that. I argue that Western notions of wilderness and property, combined with notions of what constitutes bona fide work, are to blame for this myth here and probably in most places labeled as "hunting territories." As scholars have pointed out, the perception of colonial North America as empty space was influenced by John Locke's concepts of "terra nullius," which allowed colonists to see these lands as "pure nature," empty and void of ownership. This concept, combined with other aspects of colonization, such as the doctrine of discovery, grants by the Crown, and land taken as the spoils of war, allowed European colonists who came to North America (and elsewhere) to occupy what was to them a wilderness that appeared common and free for the taking and to declare it their private property. Adam Smith's 1776 *Inquiry into the Nature and Origins of the Wealth of Nations* argued that an individual's right to private property was a common good and a condition for exchange. Private property became a basis of limited government and a source of production and even wealth. As a result, the desire for private property became the American dream.[50] Islands of poor farmland in North America, such as those in the Adirondacks, were often hunting territories. They were imagined as empty landscapes void of people and culture, and this belief served as the foundation for the erasure of the history of Aboriginal peoples that worked and sometimes lived there. To early homesteaders, places resembling the Adirondacks were as Locke described them: "pure nature," empty and void of humanity.

For Indigenous peoples, dissimilar landscapes served different purposes. For the Iroquois, the forest and village symbolically represented different things: the forest was "the space of warfare, hunting, spirits, and danger," while the village was "the space of residence, agriculture, security, and peace councils."[51] Both Iroquoian and western bands of Abenaki creation stories reflect a co-creation link with nature and a need to honor it in its various forms. The unknown was questioned, and answers were sought in order to make sense of it. As J. Edward Chamberlin claims, "Every story brings the imagination and reality together in moments of what we might as well call faith." Ghost stories and enigmatic locations explained some of the mysteries of spaces like the forest, and the Adirondacks have their share of both. For example, the southwestern portion of the Great Sacandaga Reservoir in the southern Adirondacks used to be a marsh called the Vly, probably so named by the Dutch. The Mohawk say that a star fell into the wetland there and created "a 'Great Sky Hole' of mystical power" that formed giant fish and ate creatures that came to drink.[52]

In addition, the Iroquoian legend about the creation of the "Flying Head" was set in the region. The Flying Head was created after a group of young warriors anxious to leave the Adirondacks killed their chiefs, who wanted to stay. To justify their actions, the warriors beheaded all the corpses and burned the bodies. The heads were ceremoniously placed in individual canoes and rowed out onto Sacandaga Lake by the young men. They then handed each head to their leader, who tied them by their scalp-locks in a chain, weighted them down with a rock, and threw them into the lake. As the leader threw the chain of heads overboard, he was caught in the throw and was drowned himself. His followers rowed ashore and waited. Each day, some part of a large head emerged. It started as nothing more than a stain, but by the seventh day a large head with huge eyes, no body, and wings and talons appeared, which allowed the head to fly. According to Akwesasne Mohawk hunter and guide Captain Gill, the Flying Head protected the Adirondacks from settlement. Gill told this story to sports hunters he was guiding, and the tale was documented by Charles Fenno Hoffman in his *Wild Scenes in the Forest and Prairie*. Mid-nineteenth-century Euro–North Americans used Indigenous peoples' stories to connect themselves with the North American continent. At that time, Europeans and Euro-North Americans believed one was connected to one's homeland through the past. In this instance, the non-Indigenous hunters scoffed at Captain Gill's next narration about the Stone Giants and generally grew tired of his chronicles. However, this need for connection may have been the motivation for Hoffman when he included the stories in his travel narrative. Regardless of his motivation, Hoffman did record the stories, providing us an account of them in this region. And, perhaps more important, these legends are still told by Mohawk in this place and elsewhere.[53]

Stories concretely demonstrate that a specific location is part of a people's homeland. Native peoples tell stories about place to provide symbolic importance to geographical forms and establish a relationship between the people and that landscape. These stories may also serve to remind the people about events or social offenses that occurred there, along with possible corrective responses.[54] We see this happening in the tales situated in the Adirondacks. The story of the Vly told people that the marsh was a good place to fish, but they also had to be careful. The Flying Head may have been based on a tornado going through the region. A tale about wounded warriors left to die and turning into the Stone Giants around Piseco Lake is a cautionary tale about mistaken identity, a lapse in judgment, and revenge. It also represents the terrain of the Adirondacks—rocks have been used to represent that area by Iroquoian peoples.

Not only do stories show that a place is part of a homeland, but they also provide meaning to spaces we call home, while separating us from those that are not.[55] Brian Thom argues

> "First Ancestors" and other powerful beings are inscribed in the landscape through legends. . . . Relations with these ancestral figures require reciprocity, sharing and respect for other persons, both human and non-human, who are associated with place. They create and reinforce kin-based property relations, where the land at once belongs to the ancestors who dwell there, and to those living today who encounter the ancestors. . . . Ancestors may be associated with lands in numerous locations and individuals associating with these ancestors may enjoy property rights in a number of places.[56]

Clearly, Iroquoian people had stories about the Adirondacks that represented home. European explorers and early colonists, on the other hand, relied on secondhand information. They could not even rely on their imagination to understand this place, and thus they had no stories about it. Indeed, it was the Europeans, and later their descendants, who were the wanderers; the Indigenous peoples were the settlers,[57] and, I add, proprietors of the region. These narratives demonstrate that the Adirondacks were an Indigenous homeland, and these stories provided a common bond of ancestry and shared values.

Furthermore, different conceptions of legitimate work helped to shape the myth of the Adirondacks as a hunting territory without people. We understand that both early North American and European cultures assigned labor according to concepts of gender relations and roles. However, the functions men and women performed differed dramatically between Natives and newcomers. Prior to European influences, Iroquoian women's work occurred mainly in and around the village, and the men often labored in groups outside of the community. That does not mean men did not work in the village. They were responsible for clearing new fields and building and moving communities as the need arose. But Iroquoian women did the bulk of the everyday work there. Women were in charge of and even controlled the ownership of their homes and gardens through their matrilineal and matrilocal social practices. Men did plant tobacco by spreading the seeds in the spring and drying the leaves in the fall. Clan mothers also participated in government, from providing the community's views to the chiefs to selecting and dehorning those chiefs. Similarly, Iroquoian women sometimes worked outside the village. At times some traveled with men for trade, went into the forest to process game, or accompanied military expeditions to care for supplies. Iroquoian women even traveled by themselves or in groups and participated in diplomatic missions that occurred abroad. As previously mentioned, Abenaki practices were similar, except nearly everyone traveled in family bands seasonally for their work.[58]

In European and later Euro–North American colonial homesteads, men did the farming and typically employed draft animals to plough fields. They or sometimes their wives tended livestock for their main source of protein; hunting, trapping, and fishing supplemented their agricultural and herding pursuits. Both Native and White women performed much of the same domestic labor as they cared for their families. However, married colonial women rarely owned the property their home was located on, nor were they directly involved in the governance of their community. Indigenous families' gendered labor roles complimented each other and helped Native peoples survive and adapt in their territory with minimal effect on the land. However Europeans ignored these efforts and, compared to their own homelands, saw instead a failure "to tame the wilderness," which they used as justification to conquer North America.[59] Colonists and early American settlers ignored or appropriated for their own the trails, changes to the land, artifacts, material culture, and evidence of the ancestors in places like the Adirondacks so they could eventually claim it as their own private property, even if the landscape was not ideal.

Conclusion

Contradictory beliefs about nature, property, and labor helped to create the myth that the Adirondacks were "just a hunting territory" devoid of culture and people. Combined with the piecemeal and clandestine nature of the records, these perceptions have allowed the erasure of the precolonial history of Algonquian and Iroquoian men and women in this location. I argue that Westerners need to expand their concept of work and occupancy in hunting territories equivalent to this region. I have suggested that we need a complimentary term to help many North Americans move away from their concept of these spaces as having a limited use, or, more troubling, as being a landscape for sport. Today, hunting and fishing are typically recreational activities, often performed in these places under the auspices of tourism. These practices are restricted by the state to a specific number of weeks, with limits on the kind and number of animals that can be taken. This modern view of hunting and fishing as sport, and not as subsistence, colors the majority of North Americans' perceptions of these terrains. Hunting territories were not just the local grocery store with a long commute. To put it in today's language, these spaces were Wall Street with economic and financial purposes; Main Street with economic, social, and spiritual uses; and a familiar and consistent, albeit metaphorical, extended-stay hotel, which, as the next chapter discloses, eventually became year-round homes for some.

As demonstrated in this chapter, more than hunting occurred in the Adirondacks. The variety of labor and the regularity of seasonal rounds into the region combined with political and cultural connections clearly show the Adirondacks were an Indigenous homeland. In exchange for the lands' resources, Iroquoian and Algonquian peoples offered their energy (often through their labor) as well as spiritual expressions (such as tobacco offerings), and they ceremoniously laid their dead to rest here. They also left evidence of their culture and themselves by leaving pots and creating stories about this place. All of these gestures created an imprint and reciprocal exchange with the land that made sense in their worldview. The Adirondacks, as an example of a location of exchange, should give most North Americans pause to reconsider the complexity of landscapes known as hunting territories. Such consideration should include the fact that the space's occupancy was varied and adapted over time by the Indigenous peoples who considered the area as part of their homeland.

As the next chapter notes, the Adirondacks continued to be occupied in a similar fashion for a time. Due to European contact, however, occupation also took on new and various forms. Chapter 2 describes how Mohawk, Oneida, and Abenaki peoples adapted their use of this space in response to Europeans. In addition, it looks at some of their neighbors who came to the region seeking a place of refuge to escape the violence that colonial contact had created in their own homelands during the late seventeenth and eighteenth centuries. At this time, the Adirondacks ceased to be a totally seasonally occupied space, as some chose to occupy portions of the region year round or nearly so as part of their survival strategy. The Adirondacks, too, saw its share of violence, especially in the post–Revolutionary War period and into the early nineteenth century as Native and non-Native trappers competed with one another. This situation required Algonquian and Iroquoian peoples to rely on their traditional diplomatic skills and at the same time adapt to new forms of nineteenth-century labor and occupancy, while maintaining their tenure in the Adirondacks.

2

"Couxsachrâgé"

A Contact History of Iroquoian and Algonquian Peoples in the Adirondacks to 1840

DURING THE MID-1800s, Reverend John Todd, a minister from Massachusetts, spent summers near Indian Lake and began to record a history of the area:

> Indian Lake received its name from an old Indian who came to it many years ago, bringing an only son, and who have lived there in their rude wigwam up to the present time. The old man's name is Sabael; born on the Penobscot, more than a century ago, and afterwards joining the Canada Abenaquis Indians. When, in our last war with Great Britain, the Abenaquis were induced to fight against the United States, he, being a Penobscot, left his tribe, and relinquished

Lewis Evans, *A General Map of the British Middle Colonies in America* (1755) used the word "*Couch Sachrage*" over a mostly empty region today known as the Adirondacks. A copy of this map is printed in Sulavik, *Adirondack*, 159; the original is located in the Sterling Memorial Library map collection at Yale University. The word has also been spelled *Coughsachraga*. For example, see Nathaniel Bartlett Sylvester, *Historical Sketches of Northern New York and the Adirondack Wilderness: Including Traditions of the Indians, Early Explorers, Pioneer Settlers, Hermit Hunters, &c* (Harrison, NY: Harbor Hill Books, 1877; repr. 1973), 39, interpreted as "dismal wilderness." John Fadden, e-mail message to author, Apr. 23 and Apr. 29, 2010; according to his wife, Mohawk speaker Eva Fadden, the word is probably the Mohawk *Koh-ah-sa-tsa-ra-ka* (pronounced koh-se-ra-ke), meaning "winter" or "during winter."

the yearly stipend which the Canada Indians receive from the British government, and came off through the wilderness, and settled on this lonely lake. At that time the country was well stocked with moose, beaver, otters, and deer. The two former are mostly gone, while the deer, the otter, and the bear, remain in abundance. This old Indian was in the battle at Quebec, when Wolfe fell and the city was taken. His father was a kind of chief or brave, and he was his father's cook. He knows that he was then twelve years old. The battle took place in 1759, consequently he must now be a hundred and one years old.[1]

Todd's introduction of Sabael Benedict, while not totally accurate, alludes to the complex relationship between Native peoples and the borderlands regions of the Northeast before the era of wilderness tourism. Sabael Benedict's story, which is told further in this chapter, illustrates the complexity of this early contact. This chapter focuses on the relationship between Iroquoian and Algonquian peoples and the Adirondacks after contact with Europeans and later Euro–North Americans up to the early 1840s. The precontact seasonal work and occupation by Native peoples in this homeland, discussed in chapter 1, continued during this time period. However, association with European officials, merchants, settlers, and military officers during the colonial era created other opportunities for entangled exchanges, such as work in the commercial fur trade and participation in military campaigns.

This was also an abstruse period of conflict and cooperation between the competing Indigenous groups. As the historiography of this era demonstrates, Iroquoian and Algonquian nations of the Northeast chose European allies as part of a strategy for economic and political power and, later, survival. These interactions created or exacerbated violent encounters between Iroquois and Algonquian peoples. Because European settlers avoided the Adirondacks, the region also became a place of refuge during the seventeenth and eighteenth centuries for some of those Native peoples who already occupied this place, along with others, especially southern New England Algonquian peoples fleeing from the violence brought on by colonization. The region continued its role as a place of refuge during the nineteenth century as pressures on the land and economy around nearby reserve communities increased over time. Of particular interest to the history of the Adirondacks were the former Catholic mission villages of Akwesasne (St. Regis) and Odanak (St. Francis), mostly located in Canada.

Although sparse, White settlement and resource industries expanded into most of the Adirondacks by the 1830s, which affected Iroquoian and Algonquian occupation. The lumber industry began on a small scale around 1803 and rivers were declared public highways in 1806 to accommodate this industry; lumbering was well underway by 1820. The large pines around the perimeter of the area were exhausted by 1830, so lumbermen switched to spruce. In order to get at older pine and spruce in the interior, lumbering interests began to dam rivers and lakes to send logs down these watercourses to mills such as those at Glens Falls on the Hudson River. Further, the Champlain Canal connecting Lake Champlain with the Hudson River was opened on September 10, 1823, and the Erie Canal, just south of the Adirondacks, was finished two years later. Mining began at the turn of the nineteenth century with small forges and mills, and this industry also began in earnest by the 1820s.[2] These resource extraction business efforts gradually affected the ability of Algonquian and Iroquoian peoples to traditionally occupy the region. Those who chose to stay assumed a strategy of cooperation and adapted their style of work and occupation to accommodate this Euro-American expansion. While continuing to hunt, fish, and trap, these Native settlers also began guiding homesteaders, industrialists, surveyors, scholars, and eventually tourists who made use of their knowledge of the landscape. As this chapter argues, they became "safe" Indians for eastern Euro-Americans to meet and hire, and together with local non-Native Adirondackers, some of whom learned their woodcraft from Mohawk and Abenaki neighbors, they helped set the stage for wilderness tourism in the area.

Evidence of Continued and Adapting Occupation

Indigenous peoples connected to the Adirondacks continued to use and occupy the region after contact, and their presence is notable in a variety of forms. As contact between Iroquoian and Algonquian peoples and Europeans in the Northeast became more common in the seventeenth and eighteenth centuries, the Adirondacks continued to be occupied and used as a place of resources and labor, as described in chapter 1. For example, the "Indian Council Grounds" in North Elba continued to be used during the colonial period. The area around Split Rock located in present-day Whallons Bay was well known to the Mohawk, who brought captives there during colonial wars and also mined lead nearby around Split Rock Mountain. Records indicate that a fishing encampment and settlement with an apple orchard also existed when settlers arrived at Saratoga in the mid- to late eighteenth century, as well as Indian settlements near the Mourningkill River and at the head of Ballston Lake.[3]

Late eighteenth- and early nineteenth-century records of settlers arriving in the Adirondacks reference Indian encampments and communities. For example, newcomers to Warren County noted several seasonal settlements including at "Harrisena, Dunham's Bay (at the southern extremity of Lake George), at the outlet of the Long Pond, at the Big Bend (the sweeping curve of the Hudson about three miles above Glens Falls), and at the foot of the Palmerton Mountain on the south side of the river." This last group was probably the "Palmertown" Indians, who will be discussed shortly. These camps were used during the winter for trapping and in the summer and fall for fishing and hunting. Both Natives and settlers lived together peacefully for a number of years. Newcomers arriving at present-day Horicon around 1810 tell of finding Native people, believed to be Iroquoian, living there seasonally. It is believed that Brant Lake, the centerpiece of Horicon Township, is named after an Indian family by the name of Brant who were established there. Originally, townspeople thought the lake was named for Joseph Brant, but a relative of the family living in Glens Falls told local historian William H. Brown his "Indian grandmother" was the family who lived there. This local history also notes that early residents claim there was an Indian village at Waters Swamp.[4] Warren County was not the only one with this rich history, others will be discussed below.

Fur Trade and Military Adaptions

Contact with European settlers, merchants, and military officers increased the amount and type of labor performed by Iroquoian and Algonquian peoples in the Adirondacks to include commercial trapping and military service. Little has been written about the fur trade in the area, despite the region being recognized by Europeans and Natives alike as Five Nations Iroquois land generally and, more specifically, Mohawk and Oneida hunting territory. In addition, as previously mentioned, the southeastern part of the region was Mahican country, and the northwestern section was used by the Onondaga. Oneida, Mohawk, Abenaki, Mahican, Onondaga, and other Algonquian and Iroquoian peoples worked in the Adirondacks for commercial trappers during the colonial era, either in cooperation or by competing with each other.

The beaver population in the area was purported to be nearly wiped out by 1690, although the area continued to be trapped by Native Americans and, later, Euro-Americans, which kept the beaver population low. This belief that the beaver were nearly extinct in the Northeast by the end of the seventeenth century has been called into question by William Starna and Jose Antonio Brandão in their article "From the Mohawk-Mahican War to the Beaver Wars." Starna and Brandão disagree that the beavers were played out in Iroquoia or that more northern furs were superior. Further, the beaver were, and still are, largely responsible for creating the wetlands in the Adirondacks, and decimating the beaver populations there changes the landscape. Eighteenth-century maps described the region as swampy and containing "drowned lands," which might support the case that beaver were still present enough in the area to at least continue to influence the landscape. Recall from chapter 1, even eighteenth-century mapmakers had not ventured into the area; they obtained their information from Native peoples. It is possible that there were still a number of beaver in the region, or that Native peoples were not totally truthful when describing it, perhaps to protect it from competition and settlement. Once Euro-Americans settled the region and began to dam rivers, extract resources, and drain wetlands in the nineteenth century, the landscape changed much more quickly and more obviously. The trapping and hunting of small and large animals in the region continued to be sufficiently profitable during and after the colonial period to lure Native and non-Native trappers. The commercial fur trade that the region supported during the colonial era brought about conflict and, it is likely, environmental and economic consequences.[5]

There is ample evidence in early local records that attests to Iroquoian and Algonquian peoples continuing to hunt, trap, and seasonally occupy the Adirondacks after the American Revolution. For example, in 1802, Mrs. Arabella Anderson arrived in Bolton with her father Daniel Nims. She described the area as being covered by "trackless forests" and said that "Indians roamed about the vicinity in considerable numbers."[6] An address by Charles E. Snyder entitled "John Brown's Tract, Herkimer" described this western tract in the 1830s as still being a popular hunting territory for Native peoples: "Canadian Indians from the north would gradually work their way through the forest, hunting and trapping as they went, taking their furs to the Albany market; and it was not an unfrequent [sic] sight for the early settlers at No. 4, to see at times Indians proudly walking through the forest past the settlement, guns in hand ready for an emergency, while on behind trudged the patient squaws, drawing rude sleds made of birch saplings loaded with furs and camp outfit."[7] James DeKay's *Zoology of New York* reported "St. Regis" Indians trapping three hundred beaver in 1815; they were noted on the Oswegatchie River in St. Lawrence County. DeKay attributed the large take due to the War of 1812 reducing hunting in the area and allowing the beaver to come back in the region. Even as late as 1835, the centrally located town of Raquette Lake was described as virgin territory by the brothers John and Will Constable, who also indicated "Indians were still frequenters of the lakes and surrounding wilderness."[8]

Military service–type labor in the region increased with contact. European military records indicate the region saw at least one important seventeenth-century battle as Samuel de Champlain and his allies fought the Iroquois around Crown Point or Ticonderoga in 1609. Chapter 9 of Champlain's *Voyages of Samuel de Champlain: 1604–1610* describes his expedition into Lake Champlain and this battle. In addition, the water route between Lake Champlain and the Mohawk River was used at least twice in the mid- to late 1600s by the French in campaigns against the Iroquois. By 1700, the French were using canoes on Lake Champlain to stop pelts from going to Albany. The region occasionally served as a military route, and skirmishes occurred in and around the region. For example, the Seven Years or French and Indian War (1754–63) included the Battle of Carillon or Ticonderoga (1758) and the Battle of Lake George (September 8, 1755). During the American Revolution (1775–83), fighting occurred up and down Lake Champlain in some of the first American naval battles, such as the Battle of Valcour Island (1776), as well as important land encounters, such as the Battle of Saratoga (1777), which is considered to be a turning point in the war. Besides the eastern part of the Adirondacks, other regions saw their share of intrigue and battles based on their proximity to the Mohawk River, Lake Ontario, and the St. Lawrence River. Richard Berleth claims the interior of the Adirondacks "virtually belonged to the loyalists," who used it as a route to escape to Canada.[9]

Some Mohawk and Abenaki associated with the Adirondacks were known for their military service. For example, Sabael Benedict was reportedly twelve years of age at the Battle of Quebec (1759) and acted as a cook for his father's band of warriors. Abenaki Captain Peter Sabattis (also known as Jean-Baptiste Saint-Denys, c. 1767–after 1842) was a veteran of the War of 1812 and continued to live in the Adirondacks afterward, as did Louis Watso (also known as Louis Degonzague and Watso Otondosonne, c. 1778–1885). Benoni Paul (probably Wampanoag and Mohegan) died serving in the War of 1812. His grandfather, Moses, together with his brothers John and

Samson Paul, scouted the area of Lake George for Major Israel Putnam's company during the Seven Years War. Many of the descendants of these and other Native families also fought in the American Civil War and subsequent conflicts.[10]

Indigenous men also acted as guides, scouts, and point or advance guards in military operations in and around the Adirondacks. They fought in battles and bargained with European officers over the use of their territory as throughways, and they escorted emissaries and wagons on military roads. In addition, they captured enemies, sometimes negotiated their release, and returned those captives. Furthermore, they spied, acted as informants for explorers and cartographers, and patrolled the forests around forts.[11]

As previously mentioned, the region itself served as a buffer between imperial powers, with the French in the north, the Dutch to the south in the seventeenth century (1609–64, 1673–74), and the English in the east (who later replaced the Dutch). Colonial powers tried to lure Iroquoian and Algonquian peoples to settle around the Adirondacks to create additional safeguards against their European rivals.[12] Mahican and New England Algonquian peoples were invited to settle at Schaghticoke southeast of the Adirondacks by the English colonial Governor of New York, Sir Edmund Andros, in the 1670s. He must have had some success, as the population of Schaghticoke was one thousand by 1676. Future New York Governor Thomas Dongan attempted to lure "French Indians" from Kahnawake to Saratoga in 1687 for this purpose. Two French mission communities along the St. Lawrence River just north of the Adirondacks served the same function for the French in Canada. The mission called La Présentation was founded in 1748 and was located near present-day Ogdensburg, New York. A stopping place for the voyageurs who referred to this location as La Galette, La Présentation was mostly made up of Catholic Onondaga and Cayuga and a few Oneida; it was hoped they would guard Fort Frontenac and the upper St. Lawrence River. The French mission also attempted to attract trappers away from the English at Oswego. The mission became Fort Oswegatchie under the English in 1760 and was forcibly abandoned in 1806 under that name. Some of the inhabitants moved to Akwesasne, and by that time a number of the inhabitants were Mahican and Abenaki refugees from Odanak.

The other mission community was Akwesasne, or St. Regis, which was established around 1750 by disaffected members of Kahnawake. Akwesasne became a permanent settlement around 1755, but it had been a long-held Mohawk fishing and hunting area prior to this time and became an extraregional satellite of principle communities on the Mohawk River. In addition, at least one temporary Native community sprang up near Fort Saint Frédéric at Crown Point in the 1730s, and possibly others did so around other forts in the region (for example, Fort Carillion, near today's Fort Ticonderoga, was also a trading post under the French).[13]

The records are mostly silent about Native women's roles in military service in the Adirondacks, but there is one interesting exception. During the Battle of Lake George in 1755, Theyanoguin (King Hendrick) was killed while trying to escape "by a party of bayonet-wielding Kahnawake women guarding their warrior's supplies." In other contexts, though, it is clear that Iroquoian and Algonquian women participated in warfare. The military roles of Haudenosaunee women have been described as being quite powerful and versatile, ranging from Molly Brant's diplomacy and intelligence gathering to women's withdrawal of food and their services when they did not support a war party. In general, women supported military efforts by making and mending shoes and clothing, planting crops, and providing shelter and provisions for passing warriors. Some women also accompanied the men on campaigns and performed the necessary work of camp chores. In at least one instance, the wife of an injured Oneida warrior (Thawengarakwen, or Honyery Doxtater) fought alongside her husband in the Battle of Oriskany, which occurred just south of the region in the Mohawk Valley.[14]

Place of Refuge before the American Revolution

During the colonial period, Iroquoian and Algonquian peoples' worlds became more violent because of pressure on their territories from European settlement, competition in the fur trade, and epidemics.

Warfare and colonization played a significant role in creating the need for spaces of refuge throughout the colonies of North America. Still avoided by European settlers, the Adirondacks also became a haven for a number of Algonquian peoples from New England, adding to and changing the type of occupation in the region. Several refugee communities cropped up during this time. For example, the "Palmertown" Indian community was established around Mount McGregor in northern Saratoga County prior to the Seven Years War, perhaps as early as the late seventeenth century. Its members appear to have been refugees from Connecticut who remained in the Palmertown (sometimes spelled Palmerton) Mountain range until Euro-American settlement pushed them out during the nineteenth century.

The "Podunk" Indians were located in Hogtown near the Washington and Warren County borders on the east side of Lake George. *Podunk* is an Algonquian word that is thought to mean "neck or point of land." They were also thought to be Algonquian refugees from southern New England who shared their encampment with the Mahican. It is possible these were members of the Paudunk people, who lived along the Connecticut River; their territory ranged along today's Massachusetts and Connecticut border area.

Between Lake George and Schroon Lake were the "Horikan" Indians, who lived around the previously mentioned Brant Lake. In addition, as late as 1858, a Warren County map showed an established Indian settlement between Thirteenth Lake or Pond and Puffer Pond near Johnsburg; it covered several surveyed lots. Their identity is not further known.[15] Two communities of people, thought to be Algonquian, were reported to have lived in wigwams in today's Elizabethtown at the turn of the nineteenth century. One Native village was across from where early settler Azel Abel built his log hotel between the Boquet (pronounced bo-qwet) River and the Maplewood Inn, and the other was located at or near the John Barton Homestead on Barton Brook. By 1798, the two villages were connected by "a well-worn Indian trail, a path of a foot or more in width and several inches in depth." The son of Azel Abel, Oliver Abel Sr., took the path to play with the Indian boys in the village at Barton's. In addition, the existence of many artifacts elsewhere suggests there were previous occupations, too. Euro-American settlers who arrived in Elizabethtown at this time observed these Indigenous people, who outnumbered the newcomers for a while. The obituary of Abigail Rice Johnson noted that her father was Amos Rice, an early settler to the community who arrived in 1801. The obituary claimed the Indians living there thought his arrival in a wagon was a strange sight. Oliver Abel described the Native peoples living there as never forgiving an abuse nor forgetting a kindness. They "were good natured, easy going fellows, given to the chase almost entirely. They used stone mortars and other utensils of their own invention. They hunted with bows and arrows mostly and were successful." Local historian George Levi Brown ends his first chapter by noting, "The Indians . . . who were numerous here a little over a century ago, gradually fell back before the advancing wave of civilization." He concludes by dismissing "the 'noble red man,' who once fished the streams and hunted the forests of Pleasant Valley, enjoying his natural birthright to his heart's content."[16] This suggests that Natives and newcomers lived peacefully together until the number of settlers increased to the point this growth affected the ability of these Native peoples to successfully hunt in the vicinity, forcing them to move.

The history of Parishville in St. Lawrence County records an existing Native community south of their village located in the "South Woods" near a brook. The vicinity became known as Picketville to incoming settlers whose activities eventually drove the Native community away. Town historian Emma Remington notes that what appear to be sunken graves exist in the Picketville area and that they pre-date Euro-American settlement. This may suggest that Picketville, believed to be an Abenaki community and the birthplace of Adirondack guide Mitchel Sabattis (see chapter 3), was home to those Abenaki who remained around Akwesasne after Robert Rogers' raid on Odanak on October 4, 1759.[17] Rogers and about two hundred of his "rangers" began their expedition to Odanak from Crown Point on Lake Champlain in September. Rogers claimed to have killed three hundred Abenaki, but scholars believe he exaggerated the figure to make up for the number of rangers that died. French records indicate the raid killed thirty Abenaki out of a likely population of five hundred; twenty of the dead were women and children. Many men were away fighting or hunting, but news about the raid spread quickly, and Rogers' Rangers were pursued and forced to split up with the result that Rogers lost nearly one third of his men. Nevertheless, the raid destroyed Odanak and caused the Abenaki and other Algonquian peoples who lived there to scatter, and some went to Akwesasne.[18]

Nineteenth-century wilderness guides also provided information about sites of Indian occupation. Guide Carlos Whitney (c. 1838–1917) reported that the "Saranac" Indians lived at the Indian Carry in two communities between the Upper Saranac and Stony Creek Ponds as late as the 1850s. Coreys and the Indian Carry in Franklin County were well-known and long-standing ends of a portage or "carry" between these two bodies of water prior to contact. According to Whitney, the men hunted and fished in the area, and the women grew corn. Early settlers noted that young men demonstrated feats of their masculinity by tying knots in sapling trees. In addition, the Indians there used a nearby lead mine for making bullets. Euro-American innkeepers built Coreys (or Rustic Lodge) and Hiawatha Lodge over the two communities. Carlos recalled coming upon an Indian woman who was ice fishing on the Upper Saranac, thus demonstrating the area was occupied in the wintertime as well as in the warmer weather during the nineteenth century. Abenaki Maurice Paul Dennis (Denis) claimed the "Saranac" Indians were Abenaki and that they started hunting in the Adirondacks around 1600. The word Saranac is believed to be a corruption of the Abenaki word "Salanac" which, according to anthropologist, J. Dyneley Prince, means sumac bud or cone.[19] Given the practice of settlers naming Indian peoples for their place of origin—for example, "St. Regis" Indians—it is plausible they were a group of Abenaki who had settled in the region and became known as the "Saranac" Indians.

While the region continued to support the precolonial type of occupation, as described in chapter 1, the Adirondacks clearly became a place of refuge for other Algonquian and possibly Iroquoian peoples due to the violence and settlement expansion that occurred during the colonial period. Anthropologist Robbie Ethridge and historian Sheri Shuck-Hall use the term "Mississippian shatter zone" as a framework to explain the instability of the eastern part of North America as a result of colonization and the Indian slave trade (or for captives in the case of the Iroquois and northern New England Algonquian peoples) from the late sixteenth to the early eighteenth century. New England and New York are part of this framework. Such a situation was not unique to the Adirondacks or even North America. In his study of Southeast Asia, James C. Scott uses the terms "shatter zones" and "zones of refuge" to describe a similar situation for Southeast Asian peoples who, over various periods of time, used a mountainous region that encompassed several boundaries to deliberately escape state-making and its social structures. Scott describes *shatter zones* as regions where state-making processes or natural disasters caused people to leave their homeland for more peripheral and remote areas. In the process they often created a diverse region of ethnicity, custom, and language called *zones of refuge* where people purposefully and politically place themselves out of the reach of the state. Inaccessible landscape and mobility are the two principles these refugees use to thwart state efforts to absorb them, and sometimes they also adopt ambiguous identities.[20] Refugee communities in the Adirondacks fit Scott's definitions, especially as warfare and colonization based on world capitalism created shatter zones in the homelands of Algonquian peoples in the Northeast. Affected Algonquian peoples from New England and elsewhere moved into the isolated Adirondacks, using land and water routes as a means of mobility. Further, the peoples who fled there took on ambiguous identities to escape the reach of Europeans and, perhaps, their Indigenous enemies. As a result, the Adirondacks became a more intensively used home for these refugees to escape this violence and settlement.

All the refugee communities disappeared by the mid-nineteenth century. Local historian George Levi Brown alludes to the two villages in Elizabethtown being quietly pushed out because Euro-American settlement intruded on the hunting there. It is likely all of these communities met the same fate. Yet, as these refugee communities vanished, a new zone of refuge was created as Abenaki and Mohawk individuals and families arrived to escape the pressures brought on by reservation life.

Place of Refuge after the Revolutionary War

After the American Revolution and the War of 1812, a border was established between the United States and British North America (later Canada), which created a more peaceful type of shatter zone. The Treaty of Paris in 1783 created the 45th Parallel as the border between the United States and British North America in the Northeast. The boundary was firmly established by the 1814 Treaty of Ghent which ended the War of 1812. This border separated the Abenaki communities of Odanak in Quebec and what was left of an important seasonal village, Missisquoi, in present-day northwestern Vermont. For the Kanienkehaka at Akwesasne, the border was even more invasive; it split their Mohawk community between two nation states, two provinces, and the state of New York. The border and reserves also challenged the mobility of these Algonquian and Iroquoian peoples, which they often ignored. However, what they could not ignore was the eventual land pressure from Euro-Canadian, and to some degree American, settlement.

The Abenaki of northern New England who retreated to Odanak during the violent period of the eighteenth century were not the same as the Algonquian peoples of southern New England. The latter, including the Mahican and other Algonquian-speakers in the southeastern part of today's New York State, led semisettled and agrarian lifestyles that resembled those of the Five (and later Six) Nations Iroquois. Northern New England Algonquians, which included western bands of Abenaki, had a seminomadic lifestyle. Their traditional territory was made up of today's states of Vermont, New Hampshire, and northern Massachusetts, as well as parts of southern Quebec in Canada. These differences were undoubtedly a result of the environmental variations in the landscape, climate, and soil conditions. The northern part of New England is mountainous with valleys that contain heavily forested hardwood trees and has a harsher climate than the southern part of the region, which is affected by the ocean. Traditionally, the Abenaki lived in seasonal villages near major water routes during the coldest weeks of the winter and the spring. For example, Missisquoi was an important seasonal community located in northern Vermont on the river of the same name, which flows into Lake Champlain. After their midwinter festival around February, most Abenaki families left their seasonal town and hunted moose and deer. In the spring, they returned to the village, where women tapped maple trees, gathered wild food products, and planted crops while the men fished and hunted fowl. During the summer months, many families moved to ponds or lakes. Men continued to fish and hunt while women tended their gardens, gathered plants for food and medicine, and picked berries. In the fall, most families traveled to their hunting grounds to obtain more meat for the upcoming winter.[21]

Abenaki hunting territories were clearly defined. They were based on "a system of trails related to watercourses. In the center of each hunting territory was a tributary stream of a larger river. . . . [T]he tributary served as a transportation artery, from which one could gain access to all parts of the territory." While not precisely fixed, boundaries were based on separations between watersheds. Families marked their territory often with blazes. Non–family members who wanted to hunt there needed to ask permission, which was rarely, if ever, denied among their own people. In addition, the Abenaki managed game resources by using only a portion of the territory in any given year.[22]

Politically, the Abenaki worked in family bands consisting of one to three families of fifteen to forty people. Macrobands were alliances of various family bands who worked together within a shared village and watershed. Each macroband governed with their elders, a war chief, and a civil chief, the latter being the most significant. Band leaders were chosen based on their "exceptional prowess and prestige" and continued in their position based on their ability to be persuasive and influential. Most marriages occurred between macroband members. When a marriage occurred with another macroband, the two became related to each other, which allowed them to share hunting territories, trade, and cooperate in common endeavors such as defense.[23] As a result of the dynamic nature of their communities, Abenaki leaders learned to be diplomatic and choose strategies to maintain peace and power.

During times of crisis, Abenaki bands dispersed and scattered; they regrouped when the emergency passed. During the seventeenth and eighteenth centuries they escaped to Catholic mission villages, especially to Odanak (which was created c. 1660–1700) and to seasonal villages such as Missisquoi in present-day northern Vermont. Eventually, these villages also contained Algonquian refugees from southern New England and some Mahican from the refugee village of Schaghticoke (c. 1675–1754), a community that also included southern New England Algonquian peoples. When Schaghticoke broke up, many of the inhabitants first went to Missisquoi and then on to Odanak with their Abenaki hosts. The remaining Schaghticoke residents taken during the Albany raid of 1754 went directly to Odanak. However, that did not mean the Abenaki gave up their homelands throughout northern New England and southern Quebec. Because of their affiliation with the French, the British tried to keep the Abenaki within the community of Odanak after the end of the Seven Years War (1763). This resulted in some leaving for other locations, including the Adirondacks.[24]

After the American Revolution, some Abenaki returned to their traditional territory around Missisquoi only to discover that the Levi, Ira, and Ethan Allen families had used the Abenaki's strategy of dispersal as an excuse to appropriate their land and build on it. The Allen brothers strategically called the Abenaki "Canadian Indians" and emphasized their itinerant habits to successfully weaken the latter's territorial claims. As a result, some Abenaki stayed on in Vermont, living quietly in small isolated neighborhoods, as itinerants, or hiding in environments such as swamps.[25] However, many removed or returned to Odanak, which created increased population pressure for that community. In addition, the nearby Eastern Townships opened for Loyalist settlement in 1792. This development resulted in greater pressure on the surrounding Abenaki hunting and fishing territory. In 1797, the

Abenaki petitioned for more territory, and the British "granted" them 8,150 acres in the township of Durham in 1805. By 1831, the nearby Algonquins formally protested by way of a petition to the Six Nations in Brantford, Ontario (since the Crown did not want to get involved), that the Abenaki were hunting on their territory. The Six Nations ruled in favor of the Abenaki. In addition, the Crown sold lands the Abenaki used for hunting and trapping to private clubs for sport, with the result that some Abenaki hunters became guides working for pay on their former territory. Other portions of their hunting territory were turned over to lumbering interests, where some Abenaki found wage work. By 1852, the initial phase of pulp manufacturing began on the St. Francis River and altered transportation routes, which ruined fishing and hunting. Provincial legislation began to limit the type of game and fish and when it could be taken in the 1850s. Besides land and economic pressures, the Abenaki were also facing spiritual dilemmas. A fire at the Odanak Catholic Church in 1819 resulted in arguments over whether to build separate churches for the Abenaki and Euro-Canadian Catholics in the largely Catholic community. When Dartmouth-educated Protestant Abenaki Pierre Paul (Osunkhirhine) Masta (c. 1829–58) returned home to Odanak after 1829, he began to seek converts, which had political overtones and contributed to the tension.[26] As a result of these and other changes, many Abenaki had to find different ways or places to live: one of these places was the Adirondacks, although by no means was it the only one.

The culturally and largely ethnically Mohawk of Akwesasne also experienced settlement pressure as well as social, political, and industrialization demands. After Rogers' raid on Odanak in 1759, the Kanienkehaka absorbed other Native peoples, including Abenaki and other Algonquians who had fled Odanak. By 1769, the Mohawk began to complain about the Odanak refugees still at Akwesasne, and many left; however, a few remained and intermarried with them. In addition, some of the Catholic Onondaga and Cayuga from Fort Oswegatchie (formerly La Présentation or La Galette under the French) moved there after New York State forced them to abandon their homes in 1806. As a result, Akwesasne became ethnically multicultural, although the community remained culturally Mohawk. Both the Abenaki and Oswegatchie Iroquois kept their own chiefs until the War of 1812, and Abenaki names were kept separate in records until the 1820s. Church records indicate there was a three-way movement between Akwesasne, Missisquoi, and Odanak. In addition, the residents of Akwesasne endured violent threats to their homeland during the War of 1812. While the conclusion of this war ended imperial conflicts, other changes continued to press them, such as the replacement of their communal form of agriculture with Westernized family farms. Crop failures and famine became an issue: 1816 was known as the year of no summer because of a volcano eruption in Italy, and snow remained on the ground until June. The people of Akwesasne suffered through sporadic epidemics from 1820 to 1850 and may have lost as much as half their population. Matching the Abenaki experience, from the late 1850s on the St. Regis Mohawk were also affected by provincial conservation and game laws that limited their ability to obtain game and fish near their reserve.[27]

Subsistence hunting nearby became unproductive early on as Loyalist and immigrant settlement moved near the community. Fishing, though, remained viable until the mid-twentieth century, when industrial pollution from plants on the St. Lawrence River ended that practice. By the 1850s, Akwesasne men were working in the lumbering industry and piloting rafts on the St. Lawrence River. Mohawk men began working as ironworkers near Montreal in the 1850s and later commuted to urban areas like New York City to work. Akwesasne historian Daren Bonaparte describes the landscape at that time as being deforested by settlement—"a wasteland of sorts, devoid of the very means of survival. It was during this era that many people began to relocate for much of the year and only returned to Akwesasne in the warmer seasons." Despite these many and profound changes, Mohawk people maintained their customary *style* of working and applied it to the emerging nineteenth-century economy. Men chose work that fit long-standing, pre- and early-contact practices of group travel on a temporary or seasonal basis to support their families. Kanienkehaka women mostly worked from home, and some used their traditional skills to make crafts to sell to a growing market. However, a few, often unmarried or child-less women worked in nearby town's factories, and some traveled with their men to markets, such as Indian encampments (see chapter 5).[28]

Given these and other external and internal pressures in their communities, Abenaki and Mohawk peoples had to consider other ways to support their families. Historian Frank Tough argues that "movements and intended movements of Native peoples are important indications of their response to a changing regional economy."[29] Based on the considerable movement of Abenaki and Mohawk individuals and families, one can logically conclude that the economies in and around their reserves were changing, and not for the better. As a result, some moved to the Adirondacks, a region that was familiar to them, to obtain the resources they needed. Eventually, those who came to the area were able to reasonably contend with the nineteenth-century market economy and modernity. Originally, they went to the Adirondacks in the late eighteenth and early nineteenth centuries to trap, hunt, fish, and possibly gather. They eventually began to augment these efforts by performing seasonal work in tourism and resource industries for wages.

The presence of Iroquoian and Algonquian peoples in the area during this early period is evident by the appearance of individuals in local histories, and a few even had towns or geographic features named after them. For example, Piseco Lake was named by the early nineteenth-century surveyor Joshua Brown after a "St. Regis" Mohawk he thought was named Pezeeko, who Brown found living on the western shore of the lake. According to my conversation with Parishville historian Emma Remington, Joe Indian Pond, Joe Indian Road, and Joe Indian Island in Cranberry Lake in St. Lawrence County are named for "Indian Jo" (as it should be spelled).[30]

Other Native peoples were well known by local communities, perhaps because of their Indian ancestry, and they made it into local histories. Samson Paul was mentioned in H. P. Smith's *History of Warren County* because he killed a panther with a pitchfork. Paul was part of a southern New England Wampanoag and Stockbridge family, some of whom relocated to the area after the Seven Years War.

Samson Paul married a local Euro-American woman, and they had at least one daughter, Christina, who was born in Warren County. She married Erustus (Esustus?) Jaqua, who was born in the western part of the state. The 1855 New York State Census identified them both as Indians making a living as basketmakers in Hague, the northernmost stop for Lake George steamers, which was a good location to sell baskets. Jaqua was forty-five and Christina was forty, and they had a two-month-old male child living with them with the last name of Jaqua.[31]

Other individuals were merely mentioned in passing as part of the early lore or history. For example, an Indian trapper called "Old Alec" was said to live near Duanes in Franklin County. Another allegedly "lone" Indian was the previously mentioned "Indian Jo," who lived near Parishville with his wife. Legend claimed he had been banished from his community. However, he froze to death on or next to the St. Lawrence River near Massena, which is a town just west of Akwesasne. If this is the case, it leads one to believe Jo and perhaps his wife were Mohawk and that at least he kept in touch with their community. Even less is known about the unnamed "old Indian who lived in a hut [in Derrick] and prayed in Latin and knew all about the animals."[32] Such narratives of "lone Indians" were meant to convince Euro-American settlers that Native peoples had vanished from a region, a device that anthropologist Margaret Bruchac urges needs to be countered by stressing the importance of including Aboriginal families and communities when writing histories. One such case in point in the Adirondacks is Sabael Benedict, who brought his family to the region around the time of the American Revolution. They became the first recorded family of any ethnicity to live in the interior year round. As a result, the towns of Indian Lake and Sabael in Hamilton County are named in honor of Sabael Benedict. Lewey Lake is named after Sabael's son Louis Elijah, and Squaw Brook and Squaw Brook Mountain are named for his wife, Marie Angelique Ignace.[33]

As Euro-American settlers arrived in the nineteenth century, some took up residence near the Benedicts and other Native families in communities such as Elizabethtown, Picketville, and Indian Lake. Over the course of this century, a number of Abenaki people and a few Mohawk and Oneida even moved close to tourist towns. A small group arrived at Ballston Spa as early as 1800 to make and sell baskets; more followed decades later to Saratoga Springs, Sharon Springs, Lake Luzerne, Old Forge, and Caldwell (now Lake George). All but Old Forge (which was settled later) had Indian encampments that catered to tourists. These Native newcomers moved to these encampments on a seasonal basis to take advantage of tourism's economic opportunities. A few, as in the case of the Watso and Camp families in Lake George and members of the Denis families in Lake Luzerne and Old Forge, even decided to stay more permanently. The encampments and families who worked them are discussed further in chapter 5.

Historians typically ignore small Indian communities that existed beside larger Euro-American ones because they assume these Native families assimilated into the dominant White community. However, such was not entirely the case for Adirondack Indian communities; indeed, Abenaki neighborhoods were quite visible during the nineteenth and early twentieth centuries. These Native communities sometimes consisted of an extended family living within a household, while others consisted of an actual, albeit small, neighborhood of family members and other Indigenous families living in Western-style homes on the outskirts of towns such as Caldwell and Long Lake or in tourist town encampments. For example, the 1880 federal census for the village of Caldwell lists two Abenaki families living next to each other: one household included members of the Camp, Watso, and Paul families, and the other was a household of the Benedict and Tahamont families. As we know, not all Native peoples made the census records, and some who did in the Adirondacks were misidentified as "white" or "colored." One interesting example of the use of the colored identification column was the writing of the word "copper" there to identify Abenakis John Mitchell Sr. and his son Edward in the 1905 state census for Hamilton County. Whether the community was one large household or a neighborhood, they often took advantage of their long-established skills to make money. Furthermore, Aboriginal peoples from Odanak, Akwesasne, and other Native reserves visited members of these small Native communities. At times these Indigenous visitors stayed with their Adirondack host families for extended periods, typically to work in the area. Eventually these neighborhoods also disappeared. But instead of an exodus of the entire population from Euro-American settlements, Algonquian and Iroquoian individuals and families who chose to remain lived quietly together or among their non-Native neighbors as they adapted to the nineteenth century's changing demographics and economy. Some, such as the Abenaki widow Sarah Angeline Keziah-Otondonsonne (Otôdoson) Alumkassett (1851–1925, hereinafter Sarah Angeline Keziah), even owned their own home.[34]

Euro-Americans noted the existence of Indian people in their towns; they showed up on maps, sporadically on census records, and in some local histories. Even today, many Adirondack archivists are able to point out where a local Indian community had been or where a Native family lived in the past. As the next chapters describe, these families rarely assimilated into Euro-American communities right away or even fully. Instead, some took advantage of their heritage and skills and marketed them to tourists, while others earned wages in the local economies yet were known to be "Indian."

As described above, various forms of occupation by Native people existed in the Adirondacks, and they encompassed both Indigenous and more Westernized forms. Even from a Western perspective, it is clear that Iroquoian and Algonquian peoples occupied the Adirondacks in both pre- and postcontact periods. Some continued to use the space in customary ways for labor and resources, while others used it as a haven during times of crisis. Native peoples adapted their use of the space by working in different occupations such as the military, the commercial fur trade, and, later, wage work. In addition, they created new community spaces to accommodate changing political and economic needs.

Maintaining Traditional Practices

The Family of Sabael Benedict

A clear example of late eighteenth- and early nineteenth-century occupation in the Adirondacks is that of the family of Sabael Benedict, also known as Xavier Panadis, who came to the area around the time of the

American Revolution. He and his family represent how Indigenous peoples occupied the Adirondacks as both a place of continuity and change.

Records vary regarding the nationality of Sabael Benedict, and less is known about his wife. It is thought he was either Penobscot or "western" Abenaki but we do not know for sure.[35] Given their connection to Odanak and that the Penobscot are "eastern" Abenaki peoples, I refer to Sabael Benedict and his family as being Abenaki. Sources do not indicate whether Sabael Benedict, with or without his family, had lived seasonally in the region before he brought his family to the area around Indian Lake to permanently settle, sometime before or just after the Revolutionary War. One cannot help but speculate that given his knowledge of the area and the choices he made, Sabael Benedict probably had been there before. While legend has it that Benedict and his family lived alone in the central Adirondacks, this is not correct. Many of the previously mentioned "lone" Indian hunters were staying in the region. Another example was an Akwesasne hunter and guide known as Captain Gill, who reportedly lived in a wigwam located on the Lake Pleasant outlet with a wife, Molly, and her daughter of the same name. Later reports have him living with the daughter, suggesting his wife had died. Sportsman Charles Fenno Hoffman documented that Gill and his family lived there year round. As the next section about violence and cooperation explains, a number of Abenaki and Mohawk hunters occupied the area at least part of the time after the Revolutionary War. Some of these hunters had wives and children with them.[36] In addition, some and probably all of the refugee communities described earlier in this chapter existed during this period.

Ironically, the Benedict family has been constructed by local lore as the first "settlers" in the interior of the Adirondacks. Benedict and his wife lived on Squaw Brook Point, probably where the stream entered into the western shore of Indian Lake, around the present-day town of Sabael. The body of water known as Indian Lake was smaller then than it is today. Nineteenth-century damming enlarged the Lake and changed the entrance of the brook from this period. Squaw Brook

Point is now underwater. The point was described as fertile land by the family of Laura Guenther, who settled nearby. It is possible the couple's two sons and twin daughters were born here, although this is not certain as records are contradictory. For example, Alice Mitchell Johnson (c. 1820–after 1880), the daughter of one of the twins, Catherine Benedict, and her husband John Mitchell, reported on the 1880 federal census for Chester, Warren County, that she and both of her parents were born in Canada. However, this is not definitive, as many Abenaki children were baptized in Canada (as Catherine was) but they were not born there. And there are numerous contradictions within census reporting by many Abenaki people in the Adirondacks, including ethnicity and place of birth suggesting one or both began to create barriers for them. The Benedict family lived on the point until after the children's marriages and Marie Angelique's death in the 1840s, allegedly during a diphtheria epidemic. According to Guenther and the Reverend Todd, Sabael thought the location of their home had become haunted, so by 1847 he moved to the east side of Indian Lake or to the south side of Jerry's pond. Todd met Sabael in 1850 and described his home as a sparsely furnished wigwam with a dirt floor. He also noted that Sabael kept dogs and had a black horse for which he had little use. A hunter who visited Sabael in the spring of 1853 described the centenarian as breaking ground to plant potatoes.[37]

Sabael and Marie may have had five children; we know of three that survived to adulthood. Their first son, Joseph Panadis (1795–97) was buried at the same time their second son Louis Elijah (c. 1797–c. 1855 or later) was baptized at the Catholic Church at Odanak as Lazare Panadis in May 1797. The exact whereabouts and date of birth for Louis Elijah, or Lige, are unknown, but it is believed he was still an infant when he was baptized. As an adult, Louis Elijah became Protestant, although he was not thought to have been devout. Sabael maintained a mixture of Catholic and traditional beliefs throughout his long life. Louis Elijah married Abenaki Marie or Mary Wzokhilain, at Odanak on October 16, 1820, and they had at least four children, possibly more. The known children of Louis Elijah and Mary (or Marie) were Mary Jane (born before 1836, she lived in Lake George for a time), Salomon (c. 1836–?), Samuel (1838–89, drowned in Lake George) and Edwin (1841–1901 at Odanak). There is no record of Mary coming to or living in the Adirondacks. She eventually began to call herself a widow due to her husband's long absences from Odanak; he apparently preferred living in northern New York. Mary died in 1862, and she is buried at Odanak in the Anglican Church cemetery.[38]

Sabael and Marie Angelique's twin daughters were named Catherine and Margaret. They were baptized on July 17, 1800, probably at Saint-Jean-Francois-Regis, the Catholic mission at Akwesasne. Catherine (c. 1800–before 1845?) married Abenaki John Mitchell Sr., probably known as Michel Ajean (c. 1802–?) on February 8, 1820, at Odanak in Canada, but they lived most of their lives together in the Adirondacks. They had five surviving children: Margaret, Peter, Alice, Joseph, and John Jr. (c. 1837–1920 probably born in Troy, New York, and died in Indian Lake). There may have been a son Edward who died young. John Mitchell Sr. remarried in 1846 at Odanak, so it is presumed Catherine died prior to this date. Catherine's twin, Margaret Benedict (c. 1800–?) married Euro-American John Camp Sr. (born c. 1778, died 1884 in Lake George) of Vermont probably before 1821; they may have had as many as five children. The only children we have records about are their three sons: John Jr. (born between 1823 and 1826 in Vermont, died in Lake George, date unknown), Elijah (born October 1836 in Vermont, died 1904 in Indian Lake), and George W. (born c. 1843 in New York, died c. 1919).[39]

Sabael had approximately thirteen surviving grandchildren who had many offspring of their own. Some lived in the Adirondacks, others at Odanak, and still others moved about the Northeast and the West. His children and grandchildren married into Abenaki families with names such as deGonzague O'todoson (Watso), Agent or Ajent (Mitchell), Obamsawin, and Wazmimet or Wasamemit (Emmett). All these Odanak family names appeared in the Adirondacks, especially as craft artists during the era of wilderness tourism (see chapter 5). Benedict's descendants also married into non-Abenaki families of both Indigenous and European ancestry. They often lived near each other and worked together, albeit at times only temporarily. For example, the Camp family lived near the Mitchell family in Indian Lake in the 1870s. Cousins John Mitchell Jr. and Samuel Benedict worked in a lumbering camp together in 1860.[40] Nearly all the Abenaki who came to live in the Adirondacks were related to Sabael Benedict, with the notable exception of the family of Peter Sabattis. Peter Sabattis had connections at Akwesasne and used the Catholic Church there at least for baptisms. In the early part of the nineteenth century, the Sabattis family was probably living around Parishville, less than forty miles from the Mohawk community. It may have been that Peter Sabattis and Sabael became acquainted during a Benedict family trip to Akwesasne, but there are no records to confirm or even suggest they socialized or worked together. Although there is one account of Sabael and Peter's son, Mitchel Sabattis, acting as informants for the same Queensbury historian, these interviews could have been done separately. Some have claimed the two families were related, but I have not found a connection. For whatever reason, Peter decided to bring his family to the Long Lake area, near Indian Lake, around 1830. Their family's history is featured in chapter 3.

Traditional Models of Kinship Networks and Leadership Tactics Used to Pursue and Maintain Intercultural Alliances

Both Sabael and his son Louis Elijah were hunters and trappers. Sabael sold his furs to traders in Lyons Falls by way of the Moose River, at Warren's on the Hudson River, and at Williams Store in Newton's Corners (present day Speculator), as well as to various traders coming into the region. In addition to working with each other, Sabael and Lige also worked with other Abenaki. For example, Sabael had a run-in with Euro-American trapper Nicholas Stoner in 1822 after his Abenaki companion Francis stole one of Stoner's traps and, it is likely, some pelts. It was apparent that Sabael and Stoner also knew each other. Sabael smoothed things over with the hot-tempered Stoner and probably saved Francis's life. The elder Benedict spoke Abenaki and French better than English. No records mention Louis Elijah's difficulty with English, so it is presumed he spoke that language better than his father did. As they aged, father and son lived together, although one or both were often away. There are reports that the pair occasionally drank too much; these records blamed Euro-American cultural influences and change for this behavior. Excessive alcohol consumption was not limited to Indigenous peoples in the Adirondacks, as the next chapter on guiding notes.[41]

Sabael and Louis Elijah were well-known for their hunting prowess and knowledge of the landscape, combined with a reputation for generosity. The two were sought out by White settlers, industrialists, surveyors, and eventually sports hunters to guide them. For example, Guenther described Benedict helping her pioneering family during the summer of 1847 as they homesteaded: "Old Sabael had shown Grandpa how to grind corn with stones but it was such a slow & laborious process." Sabael and Elijah's connections to Euro-American industrialists were usually made around mining interests. Prior to 1810, Sabael reportedly showed some prospectors the location of an iron ore mine near Keeseville for a basket of corn and one dollar. He or his son is credited with finding the "iron dam" at Tahawus and in 1826 revealing it to David Henderson who, along with his partners, opened the McIntyre Mine. It was probably Louis Elijah who brought the men to the location; he received a plug of tobacco and $1.50 for his efforts. There are several sometimes contradictory accounts about this incident. Perhaps the most interesting is Masten's *Story of Adirondac*, which describes the trek to the mine led by Louis Elijah. The party included Duncan McMartin Jr., David Henderson, and an African American manservant named Enoch, who was afraid of the Indian guide. The trip took from Monday afternoon to Saturday. Legend has it that Henderson was so worried Benedict would tell someone else that he made Lige travel with him to Albany to stake his claim. Sabael was thought to know of other lead mines and was rumored to know the whereabouts of a silver mine he found while trapping.

How and where Sabael died is unknown. In 1855, he left his home and headed toward Thirteenth Lake or Pond, probably to trap or perhaps to visit at the Indian Community located there. His dog was allegedly found dead in Jerry's Pond. Jerry's and Puffer Ponds were supposedly dragged, but Sabael's body was never found. He was believed to be 108 years of age at the time. How and where Louis Elijah died and is buried is also a mystery. The last two records we have about him in the Adirondacks were left in 1855, the year of his father's disappearance. The former was the 1855 state census for Queensbury, Warren County, which lists Elijah Benedick, age fifty-eight, boarding with the Abenaki family of Sarah Angeline Keziah in June of that year. There were fourteen people living in the house, and most were reported as "St. Francis" Indians who had been there for two months. The last record was a July newspaper article about Louis Elijah Benedict acting as a guide for Henry J. Raymond, who was interested in investing in a possible railroad route across the region.[42]

Nevertheless, legends of the pair's graves do exist. Keene Valley records claim to have the grave of "Sebille" at the Holt Cemetery. The person buried there was known to frequent the AuSable lakes and the area around Keene Valley in his later years. Whether the grave is that of Xavier Panadis or someone else altogether is unknown. Near Durant Lake outside the village of Blue Mountain Lake is an unmarked stone monument with a hole in the center. Some believe it is the grave of Louis Elijah Benedict, while others claim it is a 1930s Civilian Conservation Corp project that was perhaps created to memorialize him, but the centered plaque was stolen leaving its intended purpose a mystery.[43]

Indian Lake is a long and fairly narrow body of water, even as dammed. It runs north by northeast and is connected by a series of rivers and smaller lakes to create a valley just south of the Adirondacks' High Peaks region. Through a series of other lakes and rivers, one can navigate from Indian lake and connect to Lake Champlain and the Hudson, St. Lawrence, and Mohawk Rivers. These routes involve carries, as rapids and land impede direct thoroughfare. Today, dams and drainage have changed the size and flow of some of these rivers and lakes. At the end of the eighteenth century, a smaller and narrower Indian Lake was geographically a central location from which to hunt and sell furs. It was well-positioned for an Abenaki hunter who customarily looked for a body of water with tributaries to serve as transportation routes through a hunting territory.

It is not too much of a stretch to conclude that the central Adirondacks were treated as a hunting territory by Sabael Benedict, who acted as a band leader. Recall that Abenaki bands were members of several families who chose a leader based on their "exceptional prowess and prestige" and their ability to be persuasive and influential. Abenaki leaders had to be diplomatic and choose strategies to maintain peace and power. In the Adirondacks of the late eighteenth and early nineteenth centuries, Sabael Benedict found a waterway that met Abenaki hunting territory specifications. Sabael and his family also had a place they called home, where they planted a few hearty crops. From there they traveled extensively throughout the Adirondacks and across international borders for work and social purposes, probably taking advantage of the water routes. As Abenaki and others married into the Benedict family, they lived near each other and often worked together in kinship-like arrangements. Scholars have recorded three considerations for governing the negotiation of Abenaki family hunting territories during the early twentieth century, which, while later than the period Sabael Benedict was living in, are based on traditional Abenaki practices and are relevant here. The first consideration is the continuity of a family to use the same space, usually passed from father to son. Second, Abenaki families hunted in familiar places, thereby establishing a continuity of occupation of that place. And finally, the division of labor within the family meant that because men were recognized as hunters, they were the one who continued to occupy the territory.[44] It is possible Sabael invited the Sabattis family to move there; at the very least, they did not seem to bother each other. The Sabattis family may have used Long Lake, with its direct access to the Raquette and St. Lawrence Rivers, as their watershed territory. With a little imagination, one can see the Sabattis family and even a few Euro-American and Franco-Canadian families as macrobands that Sabael's family worked with, sometimes married into, and perhaps invited to the Adirondacks to live. Further, Sabael negotiated difficult situations and was influential with fellow Abenaki and trappers, incoming settlers, and industrialists. Such relationships demonstrated his "exceptional prowess and prestige" as a band leader, and he continued in this position because he was clearly persuasive and influential.

Sabael Benedict drew on centuries-old models of kinship networks and leadership tactics to pursue intercultural alliances, just as his predecessors had done in other regions. American historian Cynthia J. Van Zandt suggests that as early as 1580 Natives, Europeans, and Africans searched for ways to create alliances with each other as a way to coexist in North America. At the same time, they tried to gain as much control as possible. These efforts were sometimes misunderstood, but the ability to negotiate with multiple cultures and incorporate the Other into their social network were successful strategies that created beneficial alliances between Natives and newcomers. The "middle ground" space that the Adirondacks represented during this period allowed the Benedict family and others the opportunity to maintain a more traditional lifestyle and have some control over their lives longer than they would have at their home reserves and territories that were shrinking and under colonial imposition. Individuals like Sabael Benedict implemented a strategy of cooperation with intruding Euro-Americans—one that allowed them and their families the ability to live here in a mostly safe and initially familiar environment.[45] This strategy was not always successful, however, especially when direct competition with White hunters and trappers was involved.

Violent Encounters and Cautious Cooperation

The period following the American Revolution and into the mid-nineteenth century was at times an era of violence in the Adirondacks, particularly between Euro-American trappers and those from Akwesasne and Kahnawake. While geographically part of New York State, the region was culturally ambiguous during this period, as newly branded "Americans" and "Canadian Indians" roamed the forest for furs, squatting privileges, and, later, jobs. "Canadian Indians" was a moniker often used to identify Iroquoian and Abenaki peoples working in the area, a name that was a strategy employed by Americans to disassociate them from their homelands on the United States side of the border. In the case of the Abenaki, the United States still refuses to formally acknowledge them as "American Indians," mostly based on this argument, and the state of Vermont has only recently done so (in 2006).[46] For the Mohawk, their territory was confiscated based on their loyalty to the British, reducing their homeland on the American side to a small reservation that straddles the American–Canadian border. As loyalists, they were considered Canadian. The hostility that manifested in the Adirondacks is complicated and was a process that occurred over time.

White trappers who migrated into the region after the American Revolution were often from New England. The descendants of English colonists, these New Englanders, together with their countrymen along the eastern seaboard, had a history of fighting with and even massacring Algonquian peoples once their skills and services were no longer needed. This violence began in the Adirondack region during the early seventeenth century. New England massacres began at least as early as the Wessagusset massacre led by Miles Standish in 1622, and included the Pequot Mystic Massacre of 1637 and two massacres of Narragansett people under the leadership of Major John Talcott on July 2–3, 1676. More so than other European colonizers in North America, the English tried to maintain strict boundaries between themselves and Indigenous peoples. In the early days of colonization, this practice was based on English notions of civilization that focused on Protestant Christianity, whereas later distinctions were based on ethnic differences. Initially dependent upon local Algonquian peoples for their food and survival, early English colonists "reacted to even the slightest challenge with horrifying vengeance, and they did so in a spirit of self-righteousness." Early English settlers' responses were based on European political policies of winning at all costs. Once entrenched—and also based on their colonial experiences in Ireland and Scotland—the English applied a political hypothesis of fear to keep the local Native peoples under control. Of course, New Englanders were not the only colonists who feared and hated Native peoples. A New Yorker confirmed that no child was "allowed to grow up in that region, without imbibing . . . hatred and horror of the Indians. Tales of Indian cruelties were in the mouths of all mothers and nurses."[47]

Old animosities based on previous loyalties forged during war times were another reason for the violence in the region. A number of the Euro-American hunters and trappers who moved into the Adirondacks were soldiers during one or more of the late eighteenth and early nineteenth century wars. Native peoples either chose sides and fought in these wars or tried to remain neutral. Iroquoian peoples, only some of whom fought alongside the British during the American Revolution, were subjected to particular hostility in the region, perhaps because of the Mohawk's clear alliance with the English. New York State saw more battles on its soil than any other colony; most of these were small skirmishes or raids on settlements, lone farms, and Indian villages. Combined with operations such as the Battle of Oriskany (1777), the Cherry Valley raid (1778), and the Sullivan-Clinton campaign (1779), the fighting became personal and racialized. During the war, the Americans created a propaganda campaign describing atrocities conducted by the Iroquois, conveniently omitting their own acts. One of these atrocities was the killing and scalping of Jane McCrea in Washington County in the Adirondacks. This slaying was sensationalized by American General Horatio Gates and spread throughout the colonies as a threat to all settler women. Furthermore, prior to the War of 1812, the federal government of the new United States used newspapers and other media to produce a nationalist campaign aimed at creating loyalty to the country and away from individual states. This campaign was filled with anti-British sentiment and used images of Indians killing and scalping men, women, and children, all of which escalated tensions between Americans and Native peoples.[48]

Moreover, as increased European immigration to North America created more competition for land, some of these colonists turned into "Indian haters." These Indian-hating settlers along the western frontier at the time of the American Revolution were often Anglo-, Celtic-, and German-Americans who had lost family and property to Indian raids. They killed Indians indiscriminately, whether ally or foe, and wherever they found them. Indian haters regarded all Indigenous North Americans as standing in the way of the land they wanted, and Native peoples viewed Europeans as after their land. These

Indian haters, or "big knives," as they were sometimes called by the Indigenous peoples they fought with, imitated and lived in similar ways to Native Americans, particularly in the ways they fought and died. Indian haters distrusted people who crossed social borders and believed Native peoples could not be civilized. Meanwhile, they failed to recognize how they too crossed boundaries.[49]

Simultaneously, the English openly cultivated relationships with Aboriginal peoples so they might fight alongside them. Thus Native peoples were identified with the British enemy, regardless of whether they were involved with them. The Revolutionary War press shaped the national identity to resemble backcountry settlers, while critical documents, such as the Declaration of Independence, helped form perceptions of Indigenous peoples as non-American.[50] Furthermore, in the postrevolutionary period, America operated under the Articles of Confederation, a weak federal form of government that gave more power to the states. This process, combined with excessive war debt, meant the United States could not control its citizens, many of whom questioned the federal government's authority. As a result, the violence continued unabated for some time, and the Adirondacks were no exception.

Legends about Adirondack trappers such as Nicholas Stoner and Nat Foster often referred to them as "Indian haters" and "Indian hunters." The actions of some of these men demonstrated a propensity toward violence directed at Native peoples as the eighteenth century turned into the nineteenth. Local histories suggest that violent encounters occurred. Nathaniel Bartlett Sylvester's *Historical Sketches of Northern New York* claims there were many Indians in the Adirondacks after the Revolution who continued to hunt there either singly or in groups. He added that when Native and non-Native hunters met up, they sometimes got into disputes, and occasionally someone was killed.[51] Based on Sylvester's accounts and my research, it was the Native hunters and trappers who were killed in these encounters.

Jeptha R. Simms's 1846 *Trappers of New York or a Biography of Nicholas Stoner and Nathaniel Foster* depicts encounters between Euro-American and Mohawk hunters and describes a violent, frontier-like environment, particularly in the western part of the region. Simms interviewed Nicholas Stoner and obtained information on Nathaniel Foster through an informant named W. S. Benchley, who knew Foster well. Simms was not anti-Indian per se; however, he called both Foster and Stoner heroes and he saw his book as a tribute to them and their contemporaries. Simms's book depicts the relationship between Native and Euro-American hunters as generally unfriendly and full of suspicion. He describes the character of this period as "the rule of might and right." When a hunter believed his traps had been robbed, he saw it as a legitimate reason to take the law into his own hands.[52]

Such incidents happened despite there being law enforcement, admittedly sparse, within the region, as the case of Nicholas Stoner demonstrates. Stoner (c. 1762–1853) lived in the Broadalbin area of Fulton County and was a deputy sheriff there. He was on duty during one of the violent episodes that he initiated. In the spring of 1785, seven Kanienkehaka hunters arrived in Johnstown to sell the furs they had trapped in the Adirondacks. The Mohawk traded with a local merchant named John Grant, who had an interpreter by the name of Lieutenant Wallace. Afterward, the Mohawk stopped at Union Hall, also known as DeFonclaiere's Inn, to have dinner. They were having drinks while awaiting their meal—and treating those they wanted to befriend—when Nicholas Stoner entered looking for a Constable Nathaniel Thompson. Stoner was purported to have been drinking before his arrival. He entered into an exchange about ethnicity and mixed heritage that rapidly escalated into a brawl. By the end of the fracas Stoner had pulled the lead earring out of the ear of a man named Captain John and had thrown a heated fire poker into the neck of another hunter who allegedly bragged about killing Stoner's father. Stoner's father, Henry, a German immigrant, had been killed and scalped purportedly by Kahnawake Mohawk during the American Revolution, and his death affected his son's perception of Indian peoples. The chronicler, Simms, believed the man hit by the fire poker must have died from the wound. Stoner was arrested, and the hunters were advised to leave town. The Mohawk hired local resident Samuel

Copeland to carry them and their belongings by wagon to the Sacandaga River, "where they had left most of their rifles, their squaws and canoes" to return to Canada. Simms noted that "Indian women usually remained at the camp, and did the cooking for the hunters." As news of the tavern altercation traveled, some of the local Revolutionary War veterans broke Stoner out of jail. They enjoyed a bit of drinking at a local tavern before the jailer found the group and sent Stoner home. Simms described other incidents of Stoner killing Kanienkehaka hunters in the forest for allegedly stealing from his traps. After killing them, he typically took their furs and rifles, and on at least one occasion a canoe, as trophies.[53]

Similar tales are told about self-proclaimed Indian hater Nathaniel "Uncle Nat" Foster (c. 1766–1840), "for whom killing Natives was something of a hobby." Foster was taught to hate Native peoples by his father, and this loathing was fueled by his experiences of Revolutionary War–time raids on the family's Hinsdale, New Hampshire, home while his father was away fighting in the war in and around the Adirondacks. Just before the war ended in 1783, Nathaniel Foster Sr. moved his family northwest of Fish House in present-day Fulton County. (Fish House was a camp owned by Sir William Johnson that was destroyed when New York State flooded the region in 1930 to create the Great Sacandaga Reservoir). About two months after they arrived in the southern Adirondacks, Nathaniel Jr. witnessed the burning of the family's cabin and kidnapping of his sister Zilpha by the Mohawk. Although he and a party of neighbors recovered Zilpha by the end of the day unharmed, Foster remained bitter and angry toward Native peoples. Some "incidents" involving Foster and the killing of Indian men including a story where Foster claimed, "The best shot I ever made, I got two beaver, one otter, and fifteen martin skins; but I took the filling out of a blanket to do it!" In another incident, Foster drowned an Indian man taking a drink of water and then stole his furs and supplies. Biographer A. L. Byron Curtis tells a story of Foster tricking and murdering an Indian man with whom he was allegedly having a sharp-shooting contest. Curtis claims Hamilton County officials reported it as an accident.[54]

The best-known example of Foster's role in postwar violence was the 1833 murder of Akwesasne Mohawk Peter Waters, also known as "Drid." The pair were neighbors on the abandoned Herreshoff settlement on Brown Tract in Herkimer County. This incident became well-known because Foster was arrested and tried—probably the only individual who ever was. Despite the eyewitness accounts that Foster stood on the bank of First Lake and shot Waters while in his canoe, he was acquitted based on self defense. (The morning of the slaying, Foster and Waters had quarreled, and as the incident escalated the Mohawk had cut Foster's arm with a knife.) Initially fearful of retaliation by Waters's relatives and compatriots, Foster removed himself and his family to nearby Booneville and later to Pennsylvania before returning to the area. Mrs. Waters's brother and companions came to get her and her two children, and they buried their countryman in a flexed position, which was a traditional form of burial for the Mohawk. Mrs. Waters and her children went with them back to Canada.[55]

Euro-Americans continued to complain about Native hunters and trappers well into the nineteenth century. In this period their complaints escalated to assault and battery. In the early 1850s, a guide known as Tucker told his sportsman client, S. H. Hammond, a story about beating a "Canadian half-breed" who lived on the northwest shore of Chateaugay Lake and forcing him and his wife to leave the area. Tucker claimed he beat the man because he allowed his dogs to run deer down in the winter solely for their skins, a practice Tucker claimed he did not believe was sporting. However, his reasoning is suspect, given that the running down of deer by dogs was a popular practice used by all Adirondack guides to help their clients more easily kill their prey. The practice was initially banned by conservation legislation in 1877, but the outcry from the travel industry temporarily repealed the legislation, which was reinstated permanently in 1885 with the creation of the area as a forest preserve. This practice is described in the next chapter.[56]

Conflicts over trapping and hunting were not the only reason for violence between non-Native and Native peoples in the Adirondacks.

Racism was sometimes a factor. James Paul, brother of Samson, was pushed into an icy Lake George "one 'town meeting day'" near a tavern called Garfield's in Hague, Warren County. The timing of this incident is not clear, but was probably during the first quarter of the nineteenth century. A local newspaper reported that Paul was "semi-intoxicated," and "ruffians . . . prevented him from reaching boat, dock or shore. Finally exhausted, he folded his arms and, with typical stoicism, sank." I could not locate any other record of the incident to confirm this account or to indicate if the "ruffians" were ever prosecuted. However, the "typical stoicism" wording used to mask the violence and inevitability of the outcome—drawing on images of the vanishing Indian—suggests the murder was never prosecuted.[57]

Evidence of racialized and other types of violence in the Adirondacks continued into the early twentieth century. As late as the fall of 1912, two related Oneida men met mysterious and untimely deaths. Joe Wheelock of Old Forge had gone to a bar in Otter Creek to pay a bill when he collapsed on Saturday, September 28. He was carried onto the porch and left there on a cold, rainy night until the following afternoon; Wheelock died two days later. A physician ruled the initial cause for the collapse was a stroke, but bruises on his head and neck, plus abrasions on his arm, caused his family to believe there was foul play. After an inquest on October 15 resolved nothing, Wheelock's Oneida relative and coworker at the Iroquois Pulp and Paper Company, Alexander O. Charles of McKeever, pushed to have a second inquest. According to newspaper accounts, Charles left for Port Leyden on October 10 to witness the exhumation of Wheelock's body. He met with a Utica attorney named Sholes on October 23 and was expected to return home the next day. His body was fished out of the Erie Canal on November 13. Charles's death was initially declared an accident, but his wife insisted her husband had been murdered and that fifty dollars was missing from his wallet. On or about December 2, citing a suspicious bump on the crown of Charles's head, a coroner eventually confirmed foul play, but by February 1913 neither Wheelock's nor Charles's case had been investigated. I could find no records to indicate arrests had been made in either incident.[58]

Despite these examples, not all encounters between Euro-Americans and Native peoples during this era were violent. Their relationships were more complicated than the above confrontations suggest. French entrepreneur Peter Sailly ran a fur trade enterprise in Clinton County in 1785. Sailly's original venture was iron ore, but he found the fur trade more lucrative. He sold the furs he obtained to John Jacob Astor, who was headquartered in Albany at the time. Native peoples came to Sailly's home to trade and at times slept in his kitchen. In the late eighteenth century, Revolutionary War veteran Jonathon "Jock" Wright (c. 1746–1826) and a partner nicknamed "Crookneck" Simmons hunted and trapped in the area around Lake Champlain and Lake George, as well as the northern parts of the Hudson River. Although "Indian hunters were continually crossing their tracks," Wright and Simmons had no serious trouble with them or any other hunters. William Constable Jr. employed Oneida men to help build his house, Constable Hall, which was completed in 1819. Located at Constableville in Lewis County, his home featured an "Indian Room" built on to the ground floor. The Iroquois were known to stop over and use the room, which contained a fireplace and an old flintlock rifle for their use. "They customarily expressed their thanks for hospitality by giving a haunch of fresh meat to the Constables after a successful hunting trip." In spite of Nicholas Stoner's history, he was also known to hunt and trap with Akwesasne Mohawk hunters including Powlus, Captain Gill, and Flagg, the latter noted for wearing a loon skin for a cap. Stoner appeared to have also gotten along with Sabael and Louis Elijah Benedict.[59]

Other examples of cooperation can be found. In 1826, six-year-old Clarence Walworth gave some clothes left on the family's Saratoga Springs porch to a traveling St. Regis Mohawk. About six months later, the Mohawk returned with a gift of a youth-sized bow and arrow to repay the boy's kindness. Perhaps the most poignant example of cooperation involved William F. Wood (c. 1798–1868), a Vermonter who arrived in the Adirondacks around 1832 to work as a trapper. While working alone, he had the misfortune to fall into the icy Independence River. The timing of the accident is unclear, but it probably happened before 1839. Wood's legs were frozen, and it was several days before he was discovered by Nat Foster. Wood had to have both of his legs amputated below the knee. The surgery was "performed by Wood's Indian friends, who also nursed him back to health and provided him with heavy leather knee pads to assist crawling." (Not surprisingly, he became known as "Stumpy" Woods). The surgery and pads worked so successfully that he was able to travel, hunt, and trap in the Adirondacks during any season.[60] While this period contained many acts of violence based on inherited beliefs, real and imagined fear, wartime experiences, and competition, it is important not to overgeneralize. As noted above, many early settlers and hunters got along with the Native peoples working and living in the Adirondacks. We must recognize, however, that this period was full of tensions. These incidents of violence brought about enormous changes, especially for the Mohawk of Akwesasne who were continuing to pursue customary hunting and trapping labor in their traditional territory. The encroachment of White hunters and trappers curtailed the mobility of these hunters, and how they responded to encounters could be a matter of life and death. These were complex relationships at a very personal level.

Euro-American settlement and industry began to pervade the interior of the Adirondacks early in the nineteenth century, and tourists soon followed in their wake. As noted, some Kanienkehaka and Abenaki families and individuals were already working and living in the area. Records indicate that encounters between local Iroquoian and Algonquian peoples and new Euro-American settlers, surveyors, anthropologists, and eventually visitors were mostly friendly and cooperative. For example, an unnamed seven-foot-tall Mohawk was part of the crew for the Old Military Tract, surveyed between 1812 and 1813. In Washington County, Indian peoples showed homesteaders how to make maple sugar and told them stories about its discovery. According to local historian Fred Tracy Stiles, two stories exist about the origins of using maple sugar. The first is that the knowledge came from a dream. In the other story, a woman was taking care of an elderly man with bad teeth. She normally soaked his meat in water before cooking to tenderize it. One day she had no time to obtain water so she put the meat in a birchbark basket, which contained sap. When the meat was cooked they discovered the sweet taste of maple syrup. Encounters between Natives and newcomers in Elizabethtown were generally cordial and children played together. When a conflict occurred over a dog that had stolen meat set out to cool, the dog's Native owner replaced it with a quarter of a recently killed deer, "a payment of both principal and interest."[61]

There are no known records left by the Mohawk and Abenaki to clarify why they took the risk of coming to the region at this time or why they mostly cooperated with incoming White settlers. We know that Akwesasne and Odanak were experiencing limited possibilities based on colonization practices of settlement, legislation, and missionization that resulted in social, political, economic, and land pressures at reserve and reservation communities—factors that probably explain why some came to the area during this uncertain period. One cannot help but speculate that the Adirondack landscape, which kept Europeans away and delayed most Euro-American settlement until well after the War of 1812, felt familiar during an era of imperial upheaval as Americans and British fought and negotiated for dominion over the northern portion of the continent. Experiencing a shatter zone at their reserves, these Iroquoian and Algonquian peoples used the Adirondacks as a familiar zone of refuge, one that had been part of their homeland and that their ancestors knew well. Coming to the Adirondacks during this precarious age reflects the tension between the agency exerted by Mohawk and Abenaki peoples and the colonial practices imposed upon them. Responding to the latter, they created a new world in the Adirondacks, if only for a time, that drew on customary skills that they could use in their new reality. As a result, they became part of the fabric of Adirondack history and culture. Eventually White settlement, assisted by year-round wage work in industrial occupations, reduced the ability of Iroquoian and Algonquian hunters and trappers to work the Adirondacks for furs, hides, and meat. In many respects, the Adirondacks are an example of settler colonialism in microcosm. This history demonstrates how the process of colonial settlement did as much damage as invasion and imperial colonialism did, and that it lasted long after the events of invasion and conquest.[62]

Location of Exchange

Prior to the late 1830s, Algonquian and Iroquoian peoples were freer to move about the land and pursue seasonal activities in the Adirondacks. Even as most adapted to reservation life, they continued to cross the border for these pursuits. However, by 1840 the new world that the Mohawk, Abenaki, and others had created in the Adirondacks had become smaller and the land less useful as Euro-American settler colonialism affected their ability to successfully hunt and trap in the area. As a result, many Kanienkehaka, Oneida, and Abenaki living in and around the region adapted their labor strategies to incorporate wage employment, often as temporary contractors in some of the region's resource-type industries. The Mohawk in particular worked together in groups at lumbering, bark peeling for tanning, and on the railroad. For example, local lumberman Herbert McGee was known to have "hired Indians from up North—they apparently saved his life up there by the border at one time." The work could be dangerous: a local newspaper recorded the death of Jack Jock in 1913, who had been hit by a train on the Mohawk and Malone Railway tracks while working with a group of about sixty Kanienkehaka employed by the International Paper Company at a logging camp near Carter Station. Jock was not the only Mohawk to die this way, which may suggest continued and uninvestigated violence.[63]

Kanienkehaka from Akwesasne often lived together outside of Euro-American towns, and sometimes small shanty communities called Sientihne grew up around logging camps. (This book's cover and figure 3 illustrate Mohawk people working in these camps.) The Mohawk word *Sientihne* (pronounced zhien-tih-ne) is a hybrid based on how the Mohawk heard the English word "shanty" and the Mohawk suffix "neh," which means a building or place. There are reports of women and families in these camps. For example, George Washington Sears recorded his visit to a lumbering or bark-peeling camp headed by Akwesasne Mohawk William Bero in the summer of 1880. In addition to the crew of fifteen men were Bero's wife and adult daughter, a school teacher at Akwesasne, and four children, including an infant. Bark peeling was typically done for the tanning industry, which arrived in the area in the 1850s and was responsible for even more settlement and loss of trees. An 1871 newspaper reported fires had destroyed the camps of "a large party of Indians who were employed peeling bark" around the Moose River district. Collecting spruce gum for the chewing gum business was another industry in the central part of the region. Mohawk Johnny Leaf (1848–1908) used to earn seasonal wages collecting the gum on a crew that worked for Tim Crowley of Piseco. Leaf, sometimes spelled Lief, was also a hunter, trapper, and guide, and his sister Christina and her family made and sold baskets in the area.[64] When these jobs were done, most Mohawk workers returned to Akwesasne, although some, such as Leaf and his sister, remained. Meanwhile, others found work in the wilderness tourism industry, the subject of the next three chapters.

This chapter and those that follow clearly show that Mohawk, Oneida, and Abenaki individuals and families did not disappear from the region. Instead they continually reinvented their relationship with the area and adapted to the changing space of what the Adirondacks had to offer as a location of exchange and a familiar homeland. Those relying on the Adirondacks for traditional pursuits were eventually overrun by Euro-American settlers and industry, yet they also were able to maintain a number of their principles and practices. In resource-industry labor, Kanienkehaka men worked together, and the women who accompanied them did complementary work in the camps. This pattern of work reflected labor practices before and after contact. Sabael Benedict and his son Louis Elijah adapted their work to include trapping for wages and guiding while also continuing their subsistence hunting and living practices. A similar situation took shape in the wilderness tourism industry, as women and men carried forward their customary work practices within the new commercial venture of North American wilderness tourism. How White tourists viewed the adaptations Native peoples made to survive, and, more

3. Akwesasne Mohawk lumbering in the Adirondacks. Photograph part of the collection of the Akwesasne Library and Cultural Center. Courtesy of the Six Nations Indian Museum, Onchiota, NY.

important, how they failed to see beyond the stereotypical symbols of their own beliefs, added to the discourse of the vanishing Indian in the Northeast. But Indigenous peoples did not disappear. Instead, Algonquian and Iroquoian peoples deliberately chose which facets of their life to change and which to maintain to move forward in this new world of limited mobility and changing opportunity.

Conclusion

One of my favorite Adirondack histories is *Contested Terrain*, a book that also captures the conflict between outsiders and local Adirondackers from the late nineteenth century up to the present day. I take exception, however, with the author's statement that "the only thing that distinguished the Adirondacks from western frontier regions was that exploitation of local riches . . . did not involve the removal or slaughter of indigenous peoples." Based on my research, I argue that removal[65] and killing of indigenous peoples did happen here on a smaller scale and in a different form than we normally think. There may not have been mass slaughter such as the 1890 massacre at Wounded Knee, but many hunters (especially Mohawk) were killed in the Adirondacks without threat of penalty. While there was no forced removal similar to the 1838 Cherokee Trail of Tears, Iroquoian and Algonquian peoples' *livelihood* was removed as resource-type industries and settlers affected the amount of game in a territory that Iroquoian and Algonquian peoples needed for food and as a resource for income. Recall, settler colonialism is a process that endures long after invasion. As this chapter reveals, the Adirondacks do have a history of colonization that includes violence and economic changes; it is a history that resulted in death, removal, and entangled relations for Native peoples. Like the place itself, these incidents remained quietly isolated, seemingly only important to very regionalized, local Adirondack histories. However, as we broaden our understanding of colonization as a process that also includes forced labor changes and entanglements due to settlement, we start to see that the history of the Adirondacks clearly contributes to larger and important arguments about North American colonization history. By first acknowledging Native peoples' rights to self-determination in political, social, and economic matters, the contact history of the Adirondacks in great detail shows how self-determination was taken from them. As a result, these Iroquoian and Algonquian peoples were forced to exert their own agency and make adaptations in order to survive in and about this place.[66]

Further, the Adirondacks are an important borderlands region of the Northeast. As an indigenous homeland for Native peoples in proximity to the region, it served as a place of resources and labor, and sometimes even as a buffer zone. Before the American Revolution, the area had become a space that acted as a zone of refuge, originally for Algonquian peoples from southern New England and maybe others. After the Revolution the area served the same purpose for Abenaki with ties to Odanak and Mohawk from Akwesasne who needed to find work away from their reserve communities. As Abenaki and Mohawk hunters tried to continue their customary practices, some found crossing the political boundary created by Britain and the United States useful. In both cases, some Algonquian and Iroquoian peoples chose to use their familiarity with the Adirondacks to make it a more permanent home. This borderlands history provides insight into strategies these peoples employed during difficult times, and in some cases it suggests what happened to a few of them.

In addition, the Adirondacks continued to act as a location of exchange for some Abenaki, Kanienkehaka, and White trappers who went there to make use of its resources. Unlike the relationship between White trappers and Akwesasne Mohawk trappers, there are no records to indicate there were animosities between Mohawk and Abenaki hunters and trappers during this period up to 1840 and beyond. The Adirondacks were annexed by New York State after the Revolutionary War, but the region was ignored as most White settlers moved into the more fertile lands of Iroquoia. A number of especially Abenaki individuals and families chose to live in the area more permanently before the arrival of Euro-American and immigrant settlers into the interior. By using strategies of cooperation based on traditional Abenaki leadership and alliance-making skills, Aboriginal Adirondackers became "safe Indians"[67] in the minds of eastern Euro-Americans who moved to the region and later those urban, middle- and upper-class Whites who vacationed there. Similar to "welcoming" stories such as the first Thanksgiving, this strategy of cooperation was occurring alongside tense and sometimes violent encounters that were not part of the historical narrative. By the mid-1800s, Whites outnumbered the mostly Mohawk and Abenaki peoples occupying this space, and the Adirondacks were not always a safe place for them. Cooperation and alliance building, often with Euro-Americans who wanted to be left alone, may have been a lifesaving strategy. Meanwhile, the tensions that still existed between Indian and Euro-American hunters and trappers also made the idea of an Adirondack vacation exciting. This environment helped set the stage for wilderness tourism in the area.

If we ignore this period of violence and cooperation, we not only deny Haudenosaunee and Algonquian peoples their rightful history in the Adirondacks after the American Revolution, we also refuse to recognize a crucial piece of the region's history and the beginnings of wilderness tourism. In addition, this period portrays the initial efforts to shape the complicated relationship between Aboriginal and Euro-American settlers as they started working together instead of competing with one another or seeing each other as former adversaries. While settler colonialism was certainly occurring here, Iroquoian and Algonquian peoples who came to or left the Adirondacks for reasons of their own were not without agency. Economic need was certainly a factor, but especially Abenaki and Kanienkehaka came here and purposefully occupied this place—sometimes on their own terms, sometimes not, more often in some negotiated form of settlement. As a result, acts of reciprocity began to take place among Native and non-Native peoples and the land, acts that created opportunities for entangled exchanges within a settler colonialism context. It is important to understand this era in which, within a generation or two, Iroquoian and Abenaki peoples went from being enemies of postrevolutionary Euro-Americans who moved there to being their neighbors, spouses, and business partners who exchanged ideas. To study their lives together without knowing about this violent period conceals the breadth of distance and complexity concerning how far the two peoples had come over a short period of time. As Daniel Usner argues, to study "the imagined Indian without considering the spaces of intercultural conflict, negotiation, and exchange in which much of the imagination took place is to perpetuate the voicelessness, namelessness and facelessness . . . assigned to Indian people."[68] And these Iroquoian and Algonquian peoples would become "imagined Indians" as the nineteenth century turned into the twentieth. These encounters paved the way for Adirondackers of Aboriginal and European ancestry to come together and create communities where both could peacefully live and work. The next three chapters construct a portrait of the complex rural society and culture created by these relationships during the era of wilderness tourism.

3

"The Trustiest Guides in All the Wilderness"

Guiding for Tourists in the Adirondacks

T. S. MORRELL'S portrayal of his camping experience at Rock Pond on a Sunday morning in 1883 is a fascinating description of an Adirondack wilderness tourism adventure. Morrell, of Newark, New Jersey, was in a group that consisted of himself and two men named Atwater and Hardham, plus three guides: Mitchel Sabattis, Calvin Towns, and Lorenzo "Ren" Towns, all of Long Lake. Morrell's narrative describes in romantic terms the landscape and waking up in a homemade lean-to that morning. A devout Methodist, guide Mitchel Sabattis greeted his party's waking with an admonition to not fish that day in respect for the Sabbath. Atwater and Hardham, however, chose to ignore the reproach. Morrell did not fish; instead he accompanied Ren Towns while the guide caught minnows for bait. Upon returning to the camp, Sabattis inquired if Morrell had broken the Sabbath. Morrell denied fishing and stated that he had only floated around the lake enjoying the scenery. "Oh I see!" said Sabattis, "You have not broken it,—only bent it a little." Sensing a heavy rain by nightfall, Sabattis suggested they break camp after dinner. The guides prepared a meal of mock turtle soup (which consisted of boiled water, Liebig's

This chapter is derived, in part, from my article "Disentangling the 'Native' Guide: Indigenous and Euroamerican Guides of the Adirondacks, 1840–1920," *Cultural and Social History* 11, no. 4 (Fall 2014), available at https://www.tandf online.com/doi/abs/10.2752/147800414X14056862572104.

extract of meat, salt and pepper, cut lemon slices, and cooked egg whites), ham and eggs, canned Boston baked beans, fried and roasted brook trout, boiled salmon trout, pie and cake, plus spring water and tea, which everyone shared. The party of travelers finished off their meal with pipes and fine quality "segars" and then took an hour's nap before rolling up their blankets and putting them into the already loaded boats. The party returned to Sabattis's boardinghouse in Long Lake. By then, Morrell had come down with a chill and then a fever. He remained at the Sabattis boardinghouse for several days being treated with mustard plasters, quinine "and a hot Jamaica rum punch [that] put [him] in a sweat." The following day he was weak but on the mend. The rest of the party continued to fish until everyone left for home by way of the Raquette River toward the Saranacs.[1]

What is interesting about this wilderness travel experience is that Mitchel Sabattis (1823–1906) was a well-known Abenaki guide of the Adirondacks. The other two guides were his Euro-Canadian, now American, sons-in-law. Lorenzo Towns was born in Quebec and arrived in the area in 1853 at the age of fifteen. He married Mitchel's eldest daughter, Louisa (1849–1922), in 1872. Calvin Towns reported that he was born in English Canada and arrived in the United States in 1880 at the age of twenty. He married Mary Elizabeth Sabattis (1864–87) within a year or so of his arrival. Mary Elizabeth died in 1887, and Calvin married her older sister Emeline (1862–1915) in 1892. Mitchel and his German or Dutch-American wife, Elizabeth "Betsy" Dornburg(h) (1827–1901), ran the boardinghouse where Morrell recovered.[2] Morrell's travel account gives us a glimpse of the experience of the Adirondack wilderness tourist and the work their guides performed. It also describes the sense of humor and religious conviction that Mitchel Sabattis possessed and conveys what it might have been like to travel with him on a wilderness vacation. Further-more, it illustrates the complexity of his family and business.

As chapter 2 suggests, wilderness tourism in the Adirondacks was furthered by the tensions of encounters between Natives and new-comers, especially hunters and trappers. But there was more to wilder-ness tourism than these encounters; there were nonlocal influences as well. Setting the context for these developments is important to understanding the history of especially Mohawk and Abenaki guides in the Adirondacks and more broadly. This chapter begins with a brief discussion of the many and varied influences that helped to create and maintain wilderness tourism, including the guide and sportsmen's relationship in general, based on recent scholarship. It then focuses on the specific relationship between the "sport" (as these male sportsmen were called in the region) and guide in the Adirondacks. Next, this contextual section of the chapter provides a history of wilderness tourism in the Adirondacks, including hunting techniques and the typical experience of a wilderness vacation there.

After the contextual information, this chapter spotlights the history of Algonquian and Iroquoian peoples who worked in the Adirondacks as guides for a variety of employers, starting with the colonial era. It includes guiding for the military, early White settlers, surveyors, and, eventually, tourists. As the previous chapter argues, the family of Sabael Benedict employed customary leadership skills and a strategy of cooperation with incoming Euro-American hunters and pioneers, thereby becoming "safe Indians." Later in the century, Indigenous peoples continued this approach as they guided for tourists. Building on that argument, this chapter introduces Abenaki Mitchel Sabattis and his family. Sabattis continued this long-established tactic and as a result was sought after by nineteenth-century sportsmen, who hired Mitchel, his sons, and even grandsons to guide them.

Wilderness Tourism in the Nineteenth and Early Twentieth Century

A History of Wilderness Tourism

Wilderness tourism originally became popular as a result of the romantic movement's aesthetic appreciation of nature and for health reasons. In the Adirondacks, Ballston Spa was the first "elite retreat" for those afflicted with various diseases and conditions, especially tuberculosis. Health-conscious tourists traveled to Ballston Spa to sample nearby mineral spring waters starting in the late 1780s, which resulted in the development of inns, taverns, and hotels. Eventually nearby Saratoga Springs dominated the spa scene as it added other forms of entertainment to help draw tourists. Taking to the outdoors was used as a treatment for men with tuberculosis. Women also used outdoor environments as treatment for tuberculosis, but instead of venturing into the forest they were expected to rest, albeit sometimes outside, at institutions such as Trudeau's Adirondack Cottage Sanatorium in Saranac Lake.[3]

This earlier period was the precursor to the "wilderness cult" travel of the late nineteenth century, one bound up with concerns about masculinity. The latter type of travel was seen as a cure for the malaise of overindustrialization and urbanization, both of which sparked anxieties about modern life toward the end of the nineteenth century. During this era, many European and Euro–North American upper- and middle-class men worried that they were becoming soft and unmanly because of over civilization.

The late nineteenth century brought about many reasons for this sense of crisis. Economic depressions in the 1870s and in the 1890s thwarted the previous trend of sons working for their fathers until they had earned enough money and experience to start their own successful business, as well as upsetting the hopes of clerks who hoped to rise to management level jobs. In addition, increased immigration, labor unrest, and women's suffrage added to social, political, and cultural upheaval. Cities riddled with diseases, such as tuberculosis, cholera, and yellow fever, plus an increase in taverns, prostitution, and other forms of unsanctioned amusement caused well-to-do, mostly Protestant, urbanites to leave the cities in droves, especially during the summer, to pursue leisure activities. The relationship between Protestantism and leisure activities shifted as American Protestant culture moved from being one of work and salvation to one of therapeutic or consumer culture.[4]

By the end of the nineteenth century, historian Frederick Jackson Turner pronounced the American frontier closed. Turner suggested that the interface between wilderness and the edge of settlement, or the frontier, had created not only the American character but democracy itself. This widely acclaimed pronouncement added to the sense of crisis. Six years later, President Theodore Roosevelt coined the phrase "the strenuous life." Roosevelt believed that the Euro-American race was superior and dominant. After all, they had displaced and dispossessed the Indigenous peoples throughout the continent. However, he also believed in "racial decadence," echoing British concerns expressed a century earlier, this term implied a race lost its strength through overcivilization. These concerns created a need for escapism leading to the "cult of the wilderness," which was influenced by "primitivism." The latter held that men's happiness decreased as they became more civilized, and thus they needed authentic "primitive" experiences to compensate.[5]

All of these concerns encouraged urban, middle- and upper-class Euro-American men to leave their workplace for extended periods, mostly in the late spring, summer, or early fall, to travel to nearby wildlands for a "wilderness" experience. Regular vacations were seen as a means of relaxation. The wilderness vacation was to be strenuous and exciting, replicating the challenges of pioneering or the battlefield. Wilderness tourism became a popular way to improve a man's health and test his manhood. These men went into the wilderness as campers, hunters, and anglers. A few women also went, but in general they did not have the "authentic" experience of men because hunting was considered a male sport. Wilderness tourism has been described as a "journey to the past" that gazed upon primitive cultures in the hope of understanding their own society, which was seen as increasingly riddled with conflict. Some scholars view these actions, especially hunting, as similar to imperial ones. Late nineteenth-century sports hunting has been described as a masculine way to exert control over nature—it marked the hunter as a virile, as opposed to effeminate, imperialist. Scholars argue that wilderness tourism reflects the experience of nineteenth-century colonial expansion in North America. These hunters, like scientific and other explorers, often wrote about their experiences. Travel writers of this sort were the "capitalist vanguard" who "innocently" appropriated Indigenous knowledge and their labor to "discover" places that only became "real" once they had written about them, representing what Mary Louise Pratt terms the strategy of the "anti-conquest." The wilderness tourists who wrote about their experience in the Adirondacks during this era were no exception. Later, sports hunters were responsible for conservation laws that often affected local people's ability to practice subsistence hunting. The conservation movement's origins were part of upper-class sportsmen's efforts to protect their hunting territory and the animals contained in it. These motives, combined with the public's concern for dwindling wildlife, challenged the American myth of inexhaustibility.[6] The Adirondacks became an important location for this wilderness experience in the Northeast and reflected many of these concerns around masculinity and eventually conservation.

Wilderness tourism experiences in places like the Adirondacks were also part of an American search for a distinct cultural identity and shared past. One of the reasons well-to-do sportsmen, or "sports," came to places like the Adirondacks was to compare their lives to how people lived in a purer setting, as they searched for *the* American culture. Lakota historian Philip J. Deloria argues that Euro-Americans were still searching for their identity during the nineteenth century and that "British" and "Indianness" competed with one another for that distinction. He explains that the authentic is a social construct born out of a self-perception of being inauthentic or out of place. Seekers of authenticity often look to the Other—whether a people, place, or time period—to find authenticity. Wilderness tourism thus allowed sports to experience both identities alongside concepts of modern and primitive in their search for authenticity.[7]

As a result of this search for identity and the need to challenge one's manhood, influential outsiders purposefully manipulated cultures in and made changes to rural areas still considered untainted by urbanization. Cultural interpositions need to be looked at as interference rather than benign accidents in order to understand the politics of culture instituted by formal institutions and powerful individuals. The powerful visitors who constructed and shaped the physical, economic, and political landscapes of the Adirondacks to meet their own needs also saw the region's Aboriginal peoples, who acted as guides, artisans, entrepreneurs, and performers, as part of their own mythology. Longing for an authentic experience, they rarely noted Indians or even Euro-Americans who worked for wages in other industries.[8]

Relationship between Sportsmen and Guides

Wilderness touring in North America during the nineteenth and early twentieth centuries often required employing a guide. Indian guides were especially desired as they authenticated the sportsman's wilderness experience. Sporting narratives of this era described encounters, used Indigenous names, and characterized guides' personalities. In addition, they illustrated how Aboriginal hunting and fishing methods differed from their own methods. Many hunters and fishermen were fascinated with Indigenous culture and fancied their contacts with Indian guides as being more authentic than experiences with non-Indigenous guides, which resulted in the creation of an environment of Aboriginal culture as a commodity "at a comfortable level and at a safe distance." Simultaneously, this relationship often attempted to exercise power and control and experiments with changing masculine identities, as Euro–North American male hunters used their personae as masculine and bourgeois managers of labor to handle and denigrate their Indian guides. In response, Indigenous guides took on the roles of tricksters to resist and manipulate their arrogant customers. Each used their roles against the other as they struggled for control.[9]

Wilderness Tourism in the Adirondacks from the 1830s to the 1920s

Concepts of wilderness, masculinity, power, and authenticity are very relevant to studies about the role of Indigenous peoples working in wilderness tourism in the Adirondacks. Well-to-do tourists wrote about their experiences. They often employed the tourist gaze and engaged in behavior that involved competing with their guides, whether the latter was Indian or not. Tourists created meaning and passed judgment based on their urban sensibilities, especially about matters of authenticity with regard to Aboriginal peoples, whom they characterized based on their ideas about looks, blood quantum, and how the Abenaki and Mohawk were supposed to behave. The

Kanienkehaka and Abenaki who came to the Adirondacks to work in the tourism industry realized they were operating within a staged setting. As chapter 5 illustrates, those who came to sell their handicrafts made modifications as necessary to make a living. Wilderness guides were allowed a different sense of power than craftmakers but, as this chapter shows, even their influence had limitations.

The wilderness tourism era in the Adirondacks started as early as the mid-1830s and continued into the early twentieth century. Sometimes the sports did not bother to name their attendants, and in their writing they often kept their guides' activities vague, probably as a way of enhancing their own image. Nevertheless, these urban sports were dependent on their guides to have a wilderness-like experience. In some instances, sports even complained about a specific individual or group of guides, sometimes referred to as foresters. Their feeling of superiority over their guides was evident in their writing, a phenomenon that was not confined to the Adirondacks. Sportsmen expected to exert some control over those guiding them, and they became displeased when their guides were not fully cooperative.[10] To be sure, although sports passed judgment on and ultimately felt superior to their guides, some exhibited a real, albeit romanticized, respect for both Aboriginal and non-Aboriginal foresters. These sportsmen seemed to genuinely respect their guides, especially for their woodcraft skills, and they wrote pages or in some cases even a chapter about them. For example, Cecil Clay of Philadelphia defended Mitchel Sabattis in his column in *Field and Stream* after Sabattis and others had been accused of killing deer out of season in 1877. Clay did not believe the charge and went so far to claim if he himself saw Sabattis do such a thing he would have to put it down to "killed by special act of Providence." However, Clay did recall an incident where Sabattis, guiding a hunting party in February of 1861, had to shoot a deer out of season in order to feed the group, an act Clay felt was justified. Clay was exhibiting a form of "noblesse oblige," as Clay and other wilderness travelers did not realize it was they who put Sabattis and his neighbors in a position to be prosecuted.[11]

Adirondackers, whether Aboriginal or Euro-American, became what Ian McKay calls the "folk." They represented a more innocent time and were seen as noble, yet simultaneously simple and naive. This portrayal existed alongside Karl Jacoby's two contradictory tropes of the "pastoral" and the "primitive": the former focuses on the abundance and simple pleasures of rural life, while the latter stresses its lack of development and the deprivations. Concurrently, many of these nineteenth-century urban Americans, especially from the Northeast, began to sentimentalize about Indigenous peoples and wax nostalgic for an era when Indians roamed the (also vanishing) eastern forests.[12] Sports and industrialists who came to the area, particularly in the early to middle part of the nineteenth century, viewed the wild landscape of the Adirondacks as temporary. While they mourned its inevitable passing, these men simultaneously imagined the region becoming a more industrialized and civilized state. The contradiction of untouched wilderness and its commercialization existed side-by-side in places such as the Adirondacks. The North American landscape has a long history of being seen as a commodity, especially by European and later Euro–North American explorers and merchants. This landscape also served as the foundation for major industries, including tourism.

The region became popular for wilderness touring because of its uninviting climate and geography for farming and because of the Adirondacks proximity to major northeastern cities, such as New York City, Boston, and Philadelphia. As a result, the area maintained its wildlands setting better than most landscapes in the Northeast. As noted in earlier chapters, the earliest Westernized images of the Adirondacks were often sparse representations in seventeenth- and eighteenth-century maps and military records. These images were followed by conceptions created by naturalists, artists, and writers. Considered the media of their day for distributing information and influencing popular culture, these eighteenth- and nineteenth-century chroniclers documented parts of the region. Kalm's *Travels into North America* (1749) and Milbert's early nineteenth-century botanical history were followed by such Hudson River School artists as Thomas Cole (1801–48) and Asher B. Durand (1796–1886), who ventured into the area to paint. Another important artist was Charles Cromwell Ingham (1796–1863), who traveled with and illustrated the first regionwide geological survey in 1837. These artists captured the wilderness-like scenery and first brought the landscape of the Adirondacks to the attention of both the European and American public. Probably the most influential painter to encourage wilderness tourism was Arthur Fitzwilliam Tait, who started painting the area in 1852. His paintings depicted scenes of hunters and anglers with their guides and provided a visual understanding of these relationships.[13]

Travel writers appeared alongside the artists. Early publications encompassing at least the fringes of the Adirondacks included Theodore Dwight's *Travels in New England and New York* (1821), Gideon Davison's *The Fashionable Tour* (1822), and Henry D. Gilpin's *The Northern Tour: Being a Guide to Saratoga, Lake George, Niagara, Canada, Boston, &c* (1825). Many publications began as letters to the editor of city newspapers; authors then used these letters to compile a book. The letters of Charles Fenno Hoffman (1806–84) were published in the *New York Mirror* during the fall of 1837. Hoffman is the first known sport to chronicle his experiences in the area, and he captured the public's imagination and attention. His descriptions of camping trips with the aid of a Mohawk guide helped to spark interest in traveling to the area. Hoffman wrote about the region before it was formally known as the Adirondacks. He referred to the High Peaks as the "Aganuschion Range" or "Black Mountains" because of "sombre cedars and frowning cliffs." At the same time Ebenezer Eammons was conducting his geological survey, and his naming of the geographical space as the Adirondacks in 1838 won out over Hoffman's nomenclature.[14] Hoffman published his book *Wild Scenes in the Forest and Prairie* a year later, and other travel writers soon followed.

Early wilderness tourism within the Adirondacks was rugged: it took weeks to get there and return home, and the accommodations were rough for sports used to an urban environment. The early wilderness tourists were almost always male, and individuals often traveled as, or became part of, a party of three or four. These tourists traveled by steamer, railroad, or a combination of both to a small border city, such as Saratoga Springs, Utica, Plattsburgh, or Watertown, where they jumped off into the Adirondacks. The sports then continued by stagecoach or wagon to a small settlement where they hired a group of local men to guide them into the interior wildlands. The ratio of sports to guides varied, but it was typically one-to-one.[15]

Euro-American guides were seen in romantic ways as pioneers, and sports wrote about them, their families, and homes as if they were. In 1869, guides earned $2.50 day; by the time they organized in 1891, they earned $3.00 day plus expenses. The guides did all the heavy lifting, including portaging the transportation over a local "carry" between lakes and rivers. The party usually ventured into the forest by boat, often in an Adirondack guideboat, which was quicker and easier to row and carry alone than a canoe.[16]

Originally square at the back similar to a rowboat, the Adirondack guideboat became pointed on both ends—like a canoe—around 1875. The guideboat was (and is) not the sturdiest boat, due to its design's emphasis on speed. It is lighter than a canoe and is usually rowed from the middle when alone or paddled from the stern with a passenger in the bow. When hunting for deer using the "jacklighting" technique, described below, the guide paddled from the stern to make less noise. Seats were caned, and the center seat was removable. The interior ribbing formed a yoke to allow a guide to carry the boat over his head by himself. Early versions were painted black or dark blue on the outside and green on the inside to act as camouflage.[17]

Once the group had entered the interior, the foresters would set up a base camp for the party and themselves. If the trip included a change of region, the sports obtained a new guide from that area. As Adirondack Murray explained in his *Adventures in the Wilderness,* the region was too vast and difficult for any one person to know it all. Murray lists four areas: St. Regis and Saranac guides in the north; Potsdam and St. Lawrence guides for the west; Brown's Tract guides for the south; and Long Lake guides for the central region. By the 1880s there were approximately five hundred guides working throughout the region in as many as forty-three sub-areas.[18]

In addition to setting up the camp, foresters cooked, cleaned, and packed up camp. They led the campers into situations where they viewed sublime scenery, hunted wild animals, and fished. Sports often brought items from home that represented civilization to them, such as wearing a tie, or even dishes or bottles of spirits that the guides had to transport and carry.

Adirondack wilderness tourists primarily wanted to hunt white-tailed deer. However, they also hunted moose and often fished during the same experience. Deer hunting techniques varied in the Adirondacks, and during the warmer weather they included "jacklighting" and "hounding" (also known as "floating a deer"). Today these techniques are illegal, but for those dependent on the meat and later wages for survival, they were useful methods. Both sports and guides felt ambivalent toward these practices.

Jacklighting involved the use of a lantern at night from a boat to mesmerize deer that came out of the woods to drink. One had to mortally wound the deer in one shot with this technique. For less skilled hunters, hounding or floating a deer used dogs to run the animal into the lake where the hunter and his guide waited, often in a guideboat. The guide rowed the boat near the deer for the sport to take a shot. Sometimes the guide had to hold onto a deer's tail to allow inferior hunters more time to make a kill. If that failed, the guide might hit the deer over the head with his oar or even slit its throat with a knife. Hoffman described one of his two Euro-American foresters, Linus Catlin, making and using a "withe" to float a deer. Caitlin used a birch sapling and stripped it of all branches except two to create a noose to entangle in the deer's antlers. Dogs chased a deer into the lake, and Catlin was nearly killed using the withe when the deer pulled him into the water as it desperately tried to fight him off. Catlin survived by reaching for his hunting knife and slitting the deer's throat. According to Hoffman, they dined on the venison with a bit of cognac that evening.[19]

In the winter, deer and moose were sometimes hunted "on the crust" by hunters on snowshoes, often with dogs. "Crusting" a deer or moose in winter took advantage of an icy top crust over snow often caused by a light rain. The crust could hold a person, especially if they used snowshoes (still best made by Indians around the Canadian border, according to Hoffman) but the animal sank into the snow. Hunters could kill the poor creature even with a club. If a moose or deer escaped into a "yard" (a wooded area packed down by the moose or deer), then killing them was more difficult, especially moose, which are more aggressive and will charge at a human or other aggressor. Yards allowed the animals access to food and some safety from predators. Both two- and four-legged hunters might wait the animal out for their source of food to dwindle.[20]

The deer killed and fish caught were the main source of protein for the vacationing sports and their guides, as well as for nearby communities. Some sports were mindful of the need to practice conservation. For example, John Cheney, a Euro-American guide that Hoffman employed, shot four partridge on their way home from a foray into the wild. Cheney could not be convinced to shoot others because he did not need them, an act that Hoffman admired. We know, however, that at least a few hunters did kill game and fish excessively and left their remains to rot. One account described Mitchel Sabattis and fellow guides Alonzo "Lon" Wetherbee and Caleb Chase abandoning a sport in the late 1850s after he broke his promise not to persist in his practice of shooting too many deer and catching large amounts of trout, leaving the excesses in the woods to spoil. Warder Cadbury's introduction to Reverend John Todd's *Long Lake* describes the pastor as a wasteful hunter; the locals referred to him as a butcher of deer. By 1858 the Long Lake community asked him to stop coming there to hunt or, they warned, they would make an example of him.[21]

While sports enjoyed the idea of getting away from their work and the city, they feared getting lost in the Adirondacks amid difficult terrain and predators. Sport and Reverend Joel T. Headley described an incident of his brother getting lost: when they finally found him, he was "pale as marble" and "in a state of complete bewilderment." Sports even feared losing their minds if they got lost, reflecting their Puritan ancestors' apprehension "that life in the wilderness can lead to mental or moral degeneration."[22]

Most sports stayed a few weeks. These early travelers often noted and compared the Adirondack scenery to European epics and locations. Sports wrote about the wild scenery in Edmund Burke–like language: mountain scenery was sublime, lake scenery was beautiful. Hoffman described the region as one of a thousand lakes with outlets coming out of cataracts only comparable to Switzerland. He opined that most local hunters had never climbed Mount Marcy but was sure even they could appreciate the scene below as well as a cultivated man. Hoffman recorded the variety of plant life and geography and even mused that if the New York State Indians had chosen to live in the Adirondacks they might still be living their traditional lifestyle. Sports also described how industry, especially lumbering and mills, were juxtaposed with the wildlands and even worried about the effects these industries had on the landscape. Hoffman traveled to the McIntyre Iron Works, where he and his party stayed for several days. He described the manufacturing town as a romantic place, yet one that also was desolate because of the tree stumps, reflecting the new and incomplete nature of the community. While sports enjoyed getting away from their everyday life, they also relished returning to it. Sportsmen often wrote about the first newspaper or bit of news they obtained upon returning from the woods.[23]

After the American Civil War (1861–65), the middle class began to travel more, although they did not typically stay as long as the upper-class travelers. Professional photographers and writers penned guidebooks to provide details of the region especially for tourists. The guidebooks included schedules, places to stay, sites to see, and even recommended which guide(s) to hire within specific areas. Some of the guidebook writers and photographers for the Adirondacks included local individuals and families, such as members of the Holley family, the Taintor Brothers, E. R. Wallace, and Seneca Ray Stoddard, the latter being the most well-known photographer and guidebook writer of the Adirondacks. Stoddard became instrumental in creating concern for the environment of the Adirondacks with his "then" versus "now" photographs comparing areas after lumbering had devastated the landscape.[24]

In 1869, the New England minister known as "Adirondack Murray" wrote his *Adventures in the Wilderness*, which lured a veritable stampede of middle-class campers into the region who became known as "Murray's fools." *Harper's New Monthly* spoofed these tourists the following year and described the guides in ambiguous terms in an article entitled "The Raquette Club." This fictional tale describes a party camping in Tupper Lake who feared they were under attack by Indians after the beer they brought exploded. Boardinghouses, hotels, restaurants, and shops appeared in quick order to cater to the needs of middle-class tourists. Eventually the wilderness vacation included the entire family. Long-established resorts in towns on the outskirts of the region like Saratoga Springs competed with those being built in the interior, such as Paul Smith's Hotel, built in 1859. Men still went into the forest to hunt, but it was often for a shorter duration. Hotels began to contract with local guides to take their guests into the forest; however, these guides had an inferior reputation to the independent ones.[25] Women and children stayed at the resorts, which furnished entertainment such as boat rides, craftmaking, and social gatherings.

All of this changed the wilderness tourism environment in both landscape and experience. The wealthy, some of them Gilded Age "Robber Barons," bought large amounts of land that they privatized and then built "rustic" Great Camps to separate themselves from the masses. Modeled on European hunting estates, the Adirondack Great Camp soon became a unique regional architecture, popular among the wealthy. These camps were only lived in for as little as a few days to a few months a year, and they were maintained by a large staff that created a small community unto itself. Great Camps required a complex system of outbuildings, sanitation, water, and power, and they were extremely expensive to maintain. By the twentieth century, the man and the very occasional woman who wanted an authentic wilderness experience looked further afield for places still considered wild. The automobile eventually eliminated the era of wilderness tourism in the Adirondacks. Motels replaced hotels and resorts, and the state built facilities such as campsites and bathrooms starting in 1923. In addition, the availability of lightweight canoes that allowed people to go into remote waterways by themselves eliminated the need for a guide in many places.[26] As tourists were afforded new regions to explore and better and faster transportation to take them there, the heyday of the wilderness vacation in the Adirondacks came to an end in the 1920s.

History of Indigenous People Working as Guides in the Adirondacks

Aboriginal peoples have a long history of guiding Europeans and later Euro-Americans in the Adirondacks for a variety of purposes. They guided explorers, priests, and military officers in and around the area during the colonial period. Such work included helping Sir John Johnson and other Loyalists escape through the region to avoid arrest during the American Revolution.[27] The area remained mostly unsettled by Whites until the end of the War of 1812 as a result of continued violence and the opening up of better farmland in Iroquoia and farther west. The handful of newcomers who ventured into the Adirondacks around this period found they could rely on the assistance of the Algonquian and Iroquoian peoples already there, as discussed in chapter 2. While we need to be careful about and critically review Euro-American accounts of "helpful Indians" who helped them make a place for themselves, historians cannot ignore these references either. These accounts are often the initial contact record or even the only source of information we have about Indigenous peoples in some spaces.

Some of the earliest recorded Indigenous guides in the Adirondacks who helped early settlers and surveyors include Mohawk Captain Gill and Abenakis Peter and Mitchel Sabattis and Sabael and Louis Elijah Benedict. Former Long Lake historian Frances Seaman states that Euro-Americans who settled in the region "learned the area's secrets" sometimes from local Abenaki or Mohawk, and they too began guiding. Reverend John Todd described a Euro-American guide named Wilson around the St. Regis River who learned his craft when he accompanied an "Indian Chief" to the region for his health. Wilson decided to stay there to trap and hunt. Arguably, no one was as helpful as Sabael Benedict and his son Lige in assisting incoming

White settlers. Memories recorded by Laura Guenther describe Sabael Benedict assisting her grandfather Gideon and his cousin, Willard Porter, in the summer of 1847 when they traveled to present-day Sabael, New York, to take up residence. "They had met & talked with several native Indians, chief of whom seemed to be old Sabael. . . . He introduced them to 2 Indians, John & Lige Camp."[28]

Surveyors also used the assistance of Aboriginal guides on a local and state basis. In his field notes, John Richard's survey of the Old Military Tract during the years 1812–13 mentioned a seven-foot Mohawk blazing trees as part of the survey crew. Ebenezer Emmons's geological survey of 1836–38 employed Louis Elijah Benedict as a guide in the interior of the region, including the northern headwaters of the Hudson River. Verplanck Colvin, the state's superintendent of the Adirondack survey from 1872 to 1900, engaged Indigenous men to obtain food and Mitchel Sabattis for guiding on some of his surveys.[29]

In addition, Indigenous guides assisted with the assessment of rail routes. Henry J. Raymond, the publisher of the *New York Times*, considered investing in a railroad through the region. He hired guides to explore this possibility and published several letters in 1855 about his experience traveling with a party of financiers. They left from the southeast at Saratoga and traveled to Lowville just outside the western boundary of the Adirondacks. The group was abnormally traveling through the region with horses and wagons. According to local publisher Watson B. Berry, this party was the first to trek across the entirety of the region. Louis Elijah Benedict was Raymond's guide during much of this trip. In his first letter, published June 19, 1855, Raymond describes an incident whereby the supplies for the group were capsized en route to the camp. To compensate, Benedict caught and cooked some trout for the party.[30] A week later, Raymond published a description of the campsite Benedict created for them: "Our two huts had been built at right angles to each other—on two sides of a square. With Indian skill and unwonted care, Elijah had finished them off in superb style. They were water-proof from the roof, and a thick carpet of nicely arranged spruce boughs made a most comfortable floor. A fire of huge logs was kindled in front of each, and after an hour or two of talk we prepared for sleep. Two feet of space were allotted to each person, and each camp would thus hold eleven."[31]

Mohawk and Abenaki peoples took advantage of their awareness of the Adirondack landscape—their homeland—and used traditional skills to earn wages and create relationships with the newcomers, surveyors, anthropologists, and eventually tourists who were entering what was to them a foreign space. Indigenous peoples knew that Whites believed they had a mysterious font of cultural power, especially with regard to the land, and they used this belief to their benefit.[32] Mohawk and Abenaki guides in the Adirondacks did not hide their heritage, and some were able to gain from it. As Euro-Americans and immigrants entered the Adirondacks, Captain Gill, Sabael Benedict, and Peter Sabattis, together with the latter two's sons, developed relationships with newcomers and industrialists. These men and their families became some of the first, or at least the best known, early Indigenous guides and informants in the area. They and their descendants were active in all facets of wilderness tourism, including guiding, artisanal work, performing, and as entrepreneurs. Based on these exchanges, Gill, the Benedict family, and later the family of Peter and, in particular, Mitchel Sabattis became "safe Indians" in the imagination of eastern urban Euro-Americans who hired them as guides. These well-to-do sports wrote about the Indians with whom they came into contact, making the experience sound potentially dangerous, challenging, and exciting—all the necessary ingredients prescribed to wealthy urbanites for a wilderness remedy meant to restore their health and masculinity.

These Algonquian and Iroquoian peoples fit into the sports' nostalgic quest for an earlier period while having their safe, exciting, and "authentic" pioneering adventure. To these Indigenous guides, the Adirondacks were not a wilderness: it was their homeland. It was their deep knowledge of the landscape that made them so valuable to European and Euro–North American professionals, settlers, and eventually tourists. As a result, wilderness tourism in the Adirondacks helped to keep Iroquoian and Algonquian peoples who lived and worked there extant in the minds of Euro-Americans from the Northeast during the nineteenth century, in contrast to state and federal policies that attempted to make them disappear. Recall this was a period of federal removal of American Indian peoples through policies such as those of Andrew Jackson's administration, which compelled most Indigenous peoples living in the eastern part of the United States to move west of the Mississippi River after 1830. Even earlier, the policies of New York governor George Clinton (1777–95 and 1801–4) forced most of the Haudenosaunee and the Mahicans outside of the state's expanding boundaries.[33] Paradoxically though, wilderness accounts also helped to reinforce the notion of the disappearing Indian as tourists made those Iroquoian and Algonquian peoples living in the Adirondacks appear exotic and the last of their kind. These Aboriginal peoples were often called "Canadian Indians" or they were identified specifically as "St. Regis" or "St. Francis" Indians. Such practices reinforced their status as nonresidents and did not acknowledge they were Mohawk and Abenaki who had historically considered the Adirondacks as part of their homeland.

The Family of Mitchel Sabattis

One of the best known Aboriginal guides for wilderness tourism in the Adirondacks was Mitchel Sabattis (1821–1906). Born to Abenaki parents named Jean-Baptiste Saint-Denys, or Soniaro8ane, and Marie-Cecile on September 16, 1821, Mitchel was baptized the next day at Saint-Jean-Francois-Regis, Akwesasne's Catholic mission, as Michel Soniaro8ane. His parents used the father's first name as their child's last name, and it became the more widely used Jean-Baptiste, which eventually turned into Sabattis. This was a common Abenaki practice, and indeed Mitchel's father became known as Peter Sabattis because his French father's name was Pierre Saint-Denys (c. 1733–1811; he was adopted and raised by the Abenaki).[34]

According to local histories, Mitchel Sabattis arrived in the interior of the Adirondacks with his father, locally called Captain Peter Sabattis, about 1830. They traveled to the region with an Akwesasne Mohawk named Thompson and his son; both boys were about eight at the time. Not much is known about their lives during this early period, but local histories, an obituary, and an article dated July 22, 1900, shed some light. The obituary chronicles Adirondack Euro-American guide John Plumley's account of the first time, as a boy, he met the Sabattis father and son in the summer of 1833. He described "a small party of Indians camping at the foot of the lake." Mitchel, who was approximately eleven, was among the party and was paddling a birchbark canoe when he gestured to John and his father to take a ride with him. They accepted the offer and were taken to a camp where Peter Sabattis and several other Indigenous hunters were skinning a moose. "The Indians gave John's father a part of the moose as a sign of their friendliness."[35]

The 1900 article also referred to a story Mitchel used to tell about killing his first moose as a youth. His story described how he and his father camped during the summers and spent their winters in a settlement, including a log house in Newcomb where they stayed "many winters, but white men got in there and occupied the log house." They camped outdoors along lakes and streams as they trapped, often for marten, and sometimes they trapped moose with the use of a deadfall (a type of trap for large game that uses a weight to stun or kill the animal). At some point, Captain Peter brought other members of his family to the area where they hunted, trapped, and fished from spring to fall and then worked their way out of the mountains for the winter. Peter Sabattis sold his furs in Potsdam for the family's supplies. This account helps to support the belief that prior to the 1830s the family lived near Parishville in St. Lawrence County, that Mitchel and his siblings were probably born there, and that his mother may be buried there.[36] This article also provides a connection to Newcomb, where Mitchel and his young family first settled.

Former Colton town historian Flora Miller wrote a brief history of Peter Sabattis. She claims he fought with the American colonists in the Revolutionary War. Others claim it was Mitchel's grandfather, Pierre Saint-Denys (c. 1733–1811) who participated in the American Revolution. It is unlikely Mitchel's father was directly involved in battle during the American Revolution, but we cannot rule out that he acted as an assistant of some kind. Abenaki boys were known to act as cooks and runners and to provide other help during wartime (recall that twelve-year-old Sabael Benedict acted as a cook at the Battle of Quebec). Whatever the case, after the American Revolution Peter Sabattis worked in an early form of guiding by blazing trails for roads between Lake George and Lake Ontario during the War of 1812. Afterward, Captain Sabattis came back to the region to work by hunting, fishing, and trapping, especially up and down the Raquette River.

According to local history, Peter Sabattis was well thought of by local people in St. Lawrence County and had adopted Christianity. The baptism of his children at nearby Akwesasne attests that he had an affiliation with Catholicism. His wife died young, and it is reported his daughter Hannah took care of him in his old age. Peter Sabattis is listed on the 1840 federal census for Long Lake as head of household and being between the ages of eighty and eighty-nine, and Hannah was likely living with him, but Mitchel was not. The last account of Peter and his daughter Hannah Sabattis appears to have been written by the Reverend Joel T. Headley, who had traveled to Long Lake during the month of August sometime between 1842 and 1846.[37]

On this occasion, Headley had employed Mitchel Sabattis as his guide and consequently met Peter and Mitchel's sister Hannah. Headley was the first sport to write about hiring Mitchel Sabattis as a guide, and he employed Mitchel on later occasions. He described Hannah as barely twenty and stated that her father shook with palsy and muttered in French and an Indian language. Referring to the father, Headley claimed he was called "Old Peter" by this time and "his once powerful frame" was "now bowed and tottering." He did not think Peter could last another year. Despite emphasizing Peter's frailty, Headley noted that he still roamed the region, camped where he was when night fell, carried a canoe (although he groaned under its weight), continued to hunt using an old fowling rifle, and assessed pieces of birch bark for the making of a new canoe. Headley described Hannah as pretty, with shoulder-length, dark, wavy hair. She refused to speak to him, which might have demonstrated her distrust—belying the "well thought of" consideration of the family by local people—or perhaps her silence was an expression of modesty. Headley last saw Hannah paddling her father in a canoe; she sat in the stern while Peter occupied the middle. Local history suggests Peter died in 1861, although there are no records about him after Headley's account.[38]

Mitchel Sabattis married "Betsy" Dornburg(h) in 1844. They had at least fifteen children, although not all lived to adulthood and at least two daughters who made it into their twenties died within that decade. In order of age, the Sabattis children included Charles P. (1845–1916); John B. (1847–98); Louisa (1849–1922); Isaac, or Ike (1851–1912); Solomon (1852–56); Anett (1854–56); Byron F., sometimes referred to as Frederick B. (1857–63); Sarah Jane (1859–1907); Emmeline (1862–1915); Mary Elizabeth (1864–87); Dora, or Dorry (1867–94); Durand (1868–70); Henrietta (1869–70); Edith L. (1870–71); and Harry M. (1870–1934). The family may have adopted Alice L. (1873–96) and partially raised a granddaughter named Clara (born 1879). At least one other grandchild, Byron Thompson (1893–1933), lived with the family for a time after the death of his mother, Dora.

The family began their lives and business in Newcomb, where Mitchel and Betsy increased the value of their farm from 200 dollars in 1850 to 1,500 dollars by 1860; it is the richest property on that page of the census in the 1860 federal census for Newcomb. There is an oft-repeated legend and published reminiscence by sport and Vermont politician Lucius E. Chittenden (1824–1900) that the Vermonter bought the Sabattis's Newcomb mortgage in 1846. After discovering at the end of his wilderness adventure that the Sabattis family was about to lose their home, Chittenden offered to buy out the mortgage and give them more time to pay if Sabattis promised not to drink for the next year. Sabattis was alleged to have been drinking heavily at this time, and he kept his promise—indeed, he reportedly never drank again. As Chittenden tells it, Sabattis was a successful guide thereafter and the family lived a happy existence. Records for this transaction have not been found. However, two indentures do exist. The first, dated 1848, is for real estate located in township twenty-seven of the Totten and Crossfield Purchase (Newcomb) between Mitchel and Daniel F. Woodworth and Woodworth's wife, Elizabeth, which records that Sabattis had purchased land from the Woodworths.

Another indenture, dated 1861, between Sabattis and his wife, Betsy, and Anthony Alexander Clay of Philadelphia indicates Clay held a mortgage for the family in the amount of one thousand dollars for ten years; at the end of this period, Clay would have received two thousand dollars in return.[39] Nor do the records suggest every member of the large Sabattis family lived a happy life, but they did not appear to be any worse off than other local families. How much of the Chittenden mortgage story is true we may never know, but it certainly is an example of many sports' desire to express their "noblesse oblige" toward a guide they were fond of.

While the family lived in Newcomb from the 1840s until at least 1861, they were active in the Long Lake Methodist community. We do not know why the baptized Catholic Mitchel converted to Methodism. It is possible he changed religions because his wife's family was involved in the Long Lake Methodist church. It has been noted that Mitchel attended school for a few weeks in 1844, allegedly to catch the eye of his future wife. Thus, it would not be too much of a stretch to consider that he began attending these services to see her there as well. Regardless, the first reference to Mitchel being a Methodist is by the Reverend John Todd, a minister from Pittsfield, Massachusetts, who came to sponsor the Long Lake Methodist Church. His book *Long Lake* mentions Mitchel playing the violin for a service there as early as 1844. By 1861, Mitchel and Betsy hosted Methodist church classes in their home. In 1865, James and Mary Mulholland deeded one-quarter acre of land in Long Lake to Mitchel Sabattis for twenty-five dollars to build a meeting house. That same year, Mitchel and his son Isaac ("Ike"), along with two other members of the assembly, traveled to Philadelphia, Pittsfield, and the state of Connecticut, where Mitchel spoke before the congregations of ministers he had previously guided in order to raise money for the Long Lake Wesleyan Methodist Church. They returned with two thousand dollars, enough to build their house of worship. Mitchel was known to occasionally preach at the church.[40]

Sabattis was not the only Indigenous person to participate in Adirondack churches. For example, Stockbridge minister and Wampanoag

Anthony Paul (c. 1746–1816) was a licensed Presbyterian minister in Lake George at the end of the eighteenth century. Paul came under the influence of the Mohegan Presbyterian preacher Samson Occom and probably attended the New Lebanon School. Paul married Samson's daughter Christiana. Anthony and Christiana and four of their children were baptized at Brothertown in Oneida territory in 1784, the family originally went to Saratoga but moved to the Lake George and Bolton area in the early 1790s. Local history claims that Paul preached there until alcohol got the better of him and he was forced to give up his ministry. He tried later to work for the Baptist Society but that did not work out.[41]

The Sabattis family shows up in the Long Lake census records in 1870. Even though he was actively guiding during this period, Mitchel always noted his profession on the census as a farmer until the 1880 census, when he first listed "guide" as his occupation. Despite this, Sabattis guided plenty of sports prior to this date, including C. W. Webber in the summers of 1848 and 1849. Webber published *Spirit of the Times*, which is credited for bringing the Adirondacks to national attention. In addition to Webber, Headley, and Chittenden, all of whom Mitchel guided during the 1840s, he continued to guide sports, surveyors, and sightseers for decades. Many of his sports were ministers; they liked him and he liked them, probably because neither drank and they had similar beliefs. In 1886, Mitchel suffered a stroke, but he continued to do light guiding. He did not identify any employment on the 1892 state census for Long Lake, possibly implying that he was retired. By June of 1900, Mitchel and Betsy's youngest son Harry and his family lived with them. Within a month, Mitchel suffered a second stroke, and a local newspaper article noted that Harry was taking care of his parents thereafter. Betsy died in 1901 at the age of seventy-four. Mitchel continued to live with Harry and his family until his death on April 17, 1906, at the age of eighty-four.[42]

The census counted Mitchel as being "Indian" if it identified his ethnicity. In the case of the 1892 state census, he and his children's ethnicity was marked with an "X" in the "colored" column. His children were usually identified as being Indian except in the 1870 federal census when they were classified as "W." His wife and the wives of his sons were distinguished as being White. The grandchildren who occasionally lived with Mitchel and Betsy during a census period were, though, identified as Indian.[43] However, in the next generation, they and their offspring were sometimes recognized as Indian and at other times as being White. The 1880 Census is interesting, as Mitchel's son and a granddaughter listed on one page were identified as White while all of the children on the previous page were identified as Indian. As the children became adults and had families of their own, their status changed from census to census: one year they were classified as Indian, five or ten years later they were White, only to return to their Indian status by the next census—a typical pattern for other families of Indigenous heritage in the area. On at least one occasion, the Isaac Sabattis family identity changed on the same census as someone wrote over the initially recorded "W" and corrected it to "In." The various censuses also indicated that many family members remained geographically close to the Mitchel Sabattis homestead in Long Lake. The fluidity of these representations of the family's ethnicity accords with Lauren Basson's argument that ethnic identities are "contextual and relational" and are influenced by the stories being told about them.[44]

Accounts about Mitchel Sabattis are uniformly complimentary. No one wrote poorly about him personally; indeed, descriptions of him were glowing and stressed his honesty and devotedness. He was generally admired by the people who addressed him. While Sabattis was a physically small man and often described as reticent, other accounts describe his confidence and humor. His skill and reputation as a hunter and guide earned him the recognition of being among the top three or four best hunters and guides in the history of the Adirondacks. Mitchel's reputation as a prolific hunter was as distinctive as his prowess as a guide. He did not care for panthers and was proud of the nine he had killed in his lifetime with the help of dogs he had specially trained. Perhaps his aversion to panthers was based on his livelihood as a farmer. Romanticized reports of Sabattis noted that he was a "St. Francis" Indian and occasionally implied he was the last of his kind in the region, despite his large family, the descendants and relatives of

Sabael Benedict, and other Indigenous families who lived and worked there. As well, he was one of the few guides who crossed Adirondack regions. A multiskilled and multifaceted man, Sabattis made boats and snowshoes, and he carried the mail in a pack-basket on his back between Blue Mountain Lake and Long Lake.[45]

Sabattis also served as an informant for surveyor Verplanck Colvin and anthropologist Julius Dyneley Prince (who had a summer home in Blue Mountain Lake), as did other Abenaki in the region, such as the Benedict and Watso families. During the nineteenth century, Aboriginal peoples served as informants for ethnologists, and the Abenaki and Iroquois in New York State contributed to the new discipline of anthropology. Recording place names was a feature of this ethnographic work. Austin Wells Holden, author of *A History of the Town of Queensbury in the State of New York*, indicated he interviewed Mitchel Sabattis and Sabael Benedict around 1850 for their knowledge of place names. Mitchel and his father named some of the waterways and mountains in the area; for example, they named Long Lake "Qua-nah-ga-wah" due to its shape. Mitchel spoke Abenaki and English and possibly Mohawk and French. He did not write and probably did not read. His sons followed in his footsteps as guides and also appeared to be well thought of in that occupation. In addition, Mitchel had grandsons who became guides; for example, his son Charles's younger son, Joseph Druyea Sabattis (1878–1951), worked as a guide and was a taxidermist of some repute.[46] Despite the multiplicity of occupations and skills, it is as a guide that Mitchel Sabattis is remembered.

The records do not reflect that Mitchel or his sons resorted to stereotypes of Indians to make a living. There are no photos or written records of them in plains headdresses or other similar garb. While they were well-known as "St. Francis" Indians, it does not appear that father or sons ever marketed themselves as anything other than Adirondack guides. As mentioned, in addition to guiding, father and sons were farmers, and they participated in wage work. Yet Mitchel and his children were known to be Abenaki by both the local and the sporting community.

It was reported that Mitchel was related to the Denis or Dennis family in Lake Luzerne,[47] and as noted there were a number of Abenaki and other Indigenous families in the region. However, Mitchel married a Euro-American woman, and only one of their many children married an Aboriginal partner: Dora E., or Dorry, Sabattis (1867–94) married Frank W. Thompson (1863–?) before 1893. Thompson is believed to have been from Akwesasne, and one cannot help but speculate that he may have been related to the Thompson family that arrived in the region in 1830 with Peter and Mitchel Sabattis. Many of the Indigenous guides and their offspring married non-Aboriginal peoples. Some, like Mitchel and Betsy, had happy and long marriages, while others did not. The Camp family were particularly hard-hit when it came to troubled, ethnically mixed marriages. The family of the husband of their daughter Emma (1866–1934; Abenaki-Oneida) forced an annulment of her first marriage to their son (1882), and it is probable that they persuaded him to divorce her the second time (see chapter 4). Emma's brother Gabriel (1883–1948) wed Elsie Corscadden in 1916, and her family temporarily disowned her for marrying him. It appears the Corscadden family reconciled shortly before her father's death, but not without continued conflict. Letters between Elsie and her mother and brother indicate this reconciliation was somewhat tentative as they tried to deny her part of her father's estate because he had so recently accepted her back into the family.[48] Mitchel's son Charles's marriage ended in divorce, as did several of Mitchel's grandchildren's marriages. In addition, the children and grandchildren of these local families were not immune to the ramifications of premature deaths. When twenty-six-year-old Dorry Sabattis died from pneumonia in 1894, her son Byron K. Thompson (c. 1893–1933) went to live with his Sabattis grandparents. By 1905, he was living with the family of his Uncle Harry. By the age of seventeen, he was working for and a boarder (along with other men) of Craig Williams, foreman on a lumber job.[49]

Mitchel Sabattis's marriage raises questions about such relationships. Little has been written about interracial marriages between

Indigenous men and European or Euro-American women beyond captivity narratives, and those works that exist usually explore the period after the American Civil War and focus on middle-class relationships. One exception to the time period is Theresa Strouth Gaul's work about the marriage of New Englander Harriett Gold and Cherokee Elias Boudinot in 1826. Gaul argues that these types of marriages "tested boundaries of racial and national identity." Not only had the couple crossed ethnic boundaries, which included New England's antimiscegenation stance, but they also transgressed class lines, as Native Americans in New England at the time were considered "a dispossessed and servile underclass." Gaul argues that the act of White men marrying Indian women was less contentious and seen as a continuation of the colonial process. However, White women's status "functioned to stabilize whiteness as a racial identity," and thus White men were obliged to protect them in the name of protecting the "superior" race. Gaul suggests that for Boudinot, schooled in the ways of Protestant America, his marriage to a White woman demonstrated that he believed in American Protestant values and that he could fit into their new society. This included rejecting the matrilocal and matrilineal Cherokee traditions surrounding marriage. Boudinot quickly discovered his belief conflicted greatly with Euro-American attitudes.[50]

Later studies investigating interracial marriages between White women and Indigenous men focus on middle-class women marrying educated and professional Indian men trying to fit into Euro-American society. These studies confirm that Euro-American women were symbols of the purity and power of their race, and the few who crossed racial boundaries for love were reluctantly accepted, mostly as part of an "imperial project" or a concerted effort to assimilate Indigenous peoples into more Anglo-American ways. Ann Laura Stoler goes so far as to argue that the marriage between White women, who were thought of as the moral center of the family, and Indigenous men was acceptable because it was hoped these intermarriages would assist the country in eliminating treaty obligations.[51] I suspect this argument goes too far if one considers it a policy; however, perhaps more than one family used it as an excuse to grudgingly accept their non-White son-in-law.

None of these studies, however, describes or examines marriage between poor, rural European and later Euro-American women and Indigenous North American men. To explore these relationships, one needs to understand the marital relationship in rural areas. Nancy Grey Osterud's study of rural families focuses on a region just west of Binghamton, New York, and thus was more agriculturally focused than those communities located in the Adirondacks, but the work of women in both locations was similar. Osterud argues there was no "separate sphere of influence" for rural women in upstate New York, especially as compared to their urban middle-class counterparts. While not seen as equal to men, women's labor on the farm and elsewhere kept their influence more closely tied with rural men than their urban counterparts. At the same time, country women's kinship networks were very powerful strategies in their lives and labor.[52] As a result, the relationship between rural Euro-American women and Aboriginal men likely does not have the same meaning as other studies about these couples. Indeed, rural women's labor and relationship to their husbands' toil appear more similar to the complimentary traditional work done by Iroquoian and Algonquian women with their men's work, as well as the custom of drawing on kinship ties. The labor performed was not exactly the same, but the philosophy is.

As I have argued previously, Iroquoian and Algonquian peoples who came or returned to the Adirondacks and stayed were eventually seen as safe and cooperative Indians. Tentative relationships were created and grew into more intimate ones. Intermarriages might not have appeared unthinkable in this context. Both Indigenous and Euro-American peoples of the region lived similarly in this remote area. They planted gardens, hunted, trapped, and fished mostly for subsistence purposes. They gathered berries and plants for food, dyes, and medicines. And, they found ways to use these and other local resources for some income and later to seasonally work for wages. Successful settlement is often based on a peoples' ability to adjust their culture to the existing landscape.[53] The Adirondack landscape demanded an economy that was more akin to Indigenous ways than middle-class and urban Euro-American ones.

It is doubtful that these White women who married Algonquian and Iroquoian men during this period were concerned about imperial efforts to assimilate their husbands. Life was so harsh in the Adirondacks that a loving husband who could support a family was probably enough reason for these hardworking women. It is possible, at least in the case of Mitchel and Betsy Sabattis, that Methodism had some influence on their relationship. Mitchel and the family of Elizabeth Dornburg(h) were some of the first members of their Long Lake congregation. Early North American Methodism often attracted marginalized people; so long as one followed their strict rules, all were welcome. Interlocking networks such as religious and humanitarian circuits facilitated the necessary mobility to create intimate relationships between Indigenous and non-Indigenous peoples.[54] Did Betsy Dornburg(h) see her marriage as a Christianizing mission? It is hard to say, as there are no records to indicate what her feelings were. Nor does marriage as a Christianizing mission explain why other women of European descent married Algonquian and Iroquoian men here during the long nineteenth century; indeed, men outnumbered women in the early part of the century. It was at the end of the century that Euro-American women who married Indigenous men had the most trouble, especially with their families. After all, many of these wives were the descendants of migrating New Englanders who disliked the idea of miscegenation between races and probably originally arrived with at least a suspicion or even hatred of Indians. However, no records exist about these early marriages that suggest they invited public rebuke or discrimination. So long as the women were from a poor class of rural White families, there did not seem to be a major issue with Native and newcomer unions. It is difficult to know for certain until more in-depth study of this group has been done. As the next chapter illustrates, later in the century and once these unions involved at least one spouse from the middle class, there was more evidence of tensions around their interethnic marriages to both Indigenous men and women.

Shared values of kin networks probably helped cement these early marriages. Osterud's study of a nineteenth-century agrarian community argues that kinship was the main form of social organization in rural communities at this time. Work united the men; women were more engaged in family decisions and social activity than their urban sisters. These bonds of kinship and labor helped to create an alternate model to the Western patriarchal, middle-class separate sphere—one "of human relations based on mutual aid" and founded on kinship. This would have been a very familiar model to Indigenous societies in the Northeast. In the Adirondacks, both Aboriginal and Euro-American men and women created work and social networks that included each other. With regard to the Sabattis family, Mitchel's guiding business included several of his sons, grandsons, and Euro-American sons-in-law, as well as Euro-American neighbors. His Euro-American wife, Betsy, ran the boardinghouse. At least two of their daughters helped their mother while the men were away, as did Isaac's Euro-American wife, Arline.[55] We see here in this rural community the same kinship arrangement that Osterud describes, one that is very similar to strategies employed by Haudenosaunee and Algonquian peoples for social, political, and economic purposes.

Unlike the Benedict and other Indigenous Adirondack families, the records do not indicate that the Sabattis family maintained contact with a reservation community such as Akwesasne or Odanak. While the Benedict family traveled back and forth to Odanak (and at least once to Akwesasne) for baptisms, spouses, marriages, and even burials, the Sabattis family experienced these milestones locally. This change from depending on a reserve community to a local one occurred for many of the Abenaki (and other Indigenous) families who remained in the region, although as chapters 5 and 6 describe, this change was not always the case, nor was it final as descendants reconnected with Odanak, especially. One could probably argue that, for Mitchel Sabattis and his family, their spiritual and perhaps sociopolitical communities of Newcomb and Long Lake along with family, coworkers, and friends replaced a reservation community. It is unknown why this was so. It may have been that there was no family left at Odanak or

Akwesasne to provide a tie to those communities for Mitchel Sabattis. After all, he was born off the reservation and lived all of his life in the region. Small Adirondack towns during the nineteenth century were often isolated. Inhabitants searched for ways to be self-sufficient, including forging networks of people that helped each other survive. As a boy, Mitchel made friends with local Euro-American boys such as John Plumley and Caleb Chase of Newcomb (the latter credits Mitchel with teaching him his woodcraft). Mitchel later worked with these men, other local Euro-American guides, his sons, and his sons-in-law in guiding and other pursuits. These small-town kinship ties were public: everyone knew who you were related to and they also reflected an individual's obligations and mutual expectations between kin. The degree of flexibility or rigidity was based on particular family relationships.[56]

This does not mean Mitchel did not experience prejudice based on his being Abenaki. The records reflect he encountered at least one incident of bias when a townsperson named Isaac B. C. Robinson challenged his ability to vote in 1862. Robinson claimed the community did not have the power to allow him to vote because he was an Indian. It may be that Robinson was just following the letter of the law, or perhaps he was concerned about the way Sabattis would vote and found his ethnicity convenient. However, we cannot discount the possibility of personal prejudice. Native Americans did not get the right to vote in the United States until 1870 with the passage of the Fifteenth Amendment. Under this legislation, though, Indigenous Americans were only enfranchised if they were citizens. If they still belonged to a tribe, as many did, they could not become citizens until 1924, when the Indian Citizenship Act was passed.[57]

Moreover, occasionally sports wrote about Mitchel in stereotypical terms. An article relating an 1843 trip down the Raquette River from Long Lake refers to a teacher, probably John MacMullen, and one of his students being "guided by a passing party of 'half-breeds,' one of them believed to have been Mitchell [sic] Sabattis, famed Indian guide." The pair had to be rescued after capsizing their own craft.

This was probably Mitchel's first guiding experience, albeit an inadvertent one. Joel T. Headley described being happy to see "the swarthy and benevolent face of Mitchell [sic]." Chittenden occasionally slipped into "Indian-speak" when quoting Sabattis. He claimed Mitchel once stated "We go home—no use for waste time tonight." Yet just before that statement, Chittenden quoted him as saying, "There is no deer within two miles of Long Lake now . . . That sound would scare the devil." It is possible that Sabattis actually said the former sentence and he was "playing Indian" for the party; we do not know. Indigenous peoples often took on the persona of the trickster as a way to deal with overbearing sportsmen who had hired them as guides. Chittenden also used Indian stereotypes as a ploy to get rid of bothersome fellow travelers. At least once he threatened a fellow traveling minister with possible danger because he had angered Sabattis by failing to keep quiet as instructed. Chittenden told him that Mitchel "like all his race, was of an unforgiving nature," which contradicts all other writings about him. Chittenden also used romantic stereotypes when he described one of Mitchel's sons as having grown "up with the figure of Apollo, and when I last saw him I thought that physically he was the most perfect man I had ever seen."[58]

Mitchel Sabattis is by far the best-known Indigenous guide who worked in the Adirondacks during this period. He was born in the northern part of the region and grew up in the central Adirondacks, where he lived all of his life. His reputation as a hunter, family man, Methodist, and guide were exemplary to the point that his many other skills were overshadowed by them. His family and social ties were attached to the people and communities in the Adirondacks instead of a reserve community. Yet, for all of this, he was always known to be a "St. Francis" Indian, as were his children.

Other Indigenous Guides in the Adirondacks

Sabattis was not the only Aboriginal guide who was scrutinized by sports. George Washington Sears, also known as "Nessmuk," described an Akwesasne Mohawk guide named William Bero, who was also the foreman of a Mohawk crew peeling hemlock bark, probably for tanning. Sears complimented Bero's woodsman ability and described his fishing prowess for trout with a simple pole made of tamarack. He lauded the hard workers in Bero's camp and opined that other Indians might be lazy, "but not . . . the St. Regis or Mohawk and only in part of the Senecas and Oneidas." Hoffman characterized Mohawk guide Captain Gill as "a capital guide" when not drinking. Hoffman and a law student companion hired Gill in the late 1830s and described him as "old" and living year round in a wigwam located on the outlet of Lake Pleasant along with his daughter, Molly.

Chance meetings with Aboriginal peoples in the Adirondacks stood out for sports. While camping on Blue Mountain Lake in 1843, John Todd documented an encounter with "a young Indian and his squaw, of the St. Regis tribe" who had come from Canada to find his younger brother. Around 1850, Todd also met Sabael Benedict and described the visit at his wigwam. And, as previously mentioned, Joel Headley made a point of recording his contact with Peter and Hannah Sabattis. Not all sports limited their writing to mere observation. John Mac-Mullen's writings admired the woodcraft of his St. Regis rescuers as they made a canoe of spruce bark to replace the craft he and his student had capsized. However, MacMullen also included a description of the difference between the skin color of the full-blooded Mohawk woman ("clear, translucent, light copper-colored skin, that told at once her high health and her race") and those he considered to be half-breeds ("dull, white cheese"). A particularly harsh description of an Aboriginal family was recorded by Samuel Hammond in his *Hills, Lakes and Forest Streams*. Hammond described them as "half-breeds" and "a deterioration of both branches of the ancestral tree" who made a living by trapping, hunting, and basketmaking. He described the family as dirty, ugly, and unkempt after he and his guide, Tucker, showed up on the family's doorstep uninvited and arranged to stay overnight. Hammond chose to sleep in a bed that he described as comfortable, made of feathers and sheets "not positively dirty." In the morning, he awoke, though, complaining of being bitten by fleas and bedbugs. Despite all of this, Hammond and Tucker accepted some baked biscuits from the wife and purchased the husband's canoe for a five-dollar gold piece the next morning. Hammond opined later that Indians were similar to the wild animals of the forest: they were both destined to disappear.[59]

Such attitudes were not confined to individual sports. Early on, people of mixed ethnicity were regarded with suspicion due to their ambiguous identity, which created a threat to Euro-American acculturation. Furthermore, ethnically mixed peoples exposed the fallacy of racial assumptions and categories that nineteenth-century society and policymakers presented as normal in scientific, social, and political arenas. People of mixed Indigenous and European heritage in the United States often selectively adopted Euro-American socioeconomic practices while simultaneously maintaining some of their Indigenous way of life; still others chose between the two cultures. As well, they had a tendency to marry each other or within their Indigenous parent's nation, thereby thwarting the policy to make them Anglo-American. American policy wanted them to choose Euro-American culture and disappear as a group. Because they consciously refused to do so, ethnically mixed Indigenous peoples were condemned for not civilizing and fitting into Euro-American society and, as a result, they were especially singled out for criticism and scrutiny. Later in the century, when Euro-Americans saw Native Americans through the lens of the vanishing Indian, their multiethnic relatives were classified as inauthentic.[60] Sports writing about Indigenous peoples of mixed heritage in the Adirondacks, whether as their guides, as craftmakers, or in general, reflected this prejudice. In the Adirondacks when Abenaki and a handful of Mohawk intermarried with Euro-American Adirondackers, these unions caused the identity of Indigenous Adirondackers to vanish from the area's history. However, socially, and very locally, these individuals maintained their Indigenous identity within their community, some for a short time, while others continue to do so to this day. Chapter 6 discusses in detail the notion of rural indigenousness in the present, but as this chapter describes, this phenomenon has been going on in this place since the nineteenth century.

"Native" Guides and Sports in the Adirondacks

The work experience of both Indigenous and non-Indigenous guides in the Adirondacks was very similar in terms of their treatment by the sports. While not as callous as the Hammond example above, Euro-American Adirondack families did not escape the condescending writing of sports demonstrating that urban sportsmen focused their gaze on the difference between class and rural versus urban, too. Writings about non-Aboriginal guides were both complimentary and disparaging, the main difference being the lack of comments about their ethnicity. One exception may have been French Canadian guides; however, they are beyond the scope of this project and need a specific study of their own.[61] Richard Patrick Roth's "The Adirondack Guide" suggests these writings reflect the hunter as someone who "examines and explains." I argue these writings more clearly reflect Pratt's arguments about colonial expansion and the anti-conquest, as upper-class hunters trained their gaze on the local landscape and people and wrote about them. In the process, they reinvented a colonial space for themselves as the expert and boss. In addition, they used the experience to assert their upper-class, masculine identity. Sportsmen expressed their masculinity with guides by using work-related management techniques and treating guides as their employees. Some Adirondack travel records reflect this argument for both Aboriginal and Euro-American guides, but not always. In addition, some sports competed with their guides as another exertion of their masculinity. Canadian scholar Tina Loo reminds us that masculinity is class-based and "often defined against other men, at play as well as at work."[62] I would also add that masculinity is geographically based, as urban sports competed with their rural guides. While ethnicity and gender were (and still are) certainly factors, it is just as important for historians to consider class and the rural context when they examine contact history in the nineteenth century and later, especially when studying the occupations of both Aboriginal and non-Aboriginal peoples in regions that had become dominated by Euro-American society. Recognizing and considering these two forms of analysis alongside ethnicity and gender adds other layers of complexity and depth that are often missing from contact history.

Becoming "Native"

"Native" Adirondack guides did the same work, whether they were Abenaki, Mohawk, or Euro-American, and each was written about by their sports, sometimes glowingly and at other times disparagingly. Despite the intolerance shown toward mixed-race peoples, though, overt bigotry is not often seen in the records; stereotyping was more the norm. Adirondack typecasting of Indian peoples during this era focused on language and demeanor. For example, Sabattis was described as taciturn, and Sabael Benedict as speaking broken English. Plains Indian–style stereotyping eventually appeared in the region and, as the next two chapters demonstrate, Abenaki and Iroquoian peoples used it for marketing purposes to sell their wares. Even then, it was the generation trying to make a living in the early twentieth century that had to don headdresses. The image of Indian masculinity in North American imagination changed over time from eastern Woodland to the plains hunter at the end of the nineteenth century.[63] It was as though as each Indigenous nation was invaded by the Americans, their image was replaced with the next group to be divested of their homeland.

This early stereotyping of Indigenous peoples was little different from that used by sports, who saw their local Euro-American guides as rubes and sometimes even incompetent. Both groups of guides were accused of drinking too much. And both types of guides found ways to resist their sports if their urban employer took on too strong an air of superiority. While absolute arguments are difficult to make, it does appear that the sports' assumption of their own urban and class-based superiority marked their perceptions, as did ethnicity, when they wrote about their wilderness experience in the Adirondacks. The concept of rural was, and still is, neither settled nor consistent. Rural was defined in the nineteenth century (and often still is) by outsiders with a romanticized notion of rustic harmony, and internally defined by the behaviors and ideals of the peoples living in a specific rural region.[64]

There was not a large population of any one peoples living permanently in the Adirondacks during this period (or even now). Some of the Aboriginal families and individuals who still used the area to hunt, trap, and earn wages by working in tourism and resource-type industries often returned to their home reservation communities; such was the case, in particular, for the Mohawk from Akwesasne. As a result, for sports to report they'd had an authentic wilderness experience in the region they had to code all guides as "Native." Depictions of Adirondack guides in the travel literature were ambiguous—admired yet seen as beneath their sport. They were a romanticized holdover from a bygone era and, like the Indian, a manifestation of antimodernism's sense of loss and enthusiasm for modernity's progress. This sentiment and underlying need included contact with and references to the "folk" as well as to Indian peoples in North America. Louis Warren suggests that the non-urban American landscape was a tangible artifact of contact, including the legacy of conquest.[65] Could another of those legacies be the entanglement of identities between Indian peoples and rural Euro-Americans who lived in the same landscape and survived by practicing the same pluralistic occupations? As outlined previously, early non-Indigenous Adirondackers had to quickly learn how to survive in a nonagricultural landscape. Some brought their woodcraft skills with them from places like Northern New England and Canada, probably originally learned from Indian peoples many generations ago. Others learned such skills directly from local Abenaki and Mohawk individuals and families or each other. By this time, rural Euro-Americans living in landscapes such as the Adirondacks also knew the land intimately. As a result, it appears that the term "Native" became equal to knowledge of the Adirondack wildlands that were thought to be disappearing as quickly as Indians were believed to be by a growing nineteenth-century urban upper and middle class. Rural Whites were replacing, or at least augmenting, Indigenous peoples as part of an imagined utopian "native" American history, especially in the minds of these eastern urbanites.

Location of Exchange

During this era, upper-class tourists viewed many of the Euro-Americans living in the Adirondacks as similar to Indians. They saw them as antiquated, primitive, and living off the land to the point that these visitors referred to the local peoples as "Natives"—they differentiated those who really were Native by calling them "St. Francis" or "St. Regis" Indians, thus removing them as original inhabitants of the Adirondacks. Yet the influence of the peoples from Akwesasne and Odanak was very present in the lifeways of many local Adirondackers of European ancestry during this period. Their practices and customs were more similar to their Indigenous neighbors than to White rural commercial farmers or urbanites. This sharing of a "Native" identity became yet another example of the Adirondacks as a location of exchange, as sports affiliated these rural Euro-Americans with their Mohawk and Abenaki neighbors and connected both to the land.

The relationships between Adirondack Aboriginal guides and their Euro-American counterparts go mostly unrecorded other than the fact that they often worked together and eventually became connected through kin. As noted earlier, Mitchel Sabattis labored with his sons and sons-in-law on many occasions, and his sons and grandsons also worked with other Euro-American guides. The Raquette Lake House Register provides several examples of this collaboration as wilderness tourists checked into hotels with their guides. The register notes Isaac Sabattis (1851–1912) checking in with local Euro-American "Native" guide David Keller, also from Long Lake, on August 5, 1879. A party of eleven sports checked in on October 9, 1880, along with five guides, including Ike Sabattis. An 1881 entry includes M. Sabattis along with several other local guides working for as many sports. It appears that two of the sports, George and Henry Dale, were referred to the hotel by Abenaki guide and Indian Lake camp owner Elijah Camp.[66]

Both Aboriginal and non-Aboriginal guides had to work in other occupations during the off-season. Boatbuilding became an offshoot from guiding. Original Adirondack historian Alfred L. Donaldson recorded that Mitchel Sabattis and one of the Palmers of Long Lake designed the first Adirondack guideboat with its original square stern. In an interview, Harry Sabattis confirmed that his father Mitchel worked with Reuben Cary and Caleb Chase to design the first Adirondack guideboat. Caleb Chase of Newcomb began to manufacture the guideboat in the 1850s, and others soon followed. Isaac Sabattis worked in boatbuilding during the off-season until at least 1900, as did other local men.

Roland B. Miller's state-sponsored pamphlet "The Adirondack Pack-basket" claims Abenaki Julius Paul Denis of Old Forge told him the pack-basket was an Abenaki design. We must keep in mind that Odanak, similar to Akwesasne, was a cosmopolitan community that while linguistically and culturally made up of bands considered to be "western" Abenaki also contained other Abenaki and Algonquian peoples. The origins of the pack-basket design could easily be claimed by other Algonquian peoples or even the Haudenosaunee. Given the history of the Abenaki in the Adirondacks, however, it is certainly plausible they introduced the design to the region. During this period, the records reveal a complex interrelationship between "Native" Adirondackers of both Indigenous and Euro-American backgrounds as they navigated differences and similarities. Together, these Adirondackers probably created a new boat design, and Euro-American guides adopted the use and making of the pack-basket thought to be introduced to the area by the Abenaki.[67]

Conclusion

Sabael Benedict arrived in the Adirondacks in the late eighteenth century before Euro-American settlement into the interior, as discussed in chapter 2. He brought his family—both nuclear and extended—to stay, probably because of the familiar landscape and their ability to continue customary practices as they acclimated to the imperial changes on the continent. I believe this next generation used the region's environment with its low levels of Anglo-American population to give themselves the time they needed to adapt to the modernization changes occurring during the long nineteenth century. Native peoples chose work in rural areas because it gave them some control. The work was seasonal and allowed them to continue in customary activities. Guiding served a similar purpose. It was a form of transition employment from independent subsistence to wage work for Indigenous peoples. Guiding provided them a means to earn a good income in return for work that was familiar and used their highly developed traditional skills. Euro-American Adirondackers made similar decisions when they moved into the region. Historian Karl Jacoby describes these settlers as having a "homestead ethic," one where individuals and families valued their freedom and control over their own lives at least until 1885, when legislation promoted by the conservation movement began to curtail their practices.[68] These were very similar reasons for both peoples to be in this area during this period. The Adirondacks, as a location of exchange, provided a purposeful space where both peoples could live their lives according to their own needs and desires. Reciprocal acts occurred here to the point where it is difficult to tell which ethnic group was borrowing the most from the other. What was occurring were occasions for entangled exchanges between peoples and the land.

The history of Aboriginal guides in the Adirondacks thus may be more complex than that of other places because of the mixture of Aboriginal and Euro-American "Native" guides who competed and worked together. A great deal of suspicion and animosity had been created by the Seven Years War, the American Revolution, and the War of 1812 between Algonquian and Iroquoian hunters and trappers and the Euro-American veterans who moved to the region. Within a generation or two, these same peoples were sharing their lives in the most intimate ways by creating families together. Adirondack families of Abenaki, Oneida, Mohawk, and other Indigenous peoples have been a part of the history of many Adirondack towns since their beginnings. Despite the assumption that the Indian peoples who remained assimilated into Euro-American Adirondack communities, this was not always the case. Many families kept dual identities and histories alive as both Indigenous peoples and Adirondackers. For example, a recently deceased great-grandson of Mitchel Sabattis named Hal

Cranson (1923–2003) was interviewed in 1999 at the age of seventy-six by a reporter from the *Tupper Lake Free Press*. Mr. Cranson was very aware of the role his Abenaki family played in the development of Long Lake. A direct descendant of Isaac Sabattis, Hal heard stories about the family, learned to hunt and fish from his uncle Norman Sabattis, and continued in the family business by teaching wealthy and famous tourists to square dance.[69]

The examples in this chapter demonstrate that the Adirondacks continued to be an Indigenous homeland and a location of exchange for Algonquian and Iroquoian peoples during the long nineteenth century and now it included exchanges with rural Euro-Americans. After all, the Mohawk and in particular the Abenaki who remained there negotiated complex relationships with colleagues, neighbors, and families to create a future that made sense to them. The question then occurs: were Adirondack communities culturally more Euro-American or more Aboriginal, especially during the long nineteenth century? The two peoples experienced similar lifestyles that reflected Native social and economic traditions as much as if not more than European ones. In addition, some Indigenous peoples shared their woodcraft and technology with Euro-American neighbors and vice versa. While contacts in frontier settings were usually considered battlegrounds, they were also culturally merging and marrying grounds that affected everyone.[70] Adirondack records reveal that Native peoples who lived and worked there had a strong sense of continuity of identity, while also experiencing nineteenth-century changes that had been muted in a rural space. Together, Natives and newcomers created distinctly "Adirondack" products such as the guideboat and pack-basket, demonstrating the continuing capacity of the Indigenous peoples there to share from the bowl with one spoon. As the next chapter illustrates, this region also allowed Iroquoian and Algonquian peoples the time and space to experiment and adapt age-old entrepreneurial traditions to nineteenth- and early twentieth-century modernity.

4

"Pete Francis' Place"

Native American Entrepreneurship in the Adirondacks

MOHAWK, Peter "Pete" Francis (1810–74) opened his own restaurant in the summer of 1845. His restaurant was referred to as "Pete Francis' place" or cottage and was located on the southern shore of Saratoga Lake. It is believed that Pete was born in Schenectady. In 1828 he married Mary Speck, and the pair had a large family. Some stories claim that Pete spent his youth as an Adirondack guide and was taught to cook by a French client. Other versions indicate that Pete learned to cook from the French loyalist Andrew Berger, a chef at the posh Sans Souci Health Resort Restaurant in Ballston Spa built in 1803, one of the first luxury hotels in the region. Pete cooked there for a number of years prior to 1845, as did his sister-in-law Kate Speck.[1]

Regardless of where Pete learned to cook, he was apparently a superb and successful chef. Ballston Spa State Senator James M. Cook, a Sans Souci customer, was so impressed with Pete's abilities that he helped finance his restaurant, and many of San Souci's patrons frequented his place. "Governors, judges, members of Congress enjoyed his fish dinners and likewise enjoyed his equally famous tales of adventure." Pete was especially renowned for his Saratoga Lake bass dinners. In addition to his cooking abilities, Pete played the violin. A 1912 letter to the editor in *The Saratogian* indicates Pete was also "an Indian scout and fisherman" and had traveled widely in North and South America as well as Europe. He was described as having a kind heart and generous nature, and it was noted that he was a great swimmer and diver. He ran his business until he died in 1874. Pete's wife,

Mary, tried to keep the restaurant going but she was unsuccessful and it closed within a few years. It is unknown what happened to her; seven of their nine children grew to adulthood and some remained in the area.²

What was the likelihood that this Mohawk man could parlay his talent into running a successful restaurant? Philip J. Deloria might consider this Mohawk restaurateur an example of *Indians in Unexpected Places.* In his study, Deloria examines the expectations of American Indians in a variety of areas during the late nineteenth and early twentieth centuries. Deloria argues that Native Americans—in his case, northern plains peoples—did not miss out on turn-of-the-twentieth-century modernity, and many engaged directly with it, struggling with the same forces with which Euro-Americans grappled. Deloria argues that these seeming anomalies of the nineteenth century were not as unusual as one would think. These supposed exceptions demonstrate a new way of looking at this period. He goes on to explain that American Indians were seen in terms of assimilation and antimodern primitivism that allowed them the opportunity to shapeshift between both worlds and take advantage of "windows of possibilities" to make a living, thereby creating "secret histories of unexpectedness." This shapeshifting allowed Indian peoples the space and time to maneuver in a world that was changing not only for them but for everyone.³

However, as Native peoples became adept at being modern, that too created problems. Settler society employed a binary notion of authenticity that pitted late nineteenth-century progress and antimodernism against each other, resulting in the belief that once Indian peoples started to be modern, they stopped being authentic in the eyes of the dominant culture. Focusing on the Pacific Northwest, Canadian historian Paige Raibmon argues that "notions of authenticity that were closely related to the myth of vanishing Indian simultaneously generated and delimited opportunities for Aboriginal peoples. Indigenous peoples did not exercise much control over the terms of this discourse, but they often manipulated it to their benefit. The growth of both anthropology and tourism provided opportunities that helped Aboriginal peoples make a living under the difficult economic and political conditions created by late nineteenth century colonialism."[4]

The Adirondack region of northern New York State demonstrates that Raibmon and Deloria's arguments also apply to the northeastern part of North America, and even earlier in the nineteenth century. The Adirondacks were a place where Algonquian and Iroquoian, and, eventually, other Indigenous peoples from both Canada and the United States were able to take advantage of that "window of possibility" offered by the wilderness tourism era of the Adirondacks. Yet these possibilities may have cost them their place in the area's historical narrative over time and space, a theme that is explored here and in the next chapter. What follows are the narratives of several families who left records, and those whose efforts at entrepreneurship were a mere mention in someone else's chronicle. While labor such as basketmaking and other craftmaking skills and guiding are also entrepreneurial, this chapter focuses on those ventures that stress a commercial acumen versus, or in addition to, relying on a specific skill to sell. These families and individuals are distinguished as businessmen and women who invested in and ran a small business or perhaps a group of them. Large entrepreneurial activities such as lumbering are considered large-scale capitalist enterprises and not addressed here.

Complexity of Native Entrepreneurship in the Tourism Industry

Brief History of Native Entrepreneurship in the Northeast

Iroquoian and Algonquian peoples have been entrepreneurs for a long time, and the concept of enterprise was nothing new to them. Anthropologist Marshall Sahlins argues that Indigenous peoples' trade efforts were reciprocal gift exchanges that were social as much as they were economic. Reciprocity was considered to be a back and forth exchange of material goods that established relationships. However, the farther away the parties moved from close kin relationships vis-à-vis the household, band, nation, and inter-nation, the more businesslike the transactions became. These transactions went from being based on concepts of mutual assistance at the family and band level end of the spectrum to those of self-interest at the opposite end of the spectrum, where haggling and bartering were socially acceptable. Iroquoian and Algonquian peoples living about the Adirondacks had been active traders both before and after European contact, so nineteenth-century entrepreneurship was a matter of adapting their earlier practices of reciprocal gift exchange for unavailable goods to more contemporary market economy circumstances. For example, prior to colonization, Algonquians who lived on the Atlantic coast and around Long Island gathered whelk (white) and quahog (purple or black) shells, manufactured beads from these shells, and traded them for nonlocal goods to other Indigenous peoples without access to the ocean and these much-desired shells.[5] After contact, these coastal Algonquian-speakers diversified by incorporating the Dutch into their enterprise until European glass beads destroyed this economic endeavor. Iroquoian peoples were also well-known entrepreneurs. According to William Fenton, "Chiefs of lineages were the entrepreneurs in the Huron trade . . . which entailed elaborate arrangement of external affairs, which was a function of civil chiefs also in Iroquoia." Even Native peoples associated with the Adirondacks had a reputation as early entrepreneurs. The Abenaki used to obtain French goods and sell them to other Indigenous peoples, which irritated the French. During the colonial period, seventeenth-century Oneida women were observed trading salmon caught in rivers flowing into Lake Ontario to more eastern Mohawk villages.[6]

The Indigenous peoples of North America were well-known to be shrewd and particular traders. Prior to colonization, Native peoples were self-reliant and used the local natural resources for their economic needs, including the trading of meat and fur, mining, collection of shells especially for wampum beads, and the gathering of plants and berries. I add the practice of agriculture to this list, as we know the Huron traded excess "corn, tobacco, fishing nets and other products" for meat, hides, and dried fish from the nearby Algonquin nations. One could even include hospitality, as many North American

Aboriginal nations proffered shelter, food, and even relationships in return for the trade goods that European and later North American traders could provide to a community.[7]

Rolf Knight's seminal *Indians at Work* dedicates several pages to examining entrepreneurship in British Columbia from 1858 to 1930. Despite the different location and peoples, Knight's discussion of Indian entrepreneurs in resource-driven economies sheds light on entrepreneurship in the Adirondacks. He argues that resource extraction areas that include capitalist enterprises such as lumbering historically provided wage labor and opportunities for First Nations, in contrast to non-resource-driven economies, such as the prairies. These latter types of economies employed few people outside of the family. Knight goes on to explain that Indigenous wage laborers, independent producers, and entrepreneurs were dependent on a region and the unique opportunities of an era.[8] Following this line of thinking, the Adirondacks were the region, and wilderness tourism was the era that led to entrepreneurial opportunities for Iroquoian and Algonquian peoples there. In addition, Knight suggests that when one compares the life and labor of Native peoples with their non-Native counterparts in the same jobs within the same area and era, there are more similarities than differences. My research supports Knight's conclusion about these similarities.

When one examines the records of the Adirondacks during the wilderness tourism era, similarities between Aboriginal and local rural peoples of European descent emerge. Many of the jobs and entrepreneurial opportunities here during this era were available to both groups of peoples. A number of these families intermarried and worked together either directly or indirectly, and some became entrepreneurs in a variety of enterprises. As one of the area's earliest Indigenous entrepreneurs, Mohawk restaurateur Pete Francis must have felt he was taking a big risk by taking out a loan and running his own business. He enjoyed telling stories to entertain his customers and was even accused of some bragging during the telling. Pete also employed his kinship network by including his in-laws and wife in the business.[9] The cabins, boardinghouses, and hotels in Hamilton County, which will be described below, seemed to hold their own during the proprietor's lifetime. Thus, it is fair to say that many of these Native individuals and families were successful entrepreneurs living in a dominantly Euro-American economic and political world, albeit a rural one that still harbored some of the landscape and lifestyle with which they or their immediate ancestors were familiar. This does not mean these individuals and families did not travel outside of this protective space: they did. But in the Adirondacks they were able to experiment with entrepreneurship and even change their class status during an age of increasing urbanization and industrialization.

Iroquoian and Algonquian Pre–Wilderness Tourism Entrepreneurship in the Adirondacks

Records of entrepreneurship that include Iroquoian and Algonquian peoples in the Adirondacks date back to at least the eighteenth century. In Washington County, Colonel John Henry Lydius ran a trading post at Fort Edwards called Fort Lydius, or the Lydius House (c. 1731–44). Lydius's father was a minister to the Indians. Colonel Lydius spoke several Indian dialects and was a contemporary and rival to Sir William Johnson. Lydius's wife, Genevieve Masse, was Mohawk, probably from Kahnawake, and they had married in Montreal, where he resided from 1725 to 1730. Lydius House catered to local Mohawk and Mahican traders, but it also did well in its dealings with Huron and Algonquian peoples considered "French Indians" from Canada. One cannot help but speculate that Genevieve Masse might have had a family network that Lydius was taking advantage of, as many fur traders did in those days.[10]

In Warren County, Thomas Hammon (sometimes spelled Hammond) was described by local historian H. P. Smith as "a half-breed Oneida Indian . . . [who] kept a store here prior to and during the last war with Great Britain." Smith was referring to the War of 1812. The building still existed at the time Smith wrote his history in 1885. Hammon and his sister, Dinah, were brought to the area by Captain Green of Whipple City, now known as Greenwich in Washington County. It is unknown what Green's relationship was to the two

Oneida siblings; perhaps they were orphans and bonded to him. The records are quiet about Thomas's upbringing and are nearly nonexistent about Dinah, who is only mentioned because she arrived in the area with him and was perhaps listed in the 1810 Washington County census for Queensbury (not yet a part of Warren County). Thomas married Keziah Reynolds of Caldwell (Lake George) on March 26, 1806, at the home of her father, Solomon Reynolds—a family of European ancestry. Interestingly, Keziah's mother was Elizabeth Maria Green (and Keziah's brother James's middle name was Green), which suggests they were related to Captain Green.

Thomas and Keziah moved to nearby Queensbury, and Thomas opened a general store on a corner there. Based on a family member's communication with me, as well as local and federal records, the couple had six children—three sons and three daughters. Keziah Reynolds Hammon died in 1817, and Thomas remarried to a woman named Rebecca Wheeler. The pair had three children, all born in Warren County: Jane (born 1821), George (c. 1824), and Charles (c. 1825). According to surrogate court records dated December 18, 1831, Thomas was dead by the end of that year, and his and Keziah's youngest son, Walter S. Hammon, was appointed a guardian, which suggests he had inherited some property or assets in and around Queensbury. Walter and his half-siblings all went on to have families, though it is unknown what happened to his five full siblings.[11]

Thomas ran his general store as early as 1808 and maybe earlier. For a time, he also incorporated lumbering into his business. According to Smith, the area where Hammon's store was located became known as "the Oneida" after his Iroquoian heritage. By 1812, the Oneida had grown to be a busy place with two large and bustling inns, three stores, a large lumbering business that served nearby mills, a variety of mechanic shops, and a Baptist church and society. In addition, two local justices of the peace, Dan D. Scott and James Henderson, held their weekly tribunals there. According to Smith, "From the oft repeated expressions, 'Lets go up to the Oneida's,' 'I bought this at the Oneida's,' and 'we must send down to the Oneida's,' was derived the name which through the vicissitudes of half a century has clung like a burr to the settlement."[12] Locals today still know the area by this name.

The documents left behind about Thomas Hammon indicate that he did not always have a smooth go of it in Queensbury. In February 1814 the state filed a criminal indictment alleging Hammon was maintaining a "disorderly house occupied as a store" and that night and day men were drinking. On or about November 1, 1813, these men had apparently created a nuisance resulting in the indictment. During the nineteenth century, the divisions between types of businesses were not always clear-cut. In nearby Albany, the state's capital, a grocery store and a saloon might be part of the same business during this era.[13] Hammon also found himself the defendant in two civil lawsuits, one in 1814, and another in 1815 that stemmed from the 1814 lawsuit. However, Thomas also learned to use the justice system for his own benefit. The court records show at least three judgments in Thomas's favor against others for various amounts of money owed him from January 1817 to September 1818. Another lawsuit appeared to favor his case, but he failed to show for a subsequent hearing, thus the court found for the defendant and charged Thomas court costs. The documents do not mention whether these lawsuits were personal or part of the business, but given the multiple defendants, the lawsuits appear to be business related.[14]

According to the local history, Hammon's downfall was alcohol, and the business eventually failed. He purportedly moved to nearby French Mountain and died there "an inebriate and outcast." With the store's closure, local traffic diminished and so did the influence of the community.

This local history suggests that Hammon fit the stereotype of an Indian who succumbed to alcohol abuse when he tried to work within modern society. However, Thomas Hammon's history is more complex than this narrative admits. Warren County historian H. P. Smith regularly portrayed Native men as dying drunk and alone in the woods, when in reality he did not know the cause of their deaths. For example, in another local Indigenous family history, Smith claimed that the Presbyterian minister Reverend Anthony Paul was a drunkard, and while no one knows what happened to him the general belief was that he built, lived, and died in a hut on Lake George just below the narrows where the cliffs of Tongue Mountain almost shut off the passage. However, a 1963 article in the local *Glens Falls Post-Star* indicates Paul and his wife, Christina Occum Paul, paid a visit to Connecticut, and Reverend Paul became ill on the way home. He succumbed to his illness around Kingston, New York, where he is buried. This article acknowledges that Paul had issues with alcohol. However, Smith's accounts have the two men meeting a similar fate of going off alone and dying in the mountains, which adheres to the romantic notion of the noble savage.[15]

What we do know is that Thomas Hammon was living with his family in the town of Queensbury until at least 1830. He also owned property, although the details of his ownership are missing. While the local history tries to dilute Hammon's ethnicity by describing him as a "half-breed Oneida," his Oneida identity was so strong that, as we have seen, the neighborhood around his store became known as the Oneida. Even today, local norms have refused to change this name despite efforts to do so. It is unknown if Thomas's second wife took the younger children and left the area after his death or if they stayed. She was not listed as a parent when the surrogate court appointed Burden D. Sherman guardian of eighteen-year-old Walter, the youngest son of Thomas and Keziah. At that time, guardians were more concerned about managing property than raising a child, which suggests Walter inherited an estate from his father.[16] If Thomas decided to give up and go live in the woods, he did so within a year before his death, as according to the 1830 census he was living with and appeared to be supporting his family. How he supported them after 1818 though is unknown, as I found no other records pertaining to the store after this date.

Algonquian and Iroquoian Entrepreneurship during Adirondack Wilderness Tourism Era

The majority of the nineteenth-century records illustrate that Native peoples involved in entrepreneurial efforts began by earning an income or obtaining funds in a variety of ways to start their business. Some were guides and artisans who expanded their enterprises, while others were wage earners in some other capacity. Local history indicates that Pete Francis had been an Adirondack guide and cook for someone else before opening his restaurant. Basketmakers set up in their own places of business at the many Indian encampments in the area (see chapter 5) and around tourist destinations. For example, Abenaki Ann Jane Paul Denis Fuller (Annie Fuller) had a seasonal shop at Rainbow Lake in Franklin County to sell to patrons at the nearby Paul Smiths Hotel. By the turn of the twentieth century, Abenaki Sarah Angeline Keziah and her husband Norman Frank Johnson were operating a store in Lake George to sell their baskets. We tend to think of Natives as being victimized by these displays, but as Louis Warren notes, Indian peoples often took the initiative to play on tourists' expectations of the wilderness experience. They cultivated trade in crafts and other souvenirs, including photographs with them.[17]

Some entrepreneurial efforts were small scale, carried out on a seasonal basis, and probably meant to supplement other income. For example, Florence Emma, Emmo, or Emmeau (1848–1927), met and married a local Euro-American named David Edmonds, and they lived and raised their six children in Keene Valley, Essex County. Florence's nationality is still uncertain, but her family knows that she was born in an Indian community on a hill "above Montreal," which suggests the Lake of Two Mountains or perhaps Kanesatake. Her mother, Margaret, died when she was young, and her father sent her to live with a family in Port Henry, New York, and her sister Margaret to a family in Quebec. As an adult, Margaret and her two children joined Florence in Keene Valley to work and escape an abusive husband. Both Margaret and Florence were midwives in the area. Among other jobs, Florence worked as a domestic or in the laundry of the AuSable Club. To make some extra money, Florence grew sweet peas to sell to Interbrook Lodge for their dining room tables. Another example of a small-scale entrepreneur was Joseph D. Sabattis (c. 1878–1951), grandson of Mitchel and Betsy Sabattis, who was a professional guide as well as a taxidermist.[18]

Boardinghouses and camps became important forms of entre-preneurship in the Adirondacks during the wilderness tourism era, and Indigenous Adirondackers were involved. Mitchel and Elizabeth Sabattis owned and operated a boardinghouse first in Newcomb and later in Long Lake to complement his guiding business. Mitchel and his wife had stopped taking in boarders at their Long Lake establishment by 1878. Mitchel sold the Long Lake boardinghouse in 1896, perhaps because of a mortgage foreclosure. Another Abenaki entre-preneur in Hamilton County was John Mitchell Jr. (c. 1891–1945) who had previously been employed in the lumber industry. His fam-ily ran a camp called Cedar River Headquarters at the northern part of the Cedar River Flow west of Indian Lake, and there were several cabins on the property. The property was originally leased by a paper company that used the buildings to house loggers. The Mitchell family refurbished them to house guests. The buildings eventually burned down.[19]

The Family of Emma Camp Mead

Of all these examples, one of the best recorded instances of entre-preneurship in the Adirondacks by Native Americans belongs to the Camp family of Indian Lake. John Camp Sr. (c. 1778–1884) was purported to be an eighteenth-century English sea captain who met and married Abenaki Margaret (also known as Maria) Benedict (c. 1801–?), daughter of Sabael Benedict and his wife, Marie Angelique Ignace (see chapter 2). John and Margaret Camp had three or four children.[20] Their middle son, Elijah, married Elizabeth Kennedy (1846–1936), born on the Oneida reservation in New York to Eliza-beth "Betsy" Cooper (c. 1820–90) and Jackson Kennedy (also known as Canada or Canady).[21] They were married in 1861 at Oneida and settled in Indian Lake that same year. Elijah and Elizabeth had three children who lived to adulthood: Emma, Samuel, and Gabriel (more commonly referred to as Gabe). Elijah Camp ran a site for sportsmen called Hunter's Home (it was also known as Leige Camp, Leige being a nickname for Elijah). The building was located on Little Moose

Lake southwest of the Cedar River Flow, approximately twenty miles from Indian Lake down what is even today a back road, some of it still unpaved. Guests arrived by train at North Creek about eighteen miles southeast of Indian Lake; Elijah and eventually his son Gabe picked up their guests at the train station and transported them to the camp. Later, customers stayed at the small hotel Emma opened in Indian Lake called the Adirondack House. There was a family farm that helped to provide food for the family and guests and some small cabins on site. In addition, Elijah and later his daughter Emma owned and ran retail stores.[22]

Photographs of the Camp family and their enterprises do not resemble the usual photographs of nineteenth-century Indian peoples. Most of the typical photos of Indigenous peoples during this period were taken by anthropologists looking for a vanishing civilization or by missionaries who wished to document their transformation from paganism to Christianity and civilization. In the Camp family photos, there is more agency: they arranged and sat for the photos themselves and took pictures of their property. There is nothing in the photograph that identifies them as being Abenaki or Oneida. They are dressed similar to their customers, and they owned property. It was also apparent by the many documents left that the family was familiar and comfortable with the sports who patronized their services. Yet it was common knowledge in the community that the family was Native, and they were often identified in the census as such. For example, in the 1905 state census for Hamilton County, Elizabeth, Emma, and Gabe's occupations were described as "Indian birth." Elijah's obituary identified him as being "Indian" although the obituaries of his children and wife, who outlived her two oldest children, did not.[23]

According to the family records, sports were well pleased with their experiences at the Camp family enterprises. E. N. Foote of Northampton, Massachusetts, wrote the family in August of 1883 and told them that he had never had such a good time. He made another reservation for four and promised to send "considerable business" their way. Foote might have come through with his promise to send business, as another letter dated December 1883 from Harry Townsend, also from Northampton, acknowledged having had a pleasant time at Little Moose Lake. Another guest in April 1884 went so far as to request Elijah send him some trout and pickerel by express to Sing Sing, now Ossining, New York. A letter to Elijah's daughter Emma in June of that year acknowledged receipt of the fish. They must have had a good reputation locally, as neighboring businesses and community members sent guests to Elijah. For example, Dome Fuller of Blue Mountain Lake sent Elijah a sport along with the request that Camp personally guide the man or furnish a good one. George Harris of Ft. Edwards in Washington County wrote and asked about sending a party of three to five to stay for a week or two and inquired about charges and transportation.[24]

Elijah also ran a small store located near Leige Camp, at least for a time. There are only a couple of references to it in the records. A note dated 1884 from John McGinn of Indian Lake requested the delivery of goods and kerosene. In addition, Elijah was involved in the lumbering business. As early as November of 1884 he agreed to cut and peel logs around Lake Durant for George F. Scarritt and Ed. D. Mott. Elijah was to draw and deliver the logs by road, cut and peeled. He also got involved in mine speculation. Elijah signed a quitclaim deed in July of 1890 for five dollars to quit his half interest in a gold and silver mine at Stanton's Point, about three miles north of Indian Lake.[25] Other records about Elijah Camp indicate he was active in the community. He allowed the board of town assessors to meet at his or more likely Emma's store on March 13, 1888, and along with William Hunt, Elijah Camp was elected as overseer of the poor the following week. Despite the knowledge that he was "Indian," Elijah was allowed to vote at least locally based on a record dated March 19, 1895, in which he swore his eyesight was too poor to prepare a ballot and as a result he was assisted by John Washburn in the election process. He was probably illiterate, as his signatures on legal documents were marked with an "X"; Elizabeth and his children were all literate.[26]

Life was not always easy and profitable for Elijah Camp. In 1891, Dr. J. L. Fuller billed him for seventy-six dollars and thirty dollars for his son Sam, a substantial amount for a medical bill. He also was involved in a lawsuit in Blue Mountain Lake and settled it on May 30, 1893. This lawsuit may have been connected to Elijah and Elizabeth's sale of their property in October that year to their daughter, Emma. The sale included an agreement between Elijah and Emma to provide room and board at her farm for her parents in return for work there, so long as Emma was agreeable to it. There was no other reference for compensation otherwise. Later, Elijah was arrested in February 1899 for first-degree assault on a teamster, Elmer Osgood, who worked for him at a lumber camp. Osgood survived the attack. It was alleged Elijah had hit him in the back of the head with a wooden stick. In 1903, Elijah deeded Camp Island over to James McGinn to pay off debts.[27]

Debt, lawsuits, and poor health eventually took their toll on Elijah Camp. His son Gabe took over the running of Leige Camp and ran the family farm before Elijah died. It is unknown what happened to Elijah's small camp store, but it is likely it quietly closed during his financial hardships. Elijah Camp died in Indian Lake on April 7, 1904, at the age of sixty-eight from apoplexy. In addition to his local immediate family, Elijah Camp's funeral was attended by his older brother John Camp and his eldest son Samuel, who traveled from Pittsburgh to be present. He had been ill since March 1903, which was probably when he had his stroke. He is buried in Indian Lake.[28]

Elijah's wife, Elizabeth, continued her involvement in the family enterprises by cooking and cleaning at the boardinghouse-turned-hotel run by her daughter, Emma. This relationship was not without its conflicts. In October 1916, Sam responded to a letter from his sister, encouraging her not to scold their mother and to be patient with her. By September the following year, Elizabeth went to an attorney's office in Saratoga Springs, which resulted in the attorney writing to Emma on her mother's behalf on September 27, 1917. The letter stated that Elizabeth claimed to have been driven from her home and was looking for compensation for over the past ten years as the cook at the Adirondack House. Elizabeth subsequently traveled to Pittsburgh to stay with her son Sam and his wife Florence. Emma replied through her own attorney in Ballston Spa that her mother had been fully compensated over the years and that she had a home there. Elizabeth stayed with Sam and Florence over that winter and corresponded with her son Gabe and his wife Elsie, but there are no letters to Emma in the records for that year. While in Pittsburgh, Elizabeth worked in a store with Florence earning seven dollars for a five-day workweek before returning to Indian Lake at the end of June 1918. Mother and daughter made up, and future correspondences between Elizabeth, who often wintered in Pittsburgh, and her daughter were cordial.[29]

The Camp family narrative is filled with dramatic episodes, and the life of Emma Camp Mead was packed with complexities. Emma Jane Camp was married to Gabriel Mead of Sing Sing on December 26, 1882, in Indian Lake. She was barely sixteen years old at the time of the marriage, and her husband was six years her senior. The couple probably met when Gabriel Mead boarded with the family during the summer of 1882. They were married by the Reverend G. W. Farrington, pastor of the Methodist Episcopal Church in Indian Lake. Gabriel was the son of Robert G. Mead and part of a prosperous Ossining family who were incensed with the mixed marriage and insisted on an annulment. However, Gabriel stayed with his wife until the following spring. Accounts differ as to what happened next. A *New York Times* newspaper article stated that Gabriel returned home for a visit. Emma wrote that Gabriel's family tricked him into meeting them and spirited him away. Eventually, Emma received notice that he wanted their marriage annulled. The article suggested that the wedding was "performed when Gabriel was not in a condition to know what he was doing, and that his consent was obtained by fraud." Though she did not want the annulment, Emma, advised by General Charles Hughes, eventually gave in. According to the press, in 1883 she was awarded a ten-thousand-dollar settlement not to "fight very hard" to oppose the annulment. The district attorney of Westchester County acted as a referee and annulled the marriage.[30]

But there was more to the situation than the newspapers suggested. In 1885, Mead returned to Indian Lake and the couple remarried on October 2, 1885, again by the Reverend G. W. Farrington. According to Emma, Gabriel's parents had kidnapped him the first time and sent him to the Utica Insane Asylum to "dry out." The couple was reportedly seen in Sandy Hill (now Hudson Falls), New York, in December of that year and had registered at the Coffee House Hotel to visit General Hughes on legal business. The Mead family had supposedly finally accepted their marriage. However, Gabriel Mead only stayed for eight months and then left for good. He eventually married for a third time to a Euro-American woman, probably one from his own class, and they had several children. It was noted Mead was not home when his wife died in the fall of 1920. Although Gabriel obtained a divorce from his second marriage to Emma, she refused to recognize it. Emma did not see Mead again, although she had conceived a child during their second union. Their daughter Bessie tragically died in a fall at Emma's store on February 22, 1890, at age three years and seven months. Gabriel Mead was not present at either their daughter's birth or funeral. For his absence from the latter, Emma unsuccessfully vowed never to forgive or consider him again.[31]

Emma attempted to follow Gabriel Mead's life through the newspapers and occasionally inquired about locating him through her actress cousin Margaret Tahamont and a friend in Brooklyn. She even wrote a letter to her husband after the death of his wife in September 1920, although we do not know if she sent it. In her letter to Gabriel Mead, Emma indicated she had a friend with whom she spent time and planned to spend eternity. This phrase suggests she had at least one other romantic relationship during her lifetime, or maybe it was a spiritual reference, as her Christianity was very important to her. She also referred to two dead little sisters, a dead baby brother, and "my own darling little Bessie." Emma noted in her journal on July 17, 1933, that Gabriel had passed away on that date in Colfax, North Carolina, and was buried in Sleepy Hollow Cemetery in Ossining. Upon learning of Gabriel's death, Emma wrote the attorneys who handled his estate and told them she had never divorced him because she did not want to raise doubts about the legitimacy of their deceased daughter. She also asked if Gabriel had left her a legacy as she was suffering from heart trouble and could use the money: he had not.[32]

In spite of all her personal troubles, Emma was a shrewd businesswoman. She kept in constant communication with guests through letters, which she sometimes used for marketing purposes. In one, she offered to save the recipient their favorite room for the next season. In 1928, she went so far as to write a doctor in Brooklyn to let him know she was willing to house tuberculosis patients in two cabins during the winter. Emma even sent the gift of a basket home to the wife of a sport who had been a guest. She sold and bought land, real property, livestock, and railroad stocks. She bid on a stage coach route in 1901 and held the rights to a bridge on her property. In addition, on March 30, 1926, Emma wrote a letter to the commissioner of Indian Affairs to find out if she, as an Iroquois, was exempt from paying "any and all taxes on real estate."[33] She was not afraid to make clever use of her Indian status, although in this instance she was unsuccessful.

Emma started and managed a number of enterprises even before establishing the Adirondack House. She owned and operated Mead's Store from at least 1883 until it and other Indian Lake businesses burned in April 1891. A two-story building, the store was insured for four thousand dollars. Like many entrepreneurially minded women in the nineteenth century, Emma tried her hand at running a millinery business for a short period of time in 1885. Another enterprise included a lunchroom and basket-selling business. In the 1925 *Syracuse Post-Standard*, Emma advertised the lunchroom to let for the season along with some camps. Interested parties were to inquire of her in Nedrow "at the first house on point of reservation from Feb. 28–March 5, 1925," which indicates she was on the Onondaga reservation, at that time shared with some Oneida who remained in New York State.[34]

In addition, Emma boxed and sold herbal remedies for livestock, one called "Superior Conditioning Powders" and the other a heave powder. The front of the packages used a picture of an Indian male on horseback, and the back of the packaging described it as "a purely Indian preparation composed of roots and herbs." The label indicated the product was packaged by Camp & Co. Promotional testimonials included one from Emma under her married name as Mrs. E. Mead. A list of customers dated May 1930 indicate Emma sold at least thirty-four jars of salves. One of those customers was fellow Abenaki and relative Ed Mitchell, and another was Mrs. Johnson, who may have been her relative. Emma, her brothers, and their cousin Margaret had some knowledge of herbal medicines. Camp family records contain a recipe for rheumatism medicine. There are also a number of letters between Emma and her brother Sam in Pittsburgh and their cousin Margaret Tahamont in Hollywood asking Emma and Gabe to send various roots and plants to try and help with their ailments. In one letter, Margaret had been ill and she asked Emma to send her "some consumption weed and some lobely."[35]

As we know, Emma was a savvy businesswoman. She used media to advertise her hotel business, and she probably saw popular advertisements for Dr. Morse's Indian Root Pills manufactured by the W. H. Comstock Company located on the St. Lawrence River in Morristown, New York. She could have used the image of an Oneida woman, but instead she chose the by-then stereotyped image of a Lakota warrior on horseback, one which she knew Euro-Americans understood as "Indian." She took advantage of White culture's need to see these warriors, emblems of the past, as a cure for modernity to market her cure for livestock health needs. Interestingly, as letters reveal, she saved the medicine to heal humans for herself and her family.[36] Nor were the Camp family members the only Indigenous Adirondackers to continue to use traditional herbal cures. Annie Fuller was known to believe in witches' spells and knew of and used herbal remedies. Florence Edmonds used a poultice she got from Indians camping across from her property in Keene Valley to help heal a sore on her husband.[37]

Emma's most significant undertaking was the running of the Adirondack House. In 1898, she began by building an addition onto the family home located on Christian Hill to create a boardinghouse for workmen rebuilding the Indian Lake dam that year. Later, she opened the extra rooms for summer vacation lodging and named it the "Adirondack House," which she ran off and on until her death in 1934. A surviving hotel registry dated 1904 indicated the hotel was run seasonally; it was open from May 1 to October 30. One of the guests who signed the register in 1904 was Florence Atkinson of Pittsburgh, Pennsylvania, who married Emma's brother, Samuel Camp. The couple moved to Pittsburgh, and Emma, Gabe, and especially their mother Elizabeth visited and even wintered there with Sam and Florence over the years.

As with any enterprise, good help was difficult to find and keep. In 1916, Emma's mother, Elizabeth, who did much of the cooking, suffered from a debilitating illness. Emma described her as "being in bed so long and in such pain." For employees who were not family members, Emma went to Warrensburg to "bring home another cracked and lost one" as labor for the farm. They did not stay, however, and she claimed they wasted her time and money. Perhaps these "cracked and lost ones" did not appreciate the moralizing they might have received from Emma and her mother. Originally a Methodist, Emma became involved with the Baptist Church at the end of her life, complaining the Methodists had become too liberal. An unsigned letter dated September 26, 1916, described Emma and her mother as being devout Christians. However, the writer also constructed at least one of Emma's tendencies as unrespectable, as the writer wondered how Emma, who drove her team of horses fast, could be on the road to salvation with such an unwomanly inclination. Brother Gabe did not share his mother and sister's ardor, as the letter writer claimed, "for he is no Christian and merely stands outside the gates and scoffs." Perhaps concerned about its moral tone, the letter writer went on to ask if Gabe was running the boardinghouse yet.[38]

Gabe sometimes operated the hotel, and he also worked the 125-acre farm, plus hunting and fishing camps "along the Indian River below the lake dam." In the spring of 1918, Emma and Gabe arranged for him to lease the Adirondack House and Mead farm; he was to pay three hundred dollars rent in various installments. Emma was to keep a cottage on the premises and was to have use of the parlor and the parlor bedroom in the main farmhouse from October 1, 1918, to the end of the lease. She also had personal use of the cellar, ice house, and barn. Gabe was still running the Adirondack House in 1921 when W. R. Waddell wrote to G. E. Camp, "successor to Mrs. E. Mead."[39]

Like her father before her, Emma became involved in the community. She was appointed the secretary for local School District 3 on August 29, 1891, and was later appointed clerk (1893–94) and trustee (1895–97). She was also elected district clerk in 1899 and clerk and collector in 1901. She remained active in the school district until 1930 when the community voted to consolidate with District 1 and sell the school house.[40]

In addition to her Adirondack municipality, Emma was also involved in her Iroquoian community. She became interested in Indian affairs, especially around Oneida land claims that were made in the 1920s. She wrote letters to federal and state Indian Affairs officials chastising the government for their treatment of Indian peoples and questioning the validity of land sales. The family file contains the applications of Elizabeth Kennedy Camp, Emma Camp Mead, and Samuel and Gabriel Camp for land claims based on their being Oneida. Emma worked with William Hanyoust, who was an Oneida relative (probably her cousin), on these claims and visited him on the Onondaga Reservation in Nedrow for these purposes. Additionally, there are letters between Emma and her Oneida cousin Albert and Minnie Schanandoah pertaining to Oneida land issues and other themes including temperance. She also corresponded with Seneca archaeologist and anthropologist Arthur C. Parker when he worked for the New York State Museum.[41] Thus, despite her outward appearance of being acculturated into a rural Adirondack community, Emma clearly saw herself and her family as also being Oneida. She and other Indigenous Adirondackers often experienced these dual roles.

While Emma may have left the most records, her brother Gabriel also was active in the running of the family enterprises. He was married to Elsie Corscadden on December 14, 1916, by A. M. Woodruff, the pastor of the Methodist Church in Indian Lake. Gabe and his wife traveled to Pittsburgh shortly after their wedding. It is not clear if they went there for a honeymoon, were looking for work, or went to spend the winter with his brother, Sam. Based on a September 1917 letter from W. Hagadorn, which asked Gabe what kind of motorboat he had purchased, we know the couple had returned to Indian Lake sometime between April and September 1917. If Gabe ran the cottages or the hotel at this time, it is likely he returned in the spring. A letter from Richard C. Frandsen of New York City to "Mr. Camp" in September 1919 refers to the Camps having had a good summer with many boarders.[42] In addition to running the camps, the family farm, and occasionally the hotel, Gabe and his brother Sam also speculated in mining; they may have been following their father in that area. In August 1920, Sam wrote to his brother regarding an assay report and asking Gabe to blast down three feet deeper and to send him and the Pittsburgh Transformer Company twenty-five to thirty pounds of rock. Sam went on to state that he also was going to write to their cousin Ed Mitchell. Sam indicated that Ed's claim was "stronger than ours in gold but it has none of the other stuff, but richer." Sam concluded by asking Gabe to ask Ed to "send some of that green stone from the 3 Island mine if it is any good." In addition to mining, the brothers looked into forming a partnership in a fur business. In a letter dated December 18, 1926, Sam instructed Gabe not to buy the hides until Sam knew the cost. Sam wanted to check with the people he was working with to be sure they wanted them at that price.[43] There is no other correspondence about these enterprises, which suggests they were not profitable inquiries.

It appears also that Emma came close to selling the Adirondack House on at least two occasions. She first put it up for sale in October 1924, but by 1925 she was writing letters telling customers how to get to the Adirondack House. She also advertised to hunters in the October 1925 *Field and Stream*, noting the cost for a stay at the Adirondack House was $18–$20 per week for adults and $3.50 per day; potential customers were directed to contact Mrs. E. Mead. She continued to correspond with prospective customers into the next year as she described the particulars of the camps to lease. When the D&H Railroad applied in 1926 to stop providing service into the area except during the summer months, Emma wrote to the public service commission to complain. By 1929, Emma wanted to sell the Adirondack House for fifteen thousand dollars.[44]

Samuel J. Camp died at the age of sixty-four on July 28, 1934, in Pittsburgh, and was buried in Indian Lake. Emma soon followed him, dying on December 4 of that same year at the age of sixty-eight. The letter she wrote to her attorney shortly after Gabriel Mead's death in 1933 indicated she had heart trouble. According to her obituary, her brother Gabe was running the Adirondack House at the time of her death. Both the Methodist and Baptist ministers officiated at her funeral. In 1936, Elizabeth Kennedy Camp died from a cerebral hemorrhage at the age of ninety. The Methodist minister officiated at Elizabeth's funeral. Her obituary stated, "she was spoken of as the saint of the community." Elizabeth had been living with Gabriel and his wife, who had been taking care of her during a long illness. Gabriel Camp died ten years later on September 28, 1946, at the age of sixty-two or sixty-three. Like his mother, Gabe also died of a cerebral hemorrhage. His obituary listed him as a farmer. The entire family is buried in Indian Lake, and all but Gabriel and Elsie are in a family plot. None of the children of Elijah and Elizabeth Camp had any living children of their own. The property was left to and run by Gabe's wife Elsie for a time. Elsie eventually remarried a man named Harold Conklin, who died in 1957. Elsie outlived her second husband by two years, and she is buried next to Gabe.[45]

Complexity of Tourism and Native Peoples

By the early twentieth century, several Adirondack Native families were running commercial enterprises in housing guests, often complementing a guiding business. The Camp family was the most notable, or at least kept the best records. It appears the running of the Adirondack House got the better of Emma on more than one occasion, as she looked to sell the business at least twice; perhaps her health was an issue. Yet it is obvious that Emma had a lot of business sense. She looked for ways to save money, such as her inquiries into tax exemptions based on her Oneida heritage. She also attempted to make money in smaller enterprises and even inquired about a legacy from her deceased husband. Emma and the family's business outlasted the heyday of wilderness tourism in the Adirondacks and survived the depressions so prevalent during this era. It appears Emma did well for herself and her family, all of whom were working together.

Similarly, the Sabattis and other entrepreneurial Abenaki families continued to work together and get by, some seasons doing better than others. George Washington Sears, also known as "Nessmuk," described the Sabattis boardinghouse in letters to *Field and Stream* in 1881 and 1882. One day in August 1881, Sears paddled to Long Lake and "Mitchell Sabattis' landing," where "Auntie Sabattis will take care of you. She has been doing that sort of thing for a good many years." He described the landing as having a sandy beach—one that led to a steep path from the landing to the house. Mitchel was out guiding that day, but Sears reported that Elizabeth, Mitchel's wife, could "supplement him as camp-keeper." He mentions there were no tourists present that day but the house was full with two married daughters, their son Ike with his wife, plus eight grandchildren, all of whom kept Grandma Sabattis busy. Sears admired Elizabeth's ability to keep things under control. Both Sears and Ike were ill; Sears suffered from symptoms of tuberculosis, and Ike was down with cholera morbis or morbus, a noncontagious form of cholera now referred to as a gastrointestinal disturbance. By April 13, 1882, though, Sears described how tourists were avoiding "the old and time-honored house of Sabattis . . . because the house of Sabattis was too prolific of young half-breeds. There were nine of them when I was there."[46] As discussed in chapter 3, and again in chapter 5, those individuals known to be of mixed parentage often felt the sting of the tourists' pen as they were deemed to be less authentic and not up to the romanticized standards of some visitors to the region.

As these examples illustrate, none of these families' enterprises included the need to stereotype or market themselves as Indians, with the exception of the heave powder. Indeed, except for the Sabattis household, it is possible many of the guests did not even realize their hosts were Native. Scholars often describe Indigenous peoples' roles in tourism as that of artists and performers who were denied a "connection to a capitalist workplace and its associated wage labor."[47] In general, this argument is correct; however, this conclusion is painted with too broad a stroke. Indeed, the Native entrepreneurial families in the Adirondacks belie this conclusion. Locally their heritage was well-known, their identity remained intact, and they ran their businesses in ways similar to anyone else that lived in the Adirondacks. This is not to say stereotyping and the marketing of Indigenous peoples' culture did not occur in the Adirondacks; the next chapter demonstrates that it did. But these families and their enterprises managed to contravene the usual effects of tourism on Native peoples, and it is doubtful they were unique.

Further, depicting the tourism industry strictly as a stereotyping of cultural production for the benefit of dominant-culture tourists not only overgeneralizes but also denies Indigenous peoples their complex history of labor, entrepreneurship, and agency within that form of labor. The Adirondacks proved to be a place where some entrepreneurially minded Indian peoples could make a living and raise their families alongside their Euro-American neighbors. Some, like Pete Francis and Emma Camp Mead, even caught the attention of wealthy and powerful White men. That is not to say Algonquian and Iroquoian peoples were not marginalized; they were. The newspaper headline to attract attention to the article about Emma Camp Mead's annulment called her a "dusky maiden," and the travel writer George Washington Sears referred to the children of Mitchel Sabattis as "half-breeds." Both references clearly demonstrate the racism of the late nineteenth century. Perhaps this marginalization was the reason some of these families started their own businesses, although I found no specific evidence of such a link. The issue of their omission from the region's broad history is proof enough of their marginalization and helps to support Patricia Albers's contention that tourism served to make specific Indian cultures vanish. Yet, the tourism industry in the Adirondacks also allowed tourists and some locals to get to know Abenaki and Mohawk peoples who worked in a variety of occupations during an era when Indigenous peoples were thought to be vanishing in the Northeast. And it may have been the waning of the wilderness tourism era that vanished them from the area's history.

Motivations of Algonquian and Iroquoian Entrepreneurs

What then motivated these families to take on the risks of entrepreneurship? There are few sources that allow for a definitive statement on the subject, and there does not seem to be any one pattern in the Adirondacks. Some individuals, such as Pete Francis and Mitchel Sabattis, reportedly took advantage of a supportive patron who loaned them money because their skills were extraordinary. Others, like Emma Camp Mead, managed to obtain a considerable sum of money and risked it to start their own enterprises. Still others began small and reinvested in their ventures over time, as in the case of the Mitchell family. Individuals such as Florence Edmonds risked only their time and labor as they found ways to take advantage of local resources and turn them into petty commodity efforts for additional sources of income. For most, if not all, entrepreneurship was part of a mixed economic endeavor. None of these families was planning on getting rich from their efforts. For rural people, occupational plurality was a strategy to maintain rural family values of leaving land to next generations and to maintain cultural traditions.[48] For Indigenous families, occupational plurality was a traditional way of understanding work. Over time, one suspects some of them chose to live and work in rural areas because this style of work was familiar to them and it allowed them to maintain some cultural traditions, especially those that easily fit into rural North American society. As this chapter has suggested, entrepreneurship—often through trade and sometimes by exchanging hospitality for goods—was work Indigenous peoples were used to performing.

While there are some similarities between Iroquoian and Algonquian entrepreneurs in the Adirondacks, on the one hand, and Euro–North American entrepreneurs more generally, on the other, in terms of how they managed guesthouse businesses (such as using their home space to make money), there are also a few major differences. For one thing, the running of a boardinghouse or similar venture was considered a woman's business in White society in both rural and urban settings. In addition, the expectation of the Euro–North American businesswoman was that she would create a homelike atmosphere for her boarder(s). Further, the business was usually conducted year round and affected the family's living space nearly all of the time with little to no relief. This was not the case for Native entrepreneurs in the Adirondacks. Their undertaking was run by both women and men. The entire family helped to run the operation, and we often see men's names attached to the business, such as the Sabattis boardinghouse. These enterprises often reflected complimentary and gendered skill sets: men guided guests into the forests and set up temporary camps, or they might even have a substantial building guests stayed in. Women took care of the main home, which might house the guest for a time, and they fed and outfitted the guiding party at least initially. In some instances, men and women maintained a main house with rooms and sometimes cabins on the property. The expectation of these proprietors was to provide comfortable but rustic surroundings; this atmosphere was to be different from the boarder's home, yet still pleasant. Once the guest(s) and the male member(s) of the household ventured out into the woods, primitive and comfortable was the goal. As described in chapter 3, guides created an outdoor living environment for their sport that reflected a wilderness camp with many of the comforts of home, sometimes down to eating on china. We know that Indian peoples valued the provision of hospitality—it was part of their cultural practices, and sometimes that included exchanging hospitality for goods and the prestige it brought to the community. In addition, some scholars have argued that hospitality was a gendered type of work style typical of Native women. Indeed, fur trader Peter Sailly's 1784 diary entry notes his stop at an Oneida village was the most hospitable one they had encountered in North America and often exceeded French hospitality.[49] Thus, for these Algonquian and Iroquoian families, it was not unusual for both genders to provide hospitality, although the jobs were different.

Running a guesthouse was seasonal work for these Native entrepreneurs in the Adirondacks. At some point the family closed their home off to guests and engaged in other types of work based on the season. Many non-Indigenous Adirondackers who ran guesthouses managed their enterprises similarly. Living in an isolated area and knowing that one would eventually get their privacy and domestic space back in a few months might have made it easier for Indigenous and non-Indigenous Adirondack families to cope with the opening up of their private home for public consumption, and, in the case of the Sabattis family, even criticism. The first few weeks of catering to boarders may have even been a welcome relief from the tedium of the past winter. As this study demonstrates, both Indigenous and White Adirondackers were used to performing a variety of labor during changing seasons. Boarding tourists was probably nothing more than seasonal work for them, a way to make some income that had both advantages and disadvantages.

Location of Exchange

Over the course of this period, both Native and non-Native guest housing entrepreneurs began to appear to be living as middle-class people. They were living in larger homes that they had expanded to accommodate guests, whether seasonally or year round. Both welcomed and communicated with well-to-do city visitors, which required a certain dress and manners designed to make tourists comfortable and entice them to return the following year. These families helped the local economy by attracting urban tourists to the region—work that undoubtedly was appreciated by other businesses and the municipality. For example, it appears that Emma Camp Mead easily accepted the role of providing a welcoming atmosphere for her guests, and her Oneida heritage may have helped in this regard. Perhaps, however, Emma also looked to middle-class values as a guide to run her businesses. After all, she had lost the love of her life because of ethnic and, probably, class differences. In this instance, at least, running a small hotel may have helped to blur these lines of difference. It was also very possible she and her family helped to stimulate the economy of Indian Lake by running the Adirondack House, camps, and other enterprises. Emma's community service and work with the Methodist and Baptist churches suggest she was an accepted and active member of the community; her obituary certainly implied that she was, and it omitted the fact she was Abenaki and Oneida. Working-class people often used middle-class respectability as a tactical strategy to circumvent middle-class institutional surveillance and interference, despite their limited attachment to respectabilities' norms. The working class used these roles to take advantage of amenities and services and to keep middle-class authority figures at bay.[50] While it is not really appropriate to identify country people, even those living in non-farming communities, as working class, to date there is not a good term for scholars to use to describe the work of wage-earning (often seasonal) rural people who labor within pluralistic economies. They did share certain similarities with urban, working-class people from time to time. In particular, they both adopted and rejected middle-class values as the situation suited them.[51]

This conflict could be seen in the Camp family. Emma and her mother, Elizabeth, were ardent Christians full of evangelical beliefs, whereas Gabe rejected at least some of the tenets of middle-class respectability. Even Emma did not always epitomize middle-class respectability. It was reported that before she married Gabriel Mead she often enjoyed spending time with the tourists at her father's camp and was "thrown much in society" with Mead when he stayed with the family in 1882. As the owner and operator of her business, Emma was very visible in the enterprise. She advertised in her own name, had business cards, and personally wrote to guests to market her business for the following season. This is conduct that raised eyebrows during this period, at least in urban settings. Even in her later years, Emma was criticized for driving her horses too fast. Overall, she learned the hard way what it was like to try and circumvent middle-class values. Similar types of surveillance were being experienced by Aboriginal peoples, especially on reservations during this era, and rural peoples also were being scrutinized and judged by the urban middle class.[52] Given the capacity of Indigenous peoples to purportedly shapeshift as a survival strategy, taking on roles of middle-class respectability probably was an acceptable response as they navigated new and changing political, economic, and social frontiers. Nevertheless, these Native families' entrepreneurial efforts had consequences. The records reflect that entrepreneurial families who avoided work involving cultural stereotypes continued to have strong Algonquian and Iroquoian self-identities, but now they were becoming entangled with rural Adirondack identities. To visitors and even locals, their identity shifted from Indian to rural. Such shifts were demonstrated by their changing status on the census, obituary recordings, and erasure of them as Native peoples in the region's history.

Many Indigenous Adirondackers continued to maintain their identity as Algonquian and Haudenosaunee peoples through their relationships with each other and their continued work with customary skills such as hunting, guiding, and the making of crafts or even herbal remedies. For those families operating businesses, such persistence might have been a bit more challenging. Yet their Iroquoian and Abenaki culture, style of work, and economy were useful reference points that they could incorporate in their efforts to become successful businesswomen and men. For example, Abenaki families' work focuses around a patriarchal family unit complemented by a gendered division of labor. In the case of boardinghouse and guiding enterprises, Abenaki men took care of the hunting, fishing, and guiding needs of the sports while the women and children took care of the boardinghouse or hotel. Emma Camp Mead is an excellent example of incorporating traditional Iroquoian gendered work patterns into her enterprise. Like many Iroquoian women, Mead was a strong female voice in her home and family. She and all of the women discussed in this chapter, Native or not, worked hard to create a hospitable atmosphere for their guests. In addition, many if not all of these enterprises were seasonal and were incorporated into other ways to earn a living.

Some roles in tourism required Native Adirondackers to maintain an Indian identity through craftmaking and selling, guiding, or performing, while other opportunities such as running their own business relied less heavily on demonstrating "Indianness." This did not mean these businessmen and women had assimilated; some, like Thomas Hammon, were known for their heritage. What it does mean is those

Iroquoian and Algonquian peoples who came to work and settle in the Adirondacks had some choices. The region continued to be a location of exchange that allowed local Iroquoian and Algonquian peoples the opportunity and time to adapt to nineteenth-century modernity as they took advantage of and negotiated a series of complex relationships between Native and non-Native peoples and the land. The region became a space that allowed for Deloria's secret histories of unexpectedness, just farther east and beginning at an earlier time.

Conclusion

The latter part of the nineteenth century was a challenging period, and difficult times called for drastic measures. We must remember that the first Indigenous peoples to live year round in the Adirondacks were seeking a place of refuge (chapter 2). Those who stayed— or arrived later—chose to work within the local economy and society. Some intermarried with each other, and a few, such as Elijah Camp and Elizabeth Kennedy (Kanada), married a partner from another Native nation, while still others married Euro-Americans. Many of these individuals and families became part of Adirondack society. Some worked for wages, others sold their talents or services, and a few became entrepreneurs. In this regard, the region during the nineteenth and early twentieth century could be seen as a space for Iroquoian and Algonquian peoples to enter capitalism without losing their identity, and in some cases taking advantage of it. But this was not always easy, and some chose to hide their identity.[53]

Indigenous peoples responded to the many social, political, and economic changes that happened around them in diverse and complex ways. In the face of criticism that Native peoples who went to work or found ways to take advantage of the economy were assimilated into the dominant society, Canadian historian Rolf Knight replies, "One should give members of those generations credit for being something more than mere pawns responding to the acculturative pressures. . . . They recognized that no solution existed in a return to a past age. . . . If there is any single process which is wondrous in this account, it is the resilience and adaptability of Indian peoples during those early, chaotic, generations."[54] Knight cautions that scholars should not denigrate Indian peoples for working and seizing the opportunity to be part of the nineteenth and twentieth century world around them in spite of the restrictions facing them. As he points out, "Social change is not synonymous with 'cultural genocide.'"[55] Instead, as chapter 6 will argue, these were acts of survivance that sometimes resulted in individuals and families remaining in rural spaces and becoming Indigenous members of that usually White community.

The Iroquoian and Algonquian families who took a risk and became entrepreneurs before and during the wilderness tourism era seized a window of opportunity presented to them. They, too, created secret histories of unexpectedness concentrated in the rural region of the Adirondacks. However, there were consequences for these choices, even if unintended. Over time, their work and lives became comingled with their Euro-American neighbors, and their place in the region's history was forgotten, although many retained recognition in very local accounts. And, as the next chapter suggests, these and other blended families who chose to display their customary skills and talents as Iroquoian and Algonquian craft workers and performers became part of a North American colonizing narrative that relied on distinctions between authentic and inauthentic.[56] Such a narrative could not see past these family's adaptations, and locals and visitors alike began to fall prey to the misguided trope of the vanishing Indian in the Northeast.

5

"The Wigwam on the Hill"

Performing "Indianness" in the Nineteenth and Twentieth Centuries

AN INTRIGUING PHOTOGRAPH of Abenaki couple Cleophie Obomsawin (1877–1934) and her husband, Chief Julius Paul Denis (c. 1856 or 1866–1953) appears on a postcard located at the Goodsell Museum in Old Forge. Both are wearing pan-Indian clothing. He is aiming his bow and arrow at some unknown target in the water while the braided Cleophie in round, wire-rimmed glasses is holding a paddle, looking directly at the camera and trying not to laugh. It represents in no small way the theme of this chapter—the performative nature of marketing Native culture for the tourist industry in the Adirondacks during the wilderness tourism era.

Performance studies argue that social realities are constructed by historical and social circumstances that can be observed in the "doings" of a people that are learned, practiced, and presented over time. In other words, performance researchers examine performative components and try to determine what circumstances caused the behavior, what relationships are involved, and how the performance affects societies. Performance and cultural studies scholar Della Pollock suggests there is a complicated and broad relationship between history and performance that crosses disciplines. She argues that by crossing these fields of study one can recover the agency of historical actors, particularly their representation through historical remnants, and trace them within the metanarrative, which otherwise hides them in its shadow. Pollock goes on to define performance in conjunction with the study of history as "the process by which meanings, selves, and other effects are produced. . . . It is the embodied process of making meaning."[1]

Further, thinking of tourism as performance illustrates that roles can be selected and changed based on the stage (the site) and its location, the culture of the tourist, and the roles that tourists take on. Richard Schechner, an anthropologist and one of the founders of the field of performance studies, outlines seven often overlapping functions of human performance: to entertain, create beauty, make or change identity, make or foster community, heal, educate, and deal with spiritual or unknown realms.[2] Algonquian and Iroquoian peoples living and working in the Adirondacks during the wilderness tourism period performed a number of these types of overlapping functions. Here, evidence of the tourist gaze in the past, combined with remnants of material culture and documents still existing in the present, allows the scholar's penetrating gaze to look deeper into the meaning of these performances.

Most forms of tourist occupations employing Indigenous peoples in the Adirondacks directly linked Native culture to their labor. To be sure, this was not the case for all those who worked in tourism. Tyendinaga Mohawk John Baptiste (later Battese) of Long Lake (c. 1869–1907) was a caretaker of camps around Raquette Lake. Unmarried Mohawk girls from Akwesasne worked as waitresses, maids, and in the laundry at the Lake Placid Club and as domestics in people's homes.[3] Of course, one might argue that even these roles involved a performance in terms of their interactions with guests, employers, and fellow employees who may have compelled these workers to perform "Indianness" for them. *Indianness* refers to attributes associated with Indigenous North Americans and their cultures. Often codefined by North Americans of European and Indigenous heritage alike, the substance of Indianness was multiple and even contradictory depending on location and circumstances.[4] Even Native entrepreneurs used images to "play Indian," as we saw in Emma Camp Mead's use of a mounted Plains warrior on her packaging for an herbal remedy for livestock in chapter 4.

However, occupations tied to tourism that put Aboriginal Adirondackers on display were invariably linked to Native culture, even if it eventually was not entirely their own. These work activities are illustrative of Indigenous peoples performing culture as a way to market themselves and their goods, and to make obvious to their colonizers their continued existence. These occupations included guiding and acting as informants for scholars as well as more obvious performances, such as creating, selling, and demonstrating the making of baskets and other crafts. Other work included fortune telling, encampment demonstrations, participating in pageants, sports shows, acting, and modeling, and, by the mid-twentieth century, managing and performing in tourist attractions. All of this performance labor demonstrates historical and social circumstances that existed over time. It clearly shows agency, as participants chose to use performance as a way to make periodic (often economic) changes that would make the best possible life for themselves and their families. White tourists and locals also got involved in this production of Indianness, revealing that performance was another way to showcase the Adirondacks as a location of exchange. All of these performances are integral and necessary to tell a complete metanarrative of the region's history.

Performative Nature of "Indianness" in Occupations

The Adirondacks have an early history of Algonquian and Iroquoian peoples performing Indianness. For example, women told fortunes for tourists beginning in the mid-nineteenth century. Clairvoyance was a respected cultural trait of Mohawk and Abenaki peoples. Mohawk Tom Porter's grandmother, Konwanataha, was a seer or *teieia'taréhtha*, which means "she makes judgments or finds out something." Abenaki culture also included men and women clairvoyants, called *Wassobamit*, or "the "clear seers.""[5] This ability was used for healing purposes, but some Kanienkehaka and Abenaki seers decided to use their talents to make a living. Mohawk Elizabeth Bowen Morresy reportedly lived in a longhouse near the Kaydeross Creek in the Town of Greenfield in the mid-nineteenth century. According to her great-granddaughter Violet (or perhaps Viola) Shayne, who repeated the story told to her by her mother, Jennie Green Trimmer, tourists from nearby Saratoga Springs came by carriage to have Elizabeth tell their fortune. Jennie told her daughter about hiding under her grandmother's bed and "listening while the Mohawk matriarch told fortunes."[6]

Adirondack Indian Encampments

Advertisements in local newspapers and guidebooks noted that the art of fortune telling was also a form of entertainment at the Indian encampments that sprang up around the spas and tourist sites in the Adirondacks. These encampments included Saratoga Springs and Lake George, as well as Alexandria Bay on the St. Lawrence River north of the region, and Sharon Springs south of the Adirondacks near the old Mohawk village of Canajoharie. Writing about the 1908 Quebec tercentenary, H. V. Nelles argues that Indian encampments were sites of Indigenous domestic and social life that helped to demonstrate their culture was still very much alive, reproducing, and thriving.[7] The encampments in the Adirondacks pre-dated the Quebec tercentenary; they demonstrated that Native peoples had been staging this performance for nearly a century before.

The encampments were well known for the making and selling of baskets. Ballston Spa, then called Ballstown Springs, appears to have the earliest record of an Indian encampment in the region. In 1800, a dying Abigail May spent the summer there in the hopes of a cure. While there, the twenty-four year old kept a diary. On August 11, 1800, she took "a walk to the wigwam on the Hill" with companions. They watched an Indian family making baskets, and May described the experience: "[T]he pains bestowed and the labour required to make baskets—I thought it cruel ever to dispute the price . . . —there were three squaws and a papoose in the wigwam all whose earthly goods might have been put in a bushel. [F]or straw served them for bed chairs tables and all—an iron pot containging [sic] some indian dumplings and herrings was boiling over some coals at the door—and yet they appeared happy. [H]ow is it? [B]ut that is a question you cannot answer better than I."[8]

Indian encampments grew larger over time and expanded the use and variety of performance to attract customers. These performances eventually became a source of entertainment for tourists, and the wares being made and sold there became souvenirs. Saratoga Springs had at least three encampment locations during the nineteenth century. The first, it seems, was at Pine Grove, located on North Broadway across from the home of Chancellor Ruben Hyde Walworth. This site, which was in business at least as early as 1826 and lasted until the late 1840s, may have originally been set up as a Mohawk encampment. Some of the activities at this site included the selling of "bows and arrows, canes and baskets. Here Indians shot at pennies to show their skill."[9]

The second encampment ran from approximately 1840 to 1900, and an advertisement described its location at the corner of Congress, Circular, and Spring Streets. It, too, was considered to have originally been a Kanienkehaka encampment, but other Indigenous peoples had joined them, including those noted to be of mixed heritage. According to an oral history by Edward H. Fuller, the Akwesasne Mohawk families used the white tents, but there were also "rustic lodges." Some of the goods sold included "beaded bags and slippers and fancy colored baskets and bows and arrows." The encampment was visited by tourists who came to see "the feats of the Indians, and [who] liked to buy their handmade wares, especially moccasins and bows and arrows." Encampment participants "dressed in colourful regalia. Indian boys exhibited their skill by shooting at a cent fastened to the end of a stick stuck in the ground some 20 feet away." And it was not just boys who shot at the pennies; the 1870 federal census identified six-year-old Mary Reeves as Abenaki and indicated that for her occupation she, too, "shoots pennies."[10] It was probably this encampment that an 1883 *Saratoga Journal* article referred to as "the Picturesque Indian Village." The article described Indian Village activities that included morning parades and "first-class" entertainment:

> fancy rifle shooting by "Texas Charley" . . . Indian medicine ceremony and other descriptive acts of Indian life [which] were found of great interest. The specialty and variety programme is "simply

immense." The entire performance is free from vulgarity, the audience, in fact, being composed of many well-known citizens and guests. The children, especially, were delighted and expressed their approval again and again. Two performances will be given daily during the week under the spacious tents between Lake avenue and Circular street.[11]

According to *Lee's Guide to Saratoga, the Queen of Spas* (1883) there were two competing camps in the 1880s, this one and another on Ballston Avenue. Both were run by A. F. Mitchell and had a number of "innocent outdoor amusements," including a rifle range, bowling, and lawn croquet. The guide called the Congress Park encampment the "Indian Camp and Park" and the Ballston Avenue one the "Indian Encampment," and it cautioned the traveler not to confuse the two.[12] The Indian Camp and Park, located at Congress Park (c. 1870s-early 1900s), was later described as being "covered with tents and log houses, where the Indians camped from late spring until late autumn or until snow came. They wove baskets, embroidered fabrics and produced numerous colourful articles of their handcraft. Within the camp were a Punch and Judy Show, and glass blowers who made glass objects while the customer waited."[13] Both of these encampments included activities and performers that were not attached to Native culture, which created grumblings that the Indian encampments were no longer authentic because they did things that Native peoples were not expected to do.

Lake George also had more than one encampment during the nineteenth century, beginning as early as 1830; they were thought to be Abenaki. One was at Dieskau Street and the other along Canada Street "up from McGillis Street." Dieskau Street eventually became a year-round neighborhood for a few Abenaki families who built homes near the Catholic Church. In addition to making and selling baskets, bows and arrows, and other souvenirs, the encampments at Lake George also held basketmaking classes for tourists at upscale hotels.[14] These encampments became tourist attractions, and they may have been the precursor of the Indian villages that were part of twentieth-century roadside attractions in the Adirondacks. In addition to their commercial, entertainment, and educational value, the encampments also served as the seasonal home of the people who worked there. Some even decided to make these tourists towns their year-round home. Abenaki Andrew Joseph (1892–1978), for example, was born at the Saratoga Congress Park encampment and spent some of his youth in Saratoga Springs until the family moved to Long Lake. The Abenaki family of Louis Watso (c. 1777–1803) and his wife, the former Mary Jane Benedict Paquette, worked at the encampment at Lake George, and eventually Watso settled there.[15]

Basketmaking and Other Souvenirs

The making of baskets is seasonal and physically demanding work. Gathering the material was, and still is, more time consuming than actually weaving the baskets and other crafts. The Mohawk and the Abenaki had gendered views about the making and selling of baskets that demonstrated traditional values. Typically, the men carefully selected and felled the ash trees. Abenaki basketmaking was originally a woman's craft, but after 1880 men began to make them during the winter when they would have traditionally hunted. Mohawk men often made the larger work baskets, while the women wove the smaller, more elaborate baskets, including sweetgrass baskets. Sweetgrass adds intricacy, texture, and scent to the baskets. Found around Akwesasne and in some parts of the Adirondacks, such as Lake Placid, it was usually gathered by the women. The plant was carefully selected and harvested during the summer (the same season when black flies and snakes are so prevalent in the region), then dried in a dark place and bundled and stored for winter weaving. Before weaving could occur, sweetgrass bundles were soaked in warm water and wrapped in a towel to restore flexibility, and the grass was sometimes braided and dyed before being woven into baskets. While sweetgrass baskets were, and still are, associated with the Mohawk, many Abenaki are expert at incorporating sweetgrass into their baskets, too.[16]

Mohawk representatives took the handicrafts made at Akwesasne and traveled to the Adirondacks during the season to sell them, primarily at the encampments. The Kanienkehaka women who traveled there publically continued to make baskets and other crafts while other members of the group sold their wares and sometimes performed. At the end of the season, they usually returned home. This was not dissimilar to the pre-contact and colonial past, when the majority of Mohawk women stayed in the village to work but a few accompanied the men on hunts and military campaigns where they performed specific and usually separate jobs. As discussed in previous chapters, both the Mohawk and Abenaki adapted their customary style of work to fit contemporary economic industries, such as lumbering, and they continued this gendered practice when it came to the making and selling of wares.

Similarly, both Abenaki men and women made baskets and other souvenirs. Sometimes they made their crafts at Odanak and an individual or family brought them to the Adirondacks to sell at encampments. However, they also sold them in other varied ways, as will be discussed below. In addition, some moved to the Adirondacks to make and sell their baskets, and in a few cases they invited family and others to come to stay with them and make baskets to sell in the region. This, too, was probably representative of their customary economic practices, as the Abenaki traditionally traveled together as a family band for work instead of leaving most of the women and children in a village. Families traveled to their respective economic territories and set up camp wherever it made sense based on whatever resource(s) they were after, whether for subsistence or commercial purposes.

In the Adirondack tourism trade, it appears that Abenaki and other Algonquian families staked out specific markets as their own, and the entire family used their skills to make and sell wares. For example, the Smashwood brothers Gregory (c. 1857–87) and Frank (c. 1849–1924?) staked out Elizabethtown and nearby Keene Valley, respectively. The Smashwood brothers were believed to be Penobscot from Maine and were also called Bosso or Boss.[17] The Denis family was well-known in Old Forge, as was the Joseph family in Long Lake, for their baskets. This does not mean they did not cross into each other's craft-selling territory. For example, Julius Denis sometimes drove to Long Lake to sell baskets out of his car. Andrew Joseph sold most of his baskets to the local hardware store or in his family's gift store. The two men were friends, and Julius was known to visit at the Joseph home.[18] As in the past, it was acceptable for a friend or family member to sometimes use another's economic space if they needed to, so long as they requested permission. There are no records to let us know if Julius Denis asked Andrew Joseph for permission to sell his baskets in the Long Lake market, but given their close ties and Abenaki practice, it is probable he did or that Andrew even invited him to use the area. Thus, we see here traditional practices continuing and being adapted in the making and selling of baskets and crafts.

For Indigenous men and women in the Northeast, making and selling their baskets and other handicrafts was one of the best ways they could earn a living between 1860 and the 1890s. Many abandoned other economic pursuits to produce them, and American and Canadian tourist sites were especially good markets. Baskets were popular because they "embodied the affiliation between Aboriginal people, nature, and the past. . . . They were the perfect souvenir." Indeed, other people, such as the French in Quebec, appropriated the practice of making and selling baskets and Indian curios. As a result, in the 1890s the market became glutted. In addition, these goods also began to be manufactured by machine at a lower cost than handmade counterparts. Adding to this competition was the US-legislated *Tariff of 1890*, which for a time eliminated the duty-free status of these wares crossing the border.[19]

As a result of competition and tariff barriers, Abenaki and Mohawk peoples had to be creative in their marketing efforts. As in other parts of the Northeast, some traveled around communities and sold directly while others set up seasonal shops. For instance, Native peoples of unknown origin used to camp on family property across from the home of Florence and David Edmonds in Keene Valley. Native peoples, especially the Abenaki, including Julius Denis, were known to sell baskets in Keene Valley during the summer in the 1880s. They set up tents and usually left in the autumn. It is possible the peoples camped across from the Edmonds home were this Abenaki group there to sell crafts.[20]

Native craftspeople and sellers used Adirondack railroad and steamship stations to set up their wares to sell to tourists embarking or disembarking. Both forms of transportation were frontier markers of advancement and contributors to tourism. Tourists arriving meant money for the community, either directly or indirectly. Both Native and non-Native peoples took advantage of the arrival of railroads and steamships to sell to tourists who could not get enough of Indian crafts, which had become a fad for the well-appointed Victorian home (some even fashioned an "Indian corner"). Getting to tourists first by setting up on the docks or in the streets made a big difference.[21] An early twentieth-century photograph (later published in the *Glens Falls Post-Star*) showed a group of several men and two women dressed in Native clothing and wearing feather headdresses, waiting at the Lake George train depot to sell baskets. A 1906 photograph taken by Adirondack photographer and guidebook author Seneca Ray Stoddard shows Dennis Gill of Canada waiting at the steamboat landing in front of the Sagamore Hotel on Lake George (fig. 4). He is standing beside a large basket that the photo's caption claims contains sweetgrass baskets and birch bark, articles made by his Abenaki family to sell to tourists.[22]

In addition, Native individuals and families traveled by train or boat for commercial purposes. Although an unflattering account, Stoddard's travel guide tells us that Native peoples took a steamer on Lake Champlain, sleeping on the deck during their journey in 1874. The steamer preceded the railroad into the eastern part of the Adirondacks, and this one docked at Port Kent. At the turn of the twentieth century Annie Fuller traveled as far away as New York City by train to sell her baskets. She may have done so door-to-door, but it is more likely that she sold them at a commercial fair. Regardless, she was "discovered" by Harriet Maxwell Converse, who suggested to Ann that she could make more money in New York as an artist's model. "Falling Star," as she was often called in New York City circles, annually returned to Manhattan in the winter for at least four years to pursue

4. "Sagamore Docks," by S. R. Stoddard, c. 1906. Dennis Gill stands beside the wagon with his baskets. Courtesy of Adirondack Experience, the Museum on Blue Mountain Lake.

this endeavor. While there, she continued to make and sell baskets, moccasins, buckskin dresses, and beadwork. Fuller returned to her home in Lake Luzerne (Warren County) in the spring and fall and, as mentioned in chapter 4, during the summer she had a cabin and shop at Rainbow Lake (Franklin County). To sell her handicrafts, she dressed the part of an Indian woman, but in the summer she modified the material to a more comfortable corduroy with some beadwork for decoration.[23] Fuller's life as a model is explored later in this chapter.

Other craftspeople set up their own enterprise in various forms and expected people to come to them. For example, Abenaki Daniel Emmett, or Wasamimet (c. 1870–1952?), set up a tent under a crab apple tree at Coreys for the season. He chose this space because it was near the water, which he needed to make his canoes from local birch trees, and he carefully chose trees without knots. The late Clarence Petty, who as a boy met Daniel Emmett in 1911 or shortly thereafter, recalled Dan arriving at the landing on the Upper Saranac with baskets and balsam pillows from Odanak and, possibly, Akwesasne to sell. He had so many sweetgrass baskets that Petty recalled Emmett being "steeped in sweetgrass." Emmett traveled to the region and marketed his wares for so long that in the beginning he transported his goods from the landing to Coreys by horse and wagon; as times changed he got them there by automobile. Petty remembered that sometimes women or young men accompanied Emmett or came to visit or help him pack up and go home. Often he lived by himself in the tent but he had visitors. Emmett was also a member of and usher at the nearby Indian Carry Chapel.

Emmett was best known for the canoes he made. He used the tanned hide from a moose he had killed in Quebec the previous autumn to tie parts of the canoe together. He submerged the bark in the water to begin the process and finished by melting spruce pitch to pour onto the seams to prevent leakage. Emmett made at least three canoes every season. He also made pack-baskets and ash splint baskets from local trees. In addition, he repaired moccasins and guide boats. Sometimes called "Indian Dan" by locals and tourists, Emmett expected customers to come to him to purchase his wares. He did not dress any differently than the locals or his customers to market his products. If he still had merchandise left by the end of the season, Emmett packed it into a canoe and sold it at hotels in Axton or Long Lake. Petty recalled that it was quite a sight to see Emmett and a couple of young men, probably Abenaki, paddling birchbark canoes down the river loaded with the remaining baskets and souvenirs. Daniel Emmett returned to Quebec for the rest of the year and guided hunters, some of whom were his Adirondack customers. Wealthy families, such as the Rockefellers, were fond of him and purchased his canoes and goods.[24]

Marketing Strategies

The marketing of souvenir wares sometimes changed in form over time as the tourist area grew or as the artists became more successful. Two photographs of the Julius Denis family located at the Goodsell museum in Old Forge are illustrative. The first, a turn-of-the-century photograph probably taken in Keene Valley, shows the family standing in front of a small, portable building used to sell baskets; flags are placed on top of the building to draw peoples' attention. As well, the family is wearing Westernized clothing. Julius Denis first arrived in Old Forge in 1892 to sell baskets seasonally and later brought his family there in

1918 to live year round. According to the 1920 census records, both Julius and Cleophie could read and write, possibly French, and both spoke English (although it was not their first language).[25] The second photograph, taken around 1920, shows Julius and his third wife, Cleophie, making baskets in front of their home on North Street in Old Forge. Their son Bernard (c. 1910–25) and an unknown man watch. Julius and Cleophie are in pan-Indian garb, while Bernard and friend are in Western clothing. Old Forge had become a popular tourist destination at the turn of the century, and the family took advantage of their skills to make and sell baskets. In addition, they found other ways to perform in Old Forge, as did their son Maurice. These performances will be described further in the chapter.

However, not all Native peoples in the Adirondacks had to resort to stereotyping to sell their wares. By 1912, Sarah Angeline Keziah and her husband Norman Frank Johnson (1852–1919) had owned a basket store in Lake George village for many years, when the Abenaki couple was interviewed by the *New York Times*. Angeline wore a black dress, and neither she nor her husband, who barely spoke to the reporter, were very forthcoming about their life. She admitted not being able to read or write, and her English was said to be limited, although it did not prevent her from getting her point across in the interview. As the reporter noted, "Mrs. Johnson showed a quaint sense of humor, for at times she would look up from her work with a twinkle in her eyes to pronounce again some Indian word that was as bewildering to the neophyte [transcriptionist] as the rapidity with which she was putting the finishing touches on the dainty sweet grass basket. A proud smile of satisfaction greeted his inability to comprehend the word, and she would return to her work without proffering further assistance in solving its spelling."[26]

The difference between these two families' marketing strategy is striking. Lake George had been a well-known tourist destination since the end of the eighteenth century, whereas Old Forge was just coming into its own at the nineteenth century's end. The Johnson family had been living in the region year round for decades. Indeed, they had been there so long both husband and wife lost their status at Odanak based on the 1880 Canadian Indian Act (one of the many amendments to the original 1876 act) that limited their leave of absence to five years. Both Sarah Angeline and Norman (who had been born in Troy, New York, to Abenaki parents who returned to Odanak occasionally) had to hire an attorney to get back their Odanak property and rights. The family was reinstated successfully, but they chose to remain in the Adirondacks at least most of the time. Angeline reported that she arrived in Caldwell with her parents, who were looking for a place to sell baskets. They found Caldwell, or Lake George, to be a good place to market their wares, and it was close to Saratoga. Sarah Angeline (sometimes referred to as Angeline Sarah or Angeline) noted to the reporter that she worked until two or three o'clock in the morning making baskets during the winter to have enough to sell during the tourist season. Their shop was a well-known landmark to purchase baskets for both tourists and locals alike.[27]

One cannot help but speculate that their longevity in the well-established tourist town of Lake George allowed the Johnson family to avoid performing to stereotypical roles and exert a more direct agency, one that included resistance and humor, even demonstrating superiority to a reporter and his transcriber who could not spell their names or Abenaki references. In addition, despite their long residency in Lake George, the family still spoke Abenaki better than English, and their children spoke it as well. While the Denis family became well known and at least outwardly respected in Old Forge, their lives were different. They obviously felt compelled to resort to stereotyping to market their baskets and other wares. They also took advantage of their status as Native peoples to make money performing by posing for postcards and participating in regalia during community events. This does not mean the Denis family did not cherish their Abenaki culture; they, too, taught the language to their son Maurice. As the conclusion of this chapter demonstrates, Maurice found ways to embrace his and other Native peoples' culture, and he educated locals and tourists about it. For the Johnson and Denis families, Abenaki cultural survival lived alongside earning a living in a space that was socially, politically, and economically Euro–North American. Whether it was the difference in the age of the community and length of time the family had lived there is a matter for speculation: both families had to assess their situation and determine how to best market their wares and themselves to make a living.

Records about the Mohawk basket trade in the Adirondacks during this period are few, and the majority of documents pertaining to the making and selling of baskets are about the Abenaki. That is not to say there were not informal sales by Kanienkehaka in the Adirondacks, especially those who traveled to and lived seasonally at encampments and in lumbering camps. So far, however, no records of these informal sales have been found.[28] Akwesasne was considered to be the largest supplier of ash splint baskets in the Northeast; indeed, it sold more baskets than all reserves in the region combined. We also know the Mohawk sold baskets seasonally at the Indian encampments. It is likely the Kanienkehaka women of Akwesasne chose to make their baskets at home and sell them to middlemen to market their goods. These go-betweens, many of whom were White, purchased the baskets in large quantities from Indigenous basket weavers and either sold them in their own stores or in catalogues. An example of this practice in the Adirondacks involved the Standard Supply Company in Otter Lake. Interestingly, the large sign over the building's front door read in large letters "Indian Sweet-Grass Baskets Balsam Pillows," and right underneath this in much smaller lettering was the name of the store. The store's owner, Roscoe Norton, sent bags of local balsam by train to the St. Regis Indian Trading Company in Hogansburg, New York (the main town on the reservation), and craftmakers bought and used the balsam to make pillows for tourists. Norton then purchased the pillows and baskets from Akwesasne, and these items arrived by train to be distributed wholesale.[29] Perhaps the competition from the Abenaki in a region with a small population and highly seasonal tourist economy compelled the Mohawk to mostly ignore this market since they were able to supply to larger ones with less effort.

Beadwork

Based on the quantity of material culture evidence available, beadwork was another handicraft that was popular in the Adirondacks.

Most of the beadwork was made by Mohawk craftspeople and sold at encampments, although some Abenaki peoples were beadworkers as well.[30] As we know, Native women customarily used marine shell beads for diplomatic and decorative purposes until European glass beads were introduced and eventually became more popular. Starting in the last part of the nineteenth century, beadwork was applied to souvenir items on both Aboriginal and Westernized forms. These forms included moccasins, purses, decorative birds, and letter holders. Other souvenirs sold around the region included miniature items, such as snowshoes and boats, as well as pincushions and mementos with tourist locations beaded onto the keepsake. There are over eighty different beadwork forms created by Iroquoian beadworkers, ranging from the practical to the impractical. Souvenirs began as cardboard cut into the desired shape. The form was covered by cloth, often velvet, and the back was covered in the cheaper calico by the beadworker, or sewer as some prefer to be called. The Mohawk often used beadwork around the perimeter to hide the edges. Stuffing ranged from sawdust to sweetgrass to cattail fluff or even newspaper. Initially, the Iroquois were the only beadworkers to raise the beads above the surface of the cloth base by putting more beads on the thread than they needed to complete the pattern, thus creating an arch. Iroquois beadwork is so distinctive that experts can tell which Iroquois nation and even which family did the work.[31]

Beadworkers often used glass seed and tubular beads to create beautiful designs, the flower motif being the most popular. The Kanienkehaka also used many bird motifs.[32] Ruth B. Phillips argues that flower motifs replaced more established geometric patterns that had spiritual connotations. The flower was more acceptable to White missionaries and bureaucrats, who saw it as a symbol of "the feminine and the folk." Native peoples appropriated the floral image to replace the geometric patterns, but the meaning remained similar. Their adoption of new designs, materials, and techniques also demonstrated the versatility of Native peoples as they incorporated them into their own worldview, economies, and practices that aided them in resisting assimilation.[33]

Gilded Age and Progressive Era women treated these souvenirs as a representation of a more innocent and natural world of the past, not unlike their husbands' ideas of a wilderness vacation. Thus, the two cultures were often interconnected in gendered ways. As chapter 3 describes, White middle- and upper-class male tourists connected directly with their Indigenous male guides. White middle- and upper-class female tourists often connected less directly with female (and sometimes male) Native artists through their craftwork. Susan Stewart argues that all souvenirs are miniatures or samples that represent a secondhand experience for the possessor and act as a calendar for the individual who has taken the object from its natural place and added a narrative to it. The distance and the narrative give the object its value to the buyer. Stewart suggests that to own an "exotic" souvenir is to have a trophy that illustrates the maker had been tamed. It also provides a sense of distinction to the owner, who is trapped in a society of increasing standardization. Stewart describes miniatures as a unique product that to the purchaser embodies a nostalgic longing for preindustrial times when craftsmanship was important. Phillips's seminal work on the souvenir trade supports this argument. She demonstrates that art objects made by Native peoples during the Victorian era were "trophies of imperial possession" that naturalized European immigrants as "Native" to the land. These trophy souvenirs became markers of travel experiences that served to commemorate the demise of Indigenous peoples' culture.[34]

It is certainly possible that well-to-do buyers of Mohawk and Abenaki souvenirs in the Adirondacks purchased them for these reasons. Both the Kanienkehaka and the Abenaki were admired and remembered as having fierce reputations in the Northeast, the reputation of the Mohawk held until the conclusion of the War of 1812 and likely for a short time afterward. To own and display an item made by the Abenaki or the Mohawk could provide a unique social status to the purchaser, while also implying, however erroneously, that they were a conquered peoples whose culture was destined to disappear. As Phillips points out, however, these souvenirs also became "the object record of historical processes by which ideas of culture difference have

been constructed. They illuminated many individual acts of negotiation and cross-cultural appropriation that are not recorded in any other
place." The artwork also became the voice for the colonized, who realized their craftwork was of interest and value to Euro–North Americans. As a result, Native women modified their craftwork to meet the
dominant culture's tastes, and, sometimes, they took the opportunity
to expose "the dominant culture's contradictions and absurdities."[35]
The artwork and the artist also reminded settler society consumers
that Indian peoples were still present in places they were believed to
have disappeared from and in which they could still take center stage.

Mohawk and Abenaki performers associated with the Adirondacks, and those who worked in other towns and cities of North
America, found opportunities to incorporate their own and other
Native and non-Native peoples' cultures into ways of making a living in the tourism and entertainment industries. When the basket
market was saturated in the 1890s, they made adjustments. Abenaki
and Mohawk women crafted new types of souvenirs and decorated
them with beads, added the name of the place where the souvenir was
purchased, and adopted new motifs. These crafters took advantage
of the fads, wore pan-Indian clothing if that was what was required
to draw buyers' attention, and accepted other work when necessary
(and, as the discussion below demonstrates, they suffered when times
became lean). Abenaki and Kanienkehaka artists with connections to
the Adirondacks may have changed their artwork and their dress over
time, but their techniques and style of performance were still mostly
traditional. They kept their identity and values, traveled for work,
maintained contact with families, adapted long-established skills and
even spiritual concepts onto new forms, and kept their sense of humor
as they did so.

Staged Performers

Posing for Photographs

In addition to performing to sell baskets and other souvenir items,
some families participated in more obviously staged performances for

5. Mitchel Sabattis and guides. Photograph by Seneca Ray Stoddard. Courtesy of Adirondack Experience, the Museum on Blue Mountain Lake.

tourism and entertainment. As the opening of this chapter describes, Julius and Cleophie Denis wore pan-Indian garb and posed for postcards, and one can tell that Cleophie especially found the performance to be a bit silly. Even the guide Mitchel Sabattis posed for photographs although, notably, he did not dress in buckskin or wear a headdress; indeed, he often wore the same hat. His posing was done during an earlier period than that of the Denis family. Some of these photographs appeared in travel guides. He rarely looked forward in the photographs, and he seemed uncomfortable (fig. 5). Sabattis was also drawn by illustrated books author and historian Benson Lossing in his 1866 *The Hudson, from the Wilderness to the Sea* and by Adirondack photographer Seneca Ray Stoddard for his 1874 guidebook *The Adirondacks: Illustrated*. As well, Sabattis posed for at least one portrait that, in all likelihood, he commissioned (fig. 6). In this photo, he is seated on an elaborate fringed chair facing forward, looking directly at the camera. He wears a suit and his ever-present hat, and holds a walking stick that appears to have been whittled and smoothed.[36] By comparison, there is nothing about this photograph that makes him appear to be uncomfortable, which suggests the act of performing in other contexts was not to his liking.

6. Mitchel Sabattis, portrait. Unknown photographer. Courtesy of Adirondack Experience, Museum on Blue Mountain Lake.

Historians who have studied photography in colonial contexts have pointed to the power relations that surrounded its use. Euro–North Americans, both individuals and for commercial purposes, used photographs of Native peoples as a way to demonstrate their dispossession. Photographs and art with Indigenous North Americans as their subject were tantamount to "taking possession of the Indian image," which allowed the artist to manipulate these representations into White society's version of what authentic Indians were supposed to be. Photographs used for promotions and ethnography were done to construct cultural and ethnic differences. "Between parties of unequal status, looking was not an innocent act." Indigenous peoples realized that posing for the camera at the request of Whites offered them few benefits and was yet another encroachment they had to control.[37]

Despite these arguments, pictures can also be used to uncover hidden histories by impeaching the lack of textual evidence. Indigenous peoples adopted the use of photography early on, including having their portraits taken in large numbers. This adoption of portrait photography in particular reflected an increased economic mobility, the possession of a disposable income, and "more significantly . . . hints at increased personal control over representation of the self." The increased use of this self-representation challenged the stereotype of impoverished Indians who were increasingly becoming savvy consumers. The use of portraiture also showed that Indigenous peoples were as hard working, industrious, and affluent as their White neighbors. Following Western conventions of portraiture, these photos charted the growth and changes in a person or family, demonstrated economic stability and respectability, and showed that Native peoples understood this representation.[38]

Photographs of Iroquoian and Algonquian Adirondackers illustrate these scholarly arguments. Photographs taken for postcards and travel brochures often created a spectacle of Algonquian and Haudenosaunee peoples within the specific setting of the wild landscape, while Whites could be anywhere. Yet the photographs commissioned by Mitchel Sabattis and those contained in the Camp family records demonstrate Algonquian and Iroquoian peoples here used portraits and snapshots to define themselves and show their sophistication and respectability. Further, as Native peoples adopted and consumed photographs of themselves and their families, they demonstrated their willingness to adapt to select aspects of Euro-American culture, which contradicted White audiences' concepts of them as primitive. Overall, we must be as grateful to the families that performed for the camera in the Adirondacks as we are to those who left us their portraits. Without both of these records, we would have scant evidence of these families and their neighbors here.

Ann Jane "Annie" Paul Denis Fuller, also known as "Falling Star." When performing as actors, lecturers, and models, Native individuals and families often performed Indianness or versions of Indians based on what the dominant society imagined. Their performance often required them to dress in "Indian" regalia, although rarely, if at all, in their nation's customary dress. Inspired by Wild West shows (especially Buffalo Bill's), the Plains Indian was the image North Americans and Europeans wanted by the end of the nineteenth century.[39] Many of these performers continued to make baskets and other craftwork, which they displayed and sold in places like New York City. One such example was Annie Fuller, who was known in New York City circles as "Falling Star." She continued to make and sell her crafts during the winter months while she lived in New York City in between modeling jobs for the Metropolitan School of Fine Art and the Chase School, as well as for lesser known art schools and private artists. As a model, Fuller was very specific about what she was willing to do and could not be talked into modeling in any way she believed was immodest. For example, she refused to allow a sculptor to use her torso, posing only for the head, hands, and feet. She told a reporter, "A White woman is going to pose for the rest of the body. I wouldn't do that; you couldn't get me to for all New York. I wouldn't do it if I starved. And no Indian woman would. No Indian man would either." Fuller went on to note that she was going to sell the artist a buckskin dress she made for the White model to wear. She also described how she had referred two young men from a different tribe for a modeling job that asked them to pose nude. They refused to do it claiming, "we wouldn't do that if they would give us all the world."[40] Fuller often dressed in buckskin with a feather in her hair for these modeling jobs.

Annie Fuller rented a basement apartment on West Twenty-Fifth Street in New York City during at least one winter while she pursued her modeling and sold her handiwork. She sent the money she did not need for living expenses back to her family in Lake Luzerne.

Fuller even had business cards noting her occupation as an artist's model and seller of Indian handicrafts. In New York, she also worked as a spokesperson for at least one Adirondack hotel at a turn-of-the-century sports show there. Fuller also used her appearance as an opportunity to sell her beadwork. On one occasion, a rude customer at the show made inappropriate advances. Seeing her patron, Harriet Maxwell Converse, in the crowd, Fuller called out to her as "Chief" and asked that Converse come over "to protect that man from me." Embarrassed, the man quickly left. While Annie Fuller was willing to try new things, she was not willing to relinquish her values. She was creative in both her handicraft and marketing, she knew how to use her position to protect her dignity, and she insisted upon being treated with respect. Her modeling career ended when she was reportedly injured in a debilitating train wreck about a year before her death in January 1903. She is supposedly buried in an unmarked grave in the Anglican Church cemetery at Lake Luzerne. Her wages had paid for other relatives' markers, but no one paid for her gravestone. Despite her Anglican burial, Fuller also believed in witches' spells and knew herbal cures, according to her obituary. It is believed her mother outlived her.[41]

The presence of colonized peoples in the cities of the colonizer, and their actions there, blurred borders and provides new insights about these actors. Annie Fuller was not unlike other Native women who performed in North American cities during this era. These types of performances by Indigenous peoples were "part of the complex strategies of representation and negotiation" based on the limited opportunities available to them.[42] For example, Mohawk E. Pauline Johnson gave recitals in drawing rooms and theaters in North America and Britain. Johnson was never known as an actress and instead was described as an "elocutionist." Half of her performance was done in buckskin and the other half in Victorian, middle-class dress, representing both of her identities. Johnson was very careful about who she worked and traveled with. Even her publicity photographs were posed to present her as nonthreatening, a different stance from Native male

actors, who were often posed facing forward and staring in a challenging manner. At the turn of the century, women, whether Native or
not, had to be careful of their reputation, especially if they worked as
models or in the entertainment industry. Native women in particular
had to be conscious of middle-class stereotyped beliefs that they had
loose morals.[43] A Native woman who worked as an artist in this period
was in a very complicated occupation, one that allowed her an opportunity to earn decent wages in a creative way but also left her open
to charges of immorality. Like Johnson, Annie Fuller was very aware
of her position and how it could be portrayed; both women dressed
modestly based on Victorian and their own cultural values.

Both sexes though, were fully aware of their audiences and used
their racialized and gendered bodies, along with their knowledge of
the colonizer, for economic, educational, and political purposes. For
example, a 1902 Brooklyn newspaper reported on a performance by
Elijah "Dark Cloud" Tahamont (1861–1918), who had ties to the
Adirondacks. Tahamont lectured on Native religion to the meeting
of the Chiropean Club at the Knapp home. The Chiropean Club was
an apolitical woman's group formed in 1896 with Christian ties that
brought women together for the good of society. Tahamont told the
audience "in very fair English, not devoid of eloquence" about legends
and three great powers of rock, fire, and water. "The white man thinks
we have no religion, but we have the sweetest, most beautiful religion,
because we believed in nature—we look at the water, the trees, the
mountains: we go among the rocks to talk with the Great Spirit."
Tahamont's performance was characterized as almost arrogant, while
the women who performed were seen in domestic terms, as they presented their artwork and offered hospitality.[44]

Yet Native women were not always limited to such demure roles
as Annie Fuller's experiences demonstrate. In many ways, Fuller educated her followers by her actions as well as her artwork. Her refusal
to model for the torso provided turn-of-the-century New Yorkers an
education on Abenaki women's values and even power as she fended
off unwanted advances. In addition, she was a gifted artist, lecturer,

and businesswoman who was invited to speak in upper-class New York City circles.

Performing on the Stage and in Film

Some Aboriginal Adirondackers became musicians, models, and actors who carried out Westernized forms of performance. A few of these performers created stage names that reflected their ethnicity, which likely distinguished them from other performers. One example was Cherokee Wenonah "Princess Whitecloud" Moseley (c. 1889–1940), an accomplished musician who lived and died in Saratoga Springs. Performers like Moseley undoubtedly took advantage of the colonial agenda of demonstrating themselves as a successful example of a "civilized Indian" within this persona. However, such personas also demonstrate their desire to maintain their Indigenous identity instead of assimilating, which the colonial agenda preferred. Like many Adirondack residents, Indigenous or not, a number of Native peoples had to leave the area for work opportunities, but they often maintained residency or contact with their families in the region. Some went to New York City, where an "Indian colony" of performers and craft workers developed for a short time. Individuals such as Annie Fuller and families such as the Tahamonts (Margaret Camp Tahamont was a cousin of Emma Camp Mead) were two such examples.[45]

The Family of Elijah Tahamont and Margaret Camp. Margaret Camp (1854–1933?), great granddaughter of Sabael Benedict, cousin to Emma Camp Mead, and wife of Elijah Tahamont, was another important example of Native performers with ties to the Adirondacks. A basketmaker from Lake George turned actress, Margaret's stage names included "Soaring Dove" or "Dove Eye," and she sometimes signed letters to her cousin Emma as Margaret Dark Cloud. Her husband, Elijah, began his career as a lecturer and model for the artist Frederic Remington. Margaret, Elijah, and their two daughters Beulah (1887–1945) and Bessie (c. 1894–1909) moved from Lake George in the early 1900s to New York City, where the entire family modeled and acted. According to the Vander Weyde article "New York's Indian Colony," the family lived "within a stone's throw of Madison Square."

Bessie Tahamont, who died in Astoria, New York, at the age of fifteen, and her sister Beulah went to public school there.[46]

In 1910, Elijah went to work for American Mutoscope and Biograph (later known as Biograph). He made his first screen appearance in a movie directed by D. W. Griffith, and the family followed the director to California in 1912. Elijah appeared in thirty-five silent movies before he died in 1918, allegedly of complications from the Spanish flu. However, a letter from Margaret to Emma claims he was hit in the head by a board two weeks earlier while working at the Universal Moving Picture Company; the company provided treatment in the form of six stitches for a probable skull fracture.[47] When times were good, the pair obtained parts and put on their own productions, although at times they had to separate to pursue projects.

When the fashion to include Indigenous actors in the movies ended in the early 1930s, Margaret, who was in poor health, suffered. She and her surviving daughter Beulah carried on as best they could. During one lean period, Margaret traveled by car with other Native actors from Los Angeles to pick hops in Portland, Oregon, but there were too many there looking for work to make it profitable. Hop picking was labor-intensive work for one dollar per box; one wonders how the sickly Margaret would have fared even if she had obtained work. She may have gone to the hop fields to take advantage of the other opportunities the spectacle of hop picking had created for Indigenous peoples, which included selling baskets and curios, being paid to have their picture taken, and acting in performances. In addition, medicine men and women were known to accompany groups of their people to these locations: perhaps Margaret hoped for a treatment for her ailments.[48] Born in the Adirondacks but baptized at Odanak, Margaret was initially denied an old age pension because she could not prove she was born in the United States. Census records eventually proved her case. While Margaret did not return to the Adirondacks, she maintained a running correspondence with her cousin Emma, who sent Margaret herbs and remedies for the many ailments her cousin suffered. They stayed close through their letters; the last correspondence from Margaret is dated 1933, the year that Emma died.

She is probably buried in California. Margaret and her husband Elijah were representative of the experience of Native performers during this period. They used the stage to creatively make a living and occasionally they used the spotlight as an opportunity to educate Euro-Americans about Indian ways.

Adaptions and Questions of Authenticity

Despite the need for some Native performers to leave the Adirondacks for work prospects, others continued to travel to the region for the opportunities there. Over time, a number of the craftmakers who settled in the Adirondacks married Euro-Americans or brought their spouses, who were of European ancestry, often French Canadian. For example, French Canadian William Traversey (1867–?) married Abenaki Mary or Marie Anne Pakikan (1871–?) about 1894. When they arrived in Old Forge around 1900 they were both considered to be "Indian basketmakers."[49] Spouses of European ancestry making and selling baskets appears to have been acceptable to at least the Abenaki in Quebec, who petitioned New Hampshire resort proprietors in the 1890s not to allow anyone "but Indians *or those married to Indian women*" (emphasis added) to sell crafts at their hotels. They warned owners that French Canadians were once again appropriating their crafts and denying them their living. They cautioned proprietors to be aware that these goods were not authentic and that their guests were being sold goods of a lesser quality.[50] These Abenaki petitioners clearly separated French Canadians who married into their community from those who had not. One can easily argue this notion was a continuation of the Indigenous practice of adopting ethnically different people into their society, once embraced by the community these people became culturally part of their nation.

However, White tourists and travel writers saw these ethnically mixed families as spurious. As the next generations of multiethnic craftmakers plied their wares along with both Native and non-Native parents and contemporaries, the authenticity of all the peoples who made and sold these goods came into question. For example, the

Taintor Brothers' 1889 travel guide offered the following description of the Saratoga Springs Indian Camp near the Circular Railway:

> A number of shanties, half tent, half hut, are planted here, and a gypsy band, part Canadian, part Indian live therein, and sell such things as good Indians are suppose to wear and use. Small boys urge the visitor to set up the persuasive cent, that they may hit it with their little arrows, and pocket the same. The performance is varied by sundry domestic scenes, with appropriate dresses and motions, and the whole affair is very picturesque, and is highly instructive to the inquiring mind. To be sure, it is a little theatrical, and one has grave doubts concerning the fidelity of the display to nature; but it serves to fill an idle hour, and amuse children and others.[51]

As the encampments expanded to include such amusements as bowling, croquet, and Punch and Judy shows, the tourists began to further question the validity of the scene and those who worked there. At the same time, Aboriginal peoples living, working, and contributing to the culture of the region since before contact began to fade from the local historical memory by the end of the nineteenth century. This amnesia occurred despite the Adirondacks' early history of Algonquian and Iroquoian peoples fighting in local wars, clashing with trappers, assisting and teaching new settlers, and participating in the settlement experience with Euro-Adirondackers, which included the borrowing and adaption of each other's culture.

Playing Indian in the Adirondacks

Native peoples were not the only cultural performers of Indianness in the Adirondacks. The dime novelist Ned Buntline (1822–86; born Edward Zane Carroll Judson in Philadelphia) lived in the region for a time in a cabin he called Eagle's Nest (c. 1856–c. 1870). Not wanting to share his land or the lake on which his cabin sat, he went so far as to pretend to be an Indian to scare away trespassers. Early Adirondack historian Alfred L. Donaldson noted he danced and whooped around and occasionally shot his rifle in the air for good measure.

The Adirondack "hermit" Noah John Rondeau (1883–1967) constructed wigwams in his ghost village Cold River (population: one), which he built on abandoned lumber property. Rondeau admitted in an interview that he learned much of his woodcraft from Abenaki Daniel Emmet when Rondeau lived at Coreys. By the end of the nineteenth and into the early twentieth century, even well-to-do tourists and summer residents began to borrow from Native culture and "play Indian" throughout the Adirondacks. For example, a photograph of three young female guests on the grounds of the Irondequoit Club Inn in Piseco who were preparing for "an Adirondack adventure" featured one young woman with headband, braids, and a sidearm. As Philip Deloria argues, Euro-Americans turned to Native culture to help define themselves as other than British, and these individuals adopted the persona of the Indian as it suited their purpose.[52]

In addition, many part-time residents got into the act. Some named their "Great Camps," hunting reserves, and even their boats after Indian-sounding names. Credited with building the first Adirondack Great Camp, William West Durant (1850–1934) constructed three of them; one was named Uncas (completed in 1893) and another Sagamore (1897), which the family knew to mean "wise old chief" in an Algonquian language.[53] Durant also founded the Blue Mountain Lake and Raquette Lake Steamboats company, with vessels called *Irocosia* and *Toowahloondah* serving Blue Mountain Lake, and *Killoquah* and *Utowana* on Raquette Lake. The Lake George Steamboat Company named their evening boat the *Ganouskie* and their morning steamer the *Minne-Ha-Ha*. The latter, launched in 1857, has a namesake that still runs on the lake today. William Seward Webb (1851–1926) purchased 147,000 acres of land in the west central part of the Adirondacks. Part of this property was used for a hunting reserve that he called Ne-ha-sa-ne, which the family took to mean "beaver crossing the log." Melville Dewey named roads and buildings in and around his Lake Placid Club (1890–2002) after the Six Nations and owned a group of club houses called Theanoguen, or the Iroquois Group. This type of naming as been described as "potent symbols [representing a] region's transition from a frontier characterized by U.S.-Indian violence to a modern, industrialized society" as well as symbols of "historical memories" recast "as icons of progress and modernity."[54]

Summer Camps

Children's summer camps at the beginning of the twentieth century were late in the production, but were natural additions to the act of playing Indian. In 1905, Camp Walhalla on Lower Chateaugay Lake hired a Native basketmaker to teach female campers how to make baskets. As Bunny McBride explains, "having a "real Indian" at one's camp was a thing of prestige." Camp administrators saw Indians as the perfect model for a nature-based experience that incorporated ritual in an all-too-secular world and taught woodcraft skills to the urban children of parents who could afford to send their children for a leisure vacation. It was believed at this time that Indians had a spiritual relationship with nature that was more authentic than the dominant culture. Children playing Indian at summer camp was similar to their fathers' experiences participating in wilderness vacations or their mothers collecting souvenirs. The entire family was looking for ways to both assuage the stress of modernity and have intense experiences. These practices were gendered: boys got to rough it, while girls learned domestic skills. Once these children returned to school, however, their textbooks added such a divergent understanding of Indigenous peoples that it was difficult for the campers to reconcile the two images.[55]

Native peoples who worked for summer camps did so for a variety of reasons, which included their need or desire for seasonal work and to earn wages in ways that fit into existing economies. For men, this work, like guiding, offered opportunities to demonstrate their woodcraft skills at jobs that were less physical and dangerous than other occupations for similar wages. Further, it provided occasions for both sexes to educate White campers by "offering positive (if sometimes essentialist) portrayals of Indian life." Indeed, some camp administrators and promoters of Native, often youth, employment as camp counselors during the interwar years were motivated by the desire "to foster interracial unity and exchange."[56] The programs they ran gave some Native youth the opportunity to learn about traditional skills that had been waning on the reservation and to make contacts with White youths. Akwesasne was one of the first communities to organize such a group in the late 1940s called the Akwesasne Mohawk Counselor Organization (AMCO). Adirondacker Ray Tehanetorens Fadden was instrumental in the creation of this organization, and meetings of AMCO were held in the Adirondacks. According to Ray's son John Kahionhes Fadden, his father as a youth held jobs teaching woodcraft at summer camps. Ray Fadden and AMCO members used the organization as an incentive to teach Akwesasne youth about Kanienkehaka culture, history, and crafts, and to expose them to the outdoors. By simply hiking, camping, and so forth, AMCO participants received achievements, which were feathers. At the same time, participants gained experience they could use to obtain jobs at summer camps in the Adirondacks when they got older. AMCO initially began with both boys and girls, but eventually it became a boys-only organization, as Ray felt the mixing of the sexes was too distracting. John Fadden notes that today such a thing would be "frowned upon," but at the time it was acceptable. AMCO also collected information about Kanienkehaka history, and participants visited sites where significant events occurred. Promoters recorded that "besides supplying employment and good contacts for the young Mohawks, the Akwesasne program is making them conscious of their own cultural background. Indian traditions should be given their own rightful and dignified place in the minds of white children." Reports from camp counselors to AMCO told of White children with very stereotyped and derogatory ideas about Native peoples. Both Mohawk and often well-to-do White campers shared their histories and came away with a better understanding of each other's culture. Meanwhile, some Kanienkehaka youths became interested in obtaining a university education. In addition to these organized efforts, individual Native Adirondackers sometimes became involved in teaching for similar reasons. Maurice and Juliette Dennis were active in Old Forge's local Boy Scout and Girl Scout troops, showing the Scouts Abenaki skills.[57]

Naming and Marketing Indianness

Besides using real or imagined Indian names to label camps and boats, Native peoples' images were liberally employed for marketing purposes in the Adirondacks. For example, Glens Falls used the images of both Native and non-Native characters from *The Last of the Mohicans* because the community believed a local site known as Cooper's Cave was an inspiration for part of that story. The cave has been and still is promoted as a tourist attraction. Pageants often used the images of Native peoples. For example, Lake George's 1938 souvenir program entitled "The Romance of Lake George" features an image in the center of the page with a lone Indian figure leading other passengers off a docked steamboat while well-clad individuals look on. In the lower right corner is the image of a Native family; the male image is atop a horse with loaded traverse attached, several tipi-like homes (possibly wigwams) are set in front of a forested background. Perhaps the designer of the program thought the two images were an appropriate "then versus now" illustration. Similarly, Saratoga Springs used the likeness of an Indian man to advertise High Springs and events around the region. These images represented what Whites imagined Native peoples to be, and they were used to selectively symbolize parts of Euro–North American culture. The appropriation of the image of Indian peoples for commercial purposes serves to trivialize and domesticate Native peoples' history. Some scholars go so far as to suggest this appropriation went hand-in-hand with North American imperial efforts to dispossess Indian peoples of their countries.[58]

Pageants, Tourist Attractions, and Local Celebrations

Staged performances of Euro-Americans playing Indian also occurred in the Adirondacks. In the first decade of the twentieth century, the Sacandaga Amusement Park's Fourth of July event included a pageant in which local White men portraying Indians attacked a cabin built on the baseball field there. They shot flaming arrows at the cabin, and as the pioneers were about to be "scalped" a bugle sounded and soldiers marched from the woods and killed the attackers. Melville Dewey, a student of Iroquois society, incorporated their culture and history into the Lake Placid Club's ceremonial events. The first event was September 3, 1903, and consisted of a bonfire which became the "prelude to the annual Six Nations Council Fires during the 'Moon of Flaming Leaves' in early September of each year." The last one was held in 1953. The Iroquois roles were played by members of the Dewey family and select guests, and the audience were club members and their visitors. The Saratoga Pageant of 1912 included numerous roles for Native people in several of their scenes, but they were all played by Euro-Americans. Having vanished Native peoples from contemporary society, Euro-Americans took the opportunity "to fill the void as their remaining heirs. In doing so, they distinguished themselves—true lovers of nature—from other less enlightened elements of their society."[59]

Despite these examples, Adirondack communities also produced pageants that employed Native actors. Made popular in England in 1905, pageants quickly crossed the ocean and became fashionable in North America. Like today's reenactments, pageants were a spectacle used to commemorate historical events. They celebrated the past but were shaped by concerns about the present and future. American pageants were influenced by Progressive Era arguments against monopolies, trusts, and industrialization's dehumanization. Pageant supporters saw the form as a creative force that could bring communities together. Considered an art form by, for, and of the people, pageants quickly became institutionalized in the United States first by university program training and later through the American Pageant Association (1913). The Champlain Tercentenary celebration of the discovery of Lake Champlain by Samuel de Champlain (July 4–9, 1909) included a water pageant depicting the battle in which Champlain and his allies fought against the Iroquois; the pageant included 150 Native actors, mostly from Canada, under the leadership of L. O. Armstrong of Montreal. The participants were described as the "descendants of the tribes originally occupying the Champlain Valley." Every day the cast had to move to a different location: July 5 was in

Crown Point, July 6 in Ticonderoga, July 7 in Plattsburgh, July 8 in Burlington, Vermont, and July 9 at Isle LaMotte, Vermont. American President William Howard Taft attended the evening performance in Burlington. In addition to this reenactment, they also acted in the Longfellow play *Hiawatha*, "written to express the war-like temperament of the Algonquin." The play ran one or two showings a day from July 5 to 9 in both Adirondack and Vermont communities. Hiawatha pageants provide an interesting perspective to examine the gap between White perceptions of Indians and the actual lives of "real" Indians as they "played" Indian for settler society audiences. Many traditional Native cultural performances had been outlawed during this period (1880s–1930) by federal assimilationist policies. The Hiawatha pageants were an opportunity for Native peoples to be conspicuous and influence concepts of Indianness, even if it was only in small ways.[60]

Annual Indian pageant celebrations continued in the Adirondacks until the early 1960s. Ticonderoga's Indian pageant was larger than Dewey's Lake Placid Club productions, and it was open to the public. This annual Indian pageant was first produced in 1931 as a reenactment of the green corn ceremony among friends and lasted until 1961, although its popularity had faded by then; the last effort was taken on by Fort Ticonderoga to assist the ailing Cook family. This event started as an informal gathering and grew into formal, educational plays with a cast of 100 to 125. The pageants changed every year and were meant to portray the events and culture of the Iroquois. As the Ticonderoga Indian pageant's popularity grew, it needed to expand. Funded by H. Germain Slocum, the "Forest Theater" amphitheater was built in 1936, and it was capable of seating 2,000 to 2,500 people. Farmer Tom Cook donated twenty-five acres for the production of these plays, which included the ability to park 1,200 cars. Sponsored at first by the Champlain Valley Archaeological Society, the new productions were produced under the auspices of the Society for the Preservation of Indian Lore (1937), and the New York State Historical Association backed them and gave its approval of the plays' accuracy. The early pageants used only Euro-American actors. Eventually, though, they caught the attention of Ray Fadden. A strong supporter of the need to celebrate Haudenosaunee history and to tell it accurately, he organized youth to perform as singers, dancers, and extras in the later years of the annual Indian pageants. Ray's son John attended the pageants starting at the age of four and notes that all the Six Nations were present. It is possible that the Forest Pageant productions currently held at Six Nations in Brantville, Ontario, are a result and continuation of these plays.[61]

Ray Fadden was a school teacher at Akwesasne, and he worked fervently for both the community and its history. He also wrote and published pamphlets about Iroquois culture to educate local Mohawk and the general public. He eventually was naturalized by the community at Akwesasne and given the Mohawk name Tehanetorens. In addition to the Ticonderoga pageants, Ray became involved in the Lake Placid Club ceremonies. Ray also worked with promoters in the early 1950s to create the tourist attraction called the "Lake George Indian Village," which was meant to be a combination of a museum of the Six Nations and an attraction. The promoters were Paul Lukaris and George E. McGowan, along with Fred Lyons and John Parrott. Fadden was the curator of the museum, which housed his collection, and he presented educational lectures to visitors as part of a show. The museum was a long, log building. Ray's collection filled up one-third of the building, and the other two-thirds was used for souvenir sales. A 1952 newspaper article reported that scholars Carl E. Guthrie and William A. Ritchie were involved in helping trace lore and facts of Six Nations history; however, Ray's son John has no memory of them, and it soon became apparent to him and his father that the proprietors' desire for money was the driving factor. According to John Fadden, his family worked at the attraction for its inaugural and second years, 1952 and 1953. Ray lectured about Indigenous peoples' contributions and sometimes he included details like sign language, which he supplemented with a demonstration. He also arranged for Mohawk youths to perform social dances. Ray's lectures were part of the performance, which was meant to entertain as well as educate. John recalls that, as in the case of AMCO, Ray and his wife Christine, who also did the cooking, had to keep an eye on the youths, as the group consisted of both boys and girls. The original owners sold the attraction after the first year. The subsequent promoters were only interested in the money the attraction could make them. After several disagreements, Ray quit after the second year, taking his collection, family, and the youths with him. The attraction's promoters brought in Comanche from Oklahoma to work there the following year. John Fadden recalls visiting with them over the stockade-style fence that surrounded the performance area a year or two after his family left. The Comanche performers indicated that they, too, had problems with the proprietors and were not planning to return.[62]

During his two years at the Lake George Indian Village, Ray Fadden sold charts and pamphlets, as well as earned a salary. Ray saved as much as he could and used his savings to build the Six Nations Museum in Onchiota. The museum opened in the summer of 1954 as two rooms housing Ray's collection, together with displays on the grounds such as a longhouse. In the 1980s John, supported by his wife Eva Thompson and their sons, took over management of the museum from his parents and continued Ray's mission to educate visitors, both local and from afar, about Iroquois history and culture. Chapter 6 provides further details about this Mohawk family and the museum.

Schroon Lake's community pageant of 1957 included the early history of the relationship of the Indigenous peoples with that lake and community. The family of Chief Swift Eagle, who ran the Indian Village at nearby Frontier Town in North Hudson, took part in the event. Swift Eagle was Apache and Hopi-Tewa from New Mexico and an accomplished flutist. His wife, Clara Chee-Chee Bird Eagle (Powhatan), made jewelry and the regalia they performed in, and she also read cards to tell fortunes. The couple had met in New York City, and they had four children who performed with their parents at Frontier Town. Given that the theme of this tourist attraction was a western frontier town, it was not as odd to see this family with western and southeastern roots performing there. Swift Eagle's mission for performing at the attraction was to educate visitors about the truth regarding Native peoples.[63] Swift Eagle was the son of a medicine man in New Mexico. He was sent to a boarding school around 1911 at approximately ten years of age. He graduated from the school and stayed on for a few years to be in charge of the orchestra. Upon returning home, Swift Eagle was chosen by the elders to travel and educate Americans about their culture because of his flair for performance and storytelling. He initially traveled west and appeared at the Coconut Grove in Hollywood, where he met and became friends with athlete and part-time actor Jim Thorpe (Sac and Sauk [Fox]). Thorpe introduced him to some movie producers, and Swift Eagle found work in westerns, often playing the villain. This was not what the elders had intended for him, and he was called home and refocused. Thereafter, Swift Eagle traveled throughout the United States and Canada to speak and perform. During a performance at Frontier Town in 1954, Arthur Benson, the creator of Frontier Town, hired Swift Eagle and his family to stay and run an Indian village there. Eagle saw working at Frontier Town as an advantage because the people came to him instead of his having to travel and go to them. Swift Eagle wanted everything to be as authentic as possible at the Indian village at Frontier Town. He and his family conducted powwows, sang, and told stories. Swift Eagle occasionally expressed some resentment when audiences were difficult. In addition, he performed at school assembly programs in the Northeast. Swift Eagle described his life as a boy and demonstrated the twelve different dialects and sign language he knew to communicate with other nations.[64]

In Old Forge, the Denis/Dennis family, both Julius and later his son Maurice, often participated in local celebrations. (The family changed the spelling of Denis to Dennis after a J. Denis moved to the area that resulted in Julius's mail getting delayed, which affected his basket-selling business. This book uses Denis for Julius's last name and Dennis for Maurice and later generations.)[65] For example, a 1934 photograph shows a drum-wielding Julius with fellow Abenaki Walt LaGrave and Ana Panadis, plus probably Mohawk Josephine Ski, all in regalia, participating in what was almost certainly the opening of the Hollywood Hills Resort Hotel. Julius was so well known for his contribution in such events that his obituary stated, "He was an outstanding participant in ceremonies and pageants in the Old Forge area."

Later in the century, Maurice Dennis and sometimes his wife Juliette participated in Old Forge events, including the town's winter carnival. One year, Juliette was celebrated as the "queen" of the winter carnival to thank her and Maurice for their contributions to the event. Maurice Dennis appeared skiing while adorned in a headdress for Easter Seals and the Cadette Girl Scout "Show of Shows." The Easter Seals caption noted that Dennis was "a former member of the 10th Mt. Ski Troops." He had also been a ski instructor at nearby McCauley Mountain and a local lifeguard. The conclusion of this chapter discusses Maurice and Juliette Dennis's role running an Indian Village at the Enchanted Forest, a tourist attraction in Old Forge.[66]

Location of Exchange

These examples demonstrate that the more well-to-do Euro-Americans and even communities in the Adirondacks wanted to memorialize a Native past in the region. Originally, these efforts, especially for visitors and part-time residents, were nothing more than attaching Indianness to wilderness romanticism or for marketing purposes. As time went on, though, the motivations of those such as the Lake Placid Club's Dewey and the Ticonderoga pageant producers became more sincere, despite their erroneous belief that the Iroquois culture was disappearing. Apparently, in their minds, the Algonquian and more specifically the Abenaki connection had been severed or was less worth celebrating. How these performances of Aboriginal culture were viewed by rural, year-round residents is more of a mystery; their voices are mostly absent in these records, although some participated as cast members in the productions. That communities included Native families and performers in their local celebrations suggests these towns wanted to involve their Indigenous neighbors, even if the performance was less than historically accurate or traditional for Iroquoian and Abenaki peoples. Of course, a number of these performances were for and by the tourists. Performances of Indigenous culture by Abenaki and Mohawk peoples living in or with ties to the Adirondacks, and performances by White tourists, seasonal residents, and permanent residents, continued to support the notion of the region as a location of exchange. That is, reciprocal and complicated actions around culture, identity, change, and continuity fluctuated and became entangled with efforts to coexist and make sense of a changing world for everyone. Luckily, the performances of Native Adirondackers quietly and creatively left an imprint and a record of their persistence there.

Conclusion

A theme that is especially significant to Native history in the Northeast is the trope of the vanishing Indian. There are a number of reasons that explain this myth's occurrence. Scholars have argued this concept was used to deny Indians a future in North America, to help Euro-Americans' separate themselves from their British identity, and to address issues of contested territory.[67] Using the novels of James Fennimore Cooper, who often paired Native and non-Native characters, literary critic Thomas Hallock concludes that "any . . . lasting signs of being in between cultures get sanitized with the clear division between enemies or by a condescending sympathy for a vanishing race. Distancing a culture from its shared past, this explanation of ecological and social change mostly indulges Euro-American guilt." In addition, Native peoples' adaptations to modern society were used to marginalize them from the records. Ojibwe American historian Jean O'Brien notes that strategies of adaption caused New England Algonquian men to take on dangerous and distant work, resulting in Algonquian women intermarrying with African Americans or, less often, Euro-Americans. This practice made it difficult to track them and created the illusion Algonquian peoples in New England were vanishing.[68] Despite Euro-American efforts to see the Native peoples in the east as vanishing, many Indigenous communities developed there, in and outside of reservation settings, and continue to exist in the present. As Abenaki scholar Lisa Brooks concludes, "beneath the illusion of disappearance lay the morbid truth of displacement. Dispossession is not destiny but rather a disjuncture."[69] In a similar manner, the history of Algonquian and Iroquoian peoples who worked and lived in the Adirondacks was seen as being that of a vanishing people. Their history was thought about in romantic terms, and their authenticity was questioned because of their efforts to adapt. Fortunately, photographs, material culture, artifacts, and travel literature have helped reestablish their history in the region.

During this period, all citizens of North America experienced difficult times as they adjusted to a world of increased industrialization, urbanization, and economic uncertainty. Working people in all settings, whether urban or rural, had to adjust and make changes to survive. Yet such changes had a potential ineffable effect for Native peoples: they had to listen to Euro-Americans' and Euro-Canadians' expectations that they as a distinct people were vanishing because their culture was being replaced by a Western one. In turn, Aboriginal peoples made objects or acted in ways that appeared to support this settler society view. These Indigenous artists had to remove themselves from the traditional notion of making art for aesthetic purposes and think of that art as a commodity, whether as an object or as a performance. Indian peoples had to temporarily disconnect from their own rich culture and represent one that was simplistic and stereotyped. They had to make choices that outwardly appeared contradictory to their culture's survival even as they continued to perpetuate it privately.

Despite the US and Canadian governments' policies of assimilation, tourism demanded a stage-managed performance of exoticism and something to consume. Souvenirs filled the latter need, demonstrating a relationship of exchange and appropriation. Yet the success of these artists also reflects a strategy of resistance that helped to continue traditional practices, although the end result was often modified. While many occupations in tourism and entertainment put Indigenous peoples on display in very stereotyped ways, these industries also offered some economic, social, and political benefits for Native peoples. They allowed Iroquoian and Algonquian peoples the ability to earn respectable wages, escape the surveillance and control of reserve life, meet their own society's expectations of gender roles, and have some limited opportunities for a political voice. In the Adirondacks, the making and selling of souvenirs also identified them as Abenaki and Iroquoian peoples. For Native "performers," the Adirondacks provided a stage to educate White tourists and locals about the richness and benefits of their culture, and some of these performers found audiences in cities outside the region. These voices, then and now, told and continue to tell the North American public that their history is important to specific regions and the continent, that they are still there and plan to remain, and that their culture has something to contribute to the present.

While educating Euro-Americans, these Native performers also continued to learn, borrow, and grow as artists. In an example of intercultural exchange, Maurice Dennis (1908–1987) learned about totem poles after a trip to Alaska. He was so intrigued by them that he approached an Abenaki elder to teach him to carve. Dennis incorporated totem poles into his art and displayed them at the Indian Village, part of the Enchanted Forest in Old Forge. Maurice created and managed the village with his wife Juliette M'Saadaques (1919–2005). M'Saadaques, also an artist and educator, made and demonstrated the making of baskets and other handicrafts. Her Uncle Arthur also made baskets in the Old Forge area and lived in a tent on Big Moose Lake near the present-day Big Moose Inn. The Dennises used the Indian Village to educate tourists in the 1950s and 1960s about Native culture. Maurice Dennis was careful to explain that carving totem poles was not a customary Abenaki practice, but that carving in wood was and still is. Dennis represented the long-held practice of Indigenous peoples exchanging art, design, and other cultural forms from each other long before contact. He also continued the practice of Native peoples educating newcomers in the ways of Indigenous North America. Today, his daughter Andreé continues her father's legacy of carving and teaching, while her sister Liette continues the basketmaking tradition of their mother, Juliette.[70] These sisters, John Fadden and his family, and other Aboriginal Adirondackers continue to remind us that Native North Americans from the Northeast still exist and thrive, despite 240 years of a border that divides their territories and the bureaucracies of two nation states doing everything in their power to assimilate them. Instead these Algonquian and Iroquoian peoples have shown they are very industrious, determined, and adaptable peoples with a rich heritage and history that has contributed to local and national narratives in North America. Their long and rich history and the contributions they have made needs to be taught throughout the narrative of North America, and not just in the first chapter, which implies they "vanished." The history of the Indigenous peoples of North America existed long before Europeans arrived, and they have contributed to North American history, science, art, and culture, and they continue to engage us. The dialogues and embodied process of historical performance making meaning needs to continue. Moreover, Indian peoples need to be cast as prominent players throughout the life of the production.

6

Rural Indigenousness

Survivance in the Adirondacks

THIS CHAPTER continues the history of Indigenous peoples living in the Adirondacks into the twenty-first century. It extends the use of family histories intertwined with local history and broader topics important to contact history as well as Native American history, especially in the Northeast. It introduces the Abenaki family of Andrew Joseph and the Mohawk family of John Fadden to demonstrate that the Adirondacks remain a part of Abenaki and Kanienkehaka peoples' homelands, as well as a location of exchange for Native peoples (and others) to the present day, and they will likely continue to be. This chapter also discusses the concept of "survivance" and how Aboriginal Adirondackers fit into this notion within a rural setting that was not a reservation site. I argue for the consideration of the notion of "rural indigenousness" alongside other discourses of indigenous identity on reserves and in urban and suburban spaces.

The Adirondacks in the Twentieth and Early Twenty-First Centuries

Wilderness tourism in the Adirondacks began to wane after World War I, partly due to state policies but mostly because leisure and entertainment trends changed. As early as the turn of the twentieth century, New York State began to constrain practices that Adirondackers had been engaged in for decades to protect the wildlands of the region for all New Yorkers and visitors. For example, collecting firewood was restricted, guides had to tear down camps, and game laws were created and enforced to limit hunting and fishing numbers. These laws were not totally restrictive; the public forest preserve lands did allow for some limited exercise of subsistence hunting and fishing, but locals were denied access on private property (whether commercial or not), which had become considerable. Cars and the middle-class tourist became more frequent visitors during the twentieth century. The state of New York and the region made accommodations for them by building better roads, which spawned moderately priced hotels, followed by motels and campgrounds. New York State began to buy more land (sometimes forced through the legal process of eminent domain) and encourage tourism, and it prohibited logging in certain areas, such as the High Peaks. Elite visitors were not happy with the increase in tourism and the state's involvement.[1]

After 1920, a lengthy vacation stay in the wilderness or at a grand hotel with ballrooms, gardens, and summer activities was replaced with accommodations more useful for shorter stays. The types of leisure activities also changed. Instead of men spending weeks hunting and fishing in the woods with a trusty guide while the family idled the summer away at resorts, the family motored to the area for a long weekend or maybe a week to participate in sports like hiking, skiing, and golfing on marked and groomed trails and links. Amusements at the Indian encampments were replaced with roadside tourist attractions that catered to children. A few of the larger lakes continued to tour people in steamers that evoked nostalgia for the late nineteenth century. Communities planned events to bring in tourists and entertain their citizens. Historic sites were marked and museums established; both continued to draw seasonal visitors and locals alike. Eventually restaurants, local stores, and outlet malls sprang up to vie for tourist dollars as the allure of the amusement parks began to fade. Today, rock climbing, a ride down Mount Van Hoevenberg's bobsled run near Lake Placid, or whitewater rafting has taken the place of the nineteenth-century wilderness experience for the majority of tourists who still want to experience the sublime combined with a bit of a thrill.

As a result of these early twentieth-century changes, both Native and Euro-Americans living in the Adirondacks had to make economic adjustments. Adirondackers changed old or started new businesses that catered to these middle-class tourists. A handful of guides were (and still are) able to continue guiding for hunters and anglers in specific regions. Instead of camping in the forests, these sports sometimes stayed at the home or a cabin of their guide, or perhaps at a neighboring motel. Locals made (and still make) or produced regional goods to sell, but the products and the forum changed. Today, handmade souvenirs and local products, such as maple syrup, can be found at regional grocery stores, shops, community farmers' markets, roadside stands, and online sales. Adirondackers found work performing in seasonal roadside attractions and they participated in other forms of entertainment. Abenaki, Mohawk, and other Native families continued to contribute to these changing forms of tourism activities, many of which overlapped eras. As chapter 4 details, the Abenaki-Oneida Camp family guided, ran stores, and rented out camps and eventually rooms in their home, which they turned into a seasonal hotel as their customers changed from upper-class to middle-class sports. Daniel Emmet continued to make and sell canoes, baskets, and other crafts at Coreys until he died in 1953.[2] Starting in the 1950s, some Native families helped develop and perform in Indian villages located at regional tourist attractions. They also participated in local events with the intention of educating the public. Some even founded or contributed to museums to remind locals and tourists alike that they were part of New York State's history and still contributing to it. In addition to the Six Nations museum at Onchiota, Akwesasne has a cultural center located on the New York State side of the community. Other educational sites include the Iroquois Indian Museum at Howes Cave, New York, which is just south of the Adirondack Park as are at least two archaeological sites in the Mohawk Valley. Tom Sagogweniongwass Porter runs "Kanatsiohareke," an educational center as part of a Kanienkehaka community reestablished in 1993 near the old Mohawk village site of Canajoharie near today's Fonda, New York, in the Mohawk River Valley, southwest of the park. All the while, Native Adirondackers have lived ordinary lives that would be indistinguishable from their fellow rural New Yorkers.

And if locals thought the Mohawk had forgotten about their territory in the Adirondacks, the takeover of an abandoned Moss Lake Girl Scout camp in 1974 reminded them otherwise. The camp had been sold in 1973 to the State of New York, which planned to clear the 612 acres of all structures and make the land part of the publically held park. Hailing mostly from Kahnawake along with some from Akwesasne, the Mohawk who took over the camp were looking for a place to live a more traditional lifestyle than existed on their reserves in the 1970s, and they were interested in reclaiming Mohawk territory.[3] After three tense years, the state (in an agreement negotiated by then–Secretary of State Mario Cuomo through a series of nearly two hundred meetings) exchanged the land in the Adirondacks for the use of nearly seven hundred acres of land in the vicinity of Miner Lake near Altona in Clinton County, just north of the Blue Line. New York State considers the land as being held through an intermediary trust that allows the Mohawk to "use" it; the state did not offer title to the land. To the Mohawk, Ganienkeh is a sovereign nation.[4]

Like many fledgling endeavors, Ganienkeh has struggled over the years, but the community appears to have persevered and is planning for the future. The territory has a lumber mill, gardens, ranch, and a fish pond for subsistence purposes, as well as a holistic center, a nine-hole golf course, and a 1,500-seat Bingo Hall that pays for many bills. Ganienkeh is a drug and alcohol-free community as substance abuse and other social issues were factors in the original Moss Lake residents' desire to leave their reservations. The community began a total immersion school in 2005 to strengthen the Kanien′kehà:ka language. They govern by way of weekly community meetings where everyone has a voice, including the young. Important decisions are addressed in a formal Council of the Clans and specifically made by the Ganienkeh Council Fire. The community maintains contact with other Mohawk nations, and they have formed and reaffirmed alliances with other confederacy communities and peoples. In addition, they have done some outreach to local non-Indigenous institutions, such as policing organizations, to help educate them about Mohawk culture.[5] In the past, Iroquoian peoples created satellite communities to exert sovereignty and to emphasize "outward-facing, group-level autonomy," and Ganienkeh demonstrates this practice is still being carried on in the Adirondacks.[6]

Location of Exchange: Entangled Exchanges
Continue into the Twenty-First Century

By the twentieth century, a contradictory and complicated relationship between settler society Euro-Americans and Indigenous peoples had developed in the Adirondacks. When asked by writer Lynn Woods about working in the region, Akwesasne Mohawk elders claimed that they were not subjected to bigotry from local Adirondackers (unlike their encounters in communities near Akwesasne). However, they also did not want to talk much about these experiences, suggesting perhaps they were too polite to complain. In Woods's 1994 *Adirondack Life* article, Maurice Dennis's daughter, Andreé Dennis Newton, revealed that her parents had been subjected to prejudice by tourists in Old Forge, which may contradict accounts that imply a friendly relationship in and around the community. She described an experience her father endured when children laughed and threw stones at him on the train ride at the Enchanted Forest, where he ran the Abenaki Village.[7] Meanwhile, other Native and non-Native Adirondackers continued working together in various and less conspicuous occupations, and at times they continued to marry and raise families.

The Adirondacks of the twentieth century continued to be a place that Native peoples explored for resources, labor, and home. For example, Cherokee Joseph Pinetree and his wife, Grace Hill of Plainfield, New Jersey, moved with their son Joseph Tenderfoot Hill to Raquette Lake in 1925. Joseph Tenderfoot Hill was born in 1920 and started school in Raquette Lake, although he finished school in New York City, indicating the family had left the area at least on a year-round basis by the mid-1930s. However, Joseph Tenderfoot Hill returned to the area, and as an adult he operated excursion boats, a pickle boat, and a ferry. He was also an engineer on the Raquette Railroad that started at Blue Mountain Lake and ran north. In addition, he made baskets and other crafts from local wood and carved items for nearby churches.[8]

First Nations from Canada still crossed the border for the same reasons. Henry (1900–1963), Frank (1902–59), and Mitchell (1903–71) Nolett, the sons of Abenaki Frederick Nolett (1873–after 1930) left Odanak around 1912 to work in steel mills in the vicinity of Albany, New York. Mitchell Nolett moved for a time to Keene to sell baskets in a shop during the 1930s, but the Depression made it impossible for the family to remain there year round. Eventually, Mitchell's brother Henry opened a basket and souvenir shop on the Cascade Road (Route 73) between Keene and Lake Placid and ran it until the 1960s. At times, Mitchell and his family spent summers in Keene; his sister Germaine (or Jermaine) worked as a waitress at the Cascade Hotel, and his son Donald Sr. caddied at the AuSable Club during World War II.[9] As described in chapter 5, the family of Swift Eagle came to North Hudson in the 1950s to run the Indian village at Frontier Town, a local tourist attraction. Today, local Indigenous families, such as the Faddens and the Bruchacs, and individuals, such as Tom Sagogweniongwass Porter, Kay Ionataie:was Olan, and Denise Watso, educate the public about Iroquois and Abenaki history in the Adirondacks by creating and running museums, educational centers, and websites. They participate at regional events by speaking and telling time-honored stories. Many also write, sing, dance, and create art that reflects their culture in order to ensure the history of the original peoples are included in the Adirondacks and elsewhere.

A number of the Native families who settled in the region, as well as those who came later, kept in contact with their home reservation communities. Still others intermarried and appeared to forget about them. Sometimes subsequent generations became interested in their family and peoples' history. Mitchell Nolett wanted to forget about his Abenaki past, but his son Donald Sr. and grandson Donald Jr. were interested, and they subsequently resumed contact with Odanak.[10]

The granddaughters of Tyendinaga Mohawk John Battese (c. 1865–1904) illustrate the complexity of these family histories. Battese

224 | RURAL INDIGENOUSNESS

and his Euro-American wife, Edith Austin (1875–1942), lived in Long Lake and had a daughter named Izetta Belle (1895–1965). On at least one occasion, John brought his daughter to Tyendinaga for a ceremony, but she was afraid of the activities as she was unfamiliar with the cultural practices. According to family history, John died when Izetta was a child, and she and her mother moved in with her maternal grandfather. It is doubtful she ever returned to the reserve. Izetta later married Arthur J. Russell (1897–1936) in Long Lake, and they had nine children. When Izetta's husband died young, she moved in with her mother at Long Lake to raise her large family. Izetta's relatives knew that she and her children were part Mohawk. Indeed, visiting cousins once asked the children to perform an Indian dance, which of course they had no idea how to do, so they made something up. When Izetta passed away, the family was required to relinquish any claim to land on the Tyendinaga reserve. Today, Izetta's daughter, Beverly Locke, is interested in her Mohawk ancestry, while her sister Edith Russell is aware but not active in pursuing it.[11]

Others, such as Martha Lee Owens, are still looking for the origins of their specific Indigenous family member(s). In the meantime, they learn what they can about the Native peoples who lived and worked in the region, and they occasionally travel to investigate clues. Those seeking their family's roots express a sense of longing for that connection denied to them by their ancestors. However, they also realize there might have been good reasons for their family members' decision to give up that part of their identity to fit into the new community and era. Yet the records demonstrate that many did not, or perhaps could not, completely deny their Indian identity. Local Keene Valley lore describes Martha Lee Owens's great-grandmother, Florence Edmonds, having her babies by the river as an example of her maintaining Indigenous customs. Edmonds family history mentions that Florence used the nearby Johns Brook to clean up right after she had given birth.[12] When there is no running water in a home, a nearby brook was handy for such a task (although it probably was a cold experience). This may have been the practice of many Adirondackers, but somehow it was interpreted by the local community to express Florence's Aboriginal identity.

The Family of Andrew Joseph, Abenaki

Many of the Abenaki families who have been in the region since the late eighteenth and early nineteenth centuries are aware of their heritage and their relationship to the Adirondacks. The family of Abenaki Andrew Joseph is one example. Andrew's grandfather Pierre-Marie Magwa, or Peter Joseph, was born about 1811 in Canada to Joseph Magwa and his wife. It appears the family took on Joseph's first name for their Anglicized last name, which was not uncommon for the Abenaki. By 1870, Peter and his wife Theresa, or "Talasa," Saziboet (c. 1813–?) were living in Saratoga Springs. He was a basketmaker and she kept house, according to census records. Both claimed to be born in Canada, but Peter had become an American citizen. At least two of their children were living nearby. Theresa and Peter had three daughters born in New England states: Marie Louise (c. 1833–63?) was born in Vermont and married Vermonter Abram Burlett (1833–1909); Susan (c. 1836–before 1900) was born in Connecticut and married Quebec-born John M. Stone (c. 1834–after 1910?); and Sarah (c. 1842–1919) was born in Connecticut and married James E. Couse (c. 1843–after 1900?), who was born in New York State. All of the daughters' husbands were of European ancestry, but they were all listed as basketmakers on the 1870 federal census for Saratoga Springs. It is not entirely clear, but it appears that Louis, or Lewis, Joseph (1859–1934) was born in New York State to Sarah Joseph before she married James Couse, although it is possible he was the son of Peter and Theresa. Regardless, around 1889, Louis married fellow Abenaki Anna J. Miner (c. 1872–before 1920), born in Essex County, probably in Chesterfield. They discovered Long Lake was a good place to sell baskets, so they moved there from Saratoga by 1900. According to family history and the work of anthropologist Christopher Roy, they were distantly related through marriage to fellow Abenaki Mitchel Sabattis, who lived in the area.[13]

Louis and Anna Joseph rented a farmstead located between the farms of Mitchel Sabattis's sons Isaac and Charles. By 1900, the couple had three children, all born in New York State: James (1889–before 1979), Andrew (1892–1979), and Helen (1895–before 1979). Ten years later, the couple was still renting a house in Long Lake, and the family had grown by a daughter, Anna (1909–after 1979). Louis and his two sons James and Andrew often worked as laborers. We know from family history that Louis continued to make baskets, but neither he nor his sons ever declared basketmaking as their primary occupation. Anna Miner died between 1910 and 1920, and their two daughters continued to live with their father until at least 1920. Five years later, Louis was working as a laborer for a hotel, and his son Andrew and his family were living with him. By 1930, Andrew was the head of the household and Louis was living with his family. Louis died in 1934.[14]

Andrew Joseph was born at the Indian encampment at Saratoga Springs, and it is believed he was the last baby born there. The family moved to Long Lake by the time Andrew was eight years of age. Andrew and his mother were close, and he took her death before the age of fifty hard. Around 1918, Andrew married a Latvian immigrant by the name of Edith Savings (1896–1974), and they had six children together. The children of Andrew and Edith Joseph include Andrew "Andy" Savings (1918–91), Jane Joseph (1921–2012), Katherine "Kay" Joseph (1924–84), Edith (1927), John "Johnny" Joseph (1930), and Philip "Phil" Joseph (1934–2014).[15] Their story reflects the history of cultural continuity and change that occurred for Native families in the Adirondacks.

Fleeing from the violence in their Latvian homeland, the Savings family immigrated to New York City about 1915. Edith's father, Augustus, had been a well-to-do banker in Latvia, but they left most of their wealth behind. Edith's mother never got over her experience of forced immigration and she, like Anna Miner, died young. Edith's father eventually returned to Latvia. Edith could speak five languages (Latvian, Russian, German, French, and English) and was well-educated; she instilled in her children the need for a good education.

She came to Long Lake to work as a governess for the Johnny Schulte family. Andrew guided for Mr. Schulte through the Sagamore Hotel. According to Phil Joseph, Mr. Schulte thought Andrew would make a good husband for Edith, so he brought her with him and his family so the two could meet. Andrew apparently agreed with Mr. Schulte, as he set his sights on the young governess.[16]

Local records combined with family history demonstrate that Andrew was a hardworking and multitalented man. In addition to guiding, he was a produce dealer, a laborer, and a sought-after carpenter. He built the family home and continued to make improvements to it over time. In addition, Andrew sometimes caned seats for Adirondack guideboats, and he worked as a stone crusher during the Depression years for one dollar a day. Phil recalled his father selling vegetables and giving food to people when he knew they could not pay because he felt sorry for them, which sometimes made it hard on the family. "But that was dad's MO." His mother, Edith, felt less sorry for people, noting she had not received any handouts.[17]

As times changed, Andrew built and rented cabins and rooms in their home to accommodate sports and travelers from the early 1930s until 1953. The family's Long Lake business was known as "Joseph's Cabins." Andrew also told stories to the sports and in the community. Phil's wife, the former Wilma Black, confirmed that Andrew was a great storyteller.[18]

While hard working, Andrew was not always a sensible businessman. Phil Joseph recalled that his father refused to turn off the cabins' vacancy sign until every room was filled, even if he charged less than the cost of renting it. Phil stated that his father cut the price of an overnight stay to fill up the cabins and thought that was an achievement. However, this caused his mother to have more laundry to do, and thus they did not really make a profit. Phil's wife, Wilma, added that Andrew wanted to give his customers a lot for their money and worked many hours.[19]

Edith worked as hard as her husband. In addition to taking care of the family, she crocheted and made handiwork items such as quilts for the family and their business. Edith also sold some of these items in the family's gift shop, which she ran from the porch of their home. Once, a customer purchased a braided rug Edith made for approximately one hundred dollars. On a trip to New York City shortly thereafter, Edith discovered the rug for sale in a shop for four to five times as much as her customer had paid, which of course displeased her. The family had to occasionally send the police after guests who stole Edith's handmade quilts. In addition to the handicraft items by Andrew and Edith, the family also sold fireworks around the Fourth of July and flowers for Memorial Day. Edith helped run the cottages and guesthouse with the help of their six children. She made breakfast, lunch, and supper for the hunters and also washed towels for the Sagamore Hotel for five cents per towel. Similar to both Abenaki and rural Euro-American Adirondack families, Edith's work was gendered and complemented her husband's forms of labor and his enterprises. She was not always happy in the Adirondacks; like her mother, Edith did not want to be poor. She was a religious woman, though, and when they sold the cabins, she insisted on giving 10 percent to the Wesleyan Methodist Church. Andrew did his best to fix up their home to make his wife's life in the Adirondacks more enjoyable.[20]

Andrew Joseph was best known for his basketmaking, and he made them without a mold (fig. 7). He also made snowshoes, talking sticks, war clubs, and Abenaki wooden cups. According to his youngest son, Andrew made hundreds if not thousands of baskets during his lifetime. He learned his craft from his father, Louis. It took the pair less than a week to make eighteen to twenty-four baskets and sell them to Sullivan's, a local store in Long Lake. Father and son ferried their baskets across the lake to Sullivan's, which purchased them for nine dollars per dozen. In addition, Andrew sold some of his baskets from the gift shop at the house. Like other Native peoples during this era, Andrew occasionally donned a headdress to market his goods and to tell stories. He realized his customers wanted the headdress, and he was willing to give it to them to support his family. The headdress also signaled to his uninformed customers of Abenaki culture that these were genuine, Indian-made works of art. He was well-known in the central Adirondack region as an Abenaki, and his baskets are

7. Andrew Joseph baskets, collection of Philip Joseph. Photograph by Melissa Otis. Courtesy of the late Philip Joseph and his wife, Wilma Black Joseph.

his legacy. Unfortunately, Andrew did not usually sign his baskets, so there are many throughout the region that people do not realize he made.[21]

While many of the Joseph family's practices accommodated westernized North American culture, they also passed on Abenaki customs and skills. For example, at Phil's birth, Louis Joseph gave his grandson an Abenaki name, "Big Moose" (because he was such a large baby). Phil changed the name to "Straight Arrow" at the first opportunity, to better fit his adult life and because he disliked the name given to him at birth. Andrew taught Phil and his brothers how to fish, track, and hunt as early as the age of five. Phil believed they were skills his father thought an Abenaki man should know in order to feed his family. For example, Andrew instructed his sons to watch does feeding, as it was normal for them to precede the buck: "Bucks sent the does out to run interference." He taught his sons how to track deer and to know when an animal had been hit but kept running. (Phil explained that it's hard to track a specific deer because it is very probable it is not the only one there making tracks). On one occasion, Andrew insisted he had wounded a deer that ran off. Failing to see any evidence that the deer had been hit, Phil questioned his father's claim. Andrew brought his son to the spot where the deer was shot. They followed a deer's tracks until they found the buck's body. When asked how he knew he had hit the deer, Andrew brought Phil back to the original tracks and showed him where the deer's dew claws on the hind legs had left an imprint in the snow. Andrew could tell the buck had been hit because of the lack of stability in the deer's hind leg tracks. This is how he taught Phil not to walk on deer tracks so he could test for the stability of these claws. Phil explained that when he and his brothers hunted they sometimes became as excited as the sports; when that happened they failed to hit their target. His father rarely missed because he saw the animal as food on the table, and pro- viding for one's family required patience and composure.[22]

Phil also learned to trap and skin animals for the fur trade from his father. Phil recalled his father often taught his children to learn life's lessons through their own experience. Phil learned the hard way how to deal with different trapped animals. According to Phil, the beaver is a very intelligent animal; they are embarrassed when they get caught in a trap and bury their head in the mud. If a beaver had not drowned in the trap, Phil had to take it by the tail and "bop" it on the head. In addition to beaver, Phil and his father also trapped otter. Phil explained that the otter is offended when caught. The first time Andrew told Phil to "take care of" a trapped otter, Phil assumed he could treat the otter like a beaver. When Phil grabbed the otter by the tail it snapped at and tried to bite him. Phil complained to his father that he should have warned him about the otter's reaction, to which Andrew replied, "Now you know the difference between an otter and a beaver," and added, "now you will never forget it." Phil felt that his father always thought it was a joke when he had to teach Phil something Andrew believed an Indian should already know. This reference to animals with human emotions is representative of an Abenaki worldview that persists in the Adirondacks into the twenty-first century. These were relationships between humans and animals that needed to be respected as part of Abenaki (and other Algonquian and Iroquoian) weltanschauung.[23]

In addition, Andrew passed on his basketmaking skills to his two older sons, Andrew and John. John still makes baskets and makes sure to put his name on them. Phil, the studious son, educated others by talking to people about his family and the Abenaki. Before his death in 2014, Phil donated his father's basketmaking tools and some baskets to the Adirondack Experience museum to preserve his family's history in the area.[24] While fluent himself, Andrew chose not to teach his children the Abenaki language.

Like many in the Adirondacks, the Joseph family had to work hard and at a variety of jobs to make a comfortable living or just to make ends meet. However, non-Native Adirondackers did not have to contend with the notion their culture was destined to die out and that they were "the last." As discussed in chapter 2, declarations about Native peoples being the "last of their kind" assisted the dominant culture in clearing the landscape of its Indigenous citizens. Perhaps Edith Joseph could understand these ramifications better than most Americans, albeit from a different perspective. As an immigrant from Latvia, her family had experienced upheaval that required them to leave their homeland, and they experienced deprivations that had not previously existed. Both Andrew's and Edith's parents had struggled with the status quo, and even their generation had its difficulties. Edith did not always bear living in this rural area quietly, but her faith and her family kept her going.

The descendants of Andrew and Edith are distinctive in their upbringing, yet in a number of ways they are similar to other Adirondackers. Many have to leave the region to find work, but often one or two stay or come back, at least on a part-time basis. Edith and Andrew's children are reflective of this phenomenon. Andy and Kay remained in the Adirondacks, Edith and Phil did not move too far outside the Blue Line, while Jane and John lived in other states. Phil's life demonstrates the complexities of being a modern-day Abenaki Adirondacker. He is a card-carrying member of the Abenaki at Odanak, and his car's license plate reads "Abenaki," yet he is also a proud Adirondacker and proud of his Latvian heritage. Growing up in Long Lake had its benefits and tribulations. He was able to take advantage of the skills his Abenaki father taught him, but he also experienced prejudice in school from some of his classmates. In response, Phil chose to be studious. He became the valedictorian of his class and went to college, as did his sister Jane. Indeed, three of Andrew Joseph's children (Jane, Kay, and Phil) were the valedictorians of their class, which made their father very proud; he was known to brag about it in a town that he did not feel totally accepted him and his family. Phil went to Syracuse University and lived away from the Adirondacks for some of his adult life. In retirement, he made Indian Lake his seasonal home while wintering in Florida.[25]

The Family of John Fadden, Mohawk

John David Kahionhes Fadden's family history is similar to the Joseph family's narrative, but it is also very different. Much like other Mohawk individuals and families who lived or still live in the Adirondacks, the Fadden family maintains close ties to Akwesasne. John was born in 1938 in Massena near the reservation of Akwesasne on the New York State side of the border. His father, Ray Fadden (1910–2008), was born in the Adirondacks at his grandfather's farm in Onchiota, and he attended college at Fredonia Normal School in western New York, graduating in 1934. Ray immediately went to work as an elementary school teacher at the Tuscarora Indian School on the Tuscarora Reservation near Niagara Falls, New York. It was here that he met Mohawk Christine Chubb (1912–2014).

Born at the farm of her maternal grandparents, Louis and Katherine Back, Christine Mary Skawennati Chubb grew up on the American side of Akwesasne. Around 1924, the family moved to Niagara Falls, where her father, Mitchell Kanawakta ("near the brook") Chubb, went to work for the Carborundum plant. Christine described her grandparent's farm in Akwesasne as having huge gardens; they also probably raised dairy cattle and pigs. The Back's even tried raising sheep once, but that did not work out. Christine must have helped on the farm, as she bore a scar on the base of her chin from the horns of a cow that had lifted its head while waiting in a stanchion. Christine went to high school in Niagara Falls and held several jobs there, and she helped her mother, Louise Tewenniiosta ("good words") Back Chubb, make baskets. After a short courtship, Ray and Christine married in 1935. Ray worked in the state's Indian Education System and after a few years he was transferred to the St. Regis Mohawk School at Akwesasne. This move allowed Ray and Christine to return to the area of their births, and it was here that John, their only child, was born. John grew up mostly in Hogansburg, the main community at Akwesasne. For a brief while though, the family lived in Fort Covington, New York, a town about nine miles east of the reservation. John recalls this was the only place he ever experienced and witnessed racism toward himself and other Mohawk. Ray eventually got a job teaching seventh grade science at the Saranac Central School District, where he remained until he retired in 1967. The Fadden family spent their summers at Onchiota, and after John went to college in 1957 Ray and Christine moved there permanently.[26]

Growing up on and near the reservation and spending summers in the Adirondacks gave John an engaging childhood, and being the son of Ray Fadden was an even more compelling experience. The Fadden family originally summered with John's grandfather, Carroll Fadden Sr., in Onchiota, but eventually Ray and Christine had a house built there for themselves. As a boy, John met some of the local youths, but mostly he read a lot and went camping, often using the two birchbark canoes the family owned. Sometimes friends and family from Akwesasne came to visit, and they would canoe and go berry picking. John recalls an incident in which his Mohawk grandmother, Louise, went berry picking and did not return as quickly as the family thought she should. Concerned, Ray and his father, Carroll, went looking for her, calling out for her as they searched. Around dusk, John saw his grandmother's silhouette in the distance; she was carrying two buckets of blueberries. When she reached the house, Louise commented to her daughter, Christine, "Say, I heard some men yelling back there, I don't know what they're yelling at." When the Fadden men returned, Louise denied being lost, but Ray never believed it.

According to John, Mohawk from Akwesasne still come to the Adirondacks to pick berries and plants for medicine, especially at summer's end. For example, in the summer of 2013 a pickup truck and a car traveling in tandem pulled up next to John outside of the museum. The driver of the truck was a young Mohawk man who greeted him and indicated he was looking for John. "I'm John," Fadden replied, and the young man continued, "Oh, my grandfather Harvey said to ask you where there's turtle stocking" (a type of medicine plant). John pointed out where it would be located.[27] In many ways, John Fadden is a liaison for reservation communities and the Adirondacks as much as he is an educator for non-Native peoples about Iroquois culture in and around the region.

As chapter 5 describes, Ray Fadden was a passionate promoter of Haudenosaunee culture and history, and he included his family in his efforts. John recalls being taken to the Ticonderoga pageants at Tom Cook's farm at the age of four or five. His most vivid memory of this experience was of the White actors dressed up and walking around in Indian regalia early in the day as they waited for the pageant to begin. Being such a young child, he thought, "God this must be where the Indians live!" Recounting this memory, John was reminded of a recent occurrence: two of his granddaughters were visiting him and his wife, Eva Thompson, when somebody mentioned there were some Native people at the nearby museum. A bit later, his granddaughter Hailey arrived at the museum and asked "Where's the Indians?" She was looking for people in feathers and meanwhile, John thought, "They're all standing around her!" Hailey, now seven, was about the same age John was when he had his similar experience. John mused that as a child, "You don't even really know what [being Indian] is, you know."[28]

As a youth, John participated in several of his father's endeavors, including the Akwesasne Mohawk Counselor Organization and the Lake George Indian Village, both described in chapter 5. He was also involved in the running of the Six Nations Indian Museum, which opened in the summer of 1954 with Ray's collection housed inside the structure he built together with outside displays. Ray ran the museum with the help of his wife, Christine, as well as John, who never had another summer off until recently. Ray never kept a set schedule for the museum. He used to open as soon as anyone drove up, and he kept it open until the last person left, seven days a week. John recalls that in the early years they even worked with lamplight before the museum had electricity. Christine was in charge of ordering souvenirs and crafts, operating the small souvenir shop at the museum, and collecting admission. In addition, she made and sold her beadwork there. Christine also kept the museum clean and pointed out to Ray where repairs were needed. In describing his parents' work at the museum, John explained: "My father was more passionate about the whole thing, you know, the Indian history and so forth. My mother . . . she could get along with anybody who'd come in. She'd chitchat about the weather or whatever; she was more down to earth, I'd say, whereas my father was a person with a mission."[29]

Whether Christine minded being moved from her home at Akwesasne into the isolated hamlet of Onchiota we do not know. It most certainly was an adjustment for her, especially since she did not drive. At Akwesasne, Christine had neighbors and family nearby, and she was involved in activities, such as the Homemaker's Club. Onchiota has no town center and is nestled between ponds and state camping sites; one has to travel fifteen miles to Saranac Lake to get groceries and other necessities. Besides taking care of her family and the museum, Christine joined the Gray Ladies, a volunteer organization that helped patients at the General Hospital of Saranac Lake (now called the Adirondack Medical Center), which she enjoyed.

From 1957 to 1961, John attended the Rochester Institute of Technology, where he earned a bachelor of fine arts degree and majored in illustration. He notes that he never experienced racism there. The few times his Mohawk heritage came up, the other students found it interesting and asked thoughtful questions about what it was like. After graduating, John returned home and eventually got a job as an art teacher at the Saranac Central School District, where he taught for over thirty-two years.

In the spring of 1963, John and a friend of his from Akwesasne named Glen "Glenny" Lazore traveled with Ray to South Dakota and visited historic sites along the way, such as the Serpent Mound in Ohio and Cahokia across the river from St. Louis, Missouri. On this trip they met sculptor Korczak Ziolkowski (1908–82), who was carving a likeness of Crazy Horse into a mountainside in the Black Hills of South Dakota. Ziolkowski began working on the huge monument in 1948, and his children and now grandchildren continue working on it to this day. During their chance meeting, Ray and Korczak hit it off and spent hours talking. Both men were equally passionate about Native American history and culture, and John and Glen just sat back and listened to them. During the conversation, Ziolkowski mentioned that the Catholic Lakota wanted him to carve a monument of Mohawk Kateri Tekakwitha. However, Ziolkowski did not have any images of Mohawk women. John and Glen offered to help him by taking some photographs of Mohawk women from Akwesasne and sending them to the artist.

After the trio returned home in April, John and Glen arranged to meet in May to locate Mohawk women willing to have their photographs taken for the Ziolkowski project. On the agreed-upon date, John arrived at Akwesasne with his camera. He picked up his friend, and the pair decided Glen would talk to the girls and tell them about the project. If they were interested, John would proceed to photograph them. However, Glen never told any of the girls about the project, and John had to quickly explain to some very suspicious Kanienkehaka women why he wanted to take their photographs. Meanwhile, Glen decided this would be a good opportunity to have

John take the photograph of a young woman he thought would be a good match for John. The pair drove to the Thompson family home, where John first met Eva. Perhaps wondering who was coming to their home so early in the morning, Eva peered out of an upstairs window, "almost like Romeo and Juliet," John recalls. Eva, however, was a bit suspicious; speaking Mohawk to Glen, she asked what they wanted. Glen convinced her to come outside and have her photograph taken. John sent the photograph of Eva and other young Mohawk women to Ziolkowski, who never acknowledged receiving the photographs (John did not know if he ever used them for a sculpture nor could I find evidence Ziolkowski ever made the statue). John did not see Eva again for some months.

Meanwhile, Eva's sister Lillian moved to Lake Placid, originally to work at the Lake Placid Club. While there, she met Gary LeFebvre, who owned a dry cleaning business. Gary convinced Lillian to come to work for him, and the pair eventually married. Gary and Lillian visited the Six Nations Museum, and John got to know them a bit. One summer day in 1963 they arrived with Eva, who was visiting them. Ultimately, Gary and Lillian invited John to come to their home for a meal and to play board games. "I hate board games!" John emphatically states, "But I went because she looked kind of nice. And the rest is history."[30]

John and Eva married on July 17, 1965, at the St. Regis Mohawk Catholic Church at Akwesasne, despite John's more traditional belief system. The couple have three sons—Donald, David, and Daniel—and all three were raised at Onchiota. At the age of four or five, each boy was given a traditional Mohawk name through the Longhouse. John explains that at Akwesasne there are multiple and complex belief systems that sometimes become politicized. There are those who follow traditional beliefs and support the Mohawk Nation Council of Chiefs. They attend a cycle of ceremonies and "other elements of culture that exists within that format." Then there are Mohawk who are Christians, some of who speak Mohawk, but they do not follow any of the traditions or, if they do participate, treat the traditions as folk culture. One of these traditions is that the oldest woman in the mother's family gives a newborn their name. John's grandmother, Louise Back Chubb, gave him the name Kahionhes, which means "Long River" and was the name of her grandfather. John explains further:

> Within the Longhouse tradition, there are names that are kept, that are ancient names that go way back. . . . [T]hose names are given when a child is born. They are given according to clan. They are given either during the Mid-winter Ceremonies, or during the Strawberry Ceremony which is in the spring. The infant is brought to the ceremony, and then the person who brings the child, holds up him or her; it's like they introduce the baby to the whole community. The speaker announces who his mother is, her clan and who the child's father is and so forth. Then they would speak/pronounce his or her name, and then it's like everyone would know who it is and where he/she comes from. Whereas among the Christian Mohawks, they don't necessarily do that. They don't have an event where they hold up the baby. The closest would be when the baby gets baptized.[31]

The grandmother who gave John his Mohawk name mixed Christianity with more traditional spiritual practices, as she attended both the Catholic Church and some events at the Longhouse. In the past, the church was not supportive of this mixing of belief systems, but John believes that concern is not as strong as it used to be. In addition to Kahionhes, John was given a traditional name "from a repository of names from each of the clans, I was given one of those names from the turtle clan." However, he signs all of his artwork with Kahionhes to honor the grandmother who gave him that name. Every member of John's family has a Mohawk name, including his father. Ray was given the name Tehanetorens, meaning "he parts the pines" (splits the pitch) and was adopted by the wolf clan to honor his efforts working with the local youth at Akwesasne, as well as for his work and publications of Haudenosaunee history and culture. Christine's Mohawk name, Skawennati, means "the other side of the word," although Ray jokingly often said it meant "the last word." Eva's Mohawk name is Karonhesake, or "searching sky," and she is a member of the wolf clan, as are their three sons. John wanted the boys to be old enough to know what was happening and remember their naming ceremony at the Longhouse. Too old to be held up, each son stood for their commemoration. The two older boys were given a name by their maternal great grandmother, Christie Mitchell, and the youngest was named by Eva's mother, Elizabeth Thompson. The Mohawk names of John and Eva's sons Don, Dave, and Dan are, respectively, Tehonatake ("he has two towns"), Kanietakeron ("patches of snow"), and Kanentiio ("nice pines").[32]

John and Eva began their marriage living in Saranac Lake, where Eva worked at the American Management Association for a year while John worked at Saranac Hollow School, near Plattsburgh. In the summers he and eventually Eva worked at the museum. In the years following, the couple moved toward Onchiota, where they eventually built the home they have lived in for over forty years. Like her mother-in-law, Eva had to adjust from living in a close-knit community to being "stuck in the woods." Having been involved with the museum since it opened in 1954, John gradually inherited its management from his parents in the 1980s. Christine was happy to turn over the running of the museum to John and Eva, but Ray could not let go entirely until his health failed. As John notes, "You can't do a thing like that with that passion and just forget it."

After a season or two of following Ray's concept of no schedule, John and Eva decided to make some changes. Based on attendance records, they determined that the busiest times were between 10 a.m. and 5 p.m. and that Monday was slow, so they took Monday off and opened the other days on a regular basis between those hours in July and August. In addition, they often opened for groups and others, such as researchers. Ray was not happy with the changes, but John stood his ground. Eva took over the duties Christine had previously carried out at the museum. As a fluent speaker of Mohawk, Eva is also John's expert when it comes to language questions. Christine spoke Mohawk, too, but moving to Niagara Falls around the age of twelve gave her no one except her family to speak the language with. Her father, Mitchell Chubb, had attended a boarding school in Pennsylvania near Philadelphia called the Franklin Institute. When Mitchell returned to Akwesasne, he mispronounced words and people laughed at him, so he stopped speaking Mohawk. Mitchell understood the language, and his wife often spoke to him in Mohawk, but he responded in English. John recalls his grandmother coming to stay with them for an extended period when he was about three or four years of age. During this visit, his mother and grandmother conversed in Mohawk regularly. Unfortunately for John, once his grandmother left, his mother had no one to speak the language with at home, so he did not learn to speak Mohawk beyond a few words.

During his tenure running the museum, John found that almost everyone was open to what they had to offer; although he is quick to note that not all visitors get the same experience. "It all depends on who shows up, their observable interests and how many there are. Like if there is just one guy you're not going to sit him down and give him a forty five minute lecture. You know, you suggest that there's plenty to read and if you have any comments or you have questions about anything, just fire away."[33] They get visitors from around the world and host on-site classes for nearby schools and universities. Sometimes visitors return or keep in touch in a variety of ways, and they have made some lasting friendships as a result.[34]

However, some are not as respectful or open to the message the museum and the family offer. Ray especially ran into problems with visitors who questioned his ardent lectures, and he occasionally got into arguments with them. John seems to have inherited his mother's temperament and noted that he doubts his father ever won anyone over with his contentious style. But even John gets angry with the comments he sometimes hears. A recent example is illustrative. On a slow day during the summer of 2014, Don and Dave were standing outside on the landing of the museum enjoying the weather when a pickup truck pulled up. The driver got out and approached the Fadden brothers and inquired if they were Native. Once confirmed, he asked them their opinion about the controversy over the Washington, DC, football team's name. David explained that the name was insulting and why. He also provided other, equally insulting name examples in comparison. After listening to David's argument and examples, the pickup truck driver said "I don't think that's true. I don't believe that" and then drove away. "So that guy, he had the chance to hear; he even came looking for a Native view and he got it but he rejected it," explains John, adding with humor, in his typical moderating style, "Plus, he didn't pay admission! He didn't even come in."[35]

In addition to educating the public with the museum, many members of the Fadden family have been artists, including the women, who have expressed their creativity through craftmaking as well as other art forms. As noted previously, Ray painted and created illustrations for his pamphlets and other educational pieces, and Christine made baskets with her mother and created beadwork to sell at the museum. John's artwork has appeared in over eighty publications, posters, book cover designs, calendars, films, and videos, and his paintings have been exhibited throughout the United States and Canada and as far away as Rotterdam in the Netherlands. In the past, Eva did beadwork, was a potter and woodcarver; she sold her art at the museum and had her carvings exhibited in other venues.

All three sons grew up drawing and painting and have a flair for art. However, it is the middle son, David, who is most directly following in his father's footsteps. Dave Fadden is an artist and storyteller, and is involved in education and museum work. His artwork has been displayed in the United States and Canada. Dave has also illustrated and done covers for books. In 2013, he wrote and illustrated a children's book entitled *Kaheriio's Busy Day*, which is written in both English and a shorter Mohawk-language version. He is in the process of creating a series that will include a female lead, too. Dave plans to use the books to teach the Mohawk language and their legends. In addition, he works with the Native North American Travelling College, headquartered on Cornwall Island on the Canadian side of Akwesasne, and the Iroquois Museum at Howe's Cave, and he is also helping with the redevelopment of the Ganondagan Museum near Rochester, New York. The family is also involved with the Adirondack attraction known as the Wild Center in Tupper Lake. Along with other experts they are assisting the attraction with incorporating an Iroquoian perspective into its installations.[36] When asked if he and his family were ever thought of as Adirondack artists, John paused. "I don't know" he responded. Eva felt they were considered to be Mohawk artists. John had to agree, noting that when he has exhibited his artwork "most of the time it's been in places with other Native people exhibiting." He pointed out he has illustrated for the regional magazine *Adirondack Life*, as well as displayed his artwork at North Country Community College and the Lake Placid Council for the Arts, "but again they were about Native topics."[37]

After thirty-two years, John retired from his school teaching duties in 1994. He and Eva recently turned the full-time management of the museum over to Dave and Don. All three sons were brought up and worked there when they were young. The eldest son, Don, donates his time. Their youngest son, Dan, lives in Lake Placid with his family and works full time for the Uihlein Nursing Home. His hours are too erratic to work at the museum. In the past, Dan expressed his interest in history in a creative manner by participating as a historical reenactor together with his wife, Kim. He played the part of a Mohawk while Kim played the role of a colonial woman during the eighteenth century. They still have the attire and interest, but work and family oblige them to spend their leisure time with other pursuits.[38]

The histories of the Joseph and Fadden families illustrate that Haudenosaunee and Algonquian peoples remain part of the narrative of the Adirondacks to the present day. Their (and other Indigenous peoples') histories here continue to demonstrate the continuities and changes that exist and occur between Native peoples and the region. As the introduction and chapter 1 describe, a location of exchange is a reciprocal relationship between the land and the peoples who share it. Phil Joseph was proud of his roots in the Adirondacks and of his Abenaki heritage, and he talked to anyone who would listen about the history of his family and the Abenaki in the Adirondacks. Indeed, it was Phil's dream that the Abenaki have a recognized homeland within their territory south of the Canadian border, and this was his way of contributing toward that vision. To Phil, the telling of this history was as much a mission for him as the telling of Iroquois history was to Ray Fadden. Likewise, John Fadden and his family continue this mission through the museum, teaching, performing, and artwork that honors their Mohawk heritage. The Fadden family, like other Adirondack Mohawk families, remain closely tied to their Kanienkehaka community, especially Akwesasne. As previous chapters demonstrate, over time Abenaki families became less connected to Odanak, and some eventually chose to go to Akwesasne (especially the Catholic Church there) and eventually looked to their Adirondack communities to assume important observances such as baptisms, marriages, and burials. Although in the past their distant Native community would have filled these functions, that does not mean all Abenaki have abandoned their Odanak community; for some it just became less important in their daily lives. While many of the Adirondack Iroquois and Abenaki families can trace their roots to specific ancestors and Indigenous communities, they are also deeply connected to their Adirondack communities. These family histories go beyond the sensibility that they are "part Indian" solely as a matter of ethnic heritage.

Survivance and Rural Indigenousness

The history of Native peoples who chose to make a living in tourism by guiding, demonstrating their woodcraft at summer camps, making and selling handicrafts and souvenirs, and performing Indianness in and around the Adirondacks clearly demonstrate that the tourist marketplace of the nineteenth and early twentieth centuries essentialized their identity. Cherokee sociologist Eva Marie Garroutte defines *essentialism* as those ideas that presuppose "a connection to ancestry rooted in the individual's fundamental nature."[39] While this book has mentioned time and again that many of these Indigenous family members worked in commercial resource enterprises and other jobs, it is tourism work that is featured because the records are available and tourism has been and still is a very important industry in the Adirondacks. During the wilderness tourism era, these jobs provided a good income for Indigenous families on a seasonal basis. As I argued in earlier chapters, they took advantage of their ethnicity, which became less and less their own specific nation's identity, and some of their traditional skills, at least in a foundational sense, which they adapted to fit the place and era. American historian Boyd Cothran calls this negotiation of the borders of ethnic identity in exchange for labor and wages an "economy of authenticity." Cothran explains that this economy allowed Native peoples some agency. However, that agency was constrained by the marketplace, which was controlled by expectations of them and those who "policed the boundaries of visibility."[40]

Native American studies scholar Scott Richard Lyons (Anishinabe-Dakota) argues that when scholars talk about Indigenous identity, they need to get away from seeing Indian peoples as "being" something and instead study what it is that Indigenous peoples "do" during a given period and under specific historical conditions.[41] Lyons goes on to explain that traditions, ceremonies, principles, and values are still important, but that some aspects are negotiable and change over time. Anishinabe writer and American studies scholar Gerald Vizenor has repurposed the French term *survivance* to further explain Lyon's argument. Vizenor defines survivance as "more than the ordinary act of survival. Survivance is an active sense of native presence over absence, or sense of presence in native stories over absence of natives in histories. Survivance is a renunciation, or rejection, of the political and cultural dominance, and the unbearable sentiments of tragedy and victimry. Survivance is native courage, spirit, and native traditions."[42] American Indian studies scholar and White Earth Anishinabe Jill Doerfler contends that Indigenous peoples who selectively choose "adaptions to maintain their quality of life within a rapidly changing world" are engaging in survivance.[43]

The mostly Abenaki, Oneida, and Mohawk peoples who chose to live in the Adirondacks during the nineteenth century and later, were, and are still, clearly engaged in survivance. Further, I suggest that those Indigenous peoples living among settler society in a rural space are in a unique situation, especially as it pertains to identity issues. Living in and around a rural community is not so different from living on a rural reservation that is located near the dominant culture. As a result, some of the skills, jobs, and lifeways are similar, which may lead some to think this history is being essentialized or that all Native peoples in this situation assimilated into White, rural society.

In the Northeast, so long as an Algonquian or Iroquoian family did not (and does not) live in a rural community *near* the reservation, they mostly got (and get) along with the majority Euro-American population with whom they worked and socialized. Despite histories that suggest otherwise, some of the Native peoples in the Adirondacks and their descendants did not assimilate into rural society. Without a doubt, some did choose to acculturate, but for many Indigenous families there, and I suspect in other rural environments, their Native identities are well known within the local community, especially if they lived in the area for generations. And for many like Phil Joseph and John Fadden and his family, that distinctiveness goes beyond the sense that their Indigenous identity is nothing more than being "part Indian." I suggest that we need a concept to include Indigenous peoples, both historically and presently, who live(d) in a nonreservation space that is rural and dominated by Euro–North Americans. I offer for consideration the notion of *rural indigenousness.*

The concept of *rural* is challenging to define. Merriam Webster's definition "of or relating to the country and the people who live there instead of the city" is not particularly helpful. As discussed in the introduction, the Adirondacks are not rural in the sense that the region is an agricultural space. Instead its rurality was, and is, based on resource-driven economies and low population scattered about a large region with a challenging terrain. Thus, the environment plays a vital role in determining how a rural space is used and lived in. Also, as noted in chapter 3, rural as a concept is neither established nor constant. It takes on various understandings based on whether one lives there and is having their behavior subjected to the surveillance of their community or if the local population and the space are being gazed upon by outsiders. As a result, rural is often defined by the sparseness of population numbers: the federal governments of Canada and the United States loosely draw the line at less than ten thousand.[44] However, rural is more than a smaller version of urban; rural is as much a way of life that often involves the landscape. For example, Phil Joseph understood the techniques he learned for hunting, fishing, and trapping as Abenaki skills because these were the capabilities his Abenaki father taught him. These may or may not have been some or all of the same proficiencies any rural father would teach his son, and the occasional daughter, but to Phil these were competencies any Abenaki should know. Whether the children of Abenaki parents who moved to the Albany region to find work in factories were taught these skills or found them important beyond sport is doubtful. But, in a rural environment like the Adirondacks, hunting, fishing, and trapping were, and still are, valuable aptitudes to be familiar with to help supplement a family's wages and put protein on the table. Once Phil studied for and got a university degree and began to work with computers in Syracuse, hunting, fishing, and trapping were no longer critically important for food, but that did not change how he thought about his past. John Fadden fondly recalls canoeing, camping, and berry picking as favorite pastimes while summering in the Adirondacks as a youth. Today, his granddaughters play in the woods, and one of them, Hailey, is able to feed a chickadee from her hand. Akwesasne citizens still travel to the Adirondacks for healing plants and sweetgrass. These are not typical urban, or even suburban, practices, but they are activities for those who live in or near this rural space.

Rural is also about accepting that one has to travel for services, although a few small towns may have some essential ones, such as a grocery store, especially those communities that are county seats or larger tourist towns. Both Phil Joseph and the Fadden family accept that they have to travel a number of miles to get groceries or to access other essential services, such as healthcare and even farther to obtain luxuries like clothing, entertainment, and the like, as many Adirondackers do. Not everyone who lives in a rural space has the same experiences, but certainly these are ways of living that do not occur for the vast majority of peoples who live in urban and suburban areas. Indeed, some urbanites and suburbanites even criticize rural ways of living that they do not understand, especially activities such as hunting, fishing, and trapping.

For the purpose of considering rural indigenousness, I define *rural* as a geographic space where the landscape dictates how people live, work (whether actually there or having to commute long distances to work where the jobs are), and experience leisure activities. Essential services readily available to urbanites and suburbanites are not easily available in these spaces, so mobility is vital to survival. The population is under ten thousand people and generally sparse, although small town centers sometimes increase the density.

Rural indigenousness involves Indigenous individuals and families who live off-reservation in a rural space, as described above, and where they are a minority population among usually Euro–North Americans, whose culture currently dominates this space. These places can be part of the Indigenous person's original homeland, but this is not required.

Questions immediately arise regarding the difference between an assimilated individual who is ethnically Native American and a person who falls under the concept of rural indigenousness. Also, can the identity of a person or their family change based on their actions regarding their status, such as reconnecting with their family on reserve or leaving it? As a person who is not Indigenous to North America I cannot make this judgment call. As a historian, however, I cannot ignore what the records are clearly revealing. I can work with other scholars' ideas and ask questions based on my research, and then allow others who have more warrant than I to debate whether this notion of rural indigenousness has merit and, if so, how and where it fits into the larger discourse of Indigenous identity issues.

Indigenous identity in North America is complicated when dealing with Native peoples living on reservations and reserves. Issues of blood quantum, kinship, and band lists are often factors used to determine acceptance by or refusal into an Aboriginal community that fears the diminishment of limited resources and changing notions of sovereignty. Those Indigenous peoples living in urban, suburban, and rural spaces create an even more challenging identity discourse. Bonita Lawrence's *"Real" Indians and Others* describes how the colonial practices of the nation states of Canada and the United States came to define and regulate who was "Indian," thereby divesting Indigenous nations of their sovereignty and ability to negotiate as a society. Canada uses the Indian Act (1876) and its multiple amendments, whereas the United States bases its Indigenous population's identity on a variety of judicial and legislative decisions. Lawrence convincingly argues that all of these forms of identity framing were genocidal and meant to eventually erode power from Indigenous nations and divest them of their remaining territories. Native women who married non-Native men and their children were especially singled out in Canada; they were often the nexus for most non-status Indians in Canada. For matrilocal societies like the Haudenosaunee, "removing women . . . was key to privatizing the land base."[45] The United States was a bit less sexist; they used blood quantum to make their decision on who was a "real" Indian. Today some reservations and reserves in both countries are adopting the measurement of blood quantum to determine who belongs to their community, and who does not.

Lawrence's exploration of why some Native peoples wound up in urban areas and how they coped there is useful for my work in rural regions. Lawrence describes a variety of coping strategies that Indigenous peoples in urban spaces have used, including silence, passing as White, adapting, and resisting. All of these are very similar survival strategies employed, when they could be, by Indigenous peoples living in a rural environment. A major difference between the experiences of Native peoples in urban and rural places is that Indigenous families or individuals living in rural areas often cannot hide their heritage. In the Adirondacks, Indians generally may have been vanished from the region's history, but rarely did the identity of Native individuals and families vanish from the small town or hamlet where they lived. In addition, both rural and urban Indigenous peoples have similar issues that come with living off-reserve, such as having wide ranges of experience, increased likelihood of intermarrying with non-Indians, upward mobility, and assimilation pressures that have a negative effect on their Native identity. Some of the ranges of experience include being connected to a reservation community, or not; knowing and maintaining ties with their families on reserve, or not; and practicing traditional ways, or not. Interestingly, some of the urban Indigenous peoples who had contact with a reserve setting consider traditional beliefs to be part of practicing "a land-based process," not unlike Phil Joseph.[46]

With regard to identity discourse, where do Indigenous peoples living among the dominant society in a rural environment fit? Do individuals whose family moved to a rural setting or have lived there for generations still have an Indigenous identity? Those with direct kinship ties to a reservation can, and do, usually maintain that identity, although it is shared with their rural status as well. But what about those individuals and families who have been divested of their reserve community, or no longer know who their specific community is? These are complicated questions.

As we know, *kinship* has been an important and valuable institution for Native peoples, and it has been used in a variety of ways throughout history—including marrying or adopting non-Indigenous peoples into their nation. These ways continue in the present, as personified by Ray Fadden's experience of marrying a Mohawk woman and being adopted into the wolf clan because of his efforts to champion Mohawk history and culture. Garroutte argues that the degree of a kinship relationship is not as important as the physical relationship. She adds that "one either belongs to the ancestors or one does not, and the notion of fractionating one's essential substance . . . is untenable." To reinforce her argument, Garroutte refers to sociologist Joane Nagel's study of individuals who reclaimed their Native heritage. Nagel found that identity is "*both* optional and mandatory," meaning that while an individual can self-identify into a certain ethnicity, it is the society writ large that legitimizes or denies the individual, family, or group's assertions. This argument is similar to the concepts of "emic" and "etic" coined by the linguistic anthropologist Kenneth Pike (1954). *Emic* focuses on cultural distinctions that are meaningful to the members of a given society and *etic* relies on the scientific, or an outsiders meaning. Historian Daniel K. Richter uses the terms "emic history" and "etic history" in his 1993 article "Whose Indian History?" concerning the kinds of narratives of the past and, in his case, what the role of myth is. He characterizes the term "emic analysis" as a search to comprehend phenomena from an *insider's* perspective, whereas "etic analysis" comes from an *outsider's* standpoint.[47] Richter argues that historians, as scholars, take an etic stance. He does not distinguish whether the scholar is Indigenous or not, so it is logical to conclude it is the analysis of the historian that creates etic history. Richter then proceeds to argue that the historian's connection to the present is what turns "scholarly eticism" into an "emic purpose." Thus, my work as a scholar of history (especially since I am of European ancestry) demonstrates the etic perspective, despite any efforts I make to understand the insider's position. Yet the research is revealing and useful to consider alongside other identity discourse, therefore the sharing of my research and analysis has an emic purpose.

Indigenous peoples residing in a nonreservation rural setting exist in an unusual space and contend with complex and multifaceted notions of identity. Thus, defining rural indigenousness will inevitably be ambiguous and flexible. Those Indigenous peoples who have connections to and maintain strong ties to reservation communities, such as John Fadden and his family, obviously do have a strong Indigenous identity that needs no other support. Where identities in rural areas become problematic are the cases of those individuals and families who have lost those associations. Some, like Phil Joseph and Donald Nolett Jr., reestablished formal connections with their ancestors' community. Indeed, today, Abenaki who have direct ties to Odanak but are living elsewhere, including in the United States, can vote in their reserve elections. However, this recognition is not available to all Abenaki. Those individuals and families who cannot provide formal evidence of their family's affiliation to Odanak are not recognized as members of what has become known as Western Abenaki there. Vermonters claiming Abenaki heritage without ties to Odanak have recently received state recognition, but to date there is no federal recognition, nor does Odanak recognize them. And as Native peoples intermarry with Euro–North Americans, some may find their children or grandchildren do not have enough "blood quantum percentage" to remain enfranchised with their ancestral community, depending on the reservation. Recent Supreme Court decisions in Canada are loosening these restrictions at a federal level; however, reserves are still struggling with the ramifications of these decisions. The United

States lets reservations decide, but invariably it is blood quantum that most reservations use to make important acknowledgment decisions.

In addition, there are individuals and families who lack a formal connection to a recognized Indigenous society. Yet they, and often their rural community, sense their identity (usually based on an Aboriginal ancestor), and as a result they are accepted as a Native person or family. Some know their people or the community, but they are disconnected from one or both. If they are interested and not too timid, a few take the first steps to reconnect with their Indigenous family, but many are wary of the response they might receive. Meanwhile, others do not know who their ancestors' community is, and they use the few clues available to them to look for it. Adopting features from both Garroutte and Lawrence's work concerning identity issues, one might draw the admittedly socially constructed line of *rural indigenousness* at an individual, or individuals, whose family history connects them to known Indigenous ancestry and a shared history with an Indigenous community, nation, or band. They have an understanding of self as an Indigenous person to the point that they express it in a personal profession of their identity to their rural community and to an Indigenous one, if it is available. This personal profession of identity cannot be characterized, as it will be different for everyone, from driving a car with the license plate "Abenaki" to being recognized as a Native artist.

Recognition of this type of indigeneity and by whom is another issue that is complicated, as is the question, does it even matter? Bonita Lawrence's *Fractured Homeland* describes the multiple situations that nonstatus Ottawa Valley Algonquins find themselves in as they assert their nonreserve identity in the face of land claims. Referencing Glen Coulthard's concept of the "politics of recognition," Lawrence notes that Indigenous peoples without the benefit of reserve recognition often have their identities "distorted by misrecognition" to prevent them from thriving in a political environment that is mainly concerned with resources and sovereignty by both the nation-state and the reservation power base. The latter has to accept these definitions to receive funding, acknowledgement of their limited authority, and the like. Lawrence suggests that Indigenous peoples need to reject the nation-states' defining of Indigenous and instead look to their traditional forms and practices of citizenship.[48] Certainly recognition by a reservation or an Aboriginal community adds credence to a rural Indigenous individual or family's claim of indigeneity. As noted above, recognition by the nation-state is fraught with notions of colonialism and sovereignty issues; they are not casual observers. Concerning the notion of rural indigenousness, does it matter whether the rural district, or perhaps a region like the Adirondacks, acknowledges the individual(s) or family's Indigenous identity? After all, it is to this community that the individual and families express their indigeneity, and sometimes the community includes them in events or local decisions based on that expression. I have no prescriptive answer other than to suggest that, based on my conversations with Indigenous Adirondackers and reading the (sometimes heartbreaking) online comments that accompany articles around off-reserve indigeneity, there is a need for this discussion and perhaps some type of acknowledgement for some of these peoples' claims to indigenousness and even community. The Haudenosaunee have an interesting way to consider the position of those individuals who have been disconnected from their territory: everyone's welcome at the fire, but some sit closer than others.[49]

This recognition of rural indigenousness does have an emic purpose. On an individual basis, it may be significant to rural Indigenous peoples in terms of understanding who they are. Perhaps it will give strength to those individuals desiring to connect with their families on reservations, or reserves in Canada, but are hesitant. In addition, Indigenous peoples living in rural environments have no forum to gather and talk about their collective interests as their urban counterparts do. Would the association with a concept such as rural indigenousness offer them a concept under which to organize? More broadly, the emic purpose of this work is to challenge the trope that Indigenous peoples who move(d) to and live(d) in rural areas merely assimilate(d) into the dominant culture. Much like the history of Native peoples in the Adirondacks, Indigenous peoples belong in rural histories generally without being vanished and, perhaps more important, they belong in specific Indigenous nations' histories, too. And, hopefully, this discourse will stand beside other scholarly debates about indigeneity and give Indigenous peoples living in rural spaces a sense of belonging, whether as conceptualized here or in another deliberated form.

Conclusion

Lawrence calls for increased connections between urban and reservation communities, so that each group can help strengthen the other. Ultimately, she envisions individual Native nations regrouping as confederacies for political and social purposes. These alliances would incorporate reserve and urban Indigenous peoples, together with those who have moved to the suburbs as class mobility allowed. Lawrence argues that confederacies strengthen Indigenous communities' position because the confederacy would increase population numbers and territory, which they could use to their benefit in nation-to-nation negotiations. Confederacies also allow for citizenry acceptance throughout their collective territory, and even beyond, based on shared history and family ties instead of basing citizenry on blood quantum and where they currently reside.[50] Rural indigenous peoples could also be part of this vision, as many of these individuals and families have been living in their old territories alongside settler society members for generations. In reality, rural indigenousness members might add some leverage and could strengthen the confederacy-to-nation-state relationship much like a third leg on a stool adds stability.

As I indicated previously, as a non-Native person I cannot answer questions about Indigenous identity. However, I have to respond to the findings and ask the important questions that my research presents. In this instance, my findings demonstrate that the Indigenous identities of some Native peoples in rural spaces have not only survived, but they have persisted. Their histories are stories of survivance. They are actively present in the region's history and practice some native traditions as adapted over time. Their history and their lives need to be part of the discourse of indigeneity, and I offer my research and the stories of these rural Indigenous families as part of the discussion.

Conclusion

A Call for Education and Reconciliation
in the Twenty-First Century

SCHOLARS, if they consider Indigenous peoples who lived off-reservation in rural spaces at all, assume they assimilated into rural society. This history demonstrates otherwise. Each of the family histories of Aboriginal Adirondackers in this book, along with many others, contributed to the culture and history of the Adirondacks. However, those contributions are often unknown or ignored because time and colonial concepts of progress have concealed them. Early in the middle of the nineteenth century, this sparsely populated wildlands area with a small, scattered, and fluctuating seasonal Native population ostensibly was dominated by a Euro-American one. As the introduction and chapter 2 explain, settler colonialism is just as intrusive and devastating as the formal and purposeful type of imperial colonialism, and the history of this region clearly reveals this depredation. In the Adirondacks, both Native and non-Native peoples depended on their woodcraft expertise and at times on each other for survival. Many of the first Euro-Americans to the region were helped and taught skills by the Iroquoian and Algonquian peoples already there, but many communities today are not aware of this history. Why they assisted these early White settlers is unknown. Perhaps these Iroquoian and Algonquian peoples hoped for a shared existence with others like them who just wanted to be left alone in this wilderness-like space that was not useful for commercial agriculture. Nor did Native peoples' influence stop there. As described throughout this work, Abenaki,

Oneida, and Mohawk peoples in the Adirondacks continued to add to the region's culture during the era of wilderness tourism and later. Such may well have been the case in other rural areas where a minority Native population lived, worked with, and married into the families of Euro-American and immigrant settlers. By teasing out these family and local histories and working them into a larger metanarrative, one can discern exchanges between the cultures and see glimpses of their influence on each other. As Daniel Barr explains, "the significance of cultural interaction is more often found in the meeting than in the end result."[1] Furthermore, while not equally shared during any given era before or after European contact, the land has tried to support both Native and non-Native families. Ultimately, both peoples have influenced each other and the landscape.

The Adirondacks have always been and still are a difficult place to make a living; it is not an easy space to inhabit. This was the case even during the original occupation of the area by Native peoples who used it as a space of resources, labor, and refuge. Sometimes it is a place that can help feed and house a family, other times its usefulness is to provide nourishment for the soul. All families living within a new and different culture made, and still make, decisions about how they move forward. Some cling tenaciously to old customs, including language, occupation, and so on, while others work toward fitting into the new culture. Responses to cultural change have never been homogenous. Individuals and families borrow, adapt, and use those practices they find useful or attractive to fit their particular needs. Yet, for better or for worse, a regional society eventually acquires a character that identifies it for residents and outsiders. The customs or objects that were borrowed to create that character become part of the collective memory, and where they originated gets forgotten.

American historian David Glassberg argues that mainstream society wants history that connects people emotionally to the past and helps them to understand who they are and the place they live. He suggests historians can help the public connect to and see the value of their communities by expanding the time period they consider and by including the histories of neighbors that are often omitted. This type of history expands people's social perceptions so they know "that they are part of a larger society and environment."[2] To Glassberg's arguments I add that it is also important for individuals of specific ethnicities, genders, class, and even populated spaces—such as rural, suburban, and urban—to appreciate their own unique place within a region or society.

Initially I planned to end this book with the sixth chapter, but as I reflected on its conclusions I could not rid myself of a nagging feeling that there was one more lesson to be learned from this narrative. This troublesome sense of incomplete cognition led me to contemplate the role of North American history and history education and how these institutions treat the Indigenous peoples of North America and the entire Western hemisphere. Indigenous peoples have always engaged with the world around them, and they continue to do so. It is up to scholars of North American history to decide if we are going to pay attention and include their history and experiences in our work. Writing history is a profound and culpable practice. As historians of North American spaces, events, people, and culture, we need to ask ourselves why we choose to add or exclude peoples and their experiences in our scholarship, and what the ramifications are when we do so, especially when we eliminate the history of the peoples who are indigenous to the continent. I acknowledge that some topics are exclusive; for instance, this history is limited to Indigenous and Euro–North Americans because that is the topic of this book. However, there are many North American histories that leave out the Indigenous peoples, yet the narrative cries out for their inclusion. When historians of North America continue to omit Native peoples from our narrative, we continue the settler colonial practice of vanishing them.

Until now, the many narratives about the Adirondacks have left out the historical contributions the Indigenous peoples have made, and continue to make. Without knowing their involvement in the region's history we have no idea about their influence on iconic Adirondack symbols such as the Adirondack guide boat and pack-basket. We have little to no idea how early settlers learned to survive in this wild landscape, how they influenced wilderness tourism in the area, or how those nineteenth-century settlers to the Adirondacks became "natives." Perhaps most important of all, the Iroquoian and Algonquian peoples who have called the region home over the centuries have been denied their rightful position in the history of this place and, in some instances, their historical position in Mohawk, Oneida, and Abenaki history. It is my hope that this history of Algonquian, Iroquoian, and other Indigenous peoples who came to work and occupy a hunting territory now known as the Adirondacks demonstrates that the histories of Indigenous peoples' are rich and that they exist throughout the entire history of many North American places. The entangled exchanges that occurred between Native peoples and the Adirondacks before Europeans ever arrived and later between them and settler society reveal the endurance of the Indigenous peoples and their relationship to this place that while unique in North American history also resonates with the stories of Indigenous peoples across the continent.

The purpose of this concluding chapter is to emphasize the need for historians to not only include the histories of the Indigenous peoples when we write about the Western hemisphere but even more importantly, to include Native peoples' history *throughout the chronological narrative*. If we do not include Indigenous peoples in the writing of our histories, it is because we as historians choose to omit them, not because their history does not exist. We know this has been done intentionally in the past to divest Indigenous peoples of their homelands and to assuage Euro–North American guilt over this theft. While Native peoples' influence grows and wanes over time and in specific situations, I agree with scholars who argue one cannot tell the history of the Americas without including the peoples who were and still are indigenous to this place. Their history deserves to be included and continued over time not only because it is rich and complex but, more important, because it shapes the meaning of this hemisphere's histories.[3]

When we deny Indigenous Americans their rightful place in the history of the Western hemisphere, we purposefully conceal the true meaning of those chronicles. This argument was recently put forward and substantiated in the book *Why You Can't Teach United States History without American Indians*. The first page of this book's introduction notes that teachers claim "they would include Indians [in their teaching] if they were more central to mainstream history," and this declaration is the basis for the book. It provides teachers with a reason to include the history of Native peoples in the narrative of American history and also furnishes essays on topics that teachers can use in their classes, including explaining why a particular topic in history is important to American history as a whole. I want to add, and indeed argue, that teachers who ignore Indigenous peoples, and more importantly faculties of education that train these teachers, are creating a self-perpetuating loop: because mainstream education does not include the history of Native Americans and their proper and all-encompassing role in North American history, Indigenous peoples and their present-day issues have become less important to mainstream America. As a result, this self-perpetuating loop acts as a continuing form of settler colonialism. Ignoring Indigenous peoples and their history marginalizes them, and it clouds the facts and the real intent behind many of the events normally included in the teaching of mainstream American history. The practice of ignoring and omitting Indigenous Americans throughout North American history makes teachers and students alike think Native peoples have no history relevant to the country.[4] Even worse, some Americans today do not even realize that Native Americans still exist as a people, much less understand the issues that impact them politically, economically, and socially. Meanwhile, their population grows, all the while facing social, health-related, and educational hardships, as Americans and Canadians continue to either ignore or not fully contend with the scope of these realities.

When Europeans arrived and documented their understanding that this hemisphere existed, they should have acknowledged and been appreciative of those who invited them to share this space instead of acting like conquerors. Today, those of us who are their descendants and consider ourselves to be Americans and Canadians (for less than two hundred and fifty years) should be gratefully sharing North America with the Indigenous peoples who have called it home for thousands of years. Instead, we ignore or sugarcoat our shared past and the multitude of complicated situations this history of conquest has created for Indigenous peoples, whose homelands and vast resources we and our ancestors misappropriated in the hopes that they as a culture would (and still will) go away. Despite settler societies' best efforts, though, Indigenous populations are still here, and they are growing. We need to immediately come to terms with this history and stop ignoring it. Only then can we move forward toward reconciliation and make room for equitable decisions that affect us all. History and social studies education have a large part to play in such an important change, if teachers and faculties of education choose to embrace the task. Or, one or both can continue the status quo of settler colonialism and ignore their part in this marginalization and deprivation. But if these important facilitators of change choose the latter course, they need to remember that history will eventually judge them as part of the problem instead of as part of the solution.

Appendix
Notes
Bibliography
Index

Appendix

Place Names in the Adirondacks

Current Name	Iroquois Name (specific nation)	Algonquian Name (specific nation)	Meaning (if any)
Adirondack Mountains	Tso-non-tes-ko-wa Tsiiononteskowa (Mohawk) Latilu·taks (Oneida)	Wawobadenik, although may only mean Mt. Marcy, which they called Wawôbadenik* (White Mountain) (Abenaki)	Mountains Big Mountains (Mohawk) They're eating the trees, or beaver (Oneida)
Mohawk words that sound like Adirondacks but were not necessarily their name for the region	Ah-di-lohn-dac Rătīrōntăks		Bark eater / porcupine They eat trees
Akwesasne	Akwesasne (Mohawk)	Pŏ'kuīzās'nĕ* (Abenaki)	Place where the partridge drums (Mohawk)

* From J. Dyneley Prince's "Some Forgotten Indian Place-Names in the Adirondacks," *Journal of American Folklore* (1900), 123–28. Prince's informant was Mitchel Sabattis, then age seventy-nine.

** From Jim Reagan, "Ever Wonder about the Original Names for Places in County?" *Massena Courier* (Aug. 1, 1994).

Current Name	Iroquois Name (specific nation)	Algonquian Name (specific nation)	Meaning (if any)
			Half shriek (reference to battle) (Abenaki)
Black Lake	Otsikwá:ke	M´kazawi nĕpĕs* (Abenaki)	Where the ash trees grow with large knobs for making clubs (Mohawk)
			Black Lake (Abenaki)
Black River	Ni-ka-hi-on-ha-ko-wa** (Mohawk or other Iroquoian)		Big river
Blue Mountain Lake		Wīlôwĭ wājōĭ nĕpĕs* (Abenaki)	Blue Mountain Lake
Bog Lake		Mūkwā´kwôgā´māk* (Abenaki)	Bog Lake
Bog River		Mūkwā´kwtĕkw* (Abenaki)	Bog River
Cranberry Lake		Pŏpŏkuā nĕpĕs* (Abenaki)	Cranberry Lake
Chateaugay (place)	Kan-ah-to-he** (Mohawk or other Iroquoian)		
Chateaugay River	O-sar-he-hon** (Mohawk or other Iroquoian)		A place so close or difficult that the more one tries to extricate himself the worse off he is (probably a ref to narrow gorge near the village)

Current Name	Iroquois Name (specific nation)	Algonquian Name (specific nation)	Meaning (if any)
Forked Lake		Nīgītāwôgá′māk* (Abenaki)	Forked Lake
Grasse Lake	Osakentá:ke** (Mohawk or other Iroquoian)		Grasse Lake
Grasse River	Ni-kent-si-a-ke** (Mohawk or other Iroquoian)		Full of large fish, or where the fish live (Mohawk)
Hogansburg	Te-kas-wen-ka-ro-rens** (Mohawk)		
Hudson River	Cohatatea	Mahaganeghtuc Shatemuc	River of the mountains (Mohegan)
Lake		Nĕpĕs* (Abenaki)	lake
Lake Champlain	Caniaderiguarunte (Iroquois) Also see Ro-tsi-ich-ni** (Mohawk or other Iroquoian)	Bitawbákw (Abenaki)	The lake that is the gate of the country (Iroquois) "Coward spirit" (part of trilogy of spirits, the other two being "Good Spirit" and "Bad Spirit"; Coward Spirit lived and died on an island in Lake Champlain) The lake between (Abenaki)
Lake Clear		Wāsābāgāk*	Clear liquid (wasa means light)

Current Name	Iroquois Name (specific nation)	Algonquian Name (specific nation)	Meaning (if any)
Lake George		Andiatarocte (Mahican)	Where the lake closes
Long Lake		Qua-nah-ga-wah or Kwěnōgā´māk* (Abenaki)	About its shape (Kwěnī means long) Abenaki
Oswegatchie River	Swe-kat-si** (Huron)		Black water
Podunk		New England Algonquian	Neck or point of land
Potsdam	Te-wa-ten-e-ta-ren-ies** (Mohawk or other Iroquoian)		Place where the gravel settles under the feet in dragging a canoe.
Racquette Lake		Păpŏlpôgā´māk (Abenaki)	In and out, full of bays (deceptive)
Racquette River	Ni-ha-na-wa-te** (Mohawk or other Iroquoian)	Mas-le-a-qui (Abenaki)	Noisy river (Mohawk)
Richelieu River		Bitawbagwtegu (Abenaki)	
Round Lake		Pătěgwôgā´māk*	Round Lake
Round Pond		Pătěgwôgā´māsĭk*	Diminutive of Round Lake
Salmon River	Kent-si-a-ko-wan-ne** (Mohawk or other Iroquoian)		Big fish river

Current Name	Iroquois Name (specific nation)	Algonquian Name (specific nation)	Meaning (if any)
Saranac		S´nhălô´nĕk* (Abenaki)	Entrance of a river into a lake. Another translation is "sumac bud," but some discredit (i.e., Prince)
Saratoga	Sa-ra-ta-ke** (Mohawk or other Iroquoian)		Place where the track of a heel can be seen (reference to depressions in rocks that look like footsteps)
St. Lawrence River	Cat-a-ro-qui** (possibly Huron)	Ktsitegw (Abenaki)	
St. Regis River	Akwesasne** (Mohawk)		Where the partridge drums (Mohawk)
Ticonderoga	Tia-on-ta-ro-ken** (Mohawk or other Iroquoian)		A fork or point between two lakes
Tupper Lake	Tsitkaniatareskó:wa** (Mohawk or other Iroquoian)	Pāskāngā´māk* or Pas-kum-ga-meh (Abenaki)	The biggest lake (Mohawk) Side or branch of lake, or a lake going out from the river (Abenaki)

Current Name	Iroquois Name (specific nation)	Algonquian Name (specific nation)	Meaning (if any)
(Little) Tupper Lake	Possibly Tsikanionwareskó:wa** (Mohawk or other Iroquoian; noted as a lake below Tupper Lake, could be Sperry Pond)	Pāskāngā′māsĭk* (Abenaki)	Long Pond (Mohawk) Diminutive of side or branch of lake
Yellow Lake	Katsenekwá:o** (Mohawk or other Iroquoian)		Lake covered with yellow lilies

Notes

Introduction

1. Martin V. B. Ives, *Through the Adirondacks in Eighteen Days* (New York and Albany: Wynkoop Hallenbeck Crawford Co., State Printers, 1899), 8. Intended to be a legislative report, the size of this document became prohibitive, so the legislative committee provided the state legislator with a synopsis. The full accounting was published under this title.

2. Henry W. Raymond, *The Story of Saranac* (New York: Grafton Press, 1909), 20–21. Raymond was a summer resident of Saranac Lake, and part of his motivation for writing the book was the lack of information about Indian occupation in the region.

3. Alfred L. Donaldson, *A History of the Adirondacks*, 2 vols. (New York: Century Company, 1921; repr. Fleischmanns, NY: Purple Mountain Press, 1996), 1:21.

4. Neal Ferris, *The Archaeology of Native-Lived Colonialism: Challenging History in the Great Lakes* (Tucson, AZ: Univ. of Arizona Press, 2009), 10, citing Marshal Sahlins, *Islands of History* (Chicago: Univ. of Chicago Press, 1985), 144.

5. Andrew R. L. Cayton and Fredrika J. Teute, eds., *Contact Points: American Frontiers from the Mohawk Valley to the Mississippi, 1750–1830* (Chapel Hill: Univ. of North Carolina Press, 1998), v, 14–16. Richard White, *The Middle Ground: Indians, Empires and Republics in the Great Lakes Region, 1650–1815* (New York: Cambridge Press, 1991). Also see Daniel P. Barr, introduction to *The Boundaries between Us: Natives and Newcomers along the Frontiers of the Old Northwest Territory, 1750–1850* (Kent, OH: Kent State Univ. Press, 2006). Karl Jacoby, in *Crimes against Nature: Squatters, Poachers, Thieves, and the Hidden History of American Conservation* (Berkeley: Univ. of California Press, 2001), 21, alludes to this period when "encroaching white settlers both feuded and intermarried with the Indian people they encountered in the Adirondacks."

6. Jerry Jenkins, with Andy Keal, *The Adirondack Atlas: A Geographic Portrait of the Adirondack Park* (Syracuse, NY: Syracuse Univ. Press and Adirondack

Museum, 2004), 1, 25, 113. Jacoby, in *Crimes against Nature*, 210n18, states that "accurate population figures for the Adirondacks are surprisingly hard to come by."

7. James Axtell, *Natives and Newcomers: The Cultural Origins of North America* (New York: Oxford University Press, 2001), 309, 327.

8. Mary E. Stuckey and John M. Murphy, "By Any Other Name: Rhetorical Colonialism in North America," *American Indian Culture and Research Journal* 25, no. 4 (2001): 73–98, 75.

9. Ives Goddard, review of *Indian Names in Connecticut*, by James Hammond Trumbull, *International Journal of American Linguists* 43, no. 2 (Apr. 1977): 157–59. T. J. Brasser, "Mahican," in *Handbook of the North American Indian, Northeast*, vol. 15, ed. Bruce G. Trigger (Washington, DC: Smithsonian Institution, 1978), 198–212. Stockbridge-Munsee Community, Band of Mohican Indians (community website), accessed Jul. 26, 2012, http://www.mohican-nsn.gov.

10. Gordon M. Day, "Western Abenaki," in *Handbook of the North American Indian, Northeast*, ed. Bruce G. Trigger (Washington, DC: Smithsonian Institution, 1978), 148–59. "Conseil Des Abénakis Odanak, History," accessed July 10, 2018, https://caodanak.com/en/histoire.

11. Christopher Roy, e-mail correspondence to author, Oct. 1, 2012. Alice Nash, personal communication with author, Jun. 6, 2013.

12. Robert J. Surtees, "The Iroquois in Canada," in *The History and Culture of Iroquois Diplomacy: An Interdisciplinary Guide to the Treaties of the Six Nations and Their League*, ed. Francis Jennings et al. (Syracuse, NY: Syracuse Univ. Press, 1985), 67–83, 70, 72; James Axtell, *The Invasion Within: The Contest of Cultures in Colonial North America* (New York: Oxford Univ. Press, 1985), 62, 65, 133; Jon Parmenter, *The Edge of the Woods: Iroquoia, 1534–1701* (East Lansing: Michigan State Univ. Press, 2010), xxxiv–xxxv, 153–55.

13. Trent University, Indigenous Studies PhD, "Program Objectives," accessed Apr. 26, 2012, http://www.trentu.ca/indigenousstudiesphd/programobjectives .php. I make this decision informed by Michael Yellow Bird's "What We Want to Be Called: Indigenous Peoples' Perspectives on Racial and Ethnic Identity Labels," *American Indian Quarterly*, 23, no. 2 (Spring 1999): 1–21, and Taiaiake Alfred, *Peace, Power, Righteousness: An Indigenous Manifesto*, 2nd ed. (Don Mills, ON: Oxford Univ. Press, 2009), 23.

14. Ann Morning, "Ethnic Classification in Global Perspective: A Cross-National Survey of the 2000 Census Round," *Population Research and Policy Review* 27, no. 2 (Apr. 2008): 241–42, citing *The New Oxford American Dictionary*, ed. Elizabeth J. Jewell and Frank R. Abate (2001). Morning describes scholars suggesting race is involuntary, while ethnicity is voluntary. I tend to agree with scholars such as David J. Silverman, *Red Brethren: The Brothertown and Stockbridge Indians and the Problem of Race in Early America* (Ithaca, NY: Cornell Univ. Press, 2011),

9, who argue that race is as culturally manifested as ethnicity is, and I prefer to use the term *ethnicity*, which encompasses more than outward appearance. I disagree that ethnicity is only voluntary.

15. Frank Graham Jr., *The Adirondack Park: A Political History* (New York: Alfred A. Knopf, 1978), 3, begins with "In 1837 the village of Saratoga Springs was becoming one of the most sophisticated resorts in America."

16. Fernand Braudel, *The Identity of France, History and Environment*, trans. Siân Reynolds (London: Harper-Collins, 1988), 20.

17. For examples of US displacement, see Louis Warren, *The Hunter's Game: Poachers and Conservationists in Twentieth-Century America* (New Haven, CT: Yale Univ. Press, 1997), regarding Glacier National Park; Mark David Spence, *Dispossessing the Wilderness: Indian Removal and the Making of the National Parks* (New York: Oxford Univ. Press, 1999), regarding the removal of Native Americans from Yellowstone (Wyoming), Glacier (Montana), and Yosemite (California); and Jacoby, *Crimes against Nature*, regarding Yellowstone and the Grand Canyon. For Canada, see Bill Parenteau, "Care, Control, and Supervision: Native People in the Canadian Atlantic Salmon Fishery, 1867–1900," *Canadian Historical Review* 79, no. 1 (1998): 1–35, with reference to limitations of fishing for Native people in Atlantic Canada and Quebec; John Sandlos, "From the Outside Looking In: Aesthetics, Politics, and Wildlife Conservation in the Canadian North," *Environmental History* 6, no. 1 (2001): 6–31, about limiting the hunting of Dené and Inuit people in the North; George Colpitts, *Game in the Garden: A Human History of Wildlife in Western Canada to 1940* (Vancouver: Univ. of British Columbia Press, 2002), describing western Canada limiting Native subsistent and commercial hunters; and Theodore (Ted) Binnema and Melanie Niemi, "'Let the Line Be Drawn Now': Wilderness, Conservation, and the Exclusion of Aboriginal People from Banff National Park in Canada," *Environmental History* 11, no. 4 (Oct. 2006): 724–50, discussing the Stoney people being driven from Banff National Park; and David Calverly, "'When the Need for It No Longer Existed': Declining Wildlife and Native Hunting Rights in Ontario, 1791–1898," in *The Culture of Hunting in Canada*, ed. Jean Manore and Dale Miner (Vancouver: Univ. of British Columbia Press, 2007), 105–20; Kenneth Coates, "The Sinews of Their Lives: First Nations' Access to Resources in the Yukon, 1890–1950," in *The Culture of Hunting in Canada*, ed. Jean Manore and Dale Miner (Vancouver: Univ. of British Columbia Press, 2007), 148–66; and John Sandlos, *Hunters at the Margin: Native People and Wildlife Conservation in the Northwest Territories* (Vancouver: Univ. of British Columbia Press, 2007).

18. Nathaniel Bartlett Sylvester, *History of Saratoga County, New York with Historical Notes on Its Various Towns: Together with Biographical Sketches of Its Prominent Men and Leading Citizens* (Chicago: Gresham Publishing Co., 1893), 18–19,

75; Thomas Francis Gordon, *Gazetteer of the State of New York: Comprehending Its Colonial History* (Philadelphia: printed for author, 1836), 672. Also see William L. Stone, *Reminiscences of Saratoga and Ballston* (New York: R. Worthington, 1880), 90–94.

19. Winslow C. Watson, *Pioneer History of the Champlain Valley: Being an Account of the Settlement of the Town of Willsborough by William Gilliland, Together with His Journal and Other Papers: And a Memoir, and Historical and Illustrative Notes* ([Albany, NY?]: J. Munsell, 1863), 23–85.

20. Donaldson, *History of the Adirondacks*, 1:51–67, 2:257–60 (quote is from 1:56). For a verbatim copy of the "Indian Grant to Totten and Crossfield" dated July 15, 1772, see Donaldson's Appendix A. For conversion calculation, see Eric W. Nye, "Pounds Sterling to Dollars: Historical Conversion of Currency," Univ. of Wyoming, accessed Jun. 2, 2017, http://www.uwyo.edu/numimage/currency.htm.

21. Carl Benn, *The Iroquois in the War of 1812* (Toronto: Univ. of Toronto Press, 1998), 18–19; Barbara Graymont, *The Iroquois in the American Revolution* (Syracuse, NY: Syracuse Univ. Press, 1972), 259–64, 266–67; Isabel Thompson Kelsay, *Joseph Brant, 1743–1807: Man of Two Worlds* (Syracuse, NY: Syracuse Univ. Press, 1984), 339–41, 349–52, 357–58, 360–61, 369, 390–91.

22. Bruce Elliott Johansen and Barbara Alice Mann, eds., *Encyclopedia of the Haudenosaunee (Iroquois Confederacy)* (Westport, CT: Greenwood Press, 2000), 97–98. Also see Kelsay, *Joseph Brant*, 364–67; and Graymont, *Iroquois in the American Revolution*, 268–72.

23. Charles J. Kappler, ed., *Indian Affairs: Laws and Treaties*, vol. 2, *Treaties* (Washington, DC: Government Printing Office, 1904), 50–51, accessed Jan. 18, 2013, http://digital.library.okstate.edu/kappler/vol2/treaties/moh0050.htm; Kelsay, *Joseph Brant*, 390, 540–41, 548–52. Franklin B. Hough, *A History of St. Lawrence and Franklin Counties, New York: From the Earliest Period to the Present Time* (Albany, NY: Little and Co., 1853), 125–83. Local historian Hough provides a thorough explanation of the meetings between the delegates for the Seven Nations and New York State, including some of the speeches. Currency conversion from Nye, "Pounds Sterling to Dollars."

24. Reverend William M. Beauchamp Papers, box 27, coll. #SC 17369, folder 3, "Stockbridge Indians," New York State Library—Manuscripts and Special Collections, Albany, NY (reviewed Aug. 11, 2009). Vine Deloria Jr. and Raymond J. DeMaille, *Documents of American Indian Diplomacy: Treaties, Agreements, and Conventions, 1775–1979 (Legal History of North America)*, 2 vols. (Norman, OK: Univ. of Oklahoma, 1999), 97–100. Also see Jack Campisi and Laurence Hauptman, eds., *The Oneida Indian Experience: Two Perspectives* (Syracuse, NY: Syracuse Univ. Press, 1988), 9–10 (for original boundaries), 51–54. Ferris, *Archaeology of Native-Lived Colonialism*, 170–71.

25. Karen Flynn, *Moving beyond Borders: A History of Black Canadian and Caribbean Women in the Diaspora* (Toronto: Univ. of Toronto Press, 2011), 4.

26. Samuel de Champlain, *Voyages of Samuel de Champlain: 1604–1610* (The Prince Society, 1878), 202–3, 210–23. Gordon Day is one of the few scholars to consider this passage, and he assumed the Algonquian and Huron were lying to Champlain about the region being "thickly settled." See Gordon M. Day, "The Indian as an Ecological Factor in the Northeastern Forest," in *In Search of New England's Native Past: Selected Essays by Gordon M. Day*, ed. Michael K. Foster and William Cowan (Amherst: Univ. of Massachusetts Press, 1998), 33.

27. George Rogers Howell and Jonathan Tenney, *Bi-centennial History of Albany: History of the County of Albany, N.Y., from 1609 to 1886* (New York: W. W. Munsell and Co., 1886). Also see Warwick Stevens Carpenter, *The Summer Paradise in History: A Compilation of Fact and Tradition Covering Lake George, Lake Champlain, the Adirondack Mountains, and Other Sections Reached by the Rail and Steamer Lines of the Delaware And Hudson Company* (Albany, NY: General Passenger Department, Delaware and Hudson Co., 1914), 18, 22, 50. Alan Taylor, "Captain Hendrick Aupaumut: The Dilemmas of an Intercultural Broker," *Ethnohistory* 43, no. 3 (Summer 1996): 432. Paul Schneider, *The Adirondacks: A History of America's First Wilderness* (New York: H. Holt and Co., 1997), 18. Brasser, "Mahican," 202–3.

28. George S. Bixby, "Peter Sailly (1754–1826): A Pioneer of the Champlain Valley with Extracts from His Diary and Letters," *New York State Library History Bulletin* 12 (Albany, NY: Univ. of the State of New York, 1919), 66. Phillip G. Terrie, *Contested Terrain: A New History of Nature and People in the Adirondacks* (Syracuse, NY, Syracuse Univ. Press, 1997), 11–12. Also see Graham, *Adirondack Park*, 3. Philip J. Harris, *Adirondack, Lumber Capital of the World* (Baltimore, MD: PublishAmerica, 2008), 16, 36, 49–50, 89–90. William H. H. Murray, *Adventures in the Wilderness*, ed. William K. Verner (1869; repr., Syracuse, NY: Syracuse Univ. Press/Adirondack Museum, 1989).

29. Samuel H. Hammond, *Wild Northern Scenes; or Sporting Adventures with the Rifle and the Rod* (New York: Derby and Jackson, 1857). Henry David Thoreau, *The Maine Woods* (Boston: Ticknor and Fields, 1864; repr., New York: Penguin Books, 1988, with introduction by Edward Hoagland), 110. Nina H. Webb, *Footsteps through the Adirondacks: The Verplanck Colvin Story* (Utica, NY: North Country Books, 1996), 33–35. Graham, *Adirondack Park*, 73, 86, and ch. 9–11. Schneider, *Adirondacks*. Article VII of the 1894 NYS Constitution (now article XIV) states in part: "The lands of the state, now owned or hereafter acquired, constituting the forest preserve as now fixed by law, shall be forever kept as wild forest lands. They shall not be leased, sold or exchanged, or be taken by any corporation, public or private, nor shall the timber thereon be sold, removed or destroyed." New

York State Department of Environmental Conservation website, accessed Nov. 18, 2010, http://www.dec.ny.gov/lands/55849.html.

1. "Just a Hunting Territory?"

1. Jenkins, *Adirondack Atlas*, 1–3, 9–12, 20–21, 35. Also see New York State Office of Parks, Recreation and Historic Preservation, "Welcome to the Adirondack Region," accessed Sep. 28, 2012, http://nysparks.com/regions/adirondack/default .aspx, and Adirondacks Come to Life, "The Adirondack Park," accessed Jun. 29, 2012, http://visitadirondacks.com/adirondack-mountains/adirondack-park.html. This latter site claims there are "Seven distinct geographical regions . . . located within the Adirondacks: the Adirondack Wild, Lake George Region, Adirondack Coast, Adirondack Lakes Region, Lake Placid Region, Adirondacks-Tughill, and the Adirondack Seaway." The Adirondack Park is so large that Yellowstone, Grand Canyon, Glacier, Yosemite, and the Great Smokies National Parks could all fit within its current boundaries.

2. Schneider, *Adirondacks*, 4–5. Jenkins, *Adirondack Atlas*, 18–19.

3. Stephen B. Sulavik, *Adirondack: Of Indians and Mountains, 1535–1838* (Fleischmanns, NY: Purple Mountain Press; Blue Mt. Lake, NY: Adirondack Museum, 2005), 42, 122–23 (copy of Samuel de Champlain's *Carte Geographique De La Nouvelle France* [1612], original located at the National Library and Archives of Canada, NMC 6327), 158–59 (copy of Lewis Evans and T. Pownall's *Map of the Middle British Colonies in North America* [1755], original located in the Sterling Memorial Library map collection at Yale University), and 160–61 (copy of Richard William Seal's *New and Accurate Map of the present War in North America*, original located at the Adirondack Museum in Blue Mountain Lake, NY).

4. Guy Johnson, *To His Excellency William Tryon Esq., Captain General & Governor in Chief of the Province of New-York & this Map of the Country of the VI. Nations Proper with Part of the Adjacent Colonies* (1771), New York State Library, accessed Jul. 14, 2012, http://www.nysl.nysed.gov/scandocs/nativeamerican.htm; Sulavik, *Adirondack*, 43, 164–65; and Thomas Pownall, *A Topographical Description of the Dominions of the United States of America* (Pittsburgh: Univ. of Pittsburgh Press, 1949), 51. Thomas Hallock, *From the Fallen Tree: Frontier Narratives, Environmental Politics, and the Roots of a National Pastoral, 1749–1826* (Chapel Hill: Univ. of North Carolina Press, 2003), 41.

5. Jenkins, *Adirondack Atlas*, ix. Jacoby, *Crimes against Nature*, 20.

6. Ferris, *Archaeology of Native-Lived Colonialism*, 6.

7. Eva Marie Garroutte, *Real Indians: Identity and the Survival of Native America* (Berkeley: Univ. of California Press, 2003), 132.

8. Christopher A. Roy, "Abenaki Sociality and the Work of Family History" (PhD diss., Princeton University, 2012), especially ch. 5, "Histories of Home,"

201–57. William J. Haviland and Marjory W. Power, *The Original Vermonters: Native Inhabitant, Past and Present* (Hanover, NH: Univ. Press of New England, 1994), 31–32. Parmenter, *Edge of the Woods*, xxxviii. Andrew Gray, "Indigenous Peoples and Their Territories," in *Decolonising Indigenous Rights*, ed. Adolfo de Oliveira (New York: Routledge, 2009), 17–44, 27. Keith H. Basso, *Wisdom Sits in Places: Landscape and Language Among the Western Apache* (Albuquerque: Univ. of New Mexico Press, 1996), 7, 75, 143–45.

9. *Merriam-Webster Online Dictionary*, accessed Jul. 13, 2011, https://www.merriam-webster.com/dictionary/occupation, https://www.merriam-webster.com/dictionary/ location.

10. Dean R. Snow, *The Iroquois* (Malden, MA: Blackwell Press, 2004), 69, 129.

11. *Merriam-Webster Online Dictionary*, accessed Jul. 13, 2011 https://www.merriam-webster.com/dictionary/occupation and https://www.merriam-webster.com/dictionary/exchange.

12. Lynn Woods, "A History in Fragments: Following the Forgotten Trail of Native Adirondack Cultures," *Adirondack Life* 25, no. 7 (Nov./Dec. 1994): 30–37, 61, 68–72, 78–79. Jenkins, *Adirondack Atlas*, 19. Curt Stager of Paul Smith's College in Paul Smiths, New York, and Timothy Messner at the State University of New York at Potsdam are taking the lead on uncovering precontact evidence of Native peoples in the region.

13. "The North Woods of Old," *New York Times*, 11 May, 1890. Kay Olan, survey sponsored by the Clinton County Museum in Plattsburgh (Jul. and Aug. 1987, funded by the New York State Council on the Arts, copy at Six Nations Museum in Onchiota, New York)—I reviewed and copied all pages pertaining to New York State in August 2009 with permission. Gregory P. Otis, personal conversation with author, spring 2009 (Gregory Otis worked for the state from the 1960s to the 1980s).

14. Donaldson, *History of the Adirondacks*, 1:22. "The North Woods of Old," *New York Times*, May 11, 1890.

15. Clinton County Historical Museum, *The Original People: Native Americans in the Champlain Valley*, 5 (brochure published in conjunction with an exhibit, Jun. 10–Nov. 29, 1988), CCHA. Kay Olan's survey was conducted for this exhibit, and Dr. Peter Thomas was the archaeological consultant. National Institute of Culture and History, Institute of Archaeology, "Paleo-Indian Period," accessed Jan. 18, 2013, http://www.nichbelize.org/ia-archaeology/paleo-indian-period.html. Also see Michelle A. Hamilton, *Collections and Objections: Aboriginal Material Culture in Southern Ontario* (Montreal: McGill-Queen's Univ. Press, 2010), 23–24. Natural Resources Canada, "Deglacial History of the Champlain Sea Basin and Implications for Urbanization," *Geological Survey of Canada Open File 6947* (joint annual meeting GAC-MAC-SEG-SGA, Ottawa, Ontario, May 25–27, 2011), 1, accessed Jul. 27, 2018, http://ftp.maps.canada.ca/pub/nrcan_rncan/publications/ess

_sst/289/289555/of_6947.pdf; Haviland and Power, *Original Vermonters*, 19, 66–67. Clinton County Historical Museum, *Original People*, 8. University of Iowa, "Archaic Period," *Office of the State Archaeologist, Educational Series 2* (teacher's pamphlet), accessed Jan. 18, 2013, http://www.uiowa.edu/~osa/learn/teachers /pamphlets/Archaic-8.pdf. Snow, *Iroquois*, 15–16 (Snow does not address the Adirondacks specifically).

16. Frederick Matthew Wiseman, *The Voice of the Dawn: an Autohistory of the Abenaki Nation* (Hanover, NH: Univ. Press of New England, 2001), 13, 17, 32, and 59. Gordon Day has disputed the claim of the Adirondacks being part of Abenaki territory—see Day, "Abenaki Place-Names in the Champlain Valley," in *In Search of New England's Native Past*, ed. Michael K. Foster and William Cowan (Amherst, MA: Univ. of Massachusetts Press, 1998), 230. Jenkins, *Adirondack Atlas*, 69, contains a map called "The Iroquois and Their Neighbors, 1600," which includes the easternmost part of the Adirondacks within the territory of the "Western Abenaki" and Mahican.

17. Snow, *Iroquois*, 14–15, 19–20. Parmenter, *Edge of the Woods*, xxxvi and 299n30, indicates that Snow's "migration hypothesis" has been criticized, citing William J. Engelbrecht's "Iroquoian Ethnicity and Archaeological Taxa," in *Taming the Taxa: Toward a New Understanding of Great Lakes Archaeology*, ed. Ronald F. Williamson and Christopher M. Watts (Toronto: East End Books, 1999), 53, and others. Richard W. Hill Sr.'s "Making a Final Resting Place Final: A History of the Repatriation Experience of the Haudenosaunee," in *Cross-Cultural Collaboration: Native Peoples and Archaeology in the Northeastern United States*, ed. Jordan E. Kerber (Lincoln: Univ. of Nebraska Press, 2006), 10, refers to linguist Floyd G. Lounsbury's "Iroquois Languages," in *Handbook of North American Indians—Northeast*, vol. 15, ed. Bruce G. Trigger (Washington, DC: Smithsonian Institution Press, 1978), 336. Doug George-Kanentiio, *Iroquois Culture and Commentary* (Santa Fe, NM: Clear Light Publishers, 2000), 27–28. Wiseman, *Voice of the Dawn*, 59. Gordon Day, "The Eastern Boundaries of Iroquoia," in *In Search of New England's Native Past*, ed. Michael K. Foster and William Cowan (Hanover, NH: Univ. Press of New England, 2001), 119 (for Abenaki). Champlain, *Voyages of Samuel de Champlain*, 223n348. Champlain originally referred to it as the Lake of the Iroquois (216n343).

18. John Kahionhes Fadden, e-mail message to author, Apr. 23, 2010, as told to him by his wife Eva and her sister Marita Thompson, both of whom are Mohawk speakers (Marita Thompson teaches the Mohawk language at an Akwesasne school). "Reader 1" (review through Syracuse University Press) to author, Feb. 2, 2016, provided the term *Ah-di-lohn-dac*, and suggests the smaller territory for the Oneida. Information regarding boundaries provided by Nicolas A. Reynolds, historical researcher at the Cultural Heritage Department, Oneida Nation of Wisconsin, e-mail

message to author, Apr. 28, 2010. Loretta Metoxen, Oneida historian, Oneida Nation of Wisconsin, personal conversation with author, Aug. 18, 2010. All Oneida Nation websites concur with the oral history I received, as does the map in Karim M. Tiro's *The People of the Standing Stone: The Oneida Nation from the Revolution through the Era of Removal* (Amherst: Univ. of Massachusetts Press, 2011), facing p. 1. Also see William A. Starna, "The Oneida Homeland in the Seventeenth Century," in *The Oneida Indian Experience: Two Perspectives*, ed. Jack Campisi and Laurence M. Hauptman (Syracuse, NY: Syracuse Univ. Press, 1988), 9–10, which describes an extensive 6 million acre territory extending to the St. Lawrence River.

19. Brasser, "Mahican," 198. Also see Lisa Brooks, *The Common Pot: The Recovery of Native Space in the Northeast* (Minneapolis: Univ. of Minnesota Press, 2008), 243, which claims the Mahican identified their New York State territory extending from Manhattan to Lake Champlain. See Carroll Vincent Lonergan, *Ticonderoga: Historic Portage* (Ticonderoga, NY: Fort Mount Hope Society Press, 1959), 9–13. Melissa Jayne Fawcett, Mohegan Tribal Historian, *The Lasting of the Mohegans, Part I* (Ledyard, CT: Pequot Printing, 1995), 8–10. Jacoby, *Crimes against Nature*, 20, 25, citing Bruce G. Trigger's *The Children of Aateaentsic: A History of the Huron People to 1660* (Montreal: McGill-Queens Univ. Press, 1976), 345, 488, 618. Parmenter, *Edge of the Woods*, 5, shows their territory on a map by Nij T. Anantsuksomsri entitled "The Iroquois World, 1534–1634."

20. Rick Hill, series of e-mail messages to author, Jan. 3–14, 2011. In addition to historian, Rick is the development officer of the Indigenous Knowledge Centre, a writer, a professor at McMaster University, and a teacher at the Six Nations Polytechnic. Robert W. Venables, "The Clearings and the Woods: The Haudenosaunee (Iroquois) Landscape, Gendered *and* Balanced," in *Archaeology and Preservation of Gendered Landscapes*, ed. Sherene Baugher and Suzanne M. Spencer-Wood (New York: Springer Books, 2010), 40, citing Arthur C. Parker, *The Constitution of the Five Nations* (Albany, NY: New York State Museum, 1916). Rick Hill, e-mail message to author, Jan. 24, 2011. George-Kanentiio, *Iroquois Culture and Commentary*, 28. Elisabeth Tooker, "The League of the Iroquois: Its History, Politics, and Ritual," in *Handbook of the North American Indian, Northeast*, vol. 15, ed. Bruce G. Trigger (Washington, DC: Smithsonian Institution, 1978), 418–41, especially 418, 420–22. Also see Parmenter, *Edge of the Woods*, 17, 313–14n32, citing Victor P. Lytwyn, "A Dish with One Spoon: The Shared Hunting Grounds Agreement in the Great Lakes and St. Lawrence Valley Region," in *Papers of the Twenty-Eighth Algonquian Conference*, ed. David Pentland (Winnipeg: Univ. of Manitoba, 1997), 210–11.

21. Rick Hill, personal conversation with the author, Mar. 1, 2011, Indigenous Knowledge Centre (IKC), Six Nations Polytechnic, Six Nations Territory, Ohsweken, ON. The IKC is a partnership between Six Nations and McMaster's

University. Rick Hill, e-mail messages to author, Jan. 13 and 24, 2011. Sulavik, *Adirondack*, 38. Tom Sakokweniónkwas Porter, *And Grandma Said . . . : Iroquois Teachings as Passed Down through the Oral Tradition*, trans. and ed. Lesley Forrester (Bloomington, IN: Xlibris Corp. self-publishing, 2008), 314. Also see Alan Corbiere's "Gidonaaganinaa 'Our Dish': An Intertribal Treaty Encoded in Wampum," *Anishinabek News* 19, no. 9 (Nov. 2007): 22, http://anishinabeknews.ca/wp-content/uploads/2013/04/2007-11.pdf. Corbiere is a historian with the Ojibwe Cultural Foundation in M'Chigeeng First Nation on Manitoulin Island. Peter Kahkewaquonaby Jones, *History of the Ojebway Indians: With Especial Reference to Their Conversion to Christianity; with a Brief Memoir of the Writer* (London: A. W. Bennett, 1861), 114, 119.

22. Parmenter, *Edge of the Woods*, 29, map entitled "Iroquoia, ca. 1620" (it is the first of a number of maps by Nij T. Anantsuksomsri). William A. Starna and José António Brandão, "From the Mohawk-Mahican War to the Beaver Wars: Questioning the Pattern," *Ethnohistory* 51, no. 4 (Fall 2004): 733–39. Trigger, *Children of Aateaentsic*, 345. Robert Williams Jr., *Linking Arms Together: American Indian Treaty Visions of Law and Peace, 1600–1800* (New York: Routledge, 1999), 116, 126–28.

23. "Mortars, Used by Indians in Saratoga County for Grinding Corn, Located by John M. Corey" (unknown publication, c. Dec. 1920), located in CSSH; Frederick T. Adcock and Cynthia E. Adcock, *Images of America: Piseco Lake and Arietta* (Charleston, SC: Arcadia Publishing, 2008), 109; Paul F. Jamieson, "Highway of History: The First White Man Comes to St. Lawrence County," *The Quarterly* (St. Lawrence County Historical Assoc.) 13, no. 2 (1968): 3–4, 21–23. Parmenter, *Edge of the Woods*, xlviii and 79, with map by Nij T. Anantsuksomsri entitled "Iroquois Military Campaigns, 1650–1689," shows a route through the Adirondacks for the period of 1650–58 for a campaign against the Wendat.

24. Jenkins, *Adirondack Atlas*, 42–49. Also see Jeptha R. Simms, *Trappers of New York, or a Biography of Nicholas Stoner and Nathaniel Foster; Together with Anecdotes of Other Celebrated Hunters* (Albany, NY: J. Munsell, 1850), 272–80.

25. William Engelbrecht, *Iroquoia: The Development of a Native World* (Syracuse, NY: Syracuse Univ. Press, 2003), 9 (citing Henry T. Lewis, "Indian Fires of Spring," *Natural History* [Jan. 1980], 76–83), 10 (citing Dean Snow's *Mohawk Valley Archaeology: The Sites* [Albany, NY: Institute for Archaeological Studies, Univ. of Albany Press, 1995], 167–68), and 29. William Cronon, *Changes in the Land: Indians, Colonists, and the Ecology of New England* (New York: Hill and Wang, 1983), 50. Schneider, *Adirondacks*, 17 (citing Dutch lawyer and New Netherland landowner Adriaen Van der Donck, *A Description of New Netherlands* [1655]), and Philip G. Terrie, *Wildlife and Wilderness: A History of Adirondack Mammals* (Fleischmanns, NY: Purple Mountain Press, 1993). Fred Tracy Stiles, *From Then Till Now: History and Tales of the Adirondack Foothills* (Hudson Falls, NY: Washington

County Historical Society, 1978), 147. Peter Kalm, *Travels into North America; Containing Its Natural History, and a Circumstantial Account of Its Plantations and Agriculture in General, with the Civil, Ecclesiastical and Commercial State of the Country, the Manners of the Inhabitants, and Several Curious and Important Remarks on Various Subjects*, 3 vols., trans. John Reinhold Forster (London: The Editor, 1770–71), 3: 4–5.

26. Sulavik, *Adirondack*, 85, citing Francis Xavier Talbot, *Saints among Savages: The Life of Isaac Jogues* (New York: Harper and Brothers, 1935), 449. Parmenter, *Edge of the Woods*, xxxix. George-Kanentiio, *Iroquois Culture and Commentary*, 61. Snow, *Iroquois*, 6, 39, 69. Rick Hill, personal conversation with author, Mar. 1, 2011. Doug Kanentiio-George, "Mohawk Ceremonial Cycle," in *Encyclopedia of the Haudenosaunee (Iroquois Confederacy)*, ed. Bruce Elliott Johansen and Barbara Alice Mann (Westport, CT: Greenwood Press, 2000), 203.

27. Haviland and Power, *Original Vermonters*, 158–68, 179. Day, "Western Abenaki," 151–56.

28. Gary Warrick, *A Population History of the Huron-Petun, A.D. 500–1650* (Cambridge: Cambridge Univ. Press, 2008), 168, 171, 173. William A. Starna, "Mohawk Iroquois Populations: A Revision," *Ethnohistory* 27 (1980): 376, and Dean R. Snow and Kim M. Lanphear, "European Contact and Indian Depopulation in the Northeast: The Timing of the First Epidemics," *Ethnohistory* 35 (1988): 24. Haviland and Power, *Original Vermonters*, 162.

29. Adirondack Park Association, *The Historic Adirondacks: Historic Sketches of the Thirteen Counties of the Adirondack Park Area* (brochure, Adirondack, NY, Aug. 1970), 18. Stiles, *From Then Till Now*, 147. Thomas W. McArthur, "History of Putnam" (MS in binder, completed but not edited, 1887, appears to have been typed in 1901), 3, WCHSRL; McArthur believed it to originally have been Mohawk and later Mahican, but based on my research this would be the other way around. John Knox, "Piseco Lake," *New York State Conservationist*, reprint 106 (Albany, NY, n.d.), vertical file "Piseco," AM—BML. Other versions claim Piseco was the name of "an old Indian hermit who dwelt upon its shores." The article credits John Dunham for the explanation that it is an aboriginal word "Pi-se-co," meaning fish. Snow, *Iroquois*, 50.

30. Ralph Nading Hill, *Lake Champlain: Key to Liberty* (Montpelier, VT: Burlington Free Press, 1976), 11.

31. Ibid., 10. Hill describes Jesuits being taken to Ticonderoga for flint. Anthony Sassi and Janice Sassi, "Flint Quarry Discovered on Area Farm: Indians Found Stone for Tools and Weapons Near Fish Creek," unknown publication, Apr. 8, 1965, vertical file "Ethnic Heritage: American Indians/Native Americans-Newspaper Clippings," CSSH. Thomas Nesbitt, "Native Americans and Colonial Rivalries: First Settlers to 1774," *Warren County (NY): Its People and Their History Over Time*

(Queensbury, NY: Warren County Historical Society, 2009), 23, describes flint quarries along Wood Creek and some of its tributaries. Stiles, *From Then Till Now*, 147. Engelbrecht, *Iroquoia*, 49–50; Wiseman, *Voice of the Dawn*, 38. Dean R. Snow, Charles T. Gehring, and William A. Starna, eds., *In Mohawk Country: Early Narratives about a Native People* (Syracuse, NY: Syracuse Univ. Press, 1996), xxiii–xxiv.

32. W. H. Harwood, "The Early Settlers of that Part of the Town of Malone Now Known as Chasm Falls," *The Malone (NY) Farmer*, Apr. 8, 1903, 42–43. Morris F. Glenn, *The Story of Three Towns: Westport, Essex and Willsboro, New York* (Ann Arbor, MI: Braun-Brumfield, 1977), 42. Arthur H. Masten, *The Story of Adirondac* (1923; repr., Syracuse, NY: Syracuse Univ. Press and Adirondack Museum, 1968). Gordon, *Gazetteer*, 43.

33. D[avid] S. Kellogg, "Aboriginal Dwelling Sites in the Champlain Valley," *Proceedings of the American Association for the Advancement of Science*, 308, vertical file "Archaeology," AM-BML; G. H. Perkins, "Archaeological Researches in the Champlain Valley," *International Congress of Anthropology* (1894): 85, vertical file "Archaeology," AM-BML. Also see Hill, *Lake Champlain*, 10. Jenkins, *Adirondack Atlas*, 14–15. Mary Ann Levine, "Determining the Provenance of Native Copper Artifacts from Northeastern North America: Evidence from Instrumental Neutron Activation Analysis," *Journal of Archaeological Science* 34, no. 4 (2007): 576–82, 585. To determine where the copper came from, the pieces would have to be tested.

34. Engelbrecht, *Iroquoia*, 23. Parmenter, *Edge of the Woods*, xxxvii–xxxviii, 145. Warrick, *Population History*, 165–66. Day, "Indian as an Ecological Factor," 31. Joseph François Lafitau, *Moeurs des sauvages ameriquains comparées aux moeurs des premiers temps*, 4 vols. (Paris: Chez Saugrain l'aîné et al., 1724), 2:75–76.

35. Engelbrecht, *Iroquoia*, 31. Robert Venables (retired Cornell University historian), letter to John Fadden and his wife Eva, Oct. 5, 2009, suggests the possibility of corn being grown on the New York State side of Lake Champlain and around Lake George and south of there based on Samuel de Champlain's accounting in his *Voyages* (1609). Also see Lester St. John Thomas, assisted by Evelyn Cirino Donohue and Anita Beaudette Ranado, *Timber, Tannery and Tourists* (Lake Luzerne, NY: Committee on Publication of Local History, 1979), 21, which describes the growing of corn and then drying and pounding it around Lake Luzerne; the early pioneers called their effort "Indian meal." Christopher Angus, *The Extraordinary Adirondack Journey of Clarence Petty: Wilderness Guide, Pilot, and Conservationist* (Syracuse, NY: Syracuse Univ. Press, 2002), 3–4, 22–23, and Maitland C. DeSormo, *Summers on the Saranacs* (Saranac Lake, NY: Adirondack Yesteryears, 1980), 100, both refer to corn being grown in Franklin County. Knox, "Piseco Lake"; and Rev. John Todd, *Long Lake* (1845; repr. Fleishmanns, NY: Purple Mountain Press, 1997), 28, refer to corn in Hamilton County. Evelyn Barrett Britten, "Traces of Indian Life Remain in Area," *The Saratogian* (Sep. 1962).

36. Lee Manchester, "More from the Plains of Abraham," document transcript, accessed Jun. 16, 2012, https://www.slideshare.net/LeeManchester/more-from-the-plains-of-abraham, 19. For a description of the Plains as an uplifted plateau see Mary MacKenzie, *The Plains of Abraham: A History of North Elba and Lake Placid, Collected Writings of Mary MacKenzie*, ed. Lee Manchester (Utica, NY: Nicholas K. Burns Publishing, 2007), 11, 15.

37. Arthur C. Parker, "Iroquois Uses of Maize and Other Food Plants," *Education Department Bulletin of the New York State Museum*, No. 144 (Nov. 1, 1910), 80, 88, accessed Jul. 29, 2012, http://www.biodiversitylibrary.org/title/26294#page/126/mode/2up.

38. Knox, "Piseco Lake," 106.

39. Robert Horton, "Sabael Benedict, Indian Pioneer," *Adirondac* 54, no. 10 (Dec. 1989), 16–18. Engelbrecht, *Iroquoia*, 27, 28, 30. Stone, *Reminiscences of Saratoga and Ballston*, 59. Stiles, *From Then Till Now*, 147–48.

40. Marc D. Abrams and Gregory J. Nowacki, "Native Americans as Active and Passive Promoters of Mast and Fruit Trees in the Eastern USA," *The Holocene* 18, no. 7 (2008): 1128–29, 1132. Abrams and Nowacki do refer to a sweet crabapple tree (*Pyrus coronaria*) that was native to the eastern part of North America, but most orchard apple trees (along with pear and peach) came from Europe. Since we do not know what kind of apples this orchard contained, we cannot know if they were native to the region and/or planted prior to contact.

41. "Indian Orchard," *Saratoga Daily Forum* (Jul. 12, 1853). Stone, *Reminiscences of Saratoga and Ballston*, 59, claims the Mohawk planted the orchard around 1776.

42. Kalm, *Travels into North America*, 3:6, 14.

43. Alfred Billings Street, *The Indian Pass* (New York: Kurd and Houghton, 1869), xxv–xxvi, accessed May 4, 2013, https://archive.org/details/indianpass00strerich.

44. Philip G. Terrie, *Forever Wild: Environmental Aesthetics and the Adirondack Forest Preserve* (Philadelphia: Temple Univ. Press, 1985), 5. John W. Thieret, "Bryophytes as Economic Plants," *Economic Botany* 10, no. 1 (Jan.–Mar. 1956): 77–80.

45. Peter Bauer, "Watersheds: Twenty Decisive Moments that Made Us What We Are," *Adirondack Life* 20, no. 3 ((May/Jun. 1989): 88–101, 89. Loretta Metoxen, personal conversation with author, Aug. 18, 2010.

46. See Day, introduction, "The Eastern Boundary of Iroquoia," and "Abenaki Place-Names in the Champlain Valley" in *In Search of New England's Native Past*, 14–15, 116–22, and 229–62. Also see Alice Nash, "Théophile Panadis (1889–1966): Un guide abénaquis" (trans. Claude Gélinas), *Recherches amérindiennes au Québec* 33, no. 2 (2003), 82. English translation provided by author. Panadis referred to Ojihozo and his wife, Ojihozskwa, and said that the Abenaki used to leave tobacco or a

pipe offering to the couple when they crossed (presumably Lake Champlain, which suggests they did this before crossing the lake to go to the Adirondacks).

47. Jonathan A. Burns and Paul A. Raber, introduction to "Rockshelters in Behavioral Context: Archaeological Perspectives from Eastern North America," *North American Archaeologist* 31 (2010): 257–59.

48. Ferris, *Archaeology of Native-Lived Colonialism*, 21. Warrick, *Population History*, 202. Engelbrecht, *Iroquoia*, 11, 82, 87. Snow, *Iroquois*, 37.

49. P. Schuyler Miller, "People Looking Down," *Cloud Splitter* (Feb. 1942), 3 (newsletter published by the Adirondack Mountain Club). Miller was better known as a science fiction writer who had grown up in the Mohawk Valley. He had a passion for Iroquois culture and pursued it as an amateur archaeologist; he was a member of the New York State Archaeological Association, according to the back cover of his book *The Titan*, as noted at http://www.amazon.com/Titan-Peter-Schuyler -Miller/dp/B0007DW9TU, accessed Apr. 18, 2012. Another intact Iroquoian vessel found near Lake Pleasant in Speculator, New York, is on display at the Walter Elwood Museum at the Guy Park Manor in Amsterdam, and is photographed in Snow, *Iroquois*, 56. Rick Hill, personal conversation with author, Mar. 1, 2011, IKC.

50. Karen I. Vaughn, "John Locke and the Labor Theory of Value," *Journal of Libertarian Studies* 2, no. 4 (1978): 312–13. Also see Cronon, *Changes in the Land*, 58–80. Val Plumwood, "Wilderness Skepticism and Wilderness Dualism," in *The Great New Wilderness Debate: An Expansive Collection of Writings Defining Wilderness from John Muir to Gary Snyder*, ed. J. Baird Callicott and Michael P. Nelson (Athens, GA: Univ. of Georgia Press. 1998), 677–78. Jean O'Brien, *Firsting and Lasting: Writing Indians Out of Existence in New England* (Minneapolis: Univ. of Minnesota Press, 2010), 94. Arthur A. Goldsmith, "The State, the Market and Economic Development: A Second Look at Adam Smith in Theory and Practice," *Development and Change* 26 (1995): 637. The other two public goods and conditions for exchange were law and order and the ability to enforce contracts. Gray, "Indigenous Peoples," 23, citing Karl Marx, *Selected Writings*, ed. D. McLenna (Oxford: Oxford Univ. Press, 1977), 494. Ken Coates and William Morrison, *The Forgotten North: A History of Canada's Provincial Norths* (Toronto: James Lorimer and Co., 1992), 46.

51. Parmenter, *Edge of the Woods*, xxvii.

52. J. Edward Chamberlin, *If This Is Your Land, Where are Your Stories? Finding Common Ground* (Toronto: Alfred A. Knopf Canada, 2003), 3. Frances Sigurdsson, "The Sacandaga Saga: How the Creation of New York's Eighth-Largest Lake Left a Flood of Memories," *Adirondack Life* 33, no. 2 (Jul.–Aug. 2002): 44. Legend provided by Don Bowman, *Go Seek the Pow Wow on the Mountain* (Greenfield Center, NY: Greenfield Review Press, 1993), 41.

53. Charles Fenno Hoffman, "Ko-rea-ran-neh-neh, or the flying head. [A Legend of Sacandaga Lake]," in *Wild Scenes in the Forest and Prairie*, 2 vols. (London: Richard

Bentley, 1839), 2:39–49. According to John Kahionhes Fadden, a Mohawk storyteller, artist, and proprietor of the Six Nations Indian Museum at Onchiota, Mohawk legends used the adjacent landscape for their settings. Since the Adirondacks are located just north of the Mohawk River Valley and just south of the St. Lawrence River Valley, it is likely the area figured into other Mohawk and Oneida stories referring to mountains and forests and possibly to stories of the Onondaga, who accessed these areas easily through the eastern shores of Lake Ontario and the St. Lawrence River. Similarly, western bands of Abenaki were just across Lake Champlain, which, although 110 miles long, is only twelve miles wide; it can easily be navigated and viewed from the opposite shore. Both Abenaki and Mohawk peoples share a legend of a haunted cabin located in the Adirondacks. See Thomas C. Parkhill, *Weaving Ourselves into the Land: Charles Godfrey Leland, "Indians," and the Study of Native American Religions* (Albany, NY: State Univ. of New York Press, 1997), 91, 98, for discussion about mid-nineteenth-century use of Indigenous stories to connect Whites to North American continent.

54. Basso, *Wisdom Sits in Places*, 7, 48–49, 55. Thomas P. Grazulis, *The Tornado: Nature's Ultimate Windstorm* (Norman, OK: Univ. of Oklahoma Press, 2001), 221. Hoffmann, *Wild Scenes*, 2:178–90, for the flying head story. Rick Hill, personal conversation with author, Mar. 1, 2011, for the stone giants story, and Seneca artist Ernest Smith's map of Iroquoian places in New York State, located at the Rochester Museum and Science Center (Mr. Smith created the map for a display for the New York World's Fair in 1939).

55. Chamberlin, *If This is Your Land*, 1.

56. Brian Thom, "The Paradox of Boundaries in Coast Salish Territories," *Cultural Geographies* 16, no. 2 (Apr. 2009): 185–86.

57. Chamberlin, *If This is Your Land*, 31.

58. Snow, *Iroquois*, 62, 67–70. George-Kanentiio, *Iroquois Culture and Commentary*, 51–52, 55–56. Carl Benn, *Mohawks on the Nile: Natives among the Canadian Voyageurs in Egypt, 1884–85* (Toronto: Dundurn Press, 2009), especially ch. 4, "Mohawks as Workers," 92–111. Parmenter, *Edge of the Woods*, xi. Haviland and Power, *Original Vermonters*, 38.

59. Kathleen M. Brown, "The Anglo-Algonquian Gender Frontier," in *Negotiators of Change: Historical Perspectives on Native American Women*, ed. Nancy Shoemaker (New York and London: Routledge, 1995), 28–32.

2. "*Couxsachrâgé*"

1. Rev. John Todd, *Summer Gleanings; or, Sketches and Incidents of a Pastor's Vacation*, collected and arranged by his daughter (Northampton: Hopkins, Bridgman, and Co. 1852), 262.

2. Harris, *Adirondack*, 16, 31, 36. "Chronological Résumé of Important Laws and Events," ChamplainCanal.net, accessed Oct. 18, 2011, http://www.champlain

canal.net/Chronology-Champlain%20Canal.htm. Adirondack Experience, "Out of the Earth: Mining in the Adirondacks," accessed Oct. 18, 2011, http://www.adirondackhistory.org/adkmining/intro.html.

3. Mary MacKenzie, *The Plains of Abraham: A History of North Elba and Lake Placid, The Collected Historical Writings of Mary MacKenzie*, ed. Lee Manchester (Utica, NY: Nicholas K. Burn Publishing, 2007), 4, 24. George Levi Brown, *Pleasant Valley: A History of Elizabethtown, Essex County, New York* ([Elizabethtown, NY?]: Post and Gazette print, 1905), 1. Street, *Indian Pass*, xii–xiii. Sylvester, *Historical Sketches*, 135–36. Stone, *Reminiscences of Saratoga and Ballston*, 77–78. John Chester Booth, *Booth's History of Saratoga County, N.Y.*, ed. Violet B. Dunn, Saratoga County Historian, and Beatrice Sweeney, City Historian of Saratoga Springs (1858; repr., Saratoga Springs, NY: Saratoga County Bicentennial Commission, 1977), 33. Henry McGuier and F. B. Graham, "Indian Orchard," *Saratoga Daily Forum* (Jul. 12, 1858). Jean McGregor (a.k.a. Evelyn Barrett), "Little Remains of Old Indian Trail, Orchard," *The Saratogian*, May 27, 1949, CSSH. Britten, "Traces of Indian Life."

4. H. P. Smith, ed., *History of Warren County with Illustrations and Biographical Sketches of Some of Its Prominent—Men and Pioneers* (Syracuse, NY: D. Mason and Co., 1885), 348. William H. Brown, ed., *History of Warren County New York* (published by the Board of Supervisors of Warren County; printed by Glens Falls Post Company, 1963), 189.

5. Jenkins, *Adirondack Atlas*, 42–49, 71. According to Jenkins, we do not know how many beaver were taken from the region. He notes that in 1624, there were 7,200 beaver pelts shipped from Albany, some of them from the Adirondacks; by the 1680s approximately 80,000 pelts were exported through Albany. Also see Simms, *Trappers of New York*, 272–80. Starna and Brandão, "From the Mohawk-Mahican War," 730, 740.

6. Smith, ed., *History of Warren County*, 529–30.

7. Henry A. L. Brown and Richard J. Walton, *John Brown's Tract: Lost Adirondack Empire* (published for the Rhode Island Historical Society, Canaan, NH: Phoenix Publishing, 1988), 289–90. This John Brown should not be confused with the abolitionist of the same name. The authors cite Charles E. Snyder's *John Brown's Tract, Herkimer* (Herkimer County Historical Society Transactions, An address delivered Dec. 8, 1896), 94–108.

8. James E. DeKay, *Zoology of New York; or, The New York Fauna; comprising detailed descriptions of all the animals hitherto observed within the state of New York, with brief notices of those occasionally found near its borders, and accompanied by appropriate illustrations*, 2 vols. (Albany, NY: Carroll and Cook, 1842), 1:73, accessed Sep. 14, 2014, http://archive.org/stream/zoologyofnewyork01deka#page/72/mode/2up. Edith Pilcher, *The Constables: First Family of the Adirondacks* (Utica, NY: North Country Books, 1992), 35.

9. Champlain, *Voyages of Samuel de Champlain*, 202–3, 210–23. Parmenter, *Edge of the Woods*, 123, 191, 260. Maps entitled "The French Invasion of Mohawk Country, 1666" and "French Invasion of Iroquoia, 1687–1696" (the latter shows the 1693 Frontenac expedition using this corridor). Richard Berleth, *Bloody Mohawk: The French and Indian War and American Revolution on New York's Frontier* (Hensonville, NY: Black Dome Press, 2010), 185.

10. Harry V. Radford, "Mitchel Sabattis," *Shooting and Fishing: A Journal of the Rifle, Gun and Rod* 40, no. 3 (Apr. 26, 1906), 45–46. Watso Family file (also spelled "Watso, Watzeau, Watsaw"), ILM, and "Labor and Market," *Lake George Mirror*, Apr. 22, 1880, which reported Louis Watso had just received a pension from Canada for his service to Great Britain during the War of 1812; also see *Lake George Mirror*, May 6, 1880. Benoni Paul and his family are discussed in "Indian Biographies from Lake George," *Glens Falls Post-Star*, Dec. 14, 1963, 13–14. Also, a handwritten note in vertical file "Indians," SSHM, states "Capt. Yoke and Abram Conkspot were Indians who fought on the American side. One drew a pension and lived in Wisconsin later"; this might indicate that individual was either Mahican or Oneida. Margaret M. Bruchac, "Historical Erasure and Cultural Recovery: Indigenous People In the Connecticut River Valley," (PhD diss., University of Massachusetts, Amherst, 2007), xii footnote 17, notes her grandfather Louis or Lewis Bowman, Thomas Kesiah, and Abram Burlett (probably not Native himself he married an Abenaki woman named Mary Louise Joseph) served in the Civil War.

11. Edward P. Hamilton, ed., "A Journal of the Proceedings of Nathaniel Wheelwright appointed and commissioned by his Excellency William Shirley, Esquire, Governor and Commander in Chief in and over His Majesty's Province of the Massachusetts Bay in New England from Boston to Canada in order to redeem the captives belonging to this government in the hands of the French and Indians," *Bulletin of the Fort Ticonderoga Museum* 10, no. 4 (Feb. 1960): 260–96; Francis Parkman, *Historic Handbook of the Northern Tour: Lakes George and Champlain; Niagara; Montreal; and Quebec* (Boston: Little, Brown and Co., 1912); Bixby, "Peter Sailly"; Thomas Pray, "Wolves of the Forest, Part 2," *Lake Champlain Weekly* [Plattsburgh, NY?], n.d., but between 2000 and 2012; Anne E. Brislin, *Narratives of Old Fort Edward*, booklet published by the Members of the Board of Education, Fort Edward Public Schools (Albany, NY: Fort Orange Press, 1962), WCHSRL; Glenn, *Story of Three Towns*, 249–58.

12. Paul A. Demers, "The French Colonial Legacy of the Canada–United States Border in Eastern North America, 1650–1783," *French Colonial History* 10 (2009): 50.

13. Gordon M. Day, *The Identity of the Saint Francis Indians*, Canadian Ethnology Services, paper no. 71 (Ottawa: National Museum of Canada, 1981), 27–28, 42. Day claims the population of Schaghticoke went from one thousand around 1676 to

none by 1754; Colin G. Calloway, *The Western Abenakis of Vermont, 1600–1800: War, Migration, and the Survival of an Indian People* (Norman, OK: Univ. of Oklahoma Press, 1990), 82, 134–35. Sylvester, *Historical Sketches*, 283–84. Nicholas N. Smith, "Fort La Presentation: The Abenaki," *St. Lawrence County Historical Association Quarterly* 38, no. 1 (Winter 1993): 9–14. Also see Day, *In Search of New England's Native Past*, 164, and Gates Curtis, ed., *Our County and Its People: A Memorial Record of St. Lawrence County, New York* (Syracuse, NY: D. Mason and Company, 1894), 41–46. Johansen and Mann, *Encyclopedia of the Haudenosaunee*, 12–13. Kurt A. Jordan, "Incorporation and Colonization: Postcolumbian Iroquois Satellite Communities and Processes of Indigenous Autonomy," *American Anthropologist* 115, no. 1 (2013): 29–43. Godfrey J. Olsen, "Archeology of Ticonderoga," *Proceedings of the New York State Historical Association* 32 (1934): 407–11.

14. Jon Parmenter, "After the Mourning Wars: The Iroquois as Allies in Colonial North American Campaigns, 1676–1760," *William and Mary Quarterly*, 3d series, 64, no. 1 (Jan. 2007): 66. Also see Berleth, *Bloody Mohawk*, 47, 49. Barbara Garymont, "The Six Nations Indians in the Revolutionary War," in *Race and Gender in the Northern Colonies*, ed. Jan Noel (Toronto: Canadian Scholars Press, Inc., 2000), 185–87.

15. Nathaniel Bartlett Sylvester, *The Historic Muse on Mount MacGregor, One of the Adirondacks Near Saratoga* (Troy, NY: N. B. Sylvester, 1885), 8, and J. H. French, *Gazetteer of the State of New York: Embracing a Comprehensive View of the Geography, Geology, and General History of the State, and a Complete History and Description of Every County, City, Town, Village, and Locality with Full Tables of Statistics*, 8th ed. (Syracuse, NY: 1860), 681n6, indicate the Palmertown Mountains were named after Indian refugees from Connecticut who settled there. Bruchac, "Historical Erasure," x. Stiles, *From Then Till Now*, 147. Genevieve Woodard, "American Indians in Washington County, New York," vertical file "Indians of North America," WCHSRL. Alice Nash, communication to the author, Jun. 6, 2013. Brown, ed., *History of Warren County, NY*, 189. *1858 Chase Map of Warren County*, WCRA.

16. "Death of Abigail (Rice) Johnson, Whose Mother, Abigail (Andrews) Rice, Witnessed the Horrors of the Wyoming Massacre," Obituary, *Elizabethtown Post*, Aug. 16, 1901, 1. Brown, *Pleasant Valley*, 64–66. Brown's assessment that the people were Algonquian is based on his belief they were the people the Iroquois called the "Adirondacks."

17. Emma Remington (Parishville historian), personal conversations with author by phone, Nov. 17, 2008, and in person, Jul. 2009. Also see local history written by Emma Remington entitled *A Heritage: The American Indian Town of Parishville* (Parishville, NY: Parishville Museum, n.d.).

18. Calloway, *Western Abenakis of Vermont*, 175–81; Benn, *Iroquois in the War of 1812*, 19, 62; Smith, "Fort La Presentation," 1. Also see "A Brief History

of Akwesasne 1755–1915," *Current: The Journal of North Country Action* 5, no. 7 (Jan.–Feb. 1990): 6–7. La Présentation is also referred to as Fort de la Présentation.

19. Angus, *Extraordinary Adirondack Journey*, 3–4, 7, 22–24. Frederick J. Seaver, *Historical Sketches of Franklin County and Its Several Towns with Many Short Biographies* (Albany, NY: J. B Lyon Co., 1918), 376. "Our Adirondack Correspondence," *New York Herald*, Aug. 10, 1857; Alfred Billings Street, *Woods and Waters; or, The Saranacs and Racket* (New York: M. Doolady, 1860), 209–13. J. Dyneley Prince, "Some Forgotten Indian Place Names in the Adirondacks," *Journal of American Folklore* (1900), 125. William R. Marleau, *Big Moose Station: A Story from 1893–1983* (Van Nuys, CA: Marleau Family Press, printed by Delta Lithograph, 1986), 2, indicates Salanac was a berry. Day, "Abenaki Place-Names," 251, questions these translations but only offers a tentative alternative that Saranac is a corruption of the French "St. Helens."

20. Robbie Ethridge and Sheri M. Shuck-Hall, eds. *Mapping the Mississippian Shatter Zone: The Colonial Indian Slave Trade and Regional Instability In the American South* (Lincoln: Univ. of Nebraska Press, 2009), 2. James C. Scott, *The Art of Not Being Governed: An Anarchist History of Upland Southeast Asia* (New Haven, CT: Yale Univ. Press, 2009), 8, 22.

21. Bert Salwen, "Indians of Southern New England and Long Island: Early Period," in *Handbook of the North American Indian, Northeast*, vol. 15, edited by Bruce G. Trigger (Washington, DC: Smithsonian Institution, 1978), 160. Cronon, *Changes in the Land*, 37, 47. Haviland and Power, *Original Vermonters*, 158–68. Also see Day, "Western Abenaki," 153–54.

22. Haviland and Power, *Original Vermonters*, 161–62.

23. Ibid., 158–68, 179–80.

24. Day, "Western Abenaki," 151, 153. Dates are based on Gordon Day's claim that Odanak was a community of Indigenous immigrants that could not be older than 1660 and that the French established a mission there in 1700 under Father Jacques Bigot. Calloway, *Western Abenakis of Vermont*, 11, 14, 18, 24. Day, *Identity of the Saint Francis Indians*, 19–20, 42–43, 47–49. Also see William H. Sorrell, Attorney General for the State of Vermont and Eve Jacobs-Carnahan, Special Assistant Attorney General, *Vermont's Response to the Abenaki Nation: State of Vermont's Response to Petition for Federal Acknowledgement of the St. Francis/Sokoki Band of the Abenaki Nation of Vermont*, Dec. 2002 (2nd printing). Calloway, *Western Abenakis of Vermont*, 202. Day, *Identity of the Saint Francis Indians*, 23–24.

25. Haviland and Power, *Original Vermonters*, 245; Calloway, *Western Abenakis of Vermont*, 234–35. Wiseman, *Voice of the Dawn*, 120.

26. Day, *Identity of the Saint Francis Indians*, 55, 61. Thomas M. Charland, *Histoire Des Abénakis D'Odanak: 1675–1937* (Montreal: Les Éditions du Lévrier, 1964). Claude Gélinas, "La Mauricie des Abénaquis au XIXe siècle," *Recherches*

amérindiennes au Québec 33, no. 2 (2003), 44–56. Also see Haviland and Power, *Original Vermonters*, 239–46. Calloway, *Western Abenakis of Vermont*, 239–48; Day, *In Search of New England's Native Past*, 209; Demers, "French Colonial Legacy." "From the White Mountains," *New York Times*, Aug. 23, 1858 (ProQuest Historical Newspapers, *New York Times*). *1876 Annual Report of the Department of the Interior for the Year Ended 30th June, 1876*, accessed Jul. 16, 2018, http://central .bac-lac.gc.ca/.item/?id=1876-IAAR-RAAI&op=pdf&app=indianaffairs. For the effect of conservation game and fishing laws, see Darcy Ingram, "'Au temps et dans les quantités qui lui plaisent': Poachers, Outlaws, and Rural Banditry in Québec," *Histoire sociale/Social History* 42, no. 83 (May 2009): 1–33. For discussion of the industrialization of the area around Odanak, see Jeanne L. Manore, "The Technology of Rivers and Community Transformation: An Alternative History of the St. Francis," *Journal of Eastern Townships Studies* 23 (Fall 2003): 27–40.

27. Benn, *Iroquois in the War of 1812*, 19, 62, 192–93. Smith, "Fort La Presentation," 1. Also see "A Brief History of Akwesasne," 6–7. Sue Ellen Dow, "A History of Akwesasne," *Franklin Historical Review* 33 (1998): 9–17. Hough, *History of St. Lawrence and Franklin Counties*, 125–83. Ingram, "Au temps et dans les quantités," 10–11; Darcy Ingram, "Nature's Improvement: Wildlife, Conservation, and Conflict in Quebec, 1850–1914" (PhD diss., McGill University, 2007), 39–41, noted the Lower Canada Game Act of 1858 and the Fishery Act of 1858.

28. Daren Bonaparte, "The History of Akwesasne from Pre-Contact to Modern Times," *Wampum Chronicles*, accessed Sep. 19, 2012, http://www.wampum chronicles.com/history.html. Benn, *Mohawks on the Nile*, especially ch. 4, "Mohawks as Workers," 92–111. Also see Patricia Jasen, *Wild Things: Nature, Culture, and Tourism in Ontario, 1790–1914* (Toronto: Univ. of Toronto Press, 1995), 70–72; *Dominion of Canada Annual Report of the Department of Indian Affairs for the Year Ended 31st December, 1884*, accessed Jul. 16, 2018, http://central.bac-lac.gc .ca/.item/?id=1884-IAAR-RAAI&op=pdf&app=indianaffairs, and Bonaparte, "History of Akwesasne."

29. Frank Tough, *"As Their Natural Resources Fail": Native Peoples and the Economic History of Northern Manitoba, 1870–1930* (Vancouver: Univ. of British Columbia Press, 1996), 219.

30. Adcock and Adcock, *Images of America*, 10. Also see Knox, "Piseco Lake," 2, 106. For references to Indian Jo and map of Jo Indian Island, see Albert Vann Fowler, ed., *Cranberry Lake 1845–1959: An Adirondack Miscellany* (Blue Mountain Lake, NY: Adirondack Museum, 1959). "Joe Indian Lake Founded by Fugitive Redskin Couple," *Watertown Daily Times* (Potsdam, NY), Sep. 30, [no year]. Emma Remington, conversation with author, Nov. 17, 2008. Ms. Remington informed me the correct spelling was "Jo" and that he and his wife lived outside of the White settlement at Jo Indian Pond, which is named for him.

31. Smith, ed., *History of Warren County*, 408–9. "Indian Biographies from Lake George," *Glens Falls Post-Star*, Dec. 14, 1963, 13–14. *1855 New York State Census, Town of Hague, Warren County.*

32. Old Alec is mentioned in Seaver, *Historical Sketches*, 23–24. Emma Remington, conversation with author, Nov. 17, 2008. "Derrick Remains a Pleasant Memory," *Plattsburgh Press Republican*, Oct. 29, 1989, section C.

33. Bruchac, "Historical Erasure," 259. See also O'Brien, *Firsting and Lasting*. Horton, "Sabael Benedict," 18. Christopher Roy, personal conversation with author, May 7, 2009.

34. Daniel H. Usner Jr., *Indian Work: Language and Livelihood in Native American History* (Cambridge, MA: Harvard Univ. Press, 2009), 94–95. Garrett Clute, "Map of Lake George," dated 1891, based on survey conducted by Clute in 1810, WCCO-RCA. F. W. Beers's *County Atlas of Warren, New York 1876* (WCCO-RCA) contained the phrase "Indian Encampment" with regard to this neighborhood. *1880 US Federal Census, Village of Caldwell, Warren County.* Deed to Sally (Sarah) Keziah (Kazia), Dec. 22, 1860, Warren County, NY, Deeds, Book 7, p. 222, Glens Falls, NY, WCCO-RCA. *New York State Census, Hamilton County, NY.* Full name based on correspondence with Kevin Wolfe, descendant of Sarah Angeline Keziah-Otondonsonne (Otôdoson) Alumkassett. E-mail communication with author, January 14, 2018.

35. Christopher Roy, personal conversation with author, May 7, 2009, and e-mail to author, Oct. 1, 2012.

36. Hoffman, *Wild Scenes*, 2:21–22. Also see Simms, *Trappers of New York*, 149; Simms states Gill fought for the British during the American Revolution and for the Americans during the War of 1812.

37. "Partial History of Indian Lake Area," *Indian Lake Bulletin* (Summer 1961), papers borrowed from Scotty Miller, articles by "Laura M. Guenther. Mss.," vertical file "Indian Lake, NY," AM-BML (reviewed Apr. 29, 2009). Christopher Roy, "Looking Back on the Life and Times of John Mitchell, Abenaki of Indian Lake." *Sun Community News* http://www.suncommunitynews.com/articles/the-sun/looking-back-on-the-life-and-times-of-john/? (Elizabethtown, NY). Jun. 24, 2009. *1880 US Federal Census, Chester, Warren County, NY*, 46D. Horton "Sabael Benedict," 18. Bill Zulo (Hamilton County and Indian Lake historian), personal conversation with author, Oct. 3, 2011. Todd, *Summer Gleanings*, 261–66. Laura M. Guenther, "Glimpses of Sabael," transcript, vertical file "Surname Sabeal [sic]—Indian Lake," 2, WCHO (reviewed Nov. 17, 2009).

38. Christopher Roy, personal conversation with author, May 7, 2009, and e-mail correspondence, Oct. 1, 2012, and Feb. 24, 2013. I do not have any details on the possible fifth child. Todd, *Summer Gleanings*, 265. Anglican Church records found in *Quebec Vital and Church Records (Drouin Collection)*, 1621–1968,

Ancestry.ca. Record for Mary or Marie Benedict in the 1862 *Abenaquis Protestants P.Q. Registres Photographries au Greffe de Sorel*, Ancestry.ca records.

39. Christopher Roy, e-mail communication with author, Oct. 1, 2012. John Mitchell was the son of Captain Pierre Michele Agent and Marie Eunice Angelique.

40. The *1870 US Federal Census, Indian Lake, Hamilton County* shows Elijah and George Camp next to each other on the census. Their cousin's daughter, Mary Louise Mitchell and her husband, Charles Palmer are listed next. *1860 US Federal Census, Indian Lake, Hamilton County, NY* shows the cousins living with and working for James Cosgrove and his family along with six other non-Native men.

41. Unknown author, article about Chief Sabael, *Indian Lake Bulletin*, Jul. c. 1965, Cliff and Kelly Marl Papers, vertical file "Indian Lake, NY," AM-BML (reviewed Apr. 29, 2009). Simms, *Trappers of New York*, 153–58. Todd, *Summer Gleanings*, 263–65. Alice Nash's article "Théophile Panadis (1889–1966)," 86, indicates that even into the twentieth century most Abenaki were trilingual speakers and that English was the least known. George Levi Brown, "Sebille, the Indian," *Elizabethtown Post Gazette*, Apr. 5, 1900, from a typescript given by Mrs. Early (T. Ovitt, 6/70), biography file "Benedict family," AM-BML (reviewed Oct. 2008).

42. *1855 New York State Census, Queensbury (Glens Falls), Warren County*. Henry J. Raymond, "A Week in the Wilderness: Third Letter, The Adirondack Iron Works and Beds—Return to Raquette Lake," *New York Times*, Jul. 7, 1855, 2.

43. Guenther, "Glimpses of Sabael, NY," 3, WCHO. Todd, *Summer Gleanings*, 263–65; Horton "Sabael Benedict," 16. "A History of the McIntyre Mine near Newcomb, N.Y.," AdirondackPark.net, accessed Oct. 19, 2011, http://www.adirondack-park.net/history/mcintyre.mine.html. Masten, *Story of Adirondac*, 17. Paul Rayno, "Sabael, Indian guide," *Glens Falls Post-Star*, n.d., biography file "Sabael Benedict," AM-BML (reviewed Oct. 2008). Janet Hall (Keene Valley historian), personal conversation with author, Apr. 6, 2009, Keene Valley, NY.

44. Alice Nash, "Odanak durant les années 1920: un prisme reflétant l'histoire des abénaquis" (trans. Claude Gélinas), *Recherches amérindiennes au Québec* 32, no. 2 (2002): 24.

45. Cynthia J. Van Zandt, *Brothers among Nations: The Pursuit of Intercultural Alliances in Early America, 1580–1660* (Oxford: Oxford Univ. Press, 2008), 10, 15, 187. Cayton and Teute, eds., *Contact Points*, 2, describe a frontier as an area where settled, unsettled, and uncivilized met.

46. Haviland and Power, *Original Vermonters*, 243.

47. Karen Ordahl Kupperman, *Indians and English: Facing Off in Early America* (Ithaca, NY: Cornell Univ. Press, 2000), 31, 192–94, 213–15, 219–20, 229–30. New England colonists were usually Puritans and other marginal populations the English wanted to place at arm's length. Alan Taylor, *The Civil War of 1812: American Citizens, British Subjects, Irish Rebels, and Indian Allies* (New York: Vintage Books, 2011),

203–10 (quote p. 203). One must also keep in mind that much of the violence during this period was due to world-systems capitalism even between Indian nations. The fur trade, deerskin trade in the south, and other natural resources in North America caused a lot of violence throughout Indian country based on competition for access to European traders and goods. On a broader scale, one can include other European colonizers, such as the Dutch, French, and the Spanish to the south, but by this time and in this place, English colonization was almost exclusively influential.

48. Berleth, *Bloody Mohawk*, 115, 270–71, 283. Alan Taylor, *The Divided Ground: Indians, Settlers, and the Northern Borderland of the American Revolution* (New York: Vintage Books, 2006), 112. Philip J. Deloria, *Playing Indian* (New Haven, CT: Yale Univ. Press, 1998), 44. Jasper M. Trautsch, "'Mr. Madison's War' or the Dynamic of Early American Nationalism," *Early American Studies* (Fall 2012): 630–70, 636, 639. Trautsch argues this campaign got a majority of Republican legislators elected and forced the United States into the War of 1812, which Madison was trying to avoid. Taylor, *Civil War of 1812*, 127.

49. White, *Middle Ground*, 368–70, 377–78, 383, 388–89. Nancy Shoemaker, *A Strange Likeness: Becoming Red and White in Eighteenth-Century North America* (New York: Oxford Univ. Press, 2004), 141. Taylor, *Civil War of 1812*, 414.

50. The *Declaration of Independence* states in relevant part: "The history of the present King of Great Britain is a history of repeated injuries and usurpations, all having in direct object the establishment of an absolute Tyranny over these States. To prove this, let Facts be submitted to a candid world. . . . He has excited domestic insurrections amongst us, and has endeavoured to bring on the inhabitants of our frontiers, the merciless Indian Savages whose known rule of warfare, is an undistinguished destruction of all ages, sexes and conditions." From "The Declaration of Independence: The Want, Will, and Hopes of the People," UShistory.org, accessed Sep. 24, 2011, http://www.ushistory.org/declaration/document/.

51. White, *Middle Ground*, 413–17. Adcock and Adcock, *Images of America*, 11. Other local White trappers who were considered to be Indian hunters or haters included Shadrack Dunning and Green White. Dunning and Stoner were more often called Indian hunters. Sylvester, *Historical Sketches*, 177–78.

52. Simms, *Trappers of New York*, 18, 112, 191.

53. Ibid., 82–84, 113–22, 126–33, 143–45. It has been suggested that Stoner served as an archetype for James Fennimore Cooper's Natty Bumppo in his Leatherstocking Tales, but Alan Taylor argues the archetype was David Shipman, a squatter near the Cooper family in Otsego County. Taylor, *William Cooper's Town: Power and Persuasion on the Frontier of the Early American Republic* (New York: A. A. Knopf. Distributed by Random House, 1995), 53.

54. Schneider, *Adirondacks*, 78. A. L. Byron Curtis, *The Life and Adventures of Nat Foster: Trapper and Hunter of the Adirondacks* (Utica, NY: Press of Thomas

J. Griffiths, 1912), 26, 83–84, 94–110; and Simms, *Trappers of New York*, 175, 182, 243–48.

55. Simms, *Trappers of New York*, 200, 203, 208–48. Simms uses actual trial testimony, but I was unable to locate the testimony from Herkimer County and I was referred to this book. Schneider, *Adirondacks*, 78–80. For a similar version of the Drid/Foster story, see Sylvester, *Historical Sketches*, 181–82, who also used the court records, and Curtis, *Life and Adventures of Nat Foster*, ch. 14, "The Murder and Trial." For reference to the relatives reburying Peter Waters in their customary way, see Martin Pickands, "Cultural Resources Reconnaissance Survey," *Cultural Resource Survey Program*, Sep. 2000; and Mary Hogan photograph entitled "Peter Waters, May He Rest in Peace," Oct. 2001, showing the dedication of a monument to Peter Waters on the banks of First Lake in Old Forge on October 1, 2001. Pickands and his wife, Department of Transportation representative Marty Dwyer, local historian Mike Caltairone, St. Regis Tribal Historian Ateronhiatakon, and Chief Alma Ransom are in the photo. Document and photograph located TWHA-GM (reviewed Sep. 2009).

56. Samuel H. Hammond, *Hills, Lakes, and Forest Streams; or, a Tramp in the Chateaugay Woods* (New York: J. C. Derby, 1854), 71–75, 168–72, 235. Graham, *Adirondack Park*, 83–87.

57. "Indian Biographies from Lake George," *Glens Falls Post-Star*, Dec. 14, 1963, 14. Curtis, *Life and Adventures of Nat Foster*, 145–49.

58. "Will Hold Inquest at Fulton Chain: District Attorney Fuller Exercises Authority in Case of Indian's Death," *Utica Herald Dispatch*, Oct. 10, 1912. "Want Marks on Dead Explained," *Syracuse Journal*, Oct. 7, 1912, 5. "Attending Inquest," *Utica Herald Dispatch*, Oct. 15, 1912, 3. "Indian Joe's Inquest," *Utica Herald Dispatch*, Oct. 16, 1912, 4. "Wife Declares Charles Murdered," *Utica Herald Dispatch*, Nov. 14, 1912, 10. "Robbery Murder's Possible Motive," *Syracuse Journal*, Dec. 3, 1912, 11. "Second Indian Tragedy," *Utica Saturday Globe*, Nov. 16, 1912. "Indians Body in the Canal: Left His Home in the Adirondacks Three Weeks Ago," *Auburn Citizen*, Nov. 16, 1912, 2. "Indian Found Drowned," *Amsterdam Evening Recorder*, Nov. 1912. "Justice for Indian?" *Utica Daily Press*, Feb. 6, 1913. The murder pronouncement delay was due to striking coroners.

59. Bixby, "Peter Sailly," 11. Simms, *Trappers of New York*, 141, 148, 151–58, 258–69. Pilcher, *The Constables*, 25.

60. Jean McGregor, "Gift of Shirt to Indian Brought Bow and Arrow," *The Saratogian*, Apr. 23, 1948, CSSH. Pilcher, *The Constables*, 51. Dates of the accident are as early as 1835 to as late as 1850. Pilcher references several visitors to corroborate that the accident had occurred by 1839. Ruth Timms, *Raquette Lake: A Time to Remember* (Utica, NY: North Country Books, 1989), 12.

61. Spencer Johnson (surveyor), "Land Grants and First Settlers in Keene," *The History of Keene Valley, Bicentennial Committee*, ed. Peggy Byrne (bicentennial

lecture series, Keene Valley, NY, Jul.–Aug., 1975–76), 33–40; transcript located in vertical file "Indian Lore," KVL. According to James Bailey (Keene Valley historian, 1979–80), Richards conducted the survey of the 1812–13 Old Military Tract Townships 1 and 2, as posted on the Adirondack Realty website, "History of the Town of Keene, New York," accessed Jun. 16, 2011, http://adkrealty.com/kvhist1.html. Stiles, *From Then Till Now*, 147–48. Brown, *Pleasant Valley*, 64.

62. For scholarship on settler colonialism, see Patrick Wolfe, "Settler Colonialism and the Elimination of the Native," *Journal of Genocide Research* 84, no. 4 (2006): 387–409; Patrick Wolfe, "The Settler Complex: An Introduction," *American Indian Culture and Research Journal* 37, no. 2 (2013): 1–17; or Walter L. Hixson, *American Settler Colonialism: A History* (New York: Palgrave Macmillan, 2013).

63. Peg Masters and George Cataldo, "Howard Weiman Logging History Interview," transcript, TWHA-GM (reviewed Mar. 18, 2009). "Body of Victim Identified," *Utica Herald Dispatch*, May 28, 1913. For other examples of Mohawk working for the railroad, see Henry A Harter, *Fairy Tale Railroad: The Mohawk and Malone from the Mohawk, through the Adirondacks to the St Lawrence—The Golden Chariot Route* (Binghamton, NY: Vail-Ballou, 1979), 42; Charles H. Burnett, *Conquering the Wilderness: The Building of the Adirondack & St. Lawrence Railway by William Seward Webb, 1891–92* (Privately printed, 1932), 39; and Marleau, *Big Moose Station*, 45–47.

64. John Fadden, e-mail message to author, Oct. 29, 2009. Dan Brenan, ed., *Canoeing the Adirondacks with Nessmuk: The Adirondack Letters of George Washington Sears* (Blue Mountain Lake, NY: Adirondack Museum, 1962), 37–45. Harris, *Adirondack*, 16, 31, 36, 49–50, 89–90. Also see "Lewis County," *Utica Daily Observer*, May 26, 1871. Ted Aber and Stella King, *The History of Hamilton County* (Lake Pleasant, NY: Great Wilderness Books, 1965), 137. Christopher Roy, e-mail message to author, Apr. 21, 2009; "Jimmy Dewstop Letter," obituary for Johnny Leaf, unknown publication, but probably the *Boonville NY Herald*, Feb. 27, 1908, 9.

65. James H. Merrell argues that the term "removal" is a euphemism for ethnic cleansing in his "Second Thoughts on Colonial Historians and American Indians," *William and Mary Quarterly* 69, no. 3 (Jul. 2012): 509, citing John Mack Faragher, "'More Motley than Mackinaw': From Ethnic Mixing to Ethnic Cleansing on the Frontier of the Lower Missouri, 1783–1833," in *Contact Points: American Frontiers from the Mohawk Valley to the Mississippi, 1750–1830*, ed. Andrew R. L. Cayton and Fredrika J. Teute (Chapel Hill: Univ. of North Carolina Press, 1998), 304–26; Daniel K. Richter, *Facing East from Indian Country: A Native History of Early America* (Cambridge, MA: Harvard Univ. Press, 2003), 190, 199–206, 236; Daniel Walker Howe, *What Hath God Wrought: The Transformation of America, 1815–1848*, Oxford History of the United States (Oxford: Oxford Univ. Press, 2009), 423. Issues around the notion of deliberate versus nondeliberate ethnic cleansing are hotly debated; my

intention here is to acknowledge the debate versus drawing conclusions whether ethnic cleansing occurred in the Adirondacks.

66. Robin Brownlie and Mary-Ellen Kelm, "Desperately Seeking Absolution: Native Agency as Colonialist Alibi?," *Canadian Historical Review* 75, no. 4 (Dec. 1994): 556.

67. Philip J. Deloria, *Indians in Unexpected Places* (Lawrence: Univ. Press of Kansas, 2004), 48, 50.

68. Usner, *Indian Work*, 119, citing Joshua David Bellin, *The Demon of the Continent: Indians and the Shaping of American Literature* (Philadelphia: Univ. of Pennsylvania Press, 2001), 1–10.

3. "The Trustiest Guides in All the Wilderness"

1. "'American Angler' Article Recalls 1883 Fishing Trip to the Long Lake Area," *Tupper Lake Free Press*, Oct. 20, 1960, 8, 11.

2. Baptismal record, "Russelltown (Methodist Church and Presbyterian Church)," *Quebec Vital and Church Records (Drouin Collection), 1621–1968*, Ancestry .ca records; *1900 US Federal Census, Long Lake, Hamilton County, NY. 1910 US Federal Census, Long Lake, Hamilton County, NY.* "First Congregational Church Pulpit Bible," presented in 1842 by Rev. J. Todd, a.k.a. the "Keller Family Bible," LLA.

3. Schneider, *The Adirondacks*, 168. Both men and women convalesced here.

4. Gail Bederman, *Manliness and Civilization: A Cultural History of Gender and Race in the United States, 1880–1917* (Chicago: Univ. of Chicago Press, 1995), 12–15; Mark C. Carnes and Clyde Griffen, eds., *Meanings for Manhood: Constructions of Masculinity in Victorian America* (Chicago: Univ. of Chicago Press, 1990), 6–7; David Strauss, "Toward a Consumer Culture: 'Adirondack Murray' and the Wilderness Vacation." *American Quarterly* 39, no. 2 (Summer 1987): 270–83.

5. Frederick Jackson Turner, *The Significance of the Frontier in American History* (Indianapolis, Bobbs-Merrill, 1894), accessed Oct. 13, 2012, http://xroads .virginia.edu/~hyper/turner/home.html.

6. Cronon, *Changes in the Land*, 19–22; also see Carolyn Merchant, *Ecological Revolutions: Nature, Gender, and Science in New England*, (Chapel Hill, NC: Univ. of North Carolina Press, 1989), 11–12, 69. Gregory Eric Gillespie, *Hunting for Empire: Narratives of Sport in Rupert's Land, 1840–1870* (Vancouver: Univ. of British Columbia Press, 2007), 14. Mary Louise Pratt, *Imperial Eyes: Travel Writing and Transculturation*, 2nd ed. (New York: Routledge, 2008), 9. Strauss, "Toward a Consumer Culture," 270–83. John MacKenzie, "The Imperial Pioneer and Hunter and the British Masculine Stereotype in Late Victorian and Edwardian Times," in *Manliness and Morality: Middle Class Masculinity in Britain and North America, 1800–1940*, ed. J. A. Mangan and James Walvin (New York: St. Martin's Press, 1987), 178–79. Parenteau, "Care, Control and Supervision," 35. John F. Reiger, *American*

Sportsmen and the Origins of Conservation (Norman: Univ. of Oklahoma Press, 1986), 22, citing Stewart L. Udall's "Myth of Superabundance," in *Quiet Crisis* (1963; repr. New York, 1967).

7. Richard Patrick Roth, "The Adirondack Guide (1820–1919): Hewing Out an American Occupation," (PhD diss., Syracuse University, 1990), 52–53. Deloria, *Playing Indian*, 101.

8. David Whisnant, *All That Is Native and Fine: The Politics of Culture in an American Region* (Chapel Hill, NC: Univ. of North Carolina Press, 1983), 8, 14, 254. Also see Ian McKay, *The Quest of the Folk: Antimodernism and Cultural Selection in Twentieth-Century Nova Scotia* (Montreal: McGill-Queen's Univ. Press, 1994).

9. Parenteau, "Care, Control, and Supervision," 3, 33–34. Tina Loo, "Of Moose and Men: Hunting for Masculinities in British Columbia, 1880–1939," *Western Historical Quarterly* 32, no. 3 (Autumn 2001): 298, 310.

10. Jasen, *Wild Things*, 138.

11. Cecil Clay, "Hunting, Fishing Trips in Newcomb Are Century Ago Recalled in Old Letters," *Tupper Lake Free Press*, Jan. 4, 1960, 7. Lynda Jessup, "Landscapes of Sport, Landscapes of Exclusion: The Sportsman's Paradise in Late 19th-Century Canadian Painting," *Journal of Canadian Studies* 40, no. 1 (Winter 2006): 104.

12. McKay, *Quest of the Folk*, 10. Jacoby, *Crimes against Nature*, 19.

13. Caroline M. Welsh, "These Glorious Mountains," *Antiques and The Arts Weekly* accessed May 11, 2011, http://antiquesandthearts.com/archive/cover.htm. Roth, "Adirondack Guide," 36–49.

14. Richard H. Gassan, *The Birth of American Tourism: New York, the Hudson Valley, and American Culture, 1790–1830* (Amherst: Univ. of Massachusetts Press, 2008), 79–80, 112–14, 119–21, 140. Charles Fenno Hoffman, letters, *New York Mirror*, Sep. 23 and 30, 1837; Oct. 7, 14, 21, 28, 1837; and Dec. 16, 1837. Hoffman's letters were later reprinted in his two-volume *Wild Scenes in the Forest and Prairie*; 1:76–122 refers specifically to the Adirondacks, and he refers to the different names for the Adirondack mountains at p. 76.

15. J. Bonsall, *The Northern Tourist: An Illustrated Book of Summer Travel* (Philadelphia: John E. Potter and Co., 1879), 5–8. Murray, *Adventures in the Wilderness*, 33, 41–42. Terrie, *Forever Wild*, 46.

16. Roth, "Adirondack Guide." Clay, "Hunting, Fishing Trips," 2, 7. New York State Forest Commissioners, "Adirondack Guides," *New York State Forest Commissioners Annual Report, 1894*, 348, accessed Jul. 17, 2018, https://babel.hathitrust.org/cgi/pt?id=mdp.39015069540212;view=1up;seq=9.

17. Kenneth Durant, *Guideboat Days and Ways* (Blue Mountain Lake, NY: Adirondack Museum, 1963) as cited in Maitland DeSormo's *Summers on the Saranac*, 111. Also see Brumley, *Guides of the Adirondacks, A History: A Short Season, Hard Work Low Pay* (Utica, NY: North Country Books, 1994), 9.

18. Murray, *Adventures in the Wilderness*, appendix, 87. New York State Forest Commissioners, "Adirondack Guides," 349. "About 500 Guides Working Adirondacks by 1880s, Old Magazine Article Reports," *Tupper Lake Press*, Sep. 22, 1960. New York State Forest Commissioners, *Annual Report of the Forest Commission of the State of New York, 1893*, accessed Jul. 17, 2018, https://archive.org/details/annualreportfor04unkngoog. John J. Duquette, "The Famous Adirondack Guides' Association: Heyday of the Guides," *Adirondack Daily Enterprise* (Saranac Lake, NY), Jun. 18, 1987, 8.

19. Hoffman, *Wild Scenes*, 1:101–11. Charles Wilkins Webber, *The Hunter-Naturalist: Romance of Sporting; or Wild Scenes and Wild Hunters* (Philadelphia: J. B. Lippincott, 1867), 492–94, 515–26. Murray, "Jack-Shooting in a Foggy Night," *Adventures in the Wilderness*, 168–92.

20. Hoffman, *Wild Scenes*, 1:76, 92–99, 102–12, 117.

21. Hoffman, *Wild Scenes*, 1:92–99, 117. Todd, *Long Lake*, xxiv (introduction at xi, xiii, xxiii). Todd had set up a Methodist mission in Long Lake in the early 1840s, including the appointment of a young missionary named Parker in 1848 who did not stay long. Warder H. Cadbury's introduction to the 1997 reprint of *Long Lake* also suggests that Todd may have been the muse for Longfellow's parson in his poem "The Birds of Killingworth" in *Tales of a Wayside Inn*. Also see Clay, "Hunting, Fishing Trips."

22. Joel T. Headley, *The Adirondack; or, Life in the Woods* (New York: Baker and Scribneir, 1853), 248. Terrie, *Forever Wild*, 46–59, quote on p. 58.

23. Hoffman, *Wild Scenes*, 1:2, 23, 31, 73, 75, and 79. Also see Warder H. Cadbury, introduction to *Long Lake*, by Rev. John Todd (1845; repr., Fleishmanns, NY: Purple Mountain Press, 1997), xvii–xxiv. Another Adirondack travel writer was Samuel H. Hammond, who was one of the first to call for the preservation of the Adirondacks in 1857; see his *Wild Northern Scenes*, 83.

24. Orville L. Holley, ed., *The Picturesque Tourist: Being a Guide through the Northern and Eastern States and Canada* (New York: J. Disturnell, 1844). Henry Lee, *Lee's Guide to Saratoga, the Queen of Spas* (New York: Chas R. Parker, 1883); *The Travelers Steamboat & RR Guide to the Hudson River, Describing the Cities, Towns & Places of Interest along the Route with Maps & Engravings* (New York: Phelps & Watson, 1857). E. R. Wallace, *Descriptive Guide to the Adirondacks, and Handbook of Travel*, 10th ed. (Syracuse, NY: Watson Gill, 1882). Taintor Brothers & Co., *Saratoga illustrated—The Visitor's Guide of Saratoga Springs* (NY: Taintor Brothers and Co., 1889). *Raymond & Whitcomb Co. Guidebooks—Summer & Autumn Tours* (1911). Seneca Ray Stoddard, *The Adirondacks: Illustrated* (Albany, NY: Weed, Parsons and Co., 1874), and Seneca Ray Stoddard, *The Adirondacks: Illustrated 38th Year* (Glens Falls, NY: Published by the author, 1912). Murray's *Adventures in the Wilderness* contained many of the characteristics of a guidebook.

25. "The Raquette Club," *Harper's New Monthly Magazine*, 242 (Aug. 1870). The article states: "There were guides of all sizes, ages, nations, and degrees: lazy . . . witty . . . talkative . . . low bred . . . bragging . . . silent . . . bad . . . good . . . independent . . . hotel . . . sober . . . thirsty . . . gray-haired . . . guides well-recommended and guides without character—Frenchmen, Yankees, Irish, and Indians." Murray, *Adventures in the Wilderness*, 35; also see Brumley, *Guides of the Adirondacks*, 18.

26. Jerold Pepper, "When Men and Mountains Meet: Mapping the Adirondacks," in *Adirondack Prints and Printmakers: The Call of the Wild*, ed. Caroline Mastin Welsh (Blue Mountain Lake and Syracuse, NY: Adirondack Museum and Syracuse Univ. Press, 1998), 1–24, 10. Terrie, *Contested Terrain*, 134–35.

27. Colin G. Calloway, "Sir William Johnson, Highland Scots, and American Indians," *New York History* 89, no. 2 (Spring 2008): 163–77, 173. Local histories also include this escape, especially when referring to the naming of Raquette Lake; e.g., Donaldson, *History of the Adirondacks*, 1:42–43.

28. Frances Seaman, "Adirondack Guides Hold a Special Place in History," *Hamilton County News* (Long Lake, NY), Aug. 4, 1992, 4. Parishville Historical Association, "The Early Settlers," in *Sketches of Parishville, 1809–1976*, vertical file "Parishville," AM-BML (reviewed May 4, 2009). Todd, *Long Lake*, 59. Guenther, "Glimpses of Sabael, NY," 2. Ray Smith, former archivist of Long Lake, e-mail to author, Apr. 30, 2009, with reference to communication from Hilary to the Long Lake archivist. Smith provided a copy of some of the manuscripts and explained they appeared in installments in the *Indian Lake Bulletin* in 1961 and again in 1965 and states the title was "Glimpses of Sabael: Its First White Settlers—Their Descendants Living Nearby." John and Lige Camp were related to Sabael and were probably his son-in-law and grandson, or perhaps two grandsons.

29. Johnson, "Land Grants and First Settlers in Keene," vertical file "Indian Lore," KVL. Terrie, *Contested Terrain*, 7–8. Webb, *Footsteps through the Adirondacks*, xix, 42, 159–60. Also see "The Adirondack Region—Ascent of Mount Seward," *Albany Argus*, Nov. 21, 1870.

30. Watson B. Berry, "Start of Adirondack Journey, Saratoga to Lowville, Is Told," North Country Chronicle, *Watertown Daily Times*, Nov. 1957, published much of Raymond's letter verbatim. Berry used this and the other Raymond letters in a manuscript entitled "Addendum to Chapter 13," Watson Berry Papers, box 2, folder 4A, SLUL. The third and fourth letters by Raymond are available online.

31. Watson B. Berry, "Adirondack Mountains, Lakes Impressed Traveling Writer," North Country Chronicle, *Watertown Daily Times*, Nov. 1957, Watson Berry Papers, box 2, folder 4A, SLUL, referring to Henry J. Raymond's letter published June 26, 1855.

32. Deloria, *Playing Indian*, 178–79.

33. US Congress, *Indian Removal Act of 1830*, stat. 1, May 28, 1830, 21st Cong., session 1, chap. 148. Taylor, *Divided Ground*; Laurence M. Hauptman, *Formulating American Indian Policy in New York State, 1970–1986* (Albany: State Univ. of New York Press, 1988); Campisi and Hauptman, *Oneida Indian Experience*. Silverman, *Red Brethren*.

34. This spelling is based on Frances Seaman, "Mitchel Sabattis Honored," *Hamilton County News* (Inlet, NY), Aug. 11, 1982, 15, describing the Town of Long Lake placing a completed stone on the grave of the famous guide. This effort included research for the correct spelling of his name with one "l"; verified on a deed to convey property to the Wesleyan Church. It is unlikely he actually signed his name, as other documents indicate he did not write. Christopher Roy, e-mail to author, Jul. 18, 2011.

35. Radford, "Mitchel Sabattis," 45.

36. "An Aged Indian Hunter: Adventures of Mitchell Sabattis in the Adirondacks," *New York Sun*, Jul. 22, 1900. Frances Seaman, "Old Indian Guide Recalled," n.p., n.d., vertical file "Sabattis Family," LLA (reviewed May 2, 2009). Donaldson, *History of the Adirondacks*, 2:83. Emma Remington, conversation with author by phone, Nov. 17, 2008, and in person at the Parishville Museum, Jul. 2009.

37. Flora Miller, "Captain Peter Sabattis," 1–3, unknown publication, n.d., biography file "Mitchel Sabattis," AM-BML (reviewed Oct. 2008). Long Lake Wesleyan Methodist Church, "History," accessed Aug. 20, 2012, http://longlake wesleyan.wordpress.com/history-of-llwc/; this web page indicates that Mitchel also had a sister Betsy Ann who was fifteen years older than he was; she married a David B. Catlin, who left Long Lake after she died on December 30, 1882. This is the only reference to Betsy Ann Sabattis, and it is possible she was a cousin or an Aunt instead of Mitchel's sister (she is too old to be Hannah). The use of the term "sister" could also have been a religious term used by the Methodists. *1840 US Federal Census, Long Lake, Hamilton County, NY.* A woman between the ages of sixteen and nineteen and another man between the ages of twenty and twenty-nine lived there. The younger male could have been the eldest son known as Tomor or Solomon who was about twenty at the time, and Hannah around eighteen. Mitchel was seventeen in 1840. Todd, *Long Lake*, x, xix, xxii.

38. Headley, *Adirondack*, 249–53.

39. *1850 US Federal Census, Newcomb, Essex County, NY; 1860 US Federal Census, Newcomb.* L. E. Chittenden, *Personal Reminiscences: Including Lincoln and Others, 1840–1890* (New York: Richmond, Croscup and Co., 1893, 151–56. Chittendon embellished in his memoir; for example, he claimed Sabattis died shortly after their 1885 visit. In reality, Sabattis outlived Chittenden by nearly six years. "Woodworth Indenture," Nov. 1, 1848, deed book ff, p. 116, ECCO (reviewed Mar. 2009). "Clay Indenture," Feb. 21, 1861, Mortgage Book 4, 102–5, ECCO. *Adirondack*

Record (Elizabethtown, NY), Apr.–Jun. 1919, with New York State Supreme Court records, accessed Aug. 20, 2012, http://news2.nnyln.net/adirondack-record/1919 /adirondack-record-1919-april-june%20-%200015.pdf.

40. Todd, *Long Lake*, 80. Long Lake Wesleyan Methodist Church, "History," accessed Aug. 20, 2012, http://longlakewesleyan.wordpress.com/history-of-llwc/. Aber and King, *History of Hamilton County*, 778. "From Champlain Conference Centennial (1842–1942)," handwritten MS, vertical file "Churches," LLA. Raymond W. Smith, e-mail to author, Nov. 4, 2009, states the other two church members were Robert Shaw and James Keller. Donaldson, *History of the Adirondacks*, 2:76, and Brumley, *Guides of the Adirondacks*, 152. The Long Lake Methodist Church became part of the Champlain Conference, which began in 1845; however, the original Long Lake assembly did not last long. Later, around 1855, the church was reconstituted and remains a congregation to this day.

41. Kelly Wisecup's "Medicine, Communication, and Authority in Samson Occom's Herbal," *Early American Studies* (Fall 2012), 559, identifies Moses Paul as Wampanoag; Moses was Anthony's father. "Indian Biographies from Lake George," *Glens Falls Post-Star*, Dec. 14, 1963, 13–14. William L. Wessels, *Adirondack Profiles* (Lake George, NY: Adirondack Resorts Press, 1961), 184. DeSormo, *Summers on the Saranacs*, 103.

42. Aber and King, *History of Hamilton County*, 194, 762. "'American Angler' Article Recalls 1883 Fishing Trip to the Long Lake Area," *Tupper Lake Free Press*, Oct. 20, 1960, 8. *1850 US Federal Census, Newcomb, Essex County, New York; 1860 US Federal Census, Newcomb; 1870 US Federal Census, Long Lake, Hamilton County, NY. 1892 New York State Census, Long Lake, Hamilton County, NY. 1900 US Federal Census, Long Lake.* "An Aged Indian Hunter," *New York Sun*, Jul. 22 1900. *1905 New York State Census, Long Lake;* "Mitchel Sabattis," Obituary, *Shooting and Fishing*, Apr. 26, 1906.

43. The *1850 US Federal Census, Newcomb, Essex County, NY* does not identify ethnicity of anyone on the seven-page census of 277 people and spells the family name as Sabbates; *1860 US Federal Census, Newcomb; 1870 US Federal Census, Long Lake; 1880 US Federal Census—Long Lake; 1892 New York State Census, Long Lake; 1900 US Federal Census, Long Lake; 1905 New York State Census, Long Lake.*

44. Lauren L. Basson, "Blurring the Boundaries of Diversity: Ethnic Ambiguity and Indigenous Citizenship in Settler States," *International Journal of Diversity in Organisations, Communities and Nations* 4 (2004): 326.

45. "An Aged Indian Hunter," *New York Sun*, Jul. 22, 1900; Aber and King, *History of Hamilton County*, 24. *1850 US Federal Census, Newcomb. 1860 US Federal Census, Newcomb.* Adirondack guide boat made by Mitchel Sabattis located in storage at the Adirondack Experience, Blue Mountain Lake, New York, personal viewing and photograph taken September 30, 2010. Snowshoes made by Sabattis

for Verplanck Colvin owned by Alfred Brunner, Park Hill, Kentucky, on loan to the Adirondack Museum so long as they remain on display, L006.2001.0001 a-b ~ Snowshoe. Roland B. Miller, "The Adirondack Pack-Basket," *New York State Conservationist* 3, no. 1 (Aug.–Sep. 1948): 8–9.

46. Aber and King, *History of Hamilton County*, 522–23; Webb, *Footsteps through the Adirondacks*, 43. Day, "Abenaki Place Names in the Champlain Valley," *In Search of New England's Native Past*, 57, 233. Austin Wells Holden, *A History of the Town of Queensbury in the State of New York* (Albany: J. Munsell, 1874). Henry D. Kellogg, "Mitchell Sabattis," *Northern Monthly* 1, no. 2 (Glens Falls, NY, Jun. 1906): 14–15. Ruth V. Riley's article "Famous Adirondack Guides , No. 8, Mitchell Sabattis," *High Spots, a Magazine of the Adirondack Mountain Club* (n.d., but after 1930), 12, SLFL. "An Aged Indian Hunter," *New York Sun*, Jul. 22 1900. Sabattis's legal documents were always signed by his marking them with an "X." Murray, *Adventures in the Wilderness*, 39. "Pioneer Guides of Long Lake Fostered Development of Region in Early Days," *Adirondack Arrow* (Inlet, NY), Anniversary Old Timers' Sports Section—Part II, Jun. 16, 1938, 7.

47. "Falling Star: The Indian Beauty Who Died Last Week," Obituary, *New York Sun*, Jan. 23, 1903, 5.

48. Camp-Mead Family Records, ILM. Letter dated Apr. 25, 1924, from Elsie Camp responding to a letter from her mother, Mary Corscadden. Letter dated Apr. 27, 1925, from Mary Corscadden to Elsie Camp. Letter dated May 8, 1925, from Elsie Camp to Mary Corscadden. Letter from Mary Corscadden to Elsie Camp, May 28, 1925. Letter from Elsie Camp's attorney, Louis Crandal, to Elsie Camp, Jul. 14, 1925. An agreement dated August 10, 1925, settled the matter for two hundred dollars.

49. A Long Lake Archive report on the family noted pneumonia was the cause of Dory's death on the funeral bill paid by husband Frank Thompson to Merritt Lamos. *1900 US Federal Census, Long Lake; 1905 New York State Census, Long Lake. 1910 US Federal Census, Long Lake.*

50. Theresa Strouth Gaul, ed., *To Marry an Indian: The Marriage of Harriett Gold and Elias Boudinot in Letters, 1823–1839* (Chapel Hill: Univ. of North Carolina Press, 2005), 2, 9, 11, 21–22.

51. Katherine Ellinghaus, *Taking Assimilation to Heart: Marriages of White Women and Indigenous Men in the United States and Australia, 1887–1937* (Lincoln: Univ. of Nebraska Press, 2006), 219–20. Cathleen D. Cahill, "'You Think It Strange That I Can Love an Indian': Native Men, White Women, and Marriage in the Indian Service," *Frontiers, a Journal of Women's Studies*, 29, nos. 2–3 (2008), 106–8, 130, citing Ann Laura Stoler, *Carnal Knowledge and Imperial Power: Race and the Intimate in Colonial Rule* (Berkley: Univ. of California Press, 2002), 7, 19. Keep in mind, Gaul's *To Marry an Indian*, 15, suggests that intermarriage to

assimilate Native people had been an eighteenth-century consideration and had been rejected by the early nineteenth century.

52. Nancy Grey Osterud, *Bonds of Community: The Lives of Farm Women in Nineteenth-Century New York* (Ithaca: Cornell Univ. Press, 1991), 1–2.

53. Ruth W. Sandwell, *Contesting Rural Space: Land Policy and the Practices of Resettlement on Saltspring Island 1859–1891* (Montreal: McGill-Queen's Univ. Press, 2005), 134, citing James C. Malin, *History and Ecology: Studies of the Grassland* (Lincoln: Univ. of Nebraska Press, 1984).

54. Richter, *Facing East From Indian Country*, 239–40. Cecilia Morgan, "Creating Interracial Intimacies: British North America, Canada, and the Transatlantic World, 1830–1914," *Journal of the Canadian Historical Association/Revue de la Société historique du Canada* 19, no. 2 (2008): 101.

55. Osterud, *Bonds of Community*, 277, 279. Brennan, *Canoeing the Adirondacks with Nessmuk*, 114–22.

56. Clay, "Hunting, Fishing Trips," 7. Osterud, *Bonds of Community*, 56.

57. Aber and King, *History of Hamilton County*, 21, 25. US Constitution, Amendment XV, §1, ratified 1870, accessed at "Fifteenth Amendment to the Constitution: Primary Documents of American History," Library of Congress, Oct. 3, 2012, http://memory.loc.gov/cgi-bin/ampage?collId=llsl&fileName=015/llsl015.db&recNum=379. *US Statutes at Large* 43, ch. 233, p. 253 (1924), also known as the Indian Citizenship Act. See Charles J. Kappler, ed., *Indian Affairs: Laws and Treaties*, vol. 4 (Washington, DC: Government Printing Office, 1929), accessed Oct. 3, 2012, http://digital.library.okstate.edu/kappler/vol4/html_files/v4p0420c.html. Jacoby, *Crimes against Nature*, 48. Jacoby describes the manifestation of lawlessness by local people when it came to conservation laws in the Adirondacks and elsewhere. As well, Ingram's "'Au temps et dans les quantités" tells a similar story in that province.

58. "Guides Take Time Out at 'Tupper Lake' on 1843 Trip to Make Spruce Bark Canoe," fourth in a series on Henry J. Raymond, unknown publication, Jan. 7, 1960, 2, 7, vertical file "Guiding," LLA. Given the date and that it is part of a series running in 1960 it is probable the article was run in the *Tupper Lake Press*. "The Adirondacks in 1843," 31 TS, vertical file "Adirondacks in 1843," SLUL, appears to be a typescript of this article and was published in the *New York Evening Post*, n.d., and *St. Lawrence Plaindealer* (Canton, NY), Aug. 24, 1881, 3–5. Brumley, *Guides of the Adirondacks*, 153–54. Joel T. Headley, *Letters from the Backwoods and the Adirondac* (New York: John S. Taylor, 1850), 48. Deloria, *Playing Indian*, 178–79; Loo, "Of Moose and Men," 317. Chittenden, *Personal Reminiscences*, 143, 150.

59. Todd, *Long Lake*, 36. Todd, *Summer Gleanings*, 262–66. "Guides Take Time Out," vertical file "Guiding." LLA. Hammond, *Hills, Lakes, and Forest Streams*, 71–75, 168–72, 235.

60. Thomas N. Ingersoll, *To Intermix with Our White Brothers: Indian Mixed Bloods in the United States from Earliest Times to the Indian Removals* (Albuquerque: Univ. of New Mexico Press, 2005), xii–xiv, xvi, 40, 76, 79, citing Indian Agent John McElvain to Commissioner of Indian Affairs Hearing, 20 May 1833, National Archives M234, Roll 601, Ohio Agency, 1831–1838, 439. Lauren L. Basson, *White Enough to Be American: Race Mixing, Indigenous People, and the Boundaries of State and Nation* (Chapel Hill: North Carolina Univ. Press, 2008), 33–34, 79–80, 240, 255.

61. For examples of non-Indigenous guides being mistreated or written about condescendingly, see Donaldson, *History of the Adirondacks*, 1:124–25. Street, *Woods and Waters*, 33. Webber, *Hunter-Naturalist*, 499, 502, 512, 528, 533–35. It should be noted that Webber spelled Adirondacks as "Ariondack."

62. Roth, "Adirondack Guide," 54. Pratt, *Imperial Eyes*, 9. Loo, "Of Moose and Men," 319.

63. Elizabeth Vibert, "Real Men Hunt Buffalo: Masculinity, Race, and Class in British Fur Traders' Narratives," in *Cultures of Empire: Colonizers in Britain and the Empire of the Nineteenth and Twentieth Centuries*, ed. Catherine Hall (New York: Routledge, 2000), 281–97.

64. Sandwell, *Contesting Rural Space*, 13–14.

65. Terrie, *Contested Terrain*, 53. McKay, *Quest of the Folk*. Louis S. Warren, "The Nature of Conquest: Indians, Americans, and Environmental History," in *A Companion to American Indian History*, ed. Philip J. Deloria and Neal Salisbury (Malden, MA: Blackwell Publishing, 2004), 303.

66. Raquette Lake House Hotel Register, ILM (reviewed Oct. 19, 2008).

67. Donaldson, *History of the Adirondacks*, 2:79. William L. Wessels, "The Abenaki Indians, Early Adirondack Settlers: Architects of the Birch Bark Canoe and the Pack Basket," *Warrensburg News*, Jun. 19, 1969. King and Aber, *History of Hamilton County*, 138. Miller, "The Adirondack Pack-Basket," 8–9.

68. Coates and Morrison, *Forgotten North*, 75–77. Bruce W. Hodgins and Jamie Benidickson, *The Temagami Experience: Recreation, Resources, and Aboriginal Rights in the Northern Ontario Wilderness* (Toronto: Univ. of Toronto Press, 1989), 220. Jacoby, *Crimes against Nature*, 33.

69. Newton Greiner, "Hal Cranson Traces His Abanaki Roots to Earliest Recorded Adirondack History," *Tupper Lake Free Press*, Jan. 27, 1999, 6.

70. Gary B. Nash, "The Hidden History of Mestizo America," *Journal of American History* 87, no. 3 (Dec. 1995): 947.

4. "Pete Francis' Place"

1. Evelyn Barrett Britten, "Pete Francis, Chef Extraordinaire," *The Saratogian*, Dec. 7, 1956, SSHM (reviewed Oct. 5, 2009). F. W. Beers and Louis H. Cramer,

Combination Atlas of Saratoga and Balston: From Recent and Actual Surveys and Records (New York: J. B. Beers and Co., 1876), 64 (or possibly G4). Gassan, *Birth of American Tourism*, 5, 9, 31, 37–40, 45, 88, 160. Mary Ann Fitzgerald (Saratoga Springs historian), "'Saratoga Chips' Chronology," 2, vertical file "Saratoga County Potato Chip Stories," SCHSRL. The Speck family may be Stockbridge or Mohawk, but I could not confirm this beyond some local references and a brother George who claimed to be Mohawk. It is likely the Speck family was of mixed heritage including African, European, and Native ancestry.

2. Evelyn Barrett Britten, *Chronicles of Saratoga Springs* (Saratoga Springs, NY: published by author, 1959), 172. This book is an accumulation of Britten's newspaper column "Chronicles of Saratoga" from *The Saratogian*; some of the articles were written by her under the name Jean McGregor in the 1930s and 1940s. This particular article appeared in the newspaper under the title "Pete Francis, Chef Extraordinaire." Warren Algerond, "A Memory of Pioneer Days," Letter to the Editor, *The Saratogian*, written Aug. 23, 1912, published Aug. 24, 1912, SSPL. The article indicates Pete and Mary Francis had three sons—George, David, and Edward (who traveled to South America)—and four daughters—Sarah, Maria, Dora, and Marie Magdalene—who were still alive in 1912; two daughters, Augustus Aurelia and Cecilia, had passed away.

3. Deloria, *Indians in Unexpected Places*, 14, 234–35.

4. Paige Raibmon, *Authentic Indians: Episodes of Encounter from the Late-Nineteenth-Century Northwest Coast* (Durham, NC: Duke Univ. Press, 2005), 198.

5. Marshall Sahlins, *Stone Age Economics* (Chicago: Aldine Atherton, 1972), 185–202. Bruce G. Trigger, ed., *Handbook of North American Indians—Northeast*, vol. 15 (Washington, DC: Smithsonian Institution, 1978), 87, 166. See John Sutton Lutz, *Makúk: A New History of Aboriginal-White Relations* (Vancouver: Univ. of British Columbia Press, 2008), 219–20, for reference to trading as entrepreneurial activity.

6. William Fenton, "Northern Iroquoian Culture Patterns," in *Handbook of the North American Indians: Northeast*, vol. 15, ed. Bruce G. Trigger, 296–321 (Washington, DC: Smithsonian Institution, 1978), 315, citing Conrad E. Heidenreich's *Huronia: A History and Geography of the Huron Indians, 1600–1650* (Toronto: McClelland and Stewart, 1971), 220 ff; Olive Patricia Dickason, "The French and the Abenaki: A Study in Frontier Politics," *Vermont History* 58, no. 2 (Spring 1990): 85. William A. Starna, "Oneida Homeland," 15, based on the records of Dutch barber-surgeon Meyndertsz van den Bogaert, sent to investigate French traders in eastern Iroquoia in 1634.

7. Calvin Helin, *Dances with Dependency: Indigenous Success through Self-Reliance* (Vancouver: Orca Spirit Publishing and Communications, 2006), 80–86. Helin concludes that once colonization confined Indigenous people to reserves,

tribal self-reliance shifted to dependency on the government—a dependency that accelerated in the 1960s as social safety nets increased. Trigger, "Early Iroquoian Contacts with Europeans," *Handbook of North American Indians—Northeast*, vo. 15 (Washington, DC: Smithsonian Institution, 1978), 344. Sylvia Van Kirk, *Many Tender Ties: Women in Fur-Trade Society, 1670–1870* (1980; repr., Winnipeg: Watson and Dwyer, 1999), 46, 73–80; Jennifer S. H. Brown, *Strangers in Blood: Fur Trade Company Families in Indian Country* (Vancouver: Univ. of British Columbia Press, 1980), xvii, 1, 64. James H. Merrell, "The Indians' New World: The Catawba Experience," in *American Encounters: Natives and Newcomers from European Contact to Indian Removal, 1400–1850*, ed. Peter C. Mancall and James H. Merrell (New York: Routledge, 2007), 33; Lutz, *Makúk*, 84.

8. Rolf Knight, *Indians at Work: An Informal History of Native Labour in British Columbia, 1858–1930* (Vancouver: New Star Books, 1996), 105. See Lutz, *Makúk*, 179, 191, 219–20, for references to small scale Indigenous entrepreneurship also in the Pacific Northwest.

9. Britten, *Chronicles of Saratoga*, 172–74, as told to the author by ninety-seven-year-old Cornelius E. Durkee. Fitzgerald, "'Saratoga Chips' Chronology," 2, vertical file "Saratoga County Potato Chip Stories," SCHSRL.

10. Chrisfield Johnson, *History of Washington County New York with Illustrations and Biographical Sketches of Some of Its Prominent Men and Pioneers* (Philadelphia: J. B. Lippincott, 1878; repr., Interlaken, NY: Heart of the Lakes Publishing, 1991), 17. Also see William H. Hill, *Old Fort Edward before 1800* [An account of the historic ground now occupied by the Village of Fort Edward, New York] (Fort Edward, NY: Privately published, 1929), 27–49; and Smith, ed., *History of Warren County*, 211. Kalm, *Travels into North America*, 2:294. Also see Brislin, *Narratives of Old Fort Edward*, 9–10, WCHSRL. Johnson, *History of Washington County*, 17. For Indigenous women acting as part of a network, see Van Kirk, *Many Tender Ties*, especially 73–80. Susan Sleeper-Smith, "Women, Kin and Catholicism: New Perspectives on the Fur Trade," in *In the Days of Our Grandmothers: A Reader in Aboriginal Women's History in Canada*, ed. Mary-Ellen Kelm and Lorna Townsend (Toronto: Univ. of Toronto Press, 2006), 26.

11. Smith, ed., *History of Warren County*, 343 (referring to the War of 1812), 401–2, 409. Aletha Roberts (descendant of Thomas and Keziah through their son Walter S. Hammon), e-mail to author, Jun. 9, 2017. *1810 US Federal Census, Queensbury, Washington County* and *1830 United States Federal Census—Town of Queensbury, Warren County*. (Queensbury was originally located in Washington County but by 1830 was part of Warren County). Pamela Vogel (Warren County historian), letter to Joyce Harvey, Sep. 8, 1981, WCHO (reviewed Nov. 17, 2009); this letter provides genealogical information on Thomas Hammon, a possible descendant of Ms. Harvey. The 1810 Washington County census for Queensbury listed a Thomas

Hammon between the ages of twenty-six and forty-five living there with a female (presumably his wife) in the same age range and three other females, two under the age of ten and another between the age of sixteen and twenty-six (probably his three daughters, although one wonders if the older girl could be his sister, Dinah). Hammon is noted in the *1830 Warren County Census, Town of Queensbury*, 101, as being between the ages of fifty and sixty, and there was a woman in the household between the ages of twenty-six and forty-five (presumably Rebecca Wheeler Hammon), along with children between the ages of under five to fifteen to twenty. A Warren County Surrogate Court record regarding *Walter S. Hammond—Letters of Guardianship*, Dec. 19, 1831, indicates Thomas Hammon was "late of the Town of Queensbury" and that Walter was eighteen years old, "child of Thomas Hammon, deceased."

12. Smith, ed., *History of Warren County*, 401–2.

13. *People v. Thomas Hammon*, Criminal Indictment, Feb. 22, 1814, WCCO-RCA. Susan Ingalls Lewis, *Unexceptional Women: Female Proprietors in Mid-Nineteenth-Century Albany, New York, 1830–1885* (Columbus: Ohio State Univ. Press, 2009), 48.

14. *Benjamin Seely v. Thomas Hammon*, Record of Judgment, Warren County Pleas Court, Sep. 14, 1814; and *Joseph Lane v. Thomas Hammon*, Record of Judgment, Warren County Pleas Court, Feb. 17, 1815, WCCO-RCA. *Thomas Hammon v. Solomon Moon et al.*, Judgment, Jan. 22, 1817, awarded $84.[cents illegible] to Hammon from Solomon, Benjamin, and Robert Moon; *Thomas Hammon v. John K Parks and Luke Knapp*, Judgment, May 15, 1817, awarded $121.33, including court costs; and *Thomas Hammon v. Jeremiah Tubbs*, Judgment, Sep. 26, 1818, in the amount of $67.40. WC-RCA. Smith, ed., *History of Warren County*, 401.

15. Smith, ed., *History of Warren County*, 401, 408–9. "Indian Biographies from Lake George," *Glens Falls Post-Star*, Dec. 14, 1963, 13–14.

16. Vogel, letter to Joyce Harvey, Sep. 8, 1981, WCHO, with reference to Warren County Surrogate Court record regarding *Walter S. Hammond—Letters of Guardianship*, Dec. 19, 1831. Smith, ed., *History of Warren County*, 402. Attempts to change the name to Northville and Middleville over the years were unsuccessful.

17. "Basketmaking Indians of Lake George," *New York Times*, Sep. 8, 1912, X10; their story is more fully described in chapter 5. Warren, "Nature of Conquest," 299–301.

18. *Daily Sentinel* (unknown location, possibly Rome, NY; there was about this time a *Daily Saratoga Sentinel* in Saratoga Springs, NY) Sep. 13, 1873, SSHMA. Philip Joseph, personal conversation with author, Jul. 10, 2009. Martha Lee Edmonds Owens (Florence Edmond's great-granddaughter), conversation with author, Apr. 4, 2009, e-mail to author, Sep. 24, 2012. Also see Adrian Edmonds, *Recollections of an Adirondacker*, vol. 1, *Stories of a Keene Valley House, Adrian Edmonds to Fred and Sarah Cook on the Purchase of Their Home in Keene Valley* (Keene Valley Library Association, c. 2005), KVL. The different spellings of Florence's maiden

name show up in documents or obituaries. Christopher Roy and David Benedict, "Abenaki People in the Adirondacks—Mitchel Sabattis," *Adirondack Journal* (Warrensburg, NY) Jun. 7, 2009, accessed Jul. 1, 2009, http://www.adkmuseum.org /about_us/adirondack_journal/?id=154. "Joseph D. Sabattis," Obituary, *New York Times*, Sep. 26, 1951.

19. Aber and King, *History of Hamilton County*, 784. *Clarence F. Fuller, Plaintiff v. Elizabeth Ann Sabattis & Mitchel Sabattis her husband, Byron Thompson and Frank Thompson, Defendants*, civil records mortgage foreclosure, Dec. 1895, HCCO. Bill Zulo later became the Hamilton County historian but left the area in the fall of 2014. Also see "Kills Waitress, Ends Own Life in Suicide Pact: Camp Operator and Tahawus Woman 'Wanted to Be Together'; Bodies Found Sunday Morning," *Ticonderoga Sentinel*, Aug. 23, 1945.

20. Camp family children included Susan Camp (c. 1821–after 1892); John Camp (c. 1824–Dec. 1914), who married fellow Abenaki Susan Watso (they had five children—Margaret, Mary Ann, John, Mary Elizabeth, and Suzan—all baptized at the Church of England, Odanak, Yamaska County, Quebec); Elijah Camp (1836–1904); and George Camp (1845–?) who married Nellie[?] (1852–?). Camp family information compiled by David Benedict, a present-day descendant of Sabael and Louis Elijah Benedict. This information was given to me by the Indian Lake Museum curator and town historian, Bill Zulo. Susan Camp's place in the genealogy is somewhat assumed based on comments made by David Benedict in his records. Elijah and Elizabeth Camp marriage information is from Elizabeth Camp's obituary, Dec. 1936. Elizabeth's mother was Betsy Cooper Kennedy (a.k.a. Canada or Canady), based on Kansas land claim form, Camp-Mead file, 1927–1965, ILM.

21. Commissioner of Indian Affairs application of Elizabeth Kennedy Camp, #735, dated Mar. 1, 1903; Genealogical chart for Elizabeth "Betsy" Cooper, unknown author, handwritten, n.d., located in Camp-Mead family papers, Kansas Claim Applications, ILM.

22. Bill Zulo, personal conversation with author, May 2009; photographs part of the Camp family photograph and records collection, ILM.

23. *New York State Census, Indian Lake* (1892, 1905, 1915 and 1925), located in the Hamilton County Clerk's Office. The Camp family is not listed in the 1892 census, although Elijah had been buying and selling property in the county since the 1860s. No one was identified as "Indian" in the 1915 state census for Hamilton County—everyone was "white" despite records previous and subsequent to this census. By the 1925 state census for Hamilton County, Elizabeth is listed as the head of household, and she and her children are all identified as Indian again. Obituaries are located in Camp family notebook at ILM, no publications identified; they are taped into notebook under the year they died.

24. E. N. Foote, letter to "Friend Camp," Aug. 9, 1883 (on business letter-head of the E. N. Foote & Co., Fine Dress Buttons, Northampton, MA). Harry Townsend, letter to "Friend Elijah," Dec. 21, 1883. Camp-Mead file, 1870–1915, ILM. George N. Griffin (Hart's Drug Store, Sing Sing, NY), letter to "Friend Camp," Apr. 15, 1884; follow up letter from Griffin to Emma, June 2, 1884. Dorne Fuller, letter to Elijah Camp, Jul. 18, 1883, Blue Mountain Lake, NY. George D. Harris (Coal at Wholesale), letter to Elijah Camp, Esq. Jun. 3, 1884, Fort Edwards, NY. Camp-Mead file, 1870–1915, ILM.

25. Bill Zulo, conversation with author, c. May 2009. John McGinn, note to Elijah Camp, Jan. 30, 1884; lumbering agreement between Elijah and George F. Scarritt (?) and Edward D. Mott, Nov. 3, 1884; Quitclaim deed between Elijah Camp and Taylor J. Eldridge and Dr. James L. Fuller of Warrensburg, Jul. 28, 1890, Camp-Mead file, 1870–1915, ILM.

26. Camp-Mead file, 1870–1915, ILM. For an example of using an "X" to sign documents, see quitclaim deed, Elijah Camp to Taylor Eldridge and James Fuller, Jul. 1870.

27. Dr. J. L. Fuller of North Creek, medical bill, Feb. 26, 1891. Warranty deed from Elijah and Elizabeth Camp to Emma Mead, Oct. 13, 1893, for three hundred dollars for parts of Lots 53 and 54 in Indian Lake, about ten acres. Agreement between Elijah Camp and Emma Mead, Nov. 11, 1893. Handwritten receipt from Corlos (Carlos?) Hutchins and George Morehouse acknowledging deed to Camp Island from Elijah Camp to pay off debts owed to them, undated. Camp-Mead file, 1870–1915, ILM.

28. Journal entries of Emma Camp Mead: Apr. 4, 1904, "Father died sud-denly"; Apr. 6, 1904, "Uncle John came for father's funeral"; and Apr. 7, 1904, "Sam came home to father's funeral, which was April 7, 1904," Camp-Mead file, 1870–1915, ILM. Obituary located in Camp family notebook, Camp-Mead file, 1870–1915, ILM.

29. Samuel Camp, letter to Emma Mead, Oct. 22, 1916, Camp-Mead file, 1870–1916, ILM. Dunlavey and Sweeny (11 Arcade Bldg, Saratoga Springs, NY), letter to Emma Mead, Sep. 27, 1917; Florence Camp, letter, Oct. 1, 1917; Attorney J. S. L. A. (Ballston Spa), letter to Dunlavey and Sweeny, Oct. 2, 1917, responding to their letter of Sep. 27, 1917; Elizabeth Camp, letters to her son Gabriel Camp and his wife Elsie Camp, Feb. 10, 1918, and May 19, 1918; Elizabeth Camp, letter to Gabriel Camp, May 28, 1918; Florence Camp, letter to Gabe and Elsie Camp, Jun. 17, 1918, Camp-Mead file, 1916–1922, ILM.

30. "A Romance of the Adirondacks: The Wedding of a Wealthy Young Man and a Dusky Maiden Annulled," *New York Times*, Aug. 4, 1883. Also see "$10,000 for Release from Marriage," *Troy Times*, Jul. 30, 1883.

31. "Paleface and His Dusky Bride," *Troy Press*, Dec. 26, 1885 (originally reported in the *New York Times* on Dec. 24, 1885). Newspaper clipping from the *Citizen Sentinel* (Ossining, Westchester County, NY) c. Sep. 20, 1920, Camp-Mead File, 1916–1922, ILM. Emma Mead, letter to Attorney William Mehein (Ballston Spa), c. August 18(?), 1933, Camp-Mead file, 1927–1965. Emma Mead, letter to Mrs. Fred Payne, 1932, Camp-Mead file, 1870–1915, ILM; Emma was trying to convince Mrs. Payne to stay with her husband for the sake of their children. Note, the letter is out of date chronologically but fits into the file time period that helps to explain what happened to Emma and Gabe Mead. It is not known if the letter was a copy or one that was never sent.

32. Camp-Mead family journal entries, spring 1901, ILM; Smith Lent (NYC), letter to Emma Mead, Sep. 9, 1910, giving her information about Gabriel Mead, stating he was not drinking anymore and that he probably had truly cared about her, Camp-Mead file, 1870–1915, ILM; J. W. Hagadorn, letter to Emma Mead, Jun. 14, 1918; Emma Mead (Pittsburgh), undated letter to Gabriel Mead between a letter dated September 24, 1920, and another dated November 11, 1920, and based on the contents it was Gabe Mead's birthday when she wrote the letter, Camp-Mead file, 1916–1922, ILM. Margaret Tahmont, letter to Emma Mead, Sep. 17, 1932, responding that she could not locate Gabriel Mead as there were too many "Meads" in California, Camp-Mead file, 1927–1965; Journal entry dated Jul. 17, 1933, Camp-Mead file, ILM. Emma Mead, letter to attorney William A. Mehein (Ballston Spa), c. August 18(?), 1933, Camp-Mead file, 1927–1965, ILM.

33. Emma Mead, letter to Dr. Nackinnon (Brooklyn, NY), Jan. 17, 1928, Camp-Mead file, 1927–1965, ILM. Ella Childs, letter to "Emmy," Nov. 11, 1883, thanking her for the basket and expressing that others admired it, Camp-Mead file, 1870–1916, ILM. Warranty deed from Emma A. Depan and Tuffield D. Depan to Emma Camp, Oct. 24, 1883, for land in Indian Lake Village, Twp. 17, Lot 67, for eight hundred dollars. Deed/agreement from Isaac and Olive Kenwell to Emma Mead, May 8, 1888, for part of Lot 67 of Twp. 17, property near "Mead Store" for ten dollars. Contract for real estate between Emma Camp Mead and William P. Morehouse, 1904, and another agreement between Emma and George F. Persons, August 1904, who built cottages on the land. Note: There is a codicil to Emma's will that mentions if she owns any property in partnership with George F. Persons it is to go to her mother should she survive her, codicil No. 1 to will, Jan. 6, 1925. Diary entry, May 30, 1901, references a bid of 195 dollars for a stage route; and diary entry, March 14, 1902, mentions the purchase of one-thousand-dollar bonds in the Toronto-Hamilton-Buffalo Railroad, plus continued investments in this project. Jessie Pashley, letter to Emma Mead, c. 1900, for the sale of a cow. Agreement between P. R. Ordway (Indian Lake Commissioner of Highways) and Emma Mead, Oct. 13, 1896, for a bridge licensed to Emma and subject to her revocation at her will. Emma

Mead, letter to M. Chas H. Burke (Commissioner of Indian Affairs, Washington, DC), Mar. 30, 1926, Camp-Mead file, 1924–1926, ILM.

34. Warranty deed from Emma A. Depan and Tuffield D. Depan to Emma Camp, Oct. 24, 1883, for land in Indian Lake Village, Twp. 17, Lot 67, for eight hundred dollars. Deed/agreement from Isaac and Olive Kenwell to Emma Mead, May 8, 1888 for part of Twp. 17, Lot 67 property near "Mead Store" for 10 dollars. *Adirondack Folks*, c. Apr. 24, 1891, reported the fire that destroyed the buildings owned by Emma Mead, Neson Ste. Marie, John Ste. Marie, and T. D. Depain on that date. Mrs. J. A. Beane (Glens Falls), letter to Emma Mead, Apr. 18, 1885, and Mr. Hegeman (Glens Falls), letter to Emma Mead, May 19, 1885, Camp-Mead file, 1870–1915, ILM. Emma Mead, letter of inquiry to the *Syracuse Post-Standard*, Feb. 23, 1925. Camp-Mead file, 1924–1926, ILM.

35. Product boxes for the "Superior Conditioning Powders" and "Heave Powders" and list of clients, ILM. Margaret Tahamont, letter to Emma, Dec. 10, 1918, Camp-Mead file, 1916–1922, ILM. Margaret Tahamont, letter signed as Margaret Dark Cloud to Emma Mead, Mar. 29, 1926, referencing a prescription that Emma and Gabe had sent her. Camp-Mead file, 1924–1926, ILM.

36. See "Window Display for 'Dr Morse's Indian Root Pills' Colour Lithographs, 19th Century," *Wellcome Collection*, accessed Feb. 1, 2013, https://wellcome collection.org/works/usbmwuxp?query=Window%20Display%20for%20 %27Dr%20Morse%27s%20Indian%20Root%20Pills%27&page=1. Margaret Tahamont, letter to Emma, Dec. 10, 1918, Camp-Mead file, 1916–1922, ILM. Margaret Tahamont, letter signed as Margaret Dark Cloud to Emma Mead, Mar. 29, 1926, Camp-Mead file, 1924–1926, ILM.

37. "Falling Star: The Indian Beauty Who Died Last Week," Obituary, *New York Sun*, Jan. 23, 1903. Martha Lee Owens, personal conversation with author, Apr. 4, 2009.

38. Illegible signature (Brooklyn, NY), letter to Emma Mead, May 15, 1916. Unsigned letter to Emma Mead, Oct. 18, 1916, Camp-Mead file, 1916–1922, ILM.

39. Aber and King, *History of Hamilton County*, 521. Lease between Emma Mead (landlord) and Gabriel E. Camp (tenant), Apr. 27, 1918, Camp-Mead file, 1916–1922, ILM. W. R. Waddell., letter to G. E. Camp, successor to Mrs. E. Mead at the Adirondack House, Aug. 15, 1921, Camp-Mead file, 1916–1922, ILM.

40. Camp-Mead file, 1870–1915; Camp-Mead file, 1916–1922, ILM.

41. Sylvia, letter to Emma Mead, Dec. 1920, Nedrow, NY (the Onondaga Nation is in Nedrow), refers to Uncle William (Hanyoust) and a Council at Temperance Hall with a number of Oneida/Oneida and Tuscarora having land within the heart of Philadelphia, Pennsylvania. Camp-Mead file, 1916–1922, ILM. Also see William Hanyoust, letter to his cousin, Emma Mead, Nov. 8, 1925, Nedrow, NY Camp-Mead file, 1924–1926, ILM; they appear to be working together on the land

claims. William Hanyoust died of pneumonia in September 1927; see his obituary, Camp-Mead file, 1927–1965, ILM. Emma Camp Mead, letter to "cousin Albert" Schanandoah, Sep. 23, 1923; Emma Camp Mead, letter to Minnie Schanandoah, May 30, 1922; Emma Camp Mead, letter to Arthur C. Parker, Jun. 10, 1923, Albany, NY; all in Camp-Mead file, 1924–1926, ILM.

42. Certificate announcing wedding of Gabriel E. Camp and Elsie Corscadden signed by A. M. Woodruff, pastor at the Methodist Church, Indian Lake, NY, Dec. 14, 1916, Camp-Mead file, 1916–1922, ILM. Florence Camp, letter to Elizabeth and/or Emma, Jan. 4, 1917, Camp-Mead file, 1916–1922, ILM. Samuel Camp, letter to Elizabeth and/or Emma, Apr. 15, 1917. W. Hagadorn (Brooklyn, NY), "frog pond" letter to Gabe in Indian Lake, Sep. 3, 1917. Richard C. Frandsen (10 W. 82nd St., NYC), letter to "Mr. Camp," Sep. 6, 1919. Camp-Mead file, 1916–1922, ILM.

43. Samuel Camp (Pittsburgh, PA), letter to Gabe Camp, Aug. 29, 1920, Camp-Mead file, 1916–1922, ILM. Samuel Camp (Pittsburgh, PA), letter to Gabe Camp (Indian Lake, NY), Dec. 18, 1926. Camp-Mead file, 1924–1926, ILM.

44. Delaware & Hudson Co., letter to Emma at the Rome State School, Oct. 1924, includes reference to the cost of her advertisement to sell the hotel, land, and barns, Camp-Mead file, 1924–1926, ILM. Emma Mead, letter to Alfred T. Brown (2 Marble Hill Ave., NYC), undated, regarding her advertisement in the October 1925 issue of *Field and Stream*. Emma Mead, letter to Mrs. A. H. Walsh (115 Gray Ave. Webster Groves), Feb. 8, 1926. Notice from the D&H Railroad, Apr. 7, 1926. Certificate of Conducting Business per 4440 penal law, for the business under the name of "The Adirondack House" under the name of Emma Mead, Jul. 28, 1926, Camp-Mead file, 1924–1926, ILM. Emma Mead, undated letter in the 1929 section of the Camp-Mead file, 1927–1965, ILM, possible response to a letter from C. M. Gorden, trust officer; the letter also notes that Gabe and his wife had been in Pittsburgh for a month.

45. Obituaries located in Camp family notebook, under year of death, Camp-Mead file, 1927–1965, ILM. The family plot is located in the back of the cemetery in front of the woods with a large obelisk in the center. Aber and King, *History of Hamilton County*, 521. After Elsie's death, the property remained empty for two years until local historian Ted Aber purchased it and made it into a private home.

46. Brennan, *Canoeing the Adirondacks with Nessmuk*, 114–24. It is not known for certain but assumed the reference to "Aunty Sabattis" was Mitchell's wife, Betsy, versus his sister Hannah, or perhaps it was Betsy Sabattis who is mentioned in the Wesleyan Methodist Church records as referenced in chapter 2. For reference to cholera morbus, see *Merriam Webster Medical Dictionary* online, accessed Dec. 14, 2012, http://www.merriam-webster.com/medical/cholera%20morbus.

47. Patricia Albers, conclusion to *Native Americans and Wage Labor: Ethnohistorical Perspectives*, ed. Alice Littlefield and Martha C. Knack (Norman, OK: Univ.

of Oklahoma Press, 1996), 249; John Urry, *The Tourist Gaze*, 2nd ed. (London: Sage Publications, 2002).

48. R. W. Sandwell, "Rural Reconstruction: Towards a New Synthesis in Canadian History," *Histoire sociale/Social History* 53 (May 1994): 12, 14, 20.

49. Robbie Ethridge, *Creek Country: The Creek Indians and Their World* (Chapel Hill: Univ. of North Carolina Press, 2003), 179–94; Bixby, "Peter Sailly," 61.

50. Peter Bailey, "'Will the Real Bill Banks Please Stand Up?' Towards a Role Analysis of Mid-Victorian Working-Class Respectability," *Journal of Social History* 12, no. 3 (Spring 1979): 336, 343.

51. Ibid., 338.

52. "A Romance of the Adirondacks: The Wedding of a Wealthy Young Man and a Dusky Maiden Annulled," *New York Times*, Aug. 4, 1883. Nancy L. Gallagher, *Breeding Better Vermonters: The Eugenics Project in the Green Mountain State* (Hanover, NH: Univ. Press of New England, 1999), especially chapter 3's discussion on eugenics and Lutz Kaelber, "Vermont," in *Eugenics: Compulsory Sterilization in 50 American States*, accessed Sep. 13, 2012, http://www.uvm.edu/~lkaelber/eugenics /VT/VT.html (updated 2011).

53. An example of an individual who chose to hide their identity was Jesse Bowman, who ran a store in Greenfield, Saratoga County, just outside the Adirondack boundary. See Joseph Bruchac, *Bowman's Store: A Journey to Myself* (New York: Dial Books, 1997).

54. Knight, *Indians at Work*, 18.

55. Ibid., 197.

56. Raibmon, *Authentic Indians*, 3, 212.

5. "The Wigwam on the Hill"

1. Della Pollock, ed., *Exceptional Spaces: Essays in Performance and History* (Chapel Hill: Univ. of North Carolina Press, 1998), 9, 20.

2. Tim Edensor, "Staging Tourism: Tourists as Performers," *Annals of Tourism Research* 27, no. 2 (2000): 341–42. Richard Schechner, *Performance Studies: An Introduction* (New York: Routledge, 2002), 39. The other founding member was fellow anthropologist Victor Turner, *From Ritual to Theater: The Human Seriousness of Play* (New York: PAJ Publications, 2001).

3. Beverly Locke, e-mail communication with author, Feb. 2010, and Edith Russell, personal conversation with author, Mar. 4, 2010. Woods, "History in Fragments," 71, 78.

4. Joshua David Bellin and Laura L. Mielke, eds., *Native Acts: Indian Performance, 1603–1832* (Lincoln: Univ. of Nebraska Press, 2011), 5, 19.

5. Porter, *And Grandmother Said*, 116; Wiseman, *Voice of the Dawn*, 138.

6. Lorraine Westcott, "Indian Tales Fascinate Historian," Strands of Time, unknown publication, Feb. 3, 1988, 1c, CSSH.

7. H. V. Nelles, *The Art of Nation-Building: Pageantry and Spectacle at Quebec's Tercentenary* (Toronto: Univ. of Toronto Press, 2000), 179.

8. Abigail May, *Abigail May Journal at Ballstown Springs 1800*, transcribed by Lucretia Field Horne (New York State Historical Association, 1982), 113, Collection of Brookside Museum, SCHSRL. Abigail died at her home in Boston shortly after her return on August 30, 1800. The journal was transcribed by her adopted sister Lucretia Field Horne starting in March 1801.

9. Evelyn Barrett Britten, "3 Indian Encampments Once Located in City," *The Saratogian*, May 5, 1962, SSHMA. Also see Evelyn Barrett Britten, "Indian Encampments Stir Memories," *The Saratogian*, Dec. 5, 1959, SSHMA. George Waller, *Saratoga: Saga of an Impious Age* (Englewood Cliffs, NJ: Prentice-Hall, 1966), 71. Also see Evelyn Barrett Britten, "When the Indians Came Visiting," *The Saratogian*, Dec. 4, 1964, SSHMA.

10. Britten, "3 Indian Encampments" and "When the Indians Came Visiting," SSHMA. Also see Jean McGregor (which was the name Britten went by before she married), "Unique Memorials Mark Graves of Indians in Greenridge Cemetery," *The Saratogian*, Apr. 27, 1945, CSSH. *1870 US Federal Census, Saratoga Springs*.

11. "The Picturesque Indian Village," *Saratoga Journal*, Jul. 31, 1883, vertical file "Indians," SSPL.

12. Lee, *Lee's Guide to Saratoga*, 207, 259.

13. Britten's "When the Indians Came Visiting" claims that the exact location "occupied the block from Circular Street running from Spring Street to East Congress Street (now in our park)." Also see Britten, "3 Indian Encampments."

14. Agnes Gilligan, "News of Lake George and Vicinity Places," *Glens Falls Post-Star*, Sep. 8, 1952. Woods, "History in Fragments," 69.

15. Philip "Phil" Joseph, personal conversation with author, Jul 10, 2009. Seneca Ray Stoddard, *Lake George (Illustrated): A Book of To-Day* (Glens Falls, NY: published by the author; and Albany, NY: Van Benthuysen and Sons, 1879), 46. Also see *1880 US Federal Census, Village of Caldwell*.

16. Nina Holland, "Black Ash and Sweetgrass: Akwesasne Basketmakers Weave History and Art." *Adirondack Life* (n.d.), 30, ALCC; Sallie Benedict, "Mohawk Basketmakers of Akwesasne," *American Indian Basketry* 9, no. 3 (1983), 10–16, back cover; Miller, "The Adirondack Pack-Basket."

17. Janet Hall, personal conversation with author, Apr. 6, 2009, Keene Valley, NY. Christopher Roy, personal conversation with author, May 7, 2009. Obituary for Gregory Smashwood, *Elizabethtown Post*, Apr. 21, 1887. *1915 New York State Census, Keene, Essex County*. George L. Brown, "News in and about the County Seat," *Adirondack Record* (Elizabethtown, NY) Jun. 2, 1922. "Hurricane," *Adirondack*

Record, Jul. 26, 1923, 5, and "Keene," *Adirondack Record*, Apr. 17, 1924, 6. A third brother, Joseph, worked in the mines in Port Henry. After he divorced, Joseph moved to Burlington, Vermont, where he shortened his name to Wood according to Christopher Roy.

18. Phil Joseph, personal conversation with author, Jul. 10, 2009. Also see chapter 6.

19. Raibmon, *Authentic Indians*, 147. Ruth B. Phillips, *Trading Identities: The Souvenir in Native North American Art from the Northeast, 1700–1900* (Seattle: Univ. of Washington Press, 1998), 25, 142. US Congress, "Tariff of 1890," HR 9416, Oct. 1, 1890; also known as the "McKinley Tariff," a protectionist piece of legislation enacted October 21 of that year; it was popular with business but not with the populace. See "Up Go the Prices Now," *New York Times*, Oct. 21, 1890.

20. Martha Lee Owens, personal conversation with author, Apr. 4, 2009. According to family history and a deed, Florence purchased the land in 1881. Property deed from Eli and Eliza Crawford to Florence Edmonds, Nov. 28, 1881, Book 84, ECCO. "Bernard P. Dennis Memoir," 1–2, vertical file "Dennis Family," TWHA-GM, puts Jules in Keene Valley in the early 1880s.

21. Raibmon, *Authentic Indians*, 129, 141, 143–45.

22. "Waiting for Tourists to Roll In," photograph c. early 1900s in *Glens Falls Post-Star*, Dec. 14, 1963. S. R. Stoddard, "Sagamore Dock" (1906), photograph #1112, AM-BML.

23. Stoddard, *Adirondacks: Illustrated* (1874), 41–43. He also wrote or used a poem called "Lo! The Poor Indian," by "Shortfellow," to textualize the drawing and describes them as a noble but dying race. "Women Here and There," *New York Times*, Mar. 12, 1899, 20; "Indian Woman in New York," *New York Times*, Apr. 30, 1899, 23; "Falling Star: The Indian Beauty Who Died Last Week," Obituary, *New York Sun*, Jan. 23, 1903, 5. I have used the spelling Ann Denis, as that is the one used in the *1870 US Federal Census, Chesterfield, Essex County, NY*; it is the first record of her in the United States, and subsequent census records have her as Annie Fuller. According to her obituary, Mitchel Sabattis was her great uncle.

24. Clarence Petty, personal conversation with author, Jun. 1, 2009, Saranac Lake, NY. DeSormo, *Summers on the Saranacs*, 102. Noah John Rondeau, diary entries, Aug. 8 and Aug. 13, 1932, AM-BML. For a detailed description and photographs of Daniel Emmett at age eighty-two making a canoe, see Eugene W. Bond, "How to Build a Birchbark," *Natural History* 64, no. 5 (May 1955): 242–46. The article did not use Dan's last name and identified him as Montagnais; however, Mr. Petty was able to identify him, and I compared the article's photographs with a known photograph of Daniel Emmett at a younger age. Mr. Petty and other records confirm Dan was "Ah-BEN-a-Kee," which is the pronunciation Dan told to a youthful Clarence Petty (it was also the pronunciation used by Phil Joseph).

25. *1910 US Federal Census, Old Forge, Herkimer County, NY.* The boy, Joseph P. Denis (born c. 1898) was the son of Julius and his second wife, Marie or Mary Benedict, the great granddaughter of Sabael, granddaughter of Louis Elijah.

26. "Basketmaking Indians of Lake George," *New York Times*, Sep. 8, 1912, X10.

27. Ibid. Aboriginal Affairs and Northern Development Canada, *Indian Act, 1880*, chap. 28, §11, "Loss of Membership through Residence in a Foreign Country without Leave," accessed Aug. 18, 2014, https://www.aadnc-aandc.gc.ca/eng/110 0100010272/1100100010274. Roy, "Abenaki Sociality," 222. The "standing" included rights to shared resources and political decision-making.

28. My thanks to Sue Ellen Herne (Akwesasne Cultural Center museum director), e-mail to author, Sep. 24, 2012, for her review of this consideration and the idea of informal sales.

29. Phillips, *Trading Identities*, 67, 289, citing Harriet Converse "Reservation Indians of New York State," *Illustrated Buffalo Express* c. 1895 located in Scrapbook of Indians (unprovenanced), D72–23 at the Buffalo and Erie County Historical Society, Buffalo, New York. Converse noted the trade was so busy it employed most of the women and children at St. Regis. W. S. Tanner, "W. S. Tanner, Lawrence, Kansas, Gives Exclusive Sale to One Merchant in a City of his St. Regis Indian Fancy Baskets," photograph c. 1894, LC-USZ62-132279, Library of Congress Prints and Photographs Division, accessed Jan. 21, 2012, http://www.loc.gov/pictures/resource/cph .3c32279/. C.N. Saba and Company catalogue cover, Wellington Street, West, Toronto, Ontario, CPSH. Elizabeth Folwell, "Wish You Were Here: Hand-Tinted Memories from Standard Supply," *Adirondack Life* 20, no. 6 (Nov./Dec. 1989): 61.

30. Bruce J. Bourque and Laureen A. Labar, *Common Threads: Wabanaki Textiles, Clothing, and Costume* (Seattle: Univ. of Washington Press, 2009), 116–21.

31. Dolores Elliott, "Canoes and Horseshoes: Two Forms of Iroquois Beadwork" (paper presented at the Conference on Iroquois Research, Cortland, NY, Oct. 6, 2012); Dolores Elliott, *Birds and Beasts in Beads: 150 Years of Iroquois Beadwork* (Hamilton, NY: Longyear Museum of Anthropology, Colgate Univ., 2011), 8; and Dolores Elliott, "Iroquois Beadwork: A Haudenosaunee Tradition and Art," in *Preserving Tradition and Understanding the Past: Papers from the Conference on Iroquois Research, 2001–2005*, ed. Christine Sternberg Patrick (Albany, NY: Univ. of the State of New York, State Education Department, New York State Museum, 2010), 35–48, 38, accessed Jul. 19, 2018, http://www.nysm.nysed.gov/common/nysm/files /nysmrecord-vol1_0.pdf.

32. Elliott, *Birds and Beasts*, 10, and "Iroquois Beadwork," 37.

33. Phillips, *Trading Identities*, 157–59, 182–88, 196.

34. Susan Stewart, *On Longing: Narratives of the Miniature, the Gigantic, the Souvenir, the Collection* (Baltimore, MD: Johns Hopkins Univ. Press, 1984), 135–38, 148. Phillips, *Trading Identities*, 8.

35. Phillips, *Trading Identities*, xiii.

36. Benson J. Lossing, *The Hudson, from the Wilderness to the Sea.* (Troy, NY: H. B. Nims and Co, 1866), 13; Stoddard, *Adirondacks: Illustrated* (1874), 99. Juvenal, "Mitchell Sabattis," Letter to the Editor (under the news from Lake Placid Club, Essex County, NY), *Forest and Stream*, May 12 (no year, but Sabattis died in 1906) about the report of the death of Mitchel Sabattis.

37. Raibmon, *Authentic Indians*, 130, 203. Daniel Francis, *The Imaginary Indian: The Image of the Indian in Canadian Culture* (Vancouver: Arsenal Pulp Press, 2012), 57. Carol J. Williams, *Framing the West: Race, Gender, and the Photographic Frontier in the Pacific Northwest* (Oxford Univ. Press, 2003), 8, 144, 146.

38. Williams, *Framing the West*, 138, 141, 164–69.

39. Francis, *Imaginary Indian*, 103, 106. Other Wild West Show producers included Adam Forepaugh's Wild West Combination, Pawnee Bill's Historical Wild West Exhibition and Indian Encampment, and the 101 Wild West Show, to name a few.

40. "Indian Woman in New York," 23. "Falling Star: The Indian Beauty Who Died Last Week," Obituary, *New York Sun*, Jan. 23, 1903, 5. The sculpture for which she refused to pose for the torso was to be located in the Department of Anthropology at the Museum of Natural History.

41. "Women Here and There," 20, and "Indian Woman in New York," 23. "Falling Star: the Indian Beauty Who Died Last Week," Obituary, *New York Sun*, Jan. 23, 1903, 5. I have not been able to identify the train wreck in which she was injured, although the 1902 Park Avenue Tunnel Collision in New York City fits the timeline. There is an ongoing effort to find survivors, but she was not listed as one of the injured passengers on a website commemorating the event (http://www.roots web.ancestry.com/~nywestch/NewRoc1902/index.htm, accessed Nov. 29, 2017).

42. Cecilia Morgan, "'A Wigwam to Westminster': Performing Mohawk Identity in Imperial Britain, 1890s–1990s," *Gender and History* 15, no. 2 (Aug. 2003): 319, 336.

43. Veronica Strong-Boag and Carole Gerson, *Paddling Her Own Canoe: The Times and Texts of E. Pauline Johnson Tekahionwake* (Toronto: Univ. of Toronto Press, 2000), 20, 51, 60, 70, 81, 104–5, 113.

44. "Mohawk Chief Its Guest: Indian at Chiropean Meeting Tells of the Religion of His Race," *Brooklyn Daily Eagle*, Apr. 18, 1902; accessed Jul 19, 2018 at Brooklyn Historical Society, "Guide to the Chiropean Yearbooks ARC.164," http://dlib.nyu .edu/findingaids/html/bhs/arc_164_chiropean_yearbooks/. The article erroneously identified Tahamont as Mohawk.

45. "Princess Wenonah Whitecloud (Moseley)," Obituary, unknown publication (Apr. 1940), vertical file "Ethnic Heritage: American Indians/Native Americans—Newspaper Clippings," CSSH. William Vander Weyde, "New York's Indian Colony," unknown publication, n.d., ILM.

46. *Twelfth Census of the United States—Indian Population: Lake George, Warren County, 1900* has Elijah and Margaret living there with their two daughters and Margaret's relative Maud Benedict (age 19). Beulah became Seneca anthropologist Arthur Parker's first wife in 1904; they both remarried, she to T. W. Filson, a rail yard employee. Margaret Bruchac, e-mail to "H-AmIndian" mailing list, Apr. 25, 2005, subject line "Beulah Tahamont Parker and Bertha Parker Cody (Native archaeologist)," accessed Sep. 24, 2012, http://h-net.msu.edu/cgi-bin/logbrowse.pl?trx=vx&list=h-amindian&month=0504&week=d&msg=yD6InQQ1H%2bT2ZpRXXRGCQQ&user=&pw=. Vander Weyde, "New York's Indian Colony," ILM.

47. Hollywoodland: A Site about Hollywood and Its History, "Hollywood Forever Cemetery: Chief Dark Cloud aka Elijah Tahamont," accessed Mar. 24, 2012, http://allanellenberger.com/chief-dark-cloud-at-hollywood-forever/. Margaret Camp, letter to Emma Camp, Dec. 10, 1918, Camp-Mead file, 1916–1922, ILM.

48. Margaret Camp Tahamont, letter to Emma Camp Mead, Sep. 17, 1932, Camp-Mead file, 1927–1965, ILM. Raibmon, *Authentic Indians*, 74–97.

49. "Old Forge," *Utica Herald Dispatch*, May 26, 1905.

50. Phillips, *Trading Identities*, 52–54, 288. The petition is located in the Frank Speck papers at the American Philosophical Society in Philadelphia. Phillips describes the petition's "value as a historical documentation of concepts of property and appropriation."

51. Taintor Brothers & Co., *Saratoga Illustrated: The Visitor's Guide of Saratoga Springs* (NY: Taintor Brothers, 1889), 83.

52. Donaldson, *History of the Adirondacks*, 2:26, 121. Linda Champagne, "Noah John Rondeau Interviewed: Adirondack Hermit Part III," *Lake Placid News*, Sep. 28, 1967. For a copy of postcard with the wigwams he built, see Four Peaks, "Me & Noah Rondeau," accessed Feb. 24, 2012, http://www.4peaks.com/pprond.htm. For a hermit, Rondeau was very social; he dined with the likes of the Rockefellers, and he attended sports shows. Adcock and Adcock, *Images of America*, 45. Deloria, *Playing Indian*, 37.

53. Bob Vila, "Great Camp Sagamore," *YouTube* (video), accessed Jul. 19, 2018, https://www.youtube.com/watch?v=OI6PtZ4s7kg. The video is of Bob Vila touring the camp, and the tour guide provides him with this meaning. Alice Nash, e-mail of comments to the author, Jun. 6, 2013. Nash notes that sagamore along with "sakamo, sangheman and sachem" are all Algonquian words for leader or "chief" in various Algonquian dialects. She explains that "Sachem" is the most commonly known term because it occurs in southern New England, where the early English adopted it. However, other northeastern colonists were familiar with the term "Sagamore," which came from the region north and east of Boston.

54. Saint Hubert's Isle, "Adirondack Photos and Postcards: Raquette Lake Steamers," accessed Feb. 6, 2012, http://www.sthubertsisle.com/page170.html.

Lake George Steamboat Company, "History of the Lake George Steamboat Company," accessed Feb. 6, 2012, http://lakegeorgesteamboat.com/index.asp?lg=1&w=pages&r=26&pid=27. Untitled brochure or pamphlet, n.d., 10, vertical file "Lake George-Ft. William Henry Hotel," CPL (reviewed Nov. 2009). Dennis Aprill, "Memories of a Nehasane Trip," *Plattsburgh Press Republican*, Jul. 1, 2007, accessed Feb. 6, 2012, http://pressrepublican.com/0105_outdoor_perspective/x155086824/Memories-of-a-Nehasane-trip/print. "William Seward Webb Papers," held by the Adirondack Experience Research Library, AM-BML. Among other things Webb did with the land, he fenced about ten thousand acres and unsuccessfully experimented with breeding nonindigenous large game for hunting. David H. Ackerman, *Lake Placid Club: An Illustrated History, 1895–1980* (Lake Placid, NY: Lake Placid Education Foundation, 1998), map on cover, 63. Boyd Cothran, *Remembering the Modoc War: Redemptive Violence and the Making of American Innocence* (Chapel Hill: North Carolina Press, First Peoples New Directions in Indigenous Studies, 2014), 132.

55. Hallie E. Bond, "'Playing Indian' at Adirondack Children's Camps," TS for presentation, AM-BML (reviewed Jul. 21, 2009), citing Putnam, "Children's Camps on Chateaugay," *Chateaugay Record and Franklin County Democrat* (1905), 3. Bunny McBride, *Molly Spotted Elk: A Penobscot in Paris* (Norman, OK: Univ. of Oklahoma Press, 1996), 52. Sharon Wall, *The Nurture of Nature: Childhood, Antimodernism, and Ontario Summer Camps, 1920–55* (Vancouver: Univ. of British Columbia Press, 2009), 217, 222–23; Leslie Paris, *Children's Nature: The Rise of the American Summer Camp* (New York: New York Univ. Press, 2008), 191–94, 201, 207. Francis, *Imaginary Indian*, 171.

56. Wall, *Nurture of Nature*, 238 (quote), also see 236, 239, 242, 244. Paris, *Children's Nature*, 197, also see 217.

57. John Fadden, personal communication with author, Apr. 24, 2010, with attachment of a copy of a pamphlet by his father, Aren Akweks (Ray Fadden), "The Akwesasne Mohawk Counselor Organization," *The Record, Laws and History of the Akwesasne Mohawk Counselor Organization* (Hogansburg, NY: St. Regis Mohawk Reservation). Obituary for Ray Tehanetorens Fadden (Nov. 2008), accessed Feb. 25, 2012, http://obitsforlife.com/obituary/479854/Fadden-Ray.php. Bruce Elliott Johansen, "Grandfathers of Akwesasne Mohawk Revitalization: Ray Fadden and Ernest Benedict," *The Praeger Handbook on Contemporary Issues in Native America*, vol. 1, *Linguistic, Ethnic, and Economic Revival* (Westport, CT: Greenwood, 2007), and John Fadden, personal conversation with author, Oct. 14, 2014, Saranac Lake, NY. "Chief Maurice Dennis Instructs Girl Scout Class in Indian Lore," *Adirondack Echo* (Old Forge, NY) Jun. 3, 1966; photograph of Maurice Dennis in headdress seated in front of "Boy Scout Troop in 1948," vertical file "Dennis Family," TWHA-GM.

58. James Fennimore Cooper, *The Last of the Mohicans: A Narrative of 1757* (Philadelphia: Carey and Lea, 1826), e.g., 55, 61, 67, 70–71, 88, 91–94. Griffith Bailey Coale's "Cooper's Cave" is a large painting of the main characters from this book plus other Native men and hangs in the lobby of the Queensbury Hotel in Glens Falls. "The Romance of Lake George," Official Souvenir Program (Lake George, NY), Jul. 17–20, 1938, vertical file "Lake George Pageants," CPL. Francis, *Imaginary Indian*, 185. Cocthran, *Remembering the Modoc Wars*, 22, citing Carter Jones Myer and Diana Royer, eds., *Selling the Indian: Commercializing and Appropriating American Indian Culture* (Tucson, AZ: Univ. of Arizona Press, 2001), xi–xix.

59. Adele S. Thompson, "Sacandaga: Coney Island of the North," *Adirondack Life* (Spring 1976): 16. Ackerman, *Lake Placid Club*, 171–73. Other ceremonies included "Passing of the Warpole" and "Return of the Maize Maiden," while others focused on important Iroquoian individuals. "Pageant of Saratoga," Program (Aug. 19–24, 1912), 9–10, SSPL. The first episode, entitled "Sarachtogie: The Hunting Ground of the Mohawks," had over fifty Native parts and included a sunrise song, hunt, encampment, and dance. Wall, *Nurture of Nature*, 229.

60. Henry Wayland Hill, *The Champlain Tercentenary: Final Report of the New York Lake Champlain Tercentenary Commission* (Albany, NY: J. B. Lyon Co., 1913), 191. Todd DeGarmo, "Indian Camps and Upstate Tourism," *New York Folklore Newsletter* 14, no. 2 (1993): 5. State Commissions of New York and Vermont and of the Central Vermont Delaware & Hudson and Rutland Railroads, "Champlain Tercentenary Celebration July 4–10, 1909" (brochure), 5–7, vertical file "Vermont/New York Boundary Lines Records 1814–1985," VSAR. Michael D. McNally, "The Indian Passion Play: Contesting the Real Indian in Song of Hiawatha Pageants, 1901–1965," *American Quarterly* 58, no. 1 (Mar. 2006): 105, 107, 130–32. McNally refers especially to Deloria's *Playing Indian* for his argument about influence.

61. George H. Spring, "The Annual Indian Pageant at Ticonderoga," *North Country Life* (Summer 1948): 32–39. Arthur A. Carr, "Ticonderoga's Indian Pageant, A Historical Account," Ticonderoga Historical Society web page, accessed Dec. 8, 2017, http://ticonderogahistoricalsociety.org/ticonderogas-indian-pageant-a-historical-account/. Lonergan, *Ticonderoga*, back cover, indicates that Lonergan was very involved in the pageants and had directed and starred in several of them. Jane M. Lape, ed., *Ticonderoga: Patches and Patterns from Its Past* (Lake George, NY: Ad Resorts Press, Inc., 1969), 214–15; Cook's Farm Theater, pageant programs, 974.7538 C771 (1938, 1939, 1940, 1941), THS. The 1938 program indicates it was the seventh annual pageant. DeGarmo, "Indian Camps and Upstate Tourism," 5; Woods, "History in Fragments," 70. John Fadden, e-mail to author, July 21, 2011. For background information on Ray Fadden, see George-Kanentiio, *Iroquois Culture and Community*, 12, 214–16. "Ray Tehanetorens Fadden," Obituary, accessed

Feb. 25, 2012, http://obitsforlife.com/obituary/479854/Fadden-Ray.php; Johansen, "Grandfathers," 211.

62. Woods, "History in Fragments," 70. John Fadden, personal conversation with author, Jun. 2009. John Fadden, e-mail to author, Apr. 24, 2010, with attached copy of pamphlet "The Records, Laws, and History of the Akwesasne Mohawk Counselor Organization." Clare Audette, "Indian Village Is Being Built at Lake George," *Glens Falls Post-Star*, Jun. 16, 1952.

63. "Aquanite, 1957," transcript (Schroon Lake, NY), unknown date [1957?], and "I Remember When," program for Aqua-Nite Week-End (Schroon Lake, NY), unknown date [1957?], vertical file "Schroon Lake, NY," AM-BML. Gary Glebus (Schroon Lake historian) and his wife, Shelly Glebus, personal conversation with author, Oct. 5, 2009, Schroon Lake, NY; both Gary and Shelly personally knew "Swifty" and "Chee-Chee" and had worked at Frontier Town when they were teenagers.

64. Gary and Shelly Glebus, personal conversation with author, Oct. 5, 2009. Arthur L. Benson, *The Story of a New York City Tenderfoot and His Adirondack Mountain Adventure* (Frontier Town Productions, 1979).

65. "Bernard P. Dennis Memoir," Oct. 2007, 3, vertical file "Dennis Family," TWHA-GM.

66. Identification based on caption under a photograph labeled "Jules P. Dennis on left with his friend Ana Panadis," vertical file "Dennis Family," TWHA-GM, along with another photograph of Julius, Ana, and either Juliet M'Sadoques Dennis or Josephine Ski (Mohawk—duplicate photograph identifies the woman as Josephine) plus the torso of a young man (tentatively identified as Walt LaGrave; the photographer cut off his head, probably because he was so tall, but LaGrave was known to come to Old Forge and work with the Denis/Dennis family so this identification has merit). All are dressed in regalia, and Chief Denis is carrying a drum in the first photograph. The hotel was opened for business June 7, 1934, according to Ken Sprague's "Take a First Look at the Hollywood Hills Hotel" on the website *Adirondack Express*, accessed Jul. 24, 2018, https://www.adirondackexpress.com/take-a-first-look-at-the-hollywood-hills-hotel-by-ken-sprague/. "J. P. Dennis, Indian Chief," unknown publication (Old Forge, NY, n.d.), vertical file "Dennis Family," TWHA-GM. "Juliette Dennis, 'Queen of Winter' Saluted," *Adirondack Tourist* (Boonville, NY), Dec. 7, 1983, 3, 14; photographs of Maurice Dennis on skis wearing headdress, *Adirondack Echo* (Old Forge, NY), 1976 (Easter Seals), and Mar. 30, 1973 (Show of Shows), vertical file "Denis or Dennis family," TWHA-GM.

67. Brian W. Dippie, *The Vanishing American: White Attitude and U.S. Indian Policy* (Middletown, CT: Wesleyan Univ. Press, 1982), xii. Also see Francis, *Imaginary Indian*, especially ch. 2, "The Vanishing Canadian," 31–57. Deloria, *Playing Indian*, 37. Judith Richardson, *Possession: The History and Uses of Hauntings in the*

Hudson Valley (Cambridge, MA: Cambridge Univ. Press, 2003), 26–27, 207–8. Lisa Philips and Allan K. McDougall, "Shifting Boundaries and the Baldoon Mysteries," in *Lines Drawn upon the Water: First Nations and the Great Lakes Borders and Borderlands*, ed. Karl S. Hele (Waterloo, ON: Wilfrid Laurier Univ. Press, 2008), 131–50. Plumwood, "Wilderness Scepticism," 664.

68. Hallock, *From the Fallen Tree*, 213. Jean O'Brien, "Divorced from the Land: Accommodation Strategies of Indian Women in 18th Century New England," in *After King Philip's War: Presence and Persistence in Indian New England*, ed. Colin G. Calloway (Hanover, NH: Univ. Press of New England, 1997), 329.

69. Brooks, *Common Pot: The Recovery of Native Space*, 165.

70. Marleau, *Big Moose Station*, 3. Dick Case, "After 40 Years Old Forge Is Getting 'Too Busy,' for Totem Pole Carver," *Syracuse Herald-Journal*, Oct. 22, 1984. Also see Nash, "Théophile Panadis (1889–1966)," 84–85, which refers to Panadis carving objects with traditional tools, so it is likely the Abenaki have some tradition of carving, but not totem poles. "Maurice Paul Dennis," *Adirondack Echo* (Old Forge, NY), Dec. 30, 1987; "Andreé Newton, Old Forge Artisan, Continues a Native American Tradition," *The Adirondack Express* (Old Forge, NY) Mar. 10, 1992, 5; untitled article in *The Adirondack Express*, Oct. 11, 2005, about Andreé Newton receiving the Award of Excellence at the 26th Annual Remsen Barn Festival of the Arts, Sep. 24–25, 2005.

6. Rural Indigenousness

1. Terrie, *Contested Terrain*, 124–28, 132.

2. Christopher Roy, Letter to the Editor, *Adirondack Daily Enterprise* (Saranac Lake, NY) Jun. 23, 2009.

3. Sam Howe Verhovek, "Standoff Ends, but Not Mohawk Defiance," *New York Times*, Apr. 14, 1990, 26, accessed Mar. 25, 2016, http://www.nytimes.com/1990/04/14/nyregion/standoff-ends-but-not-mohawk-defiance.html.

4. *Ganienkeh—33 Years Later*, accessed Jun. 9, 2017, http://www.ganienkeh.net/33years/. According to the official Ganienkeh website, their territory "is a branch of the original sovereign Kanien´kehà:ka Nation located within the sovereign traditional territory of the Kanien´kehà:ka."

5. *Ganienkeh—33 Years Later*; Verhovek, "Standoff Ends." Hauptman, *Formulating American Indian Policy*, 29–32.

6. Jordan, "Incorporation and Colonization," 38.

7. Woods, "History in Fragments," 78–79; Juliette M'Saadaques, letter (from Odanak, where the couple had moved in 1986) to the Town of Webb Historical Association, Mar. 22, 1992, vertical file "Dennis Family," TWHA-GM, making it clear that her husband Maurice Dennis had willed all items donated to the association to her and that she was designating that ownership to their daughter Andreé. Compare

this to the newspaper photograph and caption describing the going away party given for the couple at the McCauley Mountain Chalet in "Farewell," *Adirondack Echo* (Old Forge, NY) Jun. 6, 1986 or Maurice Dennis's obituary entitled "Area's Friend Passes Away," unknown publication, Dec. 29, 1987, vertical file "Andreé Dennis Newton," TWHA-GM.

8. Jessie [LaPutra?] "In Our Midst . . . A Statue . . . And A Man," *Boonville Herald*, Dec. 20, 1978.

9. Martha Lee Owens, personal communication with author, Nov. 6, 2009, regarding her conversations with Donald Nolett Jr. and Donald Nolett Sr. about their families' history in Keene. Nolett was probably Wawanolette at Odanak. Mitchell eventually ran a store in Albany and thought about buying the store in Keene, but his wife was against the idea. Also see *1911 Census of Canada, Yamaska, Quebec*; 1912 List or Manifest of Alien Passengers Applying for Admission—From Canada at Port of Island Pond (St. Albans), VT, Ancestry.ca record; *1930 US Federal Census, Colonie, Albany County, NY*.

10. Martha Lee Owens, personal communication with author, Nov. 6, 2009.

11. Edith Russell, telephone conversation with author, Mar. 4, 2010. "Long Lake," *Essex County Republican* (Keeseville, NY) Apr. 2, 1915. "Boreas River," *Essex County Republican*, Jul. 7, 1916. Beverly Locke, e-mail to author, Feb. 24, 26, and 27, 2010. Also see *US Federal Census, Long Lake, Hamilton County* (1900, 1910, 1920, 1930) and *1881 Canadian Census for Hastings, Ontario*.

12. Janet Hall, personal conversation with author, Apr. 6, 2009, Keene Valley, NY; Martha Lee Owens, personal conversation with author Apr. 4, 2009, Keene Valley, New York. Norma Brown (Adrian Edmond's cousin), letter to Albertine Reynolds, Mar. 2, 1987.

13. *1870 US Federal Census, Saratoga Springs*. Roy, "Abenaki Sociality," 57, 132. Roy indicates in his footnote 34 that "Mitchel Sabattis and Andrew Joseph's maternal step-great-grandfather, Louis St. Denis, were patrilateral first cousins and likely knew each other as youths and adults." Personal correspondence between Christopher Roy and Phil Joseph, Oct. 4, 2009, shared with author on May 17, 2012.

14. *1900 US Federal Census, Long Lake*. *1910 US Federal Census, Long Lake Town*. All dates of death for the siblings of Andrew Joseph are based on whether they were alive when Andrew died in January 1979, according to his obituary, "Andrew Joseph," *The Saratogian*, Jan. 17, 1979, 3A. *1920 US Federal Census, Long Lake*. *1925 New York State Census, Long Lake Village*. *1930 US Federal Census, Long Lake*. Philip and Wilma Joseph (his wife, formerly Wilma Black), personal conversation with author, Jul. 10, 2009, Indian Lake, New York. "Phil," as he preferred to be called, was born at Mercy Hospital in Tupper Lake the same year his grandfather died, thus he did not have any memories of him.

15. Phil Joseph, personal conversation, Jul. 10, 2009.

16. Phil and Wilma Joseph, personal conversation with author, Jul. 10, 2009 and Sep. 5, 2012, Indian Lake, New York. A philosopher and atheist, Edith's father wrote a book called *Domas*, or "Thoughts," which enjoyed some popularity in Latvia. A devout Christian, Edith refused to translate the book for her children. Also see *1920 US Federal Census, Long Lake*.

17. Phil and Wilma Joseph, personal conversation with author, Jul. 10, 2009. *1920 US Federal Census, Long Lake*; *1925 New York State Census, Long Lake Village*; and *1930 US Federal Census, Long Lake*.

18. Phil and Wilma Joseph, personal conversation with author, Jul. 10, 2009.

19. Ibid.

20. Ibid.

21. Anthony Bufo, "Work Horse of the Woods: The Adirondack Pack Basket and the Man Who Made Them for Seventy Years," *Adirondack Life* (Fall 1973), 21. "Andrew Joseph," Obituary, *The Saratogian*, Jan. 17, 1979. Phil and Wilma Joseph, personal conversation with author, Jul. 10, 2009.

22. Phil and Wilma Joseph, personal conversation with author, Jul. 10, 2009.

23. For example, see A. Irving Hallowell's "Ojibwa Metaphysics of Being and the Perception of Persons," in *Person Perception and Interpersonal Behavior*, eds. Renato Tagiuri and Luigi Petrullo (Palo Alto, CA: Stanford Univ. Press, 1958), 63–85.

24. Phil and Wilma Joseph, personal conversations with author, Jul. 10, 2009, and Aug. 2, 2011. William Black eventually bought the Village Inn in Long Lake and got out of the fur business.

25. Philip Joseph, personal conversation with author, Jul. 10, 2009, and Apr. 10, 2012. Both Phil and Jane studied at Syracuse University. Jane went through grade and high school in eleven years and became a math teacher; however, most of her students were close to her age. She especially found the older girls difficult to handle. World War II offered Jane the opportunity to become an aeronautical engineer through Penn State. Kay, who was also a valedictorian, went to Mildred Elly, a business college in Albany. Sister Edith went to work for a pharmaceutical company. Andy married a granddaughter of Mitchel Sabattis and joined the army in 1944; he worked on diesel engines, and the couple raised two children. John runs two successful demolition businesses in New Jersey—John Joseph, Inc. and Explosive Supply, Inc.

26. John Fadden, accompanied by his wife, Eva Thompson Fadden, personal conversation with author, Oct. 14, 2014, Saranac Lake, New York. His mother's maternal grandparents were Louis and Katherine Back. The farm was located on Drum Street within the eastern portion of the Mohawk community of Akwesasne. His father's grandparents were Henry and Emma (Gibson) Fadden. Also see "In Memory of Christine M. 'Skawennati' Fadden," Obituary, accessed Jan. 16, 2015, http://www.donaldsonfh.com/book-of-memories/1849393/Fadden-Christine/obituary

.php?Printable=true and "Ray Tehanetorens Fadden," Obituary, accessed Jan. 16, 2015, http://www.obitsforlife.com/obituary/479854/Fadden-Ray.php.

27. John Fadden, personal conversation with author, Oct. 14, 2014.

28. Ibid.

29. Ibid.

30. Ibid. John Fadden, e-mail to author, Jan. 21, 2015.

31. John Fadden, personal conversation with author, Oct. 14, 2014.

32. Ibid. John Fadden, e-mail to author with attachment "Family Names," Nov. 27, 2014; e-mail to author, Jan. 21, 2015.

33. John Fadden, personal conversation with author, Oct. 14, 2014.

34. Ibid. "Six Nations Indian Museum" informational blurb, 2, provided by John Fadden to author by e-mail, Oct. 14, 2014.

35. Ibid.

36. Ibid. "Wild Center to Add Indigenous Perspectives," *Elizabethtown Sun*, Sep. 27, 2017. For David Fadden's book information, see "David Fadden Authors and Illustrates a Children's Book," accessed Jan. 19, 2015, http://www.indiantime .net/story/2013/05/02/news/david-fadden-authors-and-illustrates-a-childrens -book/9697.html. David is in the process of animating the book. He explains that the Mohawk version was shorter to keep the book an appropriate length.

37. John Fadden, personal conversation with author, Oct. 14, 2014. "John Fadden Resume," provided to author by e-mail, Nov. 17, 2014. Additional information from "Parade of Nations," accessed Jan. 19, 2015, http://www.paradeofnations.com /artists2.php?id=17; John Fadden, e-mail to author, Jan. 21, 2015.

38. John Fadden, personal conversation with author, Oct. 14, 2014. "John Fadden Resume," provided to author by e-mail, Nov. 17, 2014; Fadden, e-mail to author, Jan. 21, 2015.

39. Garroutte, *Real Indians*, 120.

40. Boyd Cothran, "Working the Indian Field Days: The Economy of Authenticity and the Question of Agency in Yosemite Valley," *American Indian Quarterly* 34, no. 2 (Spring 2010): 194–96, 209–10, 216–17.

41. Niigaanwewidam James Sinclair, "Kzaugin, Storying Ourselves into Life," in *Centering Anishinaabeg Studies: Understanding the World through Stories*, ed. Jill Doerfler, Niigaanwewidam James Sinclair, and Heidi Kiiwetinepinesiik Stark (East Lansing: Michigan State Univ. Press and Univ. of Manitoba Press, 2013), 85–86.

42. Gerald Vizenor, "Constitution of the White Earth Nation: Definitions of Selected Words," *Anishinaabeg Today*, Sep. 2, 2009, 19.

43. Jill Doerfler, "A Philosophy of Living: Ignatia Broker and Constitutional Reform among the White Earth Anishinaabeg," in *Centering Anishinaabeg Studies: Understanding the World through Stories*, ed. Jill Doerfler, Niigaanwewidam James

Sinclair, and Heidi Kiiwetinepinesiik Stark (East Lansing: Michigan State Univ. Press and Univ. of Manitoba Press, 2013), 173–89, 181.

44. *Merriam Webster Online Dictionary*, accessed Feb. 10, 2015, http://www .merriam-webster.com/dictionary/rural. Statistics Canada, "Urban Perspectives and Measurements," modified Nov. 30, 2015, accessed Jul. 24, 2018, https://www150 .statcan.gc.ca/n1/pub/92f0138m/92f0138m2009001-eng.htm. US Department of Health and Human Services, "Defining the Rural Population," accessed Feb. 10, 2015. http://www.hrsa.gov/ruralhealth/policy/definition_of_rural.html.

45. Bonita Lawrence, *"Real" Indians and Others: Mixed-Blood Urban Native Peoples and Indigenous Nationhood* (Vancouver: Univ. of British Columbia Press, 2004), 47. For discussion about nation states designating who was Indian, see 26–37.

46. Ibid., 26–31, 229, quote 166.

47. Garroutte, *Real Indians*, 123–24, 141. Kenneth L. Pike, *Language in Relation to a Unified Theory of the Structure of Human Behavior* (Dallas, TX: Summer Institute of Linguistics, 1954). Daniel K. Richter, "Whose Indian History?" *William and Mary Quarterly* 50, no. 2 (Apr. 1993): 387–89.

48. Bonita Lawrence, *Fractured Homeland: Federal Recognition and Algonquin Identity in Ontario* (Vancouver: Univ. of British Columbia Press, 2002), 79–81.

49. Jolene Rickard, "Intersectionality" Workshop, Centre for Transnational Cultural Analysis Series, Carleton University, Ottawa, Ontario, Nov. 18, 2016.

50. Lawrence, *"Real" Indians*, 170, 232–34, 242.

Conclusion

1. Barr, *Boundaries between Us*, xi.

2. David Glassberg, *Sense of History: The Place of the Past in American Life* (Amherst: Univ. of Massachusetts Press, 2001), 211. Glassberg focuses on the United States, but his work also reflects other countries dominated by settler societies, such as Canada, New Zealand, and Australia.

3. Philip J. Deloria and Neal Salisbury, eds., *A Companion to American Indian History* (Malden, MA: Blackwell, 2002), 4. Susan Sleeper-Smith, Juliana Barr, Jean M. O'Brien, Nancy Shoemaker, and Scott Manning Stevens, *Why You Can't Teach United States History without American Indians* (Chapel Hill: Univ. of North Carolina Press, 2015).

4. O'Brien, *Firsting and Lasting*.

Bibliography

Archives and Collections

Sources accessed at each of the following archives are listed in endnotes and (in the case of published sources) bibliographic entries, followed by the archive abbreviation.

AM-BML: Adirondack Experience, Museum on Blue Mountain Lake, Blue Mountain Lake, NY (a.k.a. the Adirondack Museum)
   Marl [Cliff and Kelly] Papers
   William Seward Webb Papers
ALCC: Akwesasne Library and Cultural Center, Hogansburg, NY
CCHA: Clinton County Historical Association and Museum, Plattsburgh, NY
CPSH: Chimney Point State Historic Site, Addison, VT
CSSH: City of Saratoga Springs Historian's Office, Saratoga Springs, NY
CPL: Crandall Public Library—Archives and Special Collections, Glens Falls, NY
ECCO: Essex County Clerk's Office, Elizabethtown, NY
HCCO: Hamilton County Clerk's Office, Lake Pleasant, NY
ILM: Indian Lake Museum, Indian Lake, NY
   Camp-Mead Family Records including transcript of Camp-Mead family journal, chronological order. Files separated by year as follows: 1870–1915; 1916–1922; 1924–1926; 1927–1965.
   Watso Family File (also spelled "Watso, Watzeau, Watsaw")
KVL: Keene Valley Library—local history collection, Keene Valley, NY
LLA: Long Lake Archives, Long Lake, NY
NYSL: New York State Library—Manuscripts and Special Collections, Albany, NY
   Reverend William M. Beauchamp Papers

SLUL: St. Lawrence University Library—Special Collections and Archives, Canton, NY
    Berry [Watson] Papers
SCHSRL: Saratoga County Historical Society's Research Library at the Brookside Museum, Ballston Spa, NY
SLFL: Saranac Lake Free Library, William Chapman White Memorial Room—Adirondack Research Center, Saranac Lake, NY
SNM-O: Six Nations Museum, Onchiota, NY
SSHMA: Saratoga Springs History Museum and Archive, Saratoga Springs, NY
SSPL: Saratoga Springs Public Library—Saratoga Room local history collection, Saratoga Springs, NY
THS: Ticonderoga Historical Society, Ticonderoga, NY
TWHA-GM: Town of Webb Historical Association—Goodsell Museum Research Room, Old Forge, NY
    Dennis Family (Jules and Cleophie, Maurice and Juliette) Records
VSAR: Vermont State Archives and Records Administration, Montpelier, VT
WCCO-RCA: Warren County Clerk's Office, Records Center and Archives, Lake George, NY
WCHO: Warren County Historian's Office, Lake George, NY
WCHSRL: Washington County Historical Society Research Library, Fort Edwards, NY

**Books, Articles, Theses, Reports,
and Other Published Sources**

Abenaquis Protestants P.Q. Registres Photographries au Greffe de Sorel. 1862. Ancestry.ca records.
Aber, Ted, and Stella King. *The History of Hamilton County.* Lake Pleasant, NY: Great Wilderness Books, 1965.
Aboriginal Affairs and Northern Development Canada. *Indian Act, 1880.* Chap. 28, §11, "Loss of Membership through Residence in a Foreign Country without Leave." Accessed Aug. 18, 2014. https://www.aadnc-aandc.gc.ca/eng/1100100010272/1100100010274.
Abrams, Marc D., and Gregory J. Nowacki. "Native Americans as Active and Passive Promoters of Mast and Fruit Trees in the Eastern USA." *The Holocene* 18, no. 7 (2008): 1123–37.

Ackerman, David H. *Lake Placid Club: An Illustrated History, 1895–1980.* Lake Placid, NY: Lake Placid Education Foundation, 1998.

Adcock, Frederick T., and Cynthia E. Adcock. *Images of America: Piseco Lake and Arietta.* Charleston SC: Arcadia Publishing, 2008.

Adirondacks Come to Life. "The Adirondack Park." Accessed Jun. 29, 2012. http://visitadirondacks.com/adirondack-mountains/Adirondack-park .html.

Akweks, Aren (Ray Fadden). "The Akwesasne Mohawk Counselor Organization." Pamphlet. *The Record, Laws and History of the Akwesasne Mohawk Counselor Organization.* Hogansburg, NY: St. Regis Mohawk Reservation. Provided to author by John Fadden.

Albers, Patricia. Conclusion to *Native Americans and Wage Labor: Ethnohistorical Perspectives,* edited by Alice Littlefield and Martha C. Knack, 245–73. Norman, OK: Univ. of Oklahoma Press, 1996.

Alfred, Taiaiake. *Peace, Power, Righteousness: An Indigenous Manifesto,* 2nd ed. Don Mills, ON: Oxford Univ. Press, 2009.

Algerond, Warren. "A Memory of Pioneer Days." Letter to the Editor. *The Saratogian.* Written Aug. 23 1912, published Aug. 24, 1912. SSPL.

Angus, Christopher. *The Extraordinary Adirondack Journey of Clarence Petty: Wilderness Guide, Pilot, and Conservationist.* Syracuse, NY: Syracuse Univ. Press, 2002.

Aprill, Dennis. "Memories of a Nehasane Trip." *Plattsburgh Press Republican.* Jul. 1, 2007. Accessed Feb. 6, 2012. http://pressrepublican.com /0105_outdoor_perspective/x155086824/Memories-of-a-Nehasane -trip/print.

Audette, Clare. "Indian Village Is Being Built at Lake George." *Glens Falls Post-Star,* Jun. 16, 1952.

Axtell, James. *The Invasion Within: The Contest of Cultures in Colonial North America.* New York: Oxford Univ. Press, 1985.

———. *Natives and Newcomers: The Cultural Origins of North America.* New York: Oxford University Press, 2001.

Bailey, Peter. "'Will the Real Bill Banks Please Stand up?' Towards a Role Analysis of Mid-Victorian Working-Class Respectability." *Journal of Social History* 12, no. 3 (Spring 1979): 336–53.

Barr, Daniel P. *The Boundaries between Us: Natives and Newcomers along the Frontiers of the Old Northwest Territory, 1750–1850.* Kent, OH: Kent State Univ. Press, 2006.

Basso, Keith H. *Wisdom Sits in Places: Landscape and Language Among the Western Apache.* Albuquerque: Univ. of New Mexico Press, 1996.

Basson, Lauren L. "Blurring the Boundaries of Diversity: Ethnic Ambiguity and Indigenous Citizenship in Settler States." *International Journal of Diversity in Organisations, Communities and Nations* 4 (2004): 325–32.

———. *White Enough to Be American: Race Mixing, Indigenous People, and the Boundaries of State and Nation.* Chapel Hill: North Carolina Univ. Press, 2008.

Bauer, Peter. "Watersheds: Twenty Decisive Moments that Made Us What We Are." *Adirondack Life* 20, no. 3 (May–Jun. 1989): 88–101.

Bederman, Gail. *Manliness and Civilization: A Cultural History of Gender and Race in the United States, 1880–1917.* Chicago: Univ. of Chicago Press, 1995.

Beers F. W. *County Atlas of Warren, New York 1876.* WCCO-RCA.

Beers, F. W., and Louis H. Cramer. *Combination Atlas of Saratoga and Balston: From Recent and Actual Surveys and Records.* New York: J. B. Beers and Co., 1876.

Bellin, Joshua David, and Laura L. Mielke, eds. *Native Acts: Indian Performance, 1603–1832.* Lincoln: Univ. of Nebraska Press, 2011.

Benedict, Sallie. "Mohawk Basketmakers of Akwesasne." *American Indian Basketry* 9, no. 3 (1983): 10–16, back cover.

Benn, Carl. *The Iroquois in the War of 1812.* Toronto: Univ. of Toronto Press, 1998.

———. *Mohawks on the Nile: Natives among the Canadian Voyageurs in Egypt, 1884–85.* Toronto: Dundurn Press, 2009.

Benson, Arthur L. *The Story of a New York City Tenderfoot and His Adirondack Mountain Adventure.* Frontier Town Productions, 1979.

Berleth, Richard. *Bloody Mohawk: The French and Indian War and American Revolution on New York's Frontier.* Hensonville, NY: Black Dome Press, 2010.

Berry, Watson B. "Adirondack Mountains, Lakes Impressed Traveling Writer." North Country Chronicle. *Watertown Daily Times,* Nov. 1957.

———. "Start of Adirondack Journey, Saratoga to Lowville, Is Told." North Country Chronicle. *Watertown Daily Times,* Nov. 1957.

Binnema, Theodore (Ted), and Melanie Niemi. "'Let the Line Be Drawn Now': Wilderness, Conservation, and the Exclusion of Aboriginal

People from Banff National Park in Canada." *Environmental History* 11, no. 4 (Oct. 2006): 724–50.

Bixby, George S. "Peter Sailly (1754–1826): A Pioneer of the Champlain Valley with Extracts from His Diary and Letters." *New York State Library History Bulletin* 12. Albany, NY: Univ. of the State of New York, 1919.

Bonaparte, Daren. "The History of Akwesasne from Pre-Contact to Modern Times," *Wampum Chronicles*. Accessed Sep. 19, 2012. http://www.wampumchronicles.com/history.html.

Bond, Eugene W. "How to Build a Birchbark." *Natural History* 64, no. 5 (May 1955): 242–46.

Bond, Hallie E. "'Playing Indian' at Adirondack Children's Camps." Transcript for presentation. AM-BML.

Bonsall, J. *The Northern Tourist: An Illustrated Book of Summer Travel*. Philadelphia: John E. Potter and Co., 1879.

Booth, John Chester. *Booth's History of Saratoga County, N.Y.* Edited by Violet B. Dunn, Saratoga County Historian, and Beatrice Sweeney, City Historian of Saratoga Springs. Saratoga Springs, NY: Saratoga County Bicentennial Commission, 1977. First published in 1858.

Bourque, J., and Laureen A. Labar. *Common Threads: Wabanaki Textiles, Clothing, and Costume*. Seattle: Univ. of Washington Press, 2009.

Bowman, Don. *Go Seek the Pow Wow on the Mountain*. Greenfield Center, NY: Greenfield Review Press, 1993.

Brasser, T. J. "Mahican." In *Handbook of the North American Indian, Northeast*, vol. 15, edited by Bruce G. Trigger, 198–212. Washington, DC: Smithsonian Institution, 1978.

Braudel, Fernand. *The Identity of France, History and Environment*. Translated by Siân Reynolds. London: Harper-Collins, 1988.

Brenan, Dan, ed. *Canoeing the Adirondacks with Nessmuk: The Adirondack Letters of George Washington Sears*. Blue Mountain Lake, NY: Adirondack Museum, 1962.

"Brief History of Akwesasne 1755–1915, A." *Current: The Journal of North Country Action* 5, no. 7 (Jan.–Feb. 1990): 6–7.

Brislin, Anne E. *Narratives of Old Fort Edward*. Booklet published by the Members of the Board of Education, Fort Edward Public Schools. Albany, NY: Fort Orange Press, 1962. WCHSRL.

Britten, Evelyn Barrett. *Chronicles of Saratoga Springs*. Saratoga Springs, NY: published by author. 1959.

———. "Indian Encampments Stir Memories." *The Saratogian*. Dec. 5, 1959. SSHMA.

———. "Pete Francis, Chef Extraordinaire." *The Saratogian*. Dec. 7, 1956. SSHMA.

———. "3 Indian Encampments Once Located in City," *The Saratogian*. May 5, 1962. SSHMA.

———. "Traces of Indian Life Remain in Area." *The Saratogian*. Sep. 1962. SSHMA.

———. "When the Indians Came Visiting." *The Saratogian*. Dec. 4, 1964. SSHMA.

Brooklyn Historical Society. "Guide to the Chiropean Yearbooks ARC.164." Accessed Jul. 19, 2019. http://dlib.nyu.edu/findingaids/html/bhs/arc _164_chiropean_yearbooks/.

Brooks, Lisa. "The Common Pot: Indigenous Writing and the Reconstruction of Native Space in the Northeast." PhD diss. Cornell University, Jan. 2004.

———. *The Common Pot: The Recovery of Native Space in the Northeast.* Minneapolis: Univ. of Minnesota Press, 2008.

Brown, George Levi. "News in and About the County Seat." *Adirondack Record* (Elizabethtown, NY). Jun. 2, 1922.

———. *Pleasant Valley: A History of Elizabethtown, Essex County, New York.* [Elizabethtown, NY?]: Post and Gazette print, 1905.

———. "Sebille, the Indian." *Elizabethtown Post Gazette.* Apr. 5, 1900. From typescript given by Mrs. Early (T. Ovitt, 6/70). Biography file "Benedict Family." AM-BML.

Brown, Henry A. L., and Richard J. Walton. *John Brown's Tract: Lost Adirondack Empire.* Published for the Rhode Island Historical Society, Canaan, NH: Phoenix Publishing, 1988.

Brown, Jennifer S. H. *Strangers in Blood: Fur Trade Company Families in Indian Country.* Vancouver: Univ. of British Columbia Press, 1980.

Brown, Kathleen. "The Anglo-Algonquian Gender Frontier." In *Negotiators of Change: Historical Perspectives on Native American Women*, edited by Nancy Shoemaker, 26–48. New York and London: Routledge, 1995.

Brown, William H., ed. *History of Warren County New York.* Published by the Board of Supervisors of Warren County; printed by Glens Falls Post Company, 1963.

Brownlie, Robin, and Mary-Ellen Kelm. "Desperately Seeking Absolution: Native Agency as Colonialist Alibi?" *Canadian Historical Review* 75, no. 4 (Dec. 1994): 543–56.

Bruchac, Joseph. *Bowman's Store: A Journey to Myself.* New York: Dial Books, 1997.

Bruchac, Margaret M. "Historical Erasure and Cultural Recovery: Indigenous People in the Connecticut River Valley." PhD diss. University of Massachusetts, Amherst, 2007.

Brumley, Charles. *Guides of the Adirondacks, A History: A Short Season, Hard Work Low Pay.* Utica, NY: North Country Books, 1994.

Bufo, Anthony. "Work Horse of the Woods: The Adirondack Pack Basket and the Man Who Made Them for Seventy Years." *Adirondack Life* (Fall 1973): 20–24.

Burnett, Charles H. *Conquering the Wilderness: The Building of the Adirondack & St. Lawrence Railway by William Seward Webb, 1891–92.* Privately printed, 1932.

Burns, Jonathan A., and Paul A. Raber. Introduction to "Rockshelters in Behavioral Context: Archaeological Perspectives from Eastern North America." *North American Archaeologist* 31 (2010): 257–85.

Cahill, Cathleen D. "'You Think It Strange That I Can Love an Indian': Native Men, White Women, and Marriage in the Indian Service." *Frontiers, a Journal of Women's Studies* 29, nos. 2–3 (2008): 106–45.

Calloway, Colin G. "Sir William Johnson, Highland Scots, and American Indians." *New York History* 89, no. 2 (Spring 2008): 163–77.

———. *The Western Abenakis of Vermont, 1600–1800: War, Migration, and the Survival of an Indian People.* Norman, OK: Univ. of Oklahoma Press, 1990.

Calverly, David. "'When the Need for It No Longer Existed': Declining Wildlife and Native Hunting Rights in Ontario, 1791–1898." In *The Culture of Hunting in Canada*, edited by Jean Manore and Dale Miner, 105–20. Vancouver: Univ. of British Columbia Press, 2007.

Campisi, Jack, and Laurence M. Hauptman, eds. *The Oneida Indian Experience: Two Perspectives.* Syracuse, NY: Syracuse Univ. Press, 1988.

Carnes, Mark C., and Clyde Griffen, eds. *Meanings for Manhood: Constructions of Masculinity in Victorian America.* Univ. of Chicago Press, 1990.

Carpenter, Warwick Stevens. *The Summer Paradise in History: A Compilation of Fact and Tradition Covering Lake George, Lake Champlain, the Adirondack Mountains, and Other Sections Reached by the Rail and Steamer Lines of the Delaware And Hudson Company.* Albany, NY: General Passenger Department, Delaware and Hudson Co., 1914.

Carr, Arthur A. "Ticonderoga's Indian Pageant, A Historical Account," Ticonderoga Historical Society web page. Accessed Dec. 8, 2017. http://ticonderogahistoricalsociety.org/ticonderogas-indian-pageant-a-historical-account/.

Case, Dick. "After 40 Years Old Forge Is Getting 'Too Busy,' for Totem Pole Carver." *Syracuse Herald-Journal.* Oct. 22, 1984.

Cayton, Andrew R. L., and Fredrika J. Teute, eds. *Contact Points: American Frontiers from the Mohawk Valley to the Mississippi, 1750–1830.* Chapel Hill: Univ. of North Carolina Press, 1998.

Chamberlin, J. Edward. *If This is Your Land, Where are Your Stories? Finding Common Ground.* Toronto: Alfred A. Knopf Canada, 2003.

Champagne, Linda. "Noah John Rondeau Interviewed: Adirondack Hermit Part III." *Lake Placid News.* Sep. 28, 1967.

Champlain, Samuel de. *Voyages of Samuel de Champlain: 1604–1610.* The Prince Society, 1878.

Charland, Thomas M. *Histoire Des Abénakis D'Odanak: 1675–1937.* Montreal: Les Éditions du Lévrier, 1964.

Chittenden, L. E. *Personal Reminiscences: Including Lincoln and Others, 1840–1890.* New York: Richmond, Croscup and Co., 1893.

Clay, Cecil. "Hunting, Fishing Trips in Newcomb Area Century Ago Recalled in Old Letters." *Tupper Lake Press.* Jan. 4, 1960.

Clute, Garrett. "Map of Lake George." Dated 1891, based on survey conducted by Clute in 1810. WCCO-RCA.

Coale, Griffith Bailey. "Cooper's Cave." Painting in the lobby of the Queensbury Hotel, Glens Falls, NY.

Coates, Kenneth. "The Sinews of Their Lives: First Nations' Access to Resources in the Yukon, 1890–1950." In *The Culture of Hunting in Canada,* edited by Jean Manore and Dale Miner, 148–66. Vancouver: Univ. of British Columbia Press, 2007.

Coates, Ken, and William Morrison. *The Forgotten North: A History of Canada's Provincial Norths.* Toronto: James Lorimer and Co., 1992.

Colpitts, George. *Game in the Garden: A Human History of Wildlife in Western Canada to 1940*. Vancouver: Univ. of British Columbia Press, 2002.

"Conseil Des Abénakis Odanak, History." Accessed July 10, 2018. https://caodanak.com/en/histoire/.

Cooper, James Fennimore. *Last of the Mohicans: A Narrative of 1757*. Philadelphia: Carey and Lea, 1826.

Corbiere, Alan. "Gidonaaganinaa 'Our Dish': An Intertribal Treaty Encoded in Wampum." *Anishinabek News* 19, no. 9 (Nov. 2007): 22, http://anishinabeknews.ca/wp-content/uploads/2013/04/2007-11.pdf.

Cothran, Boyd. *Remembering the Modoc War: Redemptive Violence and the Making of American Innocence*. Chapel Hill: North Carolina Press, First Peoples New Directions in Indigenous Studies, 2014.

———. "Working the Indian Field Days: The Economy of Authenticity and the Question of Agency in Yosemite Valley." *American Indian Quarterly* 34, no. 2 (Spring 2010): 194–223.

Cronon, William. *Changes in the Land: Indians, Colonists, and the Ecology of New England*. New York: Hill and Wang, 1983.

Curtis, A. L. Byron. *The Life and Adventures of Nat Foster: Trapper and Hunter of the Adirondacks*. Utica, NY: Press of Thomas J. Griffiths, 1912.

Curtis, Gates, ed. *Our County and Its People: A Memorial Record of St. Lawrence County, New York*. Syracuse, NY: D. Mason and Company, 1894.

Day, Gordon M. "Abenaki Place-Names in the Champlain Valley." In *In Search of New England's Native Past: Selected Essays by Gordon M. Day*, edited by Michael K. Foster and William Cowan, 229–62. Amherst, MA: Univ. of Massachusetts Press, 1998.

———. "The Eastern Boundaries of Iroquoia." In *In Search of New England's Native Past: Selected Essays by Gordon M. Day*, edited by Michael K. Foster and William Cowan, 116–22. Hanover, NH: Univ. Press of New England, 2001.

———. *The Identity of the Saint Francis Indians*. Canadian Ethnology Services, paper no. 71. Ottawa: National Museum of Canada, 1981.

———. "The Indian as an Ecological Factor in the Northeastern Forest." In *In Search of New England's Native Past: Selected Essays by Gordon M. Day*, edited by Michael K. Foster and William Cowan, 27–48. Amherst: Univ. of Massachusetts Press, 1998.

————. "Western Abenaki." In *Handbook of the North American Indian, Northeast*, vol. 15, edited by Bruce G. Trigger, 148–59. Washington, DC: Smithsonian Institution, 1978.

DeGarmo, Todd. "Indian Camps and Upstate Tourism." *New York Folklore Newsletter* 14, no. 2 (1993): 4–5, 10.

DeKay, James E. *Zoology of New York; or, The New York Fauna; comprising detailed descriptions of all the animals hitherto observed within the state of New York, with brief notices of those occasionally found near its borders, and accompanied by appropriate illustrations*, 2 vols. Albany, NY: Carroll and Cook, 1842. Accessed Sep. 14, 2014. http://archive.org /stream/zoologyofnewyork01deka#page/72/mode/2up.

Deloria, Philip J. *Indians in Unexpected Places*. Lawrence, KS: Univ. Press of Kansas, 2004.

————. *Playing Indian*. New Haven, CT: Yale Univ. Press, 1998.

Deloria, Philip J., and Neal Salisbury, eds. *A Companion to American Indian History*. Malden, MA: Blackwell, 2002.

Deloria, Vine, Jr., and Raymond J. DeMaille. *Documents of American Indian Diplomacy: Treaties, Agreements, and Conventions, 1775–1979 (Legal History of North America)* 2 vols. Norman, OK: Univ. of Oklahoma, 1999.

Demers, Paul A. "The French Colonial Legacy of the Canada–United States Border in Eastern North America, 1650–1783." *French Colonial History* 10 (2009): 35–54.

DeSormo, Maitland C. *Summers on the Saranacs*. Saranac Lake, NY: Adirondack Yesteryears, 1980.

Dickason, Olive Patricia. "The French and the Abenaki: A Study in Frontier Politics," *Vermont History* 58, no. 2 (Spring 1990): 82–98.

Dippie, Brian W. *The Vanishing American: White Attitude and U.S. Indian Policy*. Middletown, CT: Wesleyan Univ. Press, 1982.

Doerfler, Jill. "A Philosophy of Living: Ignatia Broker and Constitutional Reform among the White Earth Anishinaabeg." In *Centering Anishinaabeg Studies: Understanding the World through Stories*, edited by Jill Doerfler, Niigaanwewidam James Sinclair, and Heidi Kiiwetinepinesiik Stark, 173–89. East Lansing: Michigan State Univ. Press and Univ. of Manitoba Press, 2013.

Dominion of Canada Annual Report of the Department of Indian Affairs for the Year Ended 31st December, 1884. Accessed Jul. 16, 2018. http://central .bac-lac.gc.ca/.item/?id=1884-IAAR-RAAI&op=pdf&app=indianaffairs.

Donaldson, Alfred L. *A History of the Adirondacks,* 2 vols. Fleishchmanns, NY: Purple Mountain Press, 1992. First published in New York: Century Company, 1921.

Dow, Sue Ellen. "A History of Akwesasne." *Franklin Historical Review* 33 (1998): 9–17.

Duquette, John J. "The Famous Adirondack Guides' Association: Heyday of the Guides." *Adirondack Daily Enterprise* (Saranac Lake, NY). Jun. 18, 1987.

Edensor, Tim. "Staging Tourism: Tourists as Performers." *Annals of Tourism Research* 27, no. 2 (2000): 322–44.

Edmonds, Adrian. *Recollections of an Adirondacker.* Vol. 1, *Stories of a Keene Valley House, Adrian Edmonds to Fred and Sarah Cook on the Purchase of Their Home in Keene Valley.* Keene Valley Library Assoc., c. 2005. KVL.

Ellinghaus, Katherine. *Taking Assimilation to Heart: Marriages of White Women and Indigenous Men in the United States and Australia, 1887–1937.* Lincoln: Univ. of Nebraska Press, 2006.

Elliott, Dolores. *Birds and Beasts in Beads: 150 Years of Iroquois Beadwork.* Hamilton, NY: Longyear Museum of Anthropology, Colgate Univ., 2011.

———. "Canoes and Horseshoes: Two Forms of Iroquois Beadwork." Paper presented at the Conference on Iroquois Research, Cortland, NY, Oct. 6, 2012.

———. "Iroquois Beadwork: A Haudenosaunee Tradition and Art." In *Preserving Tradition and Understanding the Past: Papers from the Conference on Iroquois Research, 2001–2005,* edited by Christine Sternberg Patrick, 35–48. Albany, NY: Univ. of the State of New York, State Education Department, New York State Museum, 2010. Accessed Jul. 19, 2018. http://www.nysm.nysed.gov/common/nysm/files/nysmrecord-vol1_0.pdf.

Engelbrecht, William. *Iroquoia: The Development of a Native World.* Syracuse, NY: Syracuse Univ. Press, 2003.

———. "Iroquoian Ethnicity and Archaeological Taxa." In *Taming the Taxa: Toward a New Understanding of Great Lakes Archaeology,* edited by Ronald F. Williamson and Christopher M. Watts, 51–59. Toronto: East End Books, 1999.

Ethridge, Robbie. *Creek Country: The Creek Indians and Their World.* Chapel Hill: Univ. of North Carolina Press, 2003.

Ethridge, Robbie, and Sheri M. Shuck-Hall, eds. *Mapping the Mississippian Shatter Zone: The Colonial Indian Slave Trade and Regional Instability in the American South*. Lincoln: Univ. of Nebraska Press, 2009.

Fadden, Ray. See Akweks, Aren.

Faragher, John Mack. "'More Motley than Mackinaw': From Ethnic Mixing to Ethnic Cleansing on the Frontier of the Lower Missouri, 1783–1833." In *Contact Points: American Frontiers from the Mohawk Valley to the Mississippi, 1750–1830*, edited by Andrew R. L. Cayton and Fredrika J. Teute, 304–26. Chapel Hill: Univ. of North Carolina Press, 1998.

Fawcett, Melissa Jayne, Mohegan Tribal Historian. *The Lasting of the Mohegans, Part I*. Ledyard, CT: Pequot Printing, 1995.

Fenton, William. "Northern Iroquoian Culture Patterns." In *Handbook of the North American Indians: Northeast*, vol. 15, edited by Bruce G. Trigger, 296–321. Washington, DC: Smithsonian Institution, 1978.

Ferris, Neal. *The Archaeology of Native-Lived Colonialism: Challenging History in the Great Lakes*. Tucson, AZ: Univ. of Arizona Press, 2009.

Fitzgerald, Mary Ann (Saratoga Springs historian). "'Saratoga Chips' Chronology," 1–3. Vertical file "Saratoga County Potato Chip Stories." SCHSRL.

Flynn, Karen. *Moving beyond Borders: A History of Black Canadian and Caribbean Women in the Diaspora*. Toronto: Univ. of Toronto Press, 2011.

Folwell, Elizabeth. "Wish You Were Here: Hand-Tinted Memories from Standard Supply." *Adirondack Life* 20, no. 6 (Nov./Dec. 1989): 60–62.

Foster, Michael K., and William Cowan, eds. *In Search of New England's Native Past: Selected Essays by Gordon M. Day*. Amherst: Univ. of Massachusetts Press, 1998.

Fowler, Albert Vann, ed. *Cranberry Lake 1845–1959: An Adirondack Miscellany*. Blue Mountain Lake, NY: Adirondack Museum, 1959.

Francis, Daniel. *The Imaginary Indian: The Image of the Indian in Canadian Culture*. Vancouver: Arsenal Pulp Press, 2012.

French, J. H. *Gazetteer of the State of New York: Embracing a Comprehensive View of the Geography, Geology, and General History of the State, and a Complete History and Description of Every County, City, Town, Village, and Locality with Full Tables of Statistics*. 8th ed. Syracuse, NY: 1860.

Gallagher, Nancy L. *Breeding Better Vermonters: The Eugenics Project in the Green Mountain State*. Hanover, NH: Univ. Press of New England, 1999.

Ganienkeh—33 Years Later. Accessed Jun. 9, 2017. http://www.ganienkeh.net/33years/.

Garroutte, Eva Marie. *Real Indians: Identity and the Survival of Native America*. Berkeley: Univ. of California Press, 2003.

Garymont, Barbara. "The Six Nations Indians in the Revolutionary War." In *Race and Gender in the Northern Colonies*, edited by Jan Noel, 185–87. Toronto: Canadian Scholars Press, 2000.

Gassan, Richard H. *The Birth of American Tourism: New York, the Hudson Valley, and American Culture, 1790–1830*. Amherst: Univ. of Massachusetts Press, 2008.

Gaul, Theresa Strouth, ed. *To Marry an Indian: The Marriage of Harriett Gold and Elias Boudinot in Letters, 1823–1839*. Chapel Hill: Univ. of North Carolina Press, 2005.

Gélinas, Claude. "La Mauricie des Abénaquis au XIXe siécle." *Recherches amérindiennes au Québec* 33, no. 2 (2003): 44–56.

George-Kanentiio, Doug. *Iroquois Culture and Commentary*. Santa Fe, NM: Clear Light Publishers, 2000.

———. "Mohawk Ceremonial Cycle." In *Encyclopedia of the Haudenosaunee (Iroquois Confederacy)*, edited by Bruce Elliott Johansen and Barbara Alice Mann, 203. Westport, CT: Greenwood Press, 2000.

Gillespie, Gregory Eric. *Hunting for Empire: Narratives of Sport in Rupert's Land, 1840–1870*. Vancouver: Univ. of British Columbia Press, 2007.

Gilligan, Agnes. "News of Lake George and Vicinity Places." *Glens Falls Post-Star*, Sep. 8, 1952.

Glassberg, David. *Sense of History: The Place of the Past in American Life*. Amherst: Univ. of Massachusetts Press, 2001.

Glenn, Morris F. *The Story of Three Towns: Westport, Essex and Willsboro, New York*. Ann Arbor, MI: Braun-Brumfield, 1977.

Goddard, Ives. Review of *Indian Names in Connecticut* by James Hammond Trumbull. *International Journal of American Linguists* 43, no. 2 (Apr. 1977): 157–59.

Goldsmith, Arthur A. "The State, the Market and Economic Development: A Second Look at Adam Smith in Theory and Practice." *Development and Change* 26 (1995): 633–50.

Gordon, Thomas Francis. *Gazetteer of the State of New York: Comprehending Its Colonial History*. Philadelphia: printed for author, 1836.

Graham, Frank, Jr. *The Adirondack Park: A Political History.* New York: Alfred A. Knopf, 1978.

Gray, Andrew. "Indigenous Peoples and Their Territories." In *Decolonising Indigenous Rights,* edited by Adolfo de Oliveira, 17–44. New York: Routledge, 2009.

Graymont, Barbara. *The Iroquois in the American Revolution.* Syracuse, NY: Syracuse Univ. Press, 1972.

Grazulis, Thomas P. *The Tornado: Nature's Ultimate Windstorm.* Norman, OK: Univ. of Oklahoma Press, 2001.

Greiner, Newton. "Hal Cranson Traces His Abenaki Roots to Earliest Recorded Adirondack History." *Tupper Lake Free Press.* Jan. 27, 1999.

Guenther, Laura M. "Glimpses of Sabael." Transcript. Vertical file "Surname Sabeal [sic]—Indian Lake." WCHO.

Hallock, Thomas. *From the Fallen Tree: Frontier Narratives, Environmental Politics, and the Roots of a National Pastoral, 1749–1826.* Chapel Hill: Univ. of North Carolina Press, 2003.

Hallowell, A. Irving. "Ojibwa Metaphysics of Being and the Perception of Persons." In *Person Perception and Interpersonal Behavior,* edited by Renato Tagiuri and Luigi Petrullo, 63–85. Palo Alto, CA: Stanford Univ. Press, 1958.

Hamilton, Edward P., ed. "A Journal of the Proceedings of Nathaniel Wheelwright appointed and commissioned by his Excellency William Shirley, Esquire, Governor and Commander in Chief in and over His Majesty's Province of the Massachusetts Bay in New England from Boston to Canada in order to redeem the captives belonging to this government in the hands of the French and Indians." *Bulletin of the Fort Ticonderoga Museum* 10, no. 4 (Feb. 1960): 260–96.

Hamilton, Michelle A. *Collections and Objections: Aboriginal Material Culture in Southern Ontario.* Montreal: McGill-Queen's Univ. Press, 2010.

Hammond, Samuel H. *Hills, Lakes, and Forest Streams; or a Tramp in the Chateaugay Woods.* New York: J. C. Derby, 1854.

———. *Wild Northern Scenes; or Sporting Adventures with the Rifle and the Rod.* New York: Derby and Jackson, 1857.

Harris, Philip J. *Adirondack, Lumber Capital of the World.* Baltimore, MD: PublishAmerica, 2008.

Harter, Henry A. *Fairy Tale Railroad: The Mohawk and Malone from the Mohawk, through the Adirondacks to the St Lawrence—The Golden Chariot Route.* Binghamton, NY: Vail-Ballou, 1979.

Harwood, W. H. "The Early Settlers of that Part of the Town of Malone Now Known as Chasm Falls." *The Malone (NY) Farmer*, Apr. 8, 1903, 42–43.

Hauptman, Laurence M. *Formulating American Indian Policy in New York State.* Albany: State Univ. of New York Press, 1988.

Haviland, William J., and Marjory W. Power. *The Original Vermonters: Native Inhabitant, Past and Present.* Hanover, NH: Univ. Press of New England, 1994.

Headley, Joel T. *The Adirondack; or, Life in the Woods.* New York: Baker and Sciribneir, 1853.

———. *Letters from the Backwoods and the Adirondac.* New York: John S. Taylor, 1850.

Helin, Calvin. *Dances with Dependency: Indigenous Success through Self-Reliance.* Vancouver: Orca Spirit Publishing and Communications, 2006.

Hill, Henry Wayland. *The Champlain Tercentenary: Final Report of the New York Lake Champlain Tercentenary Commission.* Albany, NY: J. B. Lyon Co., 1913.

Hill, Ralph Nading. *Lake Champlain: Key to Liberty.* Montpelier, VT: Burlington Free Press, 1976.

Hill, Richard W., Sr. "Making a Final Resting Place Final: A History of the Repatriation Experience of the Haudenosaunee." In *Cross-Cultural Collaboration: Native Peoples and Archaeology in the Northeastern United States* edited by Jordan E. Kerber, 3–17. Lincoln: Univ. of Nebraska Press, 2006.

Hill, William H. *Old Fort Edward before 1800* [An account of the historic ground now occupied by the Village of Fort Edward, New York]. Fort Edward, NY: Privately published, 1929.

Historic Adirondacks, The: Historic Sketches of the Thirteen Counties of the Adirondack Park Area. Brochure. Adirondack, NY, Aug. 1970.

Hixson, Walter L. *American Settler Colonialism: A History.* New York: Palgrave Macmillan, 2013.

Hodgins, Bruce W. and Jamie Benidickson. *The Temagami Experience: Recreation, Resources, and Aboriginal Rights in the Northern Ontario Wilderness.* Toronto: Univ. of Toronto Press, 1989.

Hoffman, Charles Fenno. Letters. *New York Mirror.* Sep. 23 and 30, 1837; Oct. 7, 14, 21, and 28, 1837; and Dec. 16, 1837.

———. *Wild Scenes in the Forest and Prairie,* 2 vols. London: Richard Bentley, 1839.

Hogan, Mary. "Peter Waters, May He Rest in Peace." Photograph. Oct. 2001. TWHA-GM.

Holden, Austin Wells. *A History of the Town of Queensbury in the State of New York.* Albany: J. Munsell, 1874.

Holland, Nina. "Black Ash and Sweetgrass: Akwesasne Basketmakers Weave History and Art." *Adirondack Life* (n.d.): 30–32. Vertical file "Basketmaking." ALCC.

Holley, Orville L., ed. *The Picturesque Tourist: Being a Guide through the Northern and Eastern States and Canada.* New York: J. Disturnell, 1844.

Horton, Robert. "Sabael Benedict, Indian Pioneer." *Adirondac* 54, no. 10 (Dec. 1989): 16–18.

Hough, Franklin B. *A History of St. Lawrence and Franklin Counties, New York: From the Earliest Period to the Present Time.* Albany, NY: Little and Co., 1853.

Howe, Daniel Walker. *What Hath God Wrought: The Transformation of America, 1815–1848,* Oxford History of the United States. Oxford: Oxford Univ. Press, 2009.

Howell, George Rogers and Jonathan Tenney. *Bi-centennial History of Albany: History of the County of Albany, N.Y., from 1609 to 1886.* W. W. Munsell and Co., 1886.

Ingersoll, Thomas N. *To Intermix with Our White Brothers: Indian Mixed Bloods in the United States from Earliest Times to the Indian Removals.* Albuquerque, NM: Univ. of New Mexico Press, 2005.

Ingram, Darcy. "'Au temps et dans les quantités qui lui plaisent': Poachers, Outlaws, and Rural Banditry in Québec." *Histoire sociale/Social History* 42, no. 83 (May 2009): 1–33.

Ingram, Darcy. "Nature's Improvement: Wildlife, Conservation, and Conflict in Quebec, 1850–1914." PhD diss., McGill University, 2007.

Ives, Martin V. B. *Through the Adirondacks in Eighteen Days.* New York and Albany: Wynkoop Hallenbeck Crawford Co., State Printers, 1899.

Jacoby, Karl. *Crimes against Nature: Squatters, Poachers, Thieves, and the Hidden History of American Conservation.* Berkeley: Univ. of California Press, 2001.

Jamieson, Paul F. "Highway of History: The First White Man Comes to St. Lawrence County." *The Quarterly* (St. Lawrence County Historical Assoc.) 13, no. 2 (1968): 3–4, 21–23.

Jasen, Patricia. *Wild Things: Nature, Culture, and Tourism in Ontario, 1790–1914.* Toronto: Univ. of Toronto Press, 1995.

Jenkins, Jerry, with Andy Keal. *The Adirondack Atlas: A Geographic Portrait of the Adirondack Park.* Syracuse, NY: Syracuse Univ. Press and Adirondack Museum, 2004.

Jessup, Lynda. "Landscapes of Sport, Landscapes of Exclusion: The Sportsman's Paradise in Late 19th-Century Canadian Painting." *Journal of Canadian Studies* 40, no. 1 (Winter 2006): 71–123.

Johansen, Bruce Elliott. "Grandfathers of Akwesasne Mohawk Revitalization: Ray Fadden and Ernest Benedict." *The Praeger Handbook on Contemporary Issues in Native America.* Vol. 1, *Linguistic, Ethnic, and Economic Revival.* Westport, CT: Greenwood, 2007.

Johansen, Bruce Elliott, and Barbara Alice Mann, eds. *Encyclopedia of the Haudenosaunee (Iroquois Confederacy).* Westport, CT: Greenwood Press, 2000.

Johnson, Chrisfield. *History of Washington County New York with Illustrations and Biographical Sketches of Some of Its Prominent Men and Pioneers.* Interlaken, NY: Heart of the Lakes Publishing, 1991. First published in Philadelphia: J. B. Lippincott, 1878.

Johnson, Guy. *To His Excellency William Tryon Esq., Captain General & Governor in Chief of the Province of New-York & this Map of the Country of the VI. Nations Proper with Part of the Adjacent Colonies* (1771). New York State Library. Accessed Jul. 14, 2012. http://www.nysl.nysed.gov/scandocs/nativeamerican.htm.

Johnson, Spencer (surveyor). "Land Grants and First Settlers in Keene." *The History of Keene Valley, Bicentennial Committee,* ed. Peggy Byrne, 33–40. Bicentennial lecture series, Keene Valley, NY, Jul.–Aug. 1975–76. Vertical file "Indian Lore." KVL.

Jones, Peter Kahkewaquonaby. *History of the Ojebway Indians: With Especial Reference to Their Conversion to Christianity; with a Brief Memoir of the Writer.* London: A. W. Bennett, 1861.

Jordan, Kurt A. "Incorporation and Colonization: Postcolumbian Iroquois Satellite Communities and Processes of Indigenous Autonomy." *American Anthropologist* 115, no. 1 (2013): 29–43.

Juvenal. "Mitchell Sabattis" Letter to the Editor. *Forest and Stream*, May 12, (1906?).

Kaelber, Lutz. "Vermont." *Eugenics: Compulsory Sterilization in 50 American States*. Accessed Sep. 13, 2012. http://www.uvm.edu/~lkaelber /eugenics/VT/VT.html.

Kalm, Peter (Pehr). *Travels into North America; Containing Its Natural History, and a Circumstantial Account of Its Plantations and Agriculture in General, with the Civil, Ecclesiastical and Commercial State of the Country, the Manners of the Inhabitants, and Several Curious and Important Remarks on Various Subjects*, 3 vols. Translated by John Reinhold Forster. London: The Editor, 1770–71.

Kappler, Charles J., ed. *Indian Affairs: Laws and Treaties*. Vol. 2, *Treaties*. Washington, DC: Government Printing Office, 1904: 50–51. Accessed Jan. 18, 2013. http://digital.library.okstate.edu/kappler/vol2/treaties /moh0050.htm.

———. *Indian Affairs: Laws and Treaties*. Vol. 4. Washington, DC: Government Printing Office, 1929. Accessed Oct. 3, 2012. http://digital .library.okstate.edu/kappler/vol4/html_files/v4p0420c.html.

Kellogg, D[avid] S. "Aboriginal Dwelling Sites in the Champlain Valley." *Proceedings of the American Association for the Advancement of Science*. N.d. 308–10. Vertical file "Archaeology." AM-BML.

Kellogg, Henry D. "Mitchell Sabattis." *Northern Monthly* 1, no. 2 (Glens Falls, NY, Jun. 1906): 14–15.

Kelsay, Isabel Thompson. *Joseph Brant, 1743–1807: Man of Two Worlds*. Syracuse, NY: Syracuse Univ. Press, 1984.

Knight, Rolf. *Indians at Work: An Informal History of Native Labour in British Columbia, 1858–1930*. Vancouver: New Star Books, 1996.

Knox, John. "Piseco Lake." *New York State Conservationist*, reprint 106. Albany, NY, n.d. Vertical file "Piseco." AM-BML.

Kupperman, Karen Ordahl. *Indians and English: Facing Off in Early America*. Ithaca, NY: Cornell Univ. Press, 2000.

Lafitau, Joseph François. *Moeurs des sauvages ameriquains comparées aux moeurs des premiers temps*. 4 vols. Paris: Chez Saugrain l'aîné et al., 1724.

Lake George Steamboat Company. "History of the Lake George Steamboat Company." Accessed Feb. 6, 2012. http://lakegeorgesteamboat.com /index.asp?lg=1&w=pages&r=26&pid=27.

Lape, Jane M., ed. *Ticonderoga: Patches and Patterns from Its Past.* Lake George, NY: Ad Resorts Press, 1969.

LaPutra (? last name partly illegible), Jessie. "In Our Midst . . . A Statue . . . And A Man." *Boonville Herald,* Dec. 20, 1978.

Lawrence, Bonita. *Fractured Homeland: Federal Recognition and Algonquin Identity in Ontario.* Vancouver: Univ. of British Columbia Press, 2002.

———. *"Real" Indians and Others: Mixed-Blood Urban Native Peoples and Indigenous Nationhood.* Vancouver: Univ. of British Columbia Press, 2004.

Lee, Henry. *Lee's Guide to Saratoga, the Queen of Spas.* New York: Chas R. Parker, 1883.

Levine, Mary Ann. "Determining the Provenance of Native Copper Artifacts from Northeastern North America: Evidence from Instrumental Neutron Activation Analysis." *Journal of Archaeological Science* 34, no. 4 (2007): 572–87.

Lewis, Henry T. "Indian Fires of Spring." *Natural History* (Jan. 1980): 76–83.

Lewis, Susan Ingalls. *Unexceptional Women: Female Proprietors in Mid-Nineteenth-Century Albany, New York, 1830–1885.* Columbus: Ohio State Univ. Press, 2009.

Lonergan, Carroll Vincent. *Ticonderoga: Historic Portage.* Ticonderoga, NY: Fort Mount Hope Society Press, 1959.

Long Lake Wesleyan Methodist Church. "History." Accessed Aug. 20, 2012, http://longlakewesleyan.wordpress.com/history-of-llwc/.

Loo, Tina. "Of Moose and Men: Hunting for Masculinities in British Columbia, 1880–1939." *Western Historical Quarterly* 32, no. 3 (Autumn 2001): 296–313.

Lossing, Benson J. *The Hudson, from the Wilderness to the Sea.* Troy, NY: H. B. Nims and Co, 1866.

Lounsbury, Floyd G. "Iroquois Languages." In *Handbook of North American Indians—Northeast,* vol. 15, edited by Bruce G. Trigger, 334–43. Washington, DC, Smithsonian Institution Press, 1978.

Lutz, John Sutton. *Makúk: A New History of Aboriginal—White Relations.* Vancouver and Toronto: Univ. of British Columbia Press, 2008.

Lytwyn, Victor P. "A Dish with One Spoon: The Shared Hunting Grounds Agreement in the Great Lakes and St. Lawrence Valley Region." In *Papers of the Twenty-Eighth Algonquian Conference,* edited by David Pentland, 210–11. Winnipeg: Univ. of Manitoba, 1997.

MacKenzie, John. "The Imperial Pioneer and Hunter and the British Masculine Stereotype in Late Victorian and Edwardian Times." In *Manliness and Morality: Middle Class Masculinity in Britain and North America, 1800–1940*, ed. J. A. Mangan and James Walvin, 176–98. New York: St. Martin's Press, 1987.

MacKenzie, Mary. *The Plains of Abraham: A History of North Elba and Lake Placid, The Collected Historical Writings of Mary MacKenzie*. Edited by Lee Manchester. Utica, NY: Nicholas K. Burn Publishing, 2007.

Manchester, Lee. "More from the Plains of Abraham." Document transcript. Accessed Jun. 16, 2012. http://www.slideshare.net/LeeManchester/more-from-the-plains-of-abraham.

Manore, Jeanne L. "The Technology of Rivers and Community Transformation: An Alternative History of the St. Francis." *Journal of Eastern Townships Studies* (Fall 2003): 27–40.

Manore, Jean L., and Dale Miner, eds. *The Culture of Hunting in Canada*. Vancouver: Univ. of British Columbia Press, 2007.

Marleau, William R. *Big Moose Station: A Story from 1893–1983*. Van Nuys, CA: Marleau Family Press, printed by Delta Lithograph, 1986.

Masten, Arthur H. *The Story of Adirondac*. Syracuse, NY: Syracuse Univ. Press and Adirondack Museum, 1968. First published in 1923.

Masters, Peg, and George Cataldo. "Howard Weiman Logging History Interview." Transcript. TWHA-GM.

May, Abigail. *Abigail May Journal at Ballstown Springs 1800*. Transcribed from the original by Field Horne. New York State Historical Association, 1982. Collection of Brookside Museum. SCHSRL.

McArthur, Thomas W. "History of Putnam." Manuscript in binder (completed but not edited, 1887, appears to have been typed in 1901). WCHSRL.

McBride, Bunny. *Molly Spotted Elk: A Penobscot in Paris*. Norman, OK: Univ. of Oklahoma Press, 1996.

McBride, Kari Boyd. "A (Boarding) House Is Not a Home: Women's Work and Woman's Worth on the Margins of Domesticity." *Frontiers* 17:1 (1996): 91–112.

McGregor, Jean (a.k.a. Evelyn Barrett). "Gift of Shirt to Indian Brought Bow and Arrow." *The Saratogian*, Apr. 23, 1948. CSSH.

———. "Little Remains of Old Indian Trail, Orchard." *The Saratogian*, May 27, 1949. CSSH.

———. "Unique Memorials Mark Graves of Indians in Greenridge Cemetery." *The Saratogian*, Apr. 27, 1945. CSSH.

McGuier, Henry, and F. B. Graham. "Indian Orchard." *Saratoga Daily Forum*, Jul. 12, 1858.

McKay, Ian. *The Quest of the Folk: Antimodernism and Cultural Selection in Twentieth-Century Nova Scotia*. Montreal: McGill-Queen's Univ. Press, 1994.

McNally, Michael D. "The Indian Passion Play: Contesting the Real Indian in Song of Hiawatha Pageants, 1901–1965." *American Quarterly* 58, no. 1 (Mar. 2006): 105–36.

Merchant, Carolyn. *Ecological Revolutions: Nature, Gender, and Science in New England*. Chapel Hill, NC: Univ. of North Carolina Press, 1989.

Merrell, James H. "The Indians' New World: The Catawba Experience." In *American Encounters: Natives and Newcomers from European Contact to Indian Removal, 1400–1850*, edited by Peter C. Mancall and James H. Merrell, 26–48. New York: Routledge, 2007.

———. "Second Thoughts on Colonial Historians and American Indians." *William and Mary Quarterly* 69, no. 3 (Jul. 2012): 451–512.

Miller, Flora. "Captain Peter Sabattis." Unknown publication. n.d. Biography file "Mitchel Sabattis." AM-BML.

Miller, P. Schuyler. "People Looking Down." *Cloud Splitter* (Feb. 1942): 2–3. Newsletter published by the Adirondack Mountain Club.

Miller, Roland B. "The Adirondack Pack-Basket." *New York State Conservationist* 3, no. 1 (Aug.–Sep. 1948): 8–9.

Morgan, Cecilia. "Creating Interracial Intimacies: British North America, Canada, and the Transatlantic World, 1830–1914." *Journal of the Canadian Historical Association/Revue de la Société historique du Canada* 19, no. 2 (2008): 76–104.

———. "'A Wigwam to Westminster': Performing Mohawk Identity in Imperial Britain, 1890s–1990s." *Gender and History* 15, no. 2 (Aug. 2003): 319–41.

Morning, Ann. "Ethnic Classification in Global Perspective: A Cross-National Survey of the 2000 Census Round." *Population Research and Policy Review* 27:2 (Apr. 2008): 239–72.

Murray, William H. H. *Adventures in the Wilderness*, edited by William K. Verner. Syracuse, NY: Syracuse Univ. Press/Adirondack Museum, 1989. First published in 1869.

Nash, Alice. "Odanak durant les années 1920: un prisme reflétant l'histoire des abénaquis" (translated by Claude Gélinas). *Recherches amérindiennes au Québec* 32, no. 2 (2002): 17–34.

———. "Théophile Panadis (1889–1966): Un guide abénaquis" (translated by Claude Gélinas). *Recherches amérindiennes au Québec* 33, no. 2 (2003): 75–92.

Nash, Gary B. "The Hidden History of Mestizo America." *Journal of American History* 87, no. 3 (Dec. 1995): 941–96.

National Institute of Culture and History, Institute of Archaeology. "Paleo-Indian Period." Accessed Jan. 18, 2013. http://www.nichbelize.org/ia-archaeology/paleo-indian-period.html.

Natural Resources Canada. "Deglacial History of the Champlain Sea Basin and Implications for Urbanization." *Geological Survey of Canada Open File 6947*. Joint annual meeting GAC-MAC-SEG-SGA, Ottawa, Ontario, May 25–27, 2011. Accessed Jul. 27, 2018. http://ftp.maps.canada.ca/pub/nrcan_rncan/publications/ess_sst/289/289555/of_6947.pdf.

Nelles, H. V. *The Art of Nation-Building: Pageantry and Spectacle at Quebec's Tercentenary*. Toronto: Univ. of Toronto Press, 2000.

Nesbitt, Thomas. "Native Americans and Colonial Rivalries: First Settlers to 1774." In *Warren County (NY): Its People and Their History Over Time*. Queensbury, NY: Warren County Historical Society, 2009.

New York State Constitution, Article VII (1894) (now article XIV). Accessed at New York State Department of Environmental Conservation "Article XIV of the New York State Constitution," Nov. 18, 2010. http://www.dec.ny.gov/lands/55849.html.

New York State Forest Commissioners. "Adirondack Guides." *New York State Forest Commissioners Annual Report, 1894*. Accessed Jul. 17, 2018. https://babel.hathitrust.org/cgi/pt?id=mdp.39015069540212;view=1up;seq=9.

———. *Annual Report of the Forest Commission of the State of New York, 1893*. Accessed Jul. 17, 2018. https://archive.org/details/annualreportforo4unkngoog.

New York State Office of Parks, Recreation and Historic Preservation. "Welcome to the Adirondack Region." Accessed Sep. 28, 2012. http://nysparks.com/regions/adirondack/default.aspx.

Nye, Eric W. "Pounds Sterling to Dollars: Historical Conversion of Currency." Univ. of Wyoming. Accessed Jun. 2, 2017, http://www.uwyo.edu/numimage/currency.htm.

O'Brien, Jean M. "Divorced from the Land: Accommodation Strategies of Indian Women in 18th Century New England." In *After King Philip's War: Presence and Persistence in Indian New England,* edited by Colin G. Calloway, 319–34. Hanover, NH: Univ. Press of New England, 1997.

———. *Firsting and Lasting: Writing Indians Out of Existence in New England.* Minneapolis: Univ. of Minnesota Press, 2010.

Olan, Kay. Survey sponsored by the Clinton County Museum in Plattsburgh. Funded by the New York State Council on the Arts. Jul. and Aug. 1987. SNM-O.

Olsen, Godfrey J. "Archeology of Ticonderoga." *Proceedings of the New York State Historical Association* 32 (1934): 407–11.

Osterud, Nancy Grey. *Bonds of Community: The Lives of Farm Women in Nineteenth-Century New York.* Ithaca, NY: Cornell Univ. Press, 1991.

Parenteau, Bill. "Care, Control, and Supervision: Native People in the Canadian Atlantic Salmon Fishery, 1867–1900." *Canadian Historical Review* 79, no. 1 (1998): 1–35.

Paris, Leslie. *Children's Nature: The Rise of the American Summer Camp.* New York: New York Univ. Press, 2008.

Parishville Historical Association, "The Early Settlers," in *Sketches of Parishville, 1809–1976.* Vertical file "Parishville." AM-BML.

Parker, Arthur C. *The Constitution of the Five Nations.* Albany, NY: New York State Museum, 1916.

———. "Iroquois Uses of Maize and Other Food Plants." *Education Department Bulletin of the New York State Museum,* No. 144. Nov. 1, 1910. Accessed Jul. 29, 2012. http://www.biodiversitylibrary.org/title/26294#page/126/mode/2up.

Parkhill, Thomas C. *Weaving Ourselves into the Land: Charles Godfrey Leland, "Indians," and the Study of Native American Religions.* Albany, NY: State Univ. of New York Press, 1997.

Parkman, Francis. *Historic Handbook of the Northern Tour: Lakes George and Champlain; Niagara; Montreal; and Quebec.* Boston: Little, Brown and Co., 1912.

Parmenter, Jon. "After the Mourning Wars: The Iroquois as Allies in Colonial North American Campaigns, 1676–1760." *William and Mary Quarterly*, 3d series, 64, no. 1 (Jan. 2007): 39–82.

———. *The Edge of the Woods: Iroquoia, 1534–1701*. East Lansing: Michigan State Univ. Press, 2010.

Pepper, Jerold. "When Men and Mountains Meet: Mapping the Adirondacks." In *Adirondack Prints and Printmakers: The Call of the Wild* edited by Caroline Mastin Welsh, 1–24. Blue Mountain Lake and Syracuse, NY: Adirondack Museum and Syracuse Univ. Press, 1998.

Perkins, G. H. "Archaeological Researches in the Champlain Valley." *International Congress of Anthropology* (1894): 84–91. Vertical file "Archaeology." AM-BML.

Philips, Lisa, and Allan K. McDougall. "Shifting Boundaries and the Baldoon Mysteries." In *Lines Drawn upon the Water: First Nations and the Great Lakes Borders and Borderlands*, edited by Karl S. Hele, 131–50. Waterloo, ON: Wilfrid Laurier Univ. Press, 2008.

Phillips, Ruth B. *Trading Identities: The Souvenir in Native North American Art from the Northeast, 1700–1900*. Seattle: Univ. of Washington Press, 1998.

Pickands, Martin. "Cultural Resources Reconnaissance Survey." *Cultural Resource Survey Program*. Sep. 2000. TWHA-GM.

Pike, Kenneth L. *Language in Relation to a Unified Theory of the Structure of Human Behavior*. Dallas, TX: Summer Institute of Linguistics, 1954.

Pilcher, Edith. *The Constables: First Family of the Adirondacks*. Utica, NY: North Country Books, 1992.

Plumwood, Val. "Wilderness Skepticism and Wilderness Dualism." In *The Great New Wilderness Debate: An Expansive Collection of Writings Defining Wilderness from John Muir to Gary Snyder*, edited by J. Baird Callicott and Michael P. Nelson, 652–90. Athens, GA: Univ. of Georgia Press, 1998.

Pollock, Della, ed. *Exceptional Spaces: Essays in Performance and History*. Chapel Hill: Univ. of North Carolina Press, 1998.

Porter, Tom Sakokweniónkwas. *And Grandma Said . . . : Iroquois Teachings as Passed Down through the Oral Tradition*. Transcribed and edited by Lesley Forrester. Bloomington, IN: Xlibris Corp. self-publishing, 2008.

Pownall, Thomas. *A Topographical Description of the Dominions of the United States of America*. Pittsburgh: Univ. of Pittsburgh Press, 1949.

Pratt, Mary Louise. *Imperial Eyes: Travel Writing and Transculturation*, 2nd ed. New York: Routledge, 2008.

Pray, Thomas. "Wolves of the Forest, Part 2." *Lake Champlain Weekly* [Plattsburgh, NY?], n.d.

Prince, J. Dyneley. "Some Forgotten Indian Place Names in the Adirondacks." *Journal of American Folklore* (1900): 123–28.

Québec Vital and Church Records (Drouin Collection). 1621–1968. Ancestry .ca records.

Radford, Harry V. "Mitchel Sabattis." *Shooting and Fishing: A Journal of the Rifle, Gun and Rod* 40, no. 3 (Apr. 26, 1906): 45–56.

Raibmon, Paige. *Authentic Indians: Episodes of Encounter from the Late-Nineteenth-Century Northwest Coast.* Durham, NC: Duke Univ. Press, 2005.

Raymond & Whitcomb Co. Guidebooks—Summer & Autumn Tours. 1911.

Raymond, Henry J. "A Week in the Wilderness: Fourth Letter." *New York Daily Times*, Jul. 24, 1855.

———. "A Week in the Wilderness: Third Letter, The Adirondack Iron Works and Beds—Return to Raquette Lake." *New York Times*, Jul. 7, 1855, 2.

Raymond, Henry W. *The Story of Saranac.* New York: Grafton Press, 1909.

Rayno, Paul. "Sabael, Indian guide," *Glens Falls Post-Star*, n.d. Biography file "Sabael Benedict." AM-BML.

Reagan, Jim. "Ever Wonder about the Original Names for Places in County?" *Massena Courier* (Aug. 1, 1994).

Reiger, John F. *American Sportsmen and the Origins of Conservation.* Norman, OK: Univ. of Oklahoma Press, 1986.

Remington, Emma. *A Heritage: The American Indian Town of Parishville.* (Parishville, NY: Parishville Museum, n.d.).

Richardson, Judith. *Possession: The History and Uses of Hauntings in the Hudson Valley.* Cambridge, MA: Cambridge Univ. Press, 2003.

Richter, Daniel K. *Facing East from Indian Country: A Native History of Early America.* Cambridge, MA: Harvard Univ. Press, 2003.

———. "Whose Indian History?" *William and Mary Quarterly* 50, no. 2 (Apr. 1993): 379–93.

Rickard, Jolene. "Intersectionality" Workshop. Centre for Transnational Cultural Analysis Series, Carleton University, Ottawa, Ontario, Nov. 18, 2016.

Riley, Ruth V. "Famous Adirondack Guides, No. 8, Mitchell Sabattis." *High Spots, a Magazine of the Adirondack Mountain Club* (n.d., but after 1930), 11–12. SLFL.

Roth, Richard Patrick. "The Adirondack Guide (1820–1919): Hewing Out an American Occupation." PhD diss., Syracuse University, 1990.

Roy, Christopher A. "Abenaki Sociality and the Work of Family History." PhD diss., Princeton University, 2012.

———. Letter to the Editor. *Adirondack Daily Enterprise* (Saranac Lake, NY). Jun. 23, 2009.

———. "Looking Back on the Life and Times of John Mitchell, Abenaki of Indian Lake." *Sun Community News* http://www.suncommunitynews .com/articles/the-sun/looking-back-on-the-life-and-times-of-john/? (Elizabethtown, NY). Jun. 24, 2009.

Roy, Christopher, and David Benedict. "Abenaki People in the Adirondacks—Mitchel Sabattis." *Adirondack Journal* (Warrensburg, NY). Jun. 7, 2009. Accessed Jul. 1, 2009. http://www.adkmuseum.org/about _us/adirondack_journal/?id=154.

Sahlins, Marshal. *Islands of History.* Chicago: Univ. of Chicago Press, 1985.

———. *Stone Age Economics.* Chicago: Aldine Atherton, 1972.

Salwen, Bert. "Indians of Southern New England and Long Island: Early Period." In *Handbook of the North American Indian, Northeast,* vol. 15, edited by Bruce G. Trigger, 160–76. Washington, DC: Smithsonian Institution, 1978.

Sandlos, John. "From the Outside Looking In: Aesthetics, Politics, and Wildlife Conservation in the Canadian North." *Environmental History* 6, no. 1 (2001): 6–31.

———. *Hunters at the Margin: Native People and Wildlife Conservation in the Northwest Territories.* Vancouver: Univ. of British Columbia Press, 2007.

Sandwell, Ruth W. *Contesting Rural Space: Land Policy and the Practices of Resettlement on Saltspring Island 1859–1891.* Montreal: McGill-Queen's Univ. Press, 2005.

———. "Rural Reconstruction: Towards a New Synthesis in Canadian History." *Histoire sociale/Social History* 53 (May 1994): 1–32.

Sassi, Anthony, and Janice Sassi. "Flint Quarry Discovered on Area Farm: Indians Found Stone for Tools and Weapons Near Fish Creek." Unknown publication, Apr. 8, 1965. Vertical file "Ethnic Heritage: American Indians/Native Americans-Newspaper Clippings." CSSH.

Schechner, Richard. *Performance Studies: An Introduction*. New York: Routledge, 2002.

Schneider, Paul. *The Adirondacks: A History of America's First Wilderness*. New York: H. Holt and Co., 1997.

Scott, James C. *The Art of Not Being Governed: An Anarchist History of Upland Southeast Asia*. New Haven, CT: Yale Univ. Press, 2009.

Seaman, Frances. "Adirondack Guides Hold a Special Place in History." *Hamilton County News* (Long Lake, NY), Aug. 4, 1992.

———. "Mitchel Sabattis Honored." *Hamilton County News* (Inlet, NY). Aug. 11, 1982.

———. "Old Indian Guide Recalled," n.p., n.d. Vertical file "Sabattis Family." LLA.

Seaver, Frederick J. *Historical Sketches of Franklin County and Its Several Towns with Many Short Biographies*. Albany, NY: J. B Lyon Co., 1918.

Shoemaker, Nancy. *A Strange Likeness: Becoming Red and White in Eighteenth-Century North America*. New York: Oxford Univ. Press, 2004.

Sigurdsson, Frances. "The Sacandaga Saga: How the Creation of New York's Eighth-Largest Lake Left a Flood of Memories." *Adirondack Life* 33, no. 2 (Jul.–Aug. 2002): 39–45, 70.

Silverman, David J. *Red Brethren: The Brothertown and Stockbridge Indians and the Problem of Race in Early America*. Ithaca, NY: Cornell Univ. Press, 2011.

Simms, Jeptha R. *Trappers of New York, or a Biography of Nicholas Stoner and Nathaniel Foster; Together with Anecdotes of Other Celebrated Hunters*. Albany, NY: J. Munsell, 1850.

Sinclair, Niigaanwewidam James. "Kzaugin, Storying Ourselves into Life." In *Centering Anishinaabeg Studies: Understanding the World through Stories*, edited by Jill Doerfler, Niigaanwewidam James Sinclair, and Heidi Kiiwetinepinesiik Stark, 81–102. East Lansing: Michigan State Univ. Press and Univ. of Manitoba Press, 2013.

Sleeper-Smith, Susan. "Women, Kin and Catholicism: New Perspectives on the Fur Trade." In *In the Days of Our Grandmothers: A Reader in Aboriginal Women's History in Canada*, edited by Mary-Ellen Kelm and Lorna Townsend, 26–55. Toronto: Univ. of Toronto Press, 2006.

Sleeper-Smith, Susan, Juliana Barr, Jean M. O'Brien, Nancy Shoemaker, and Scott Manning Stevens. *Why You Can't Teach United States History without American Indians.* Chapel Hill: Univ. of North Carolina Press, 2015.

Smashwood, Gregory. Obituary. *Elizabethtown Post,* Apr. 21, 1887.

Smith, H. P., ed. *History of Warren County with Illustrations and Biographical Sketches of Some of Its Prominent—Men and Pioneers.* Syracuse, NY: D. Mason and Co., 1885.

Smith, Nicholas N. "Fort La Presentation: The Abenaki." *St. Lawrence County Historical Association Quarterly* 38, no. 1 (Winter 1993): 9–14.

Snow, Dean R. *The Iroquois.* Malden, MA: Blackwell Press, 2004.

———. *Mohawk Valley Archaeology: The Sites.* Albany, NY: Institute for Archaeological Studies, Univ. of Albany Press, 1995.

Snow, Dean R., Charles T. Gehring, and William A. Starna, eds. *In Mohawk Country: Early Narratives about a Native People.* Syracuse, NY: Syracuse Univ. Press, 1996.

Snow, Dean R., and Kim M. Lanphear. "European Contact and Indian Depopulation in the Northeast: The Timing of the First Epidemics." *Ethnohistory* 35 (1988): 15–33.

Sorrell, William H. Attorney General for the State of Vermont and Eve Jacobs—Carnahan, Special Assistant Attorney General. *Vermont's Response to the Abenaki Nation: State of Vermont's Response to Petition for Federal Acknowledgement of the St. Francis/Sokoki Band of the Abenaki Nation of Vermont.* Dec. 2002 (2nd printing).

Spence, Mark David. *Dispossessing the Wilderness: Indian Removal and the Making of National Parks.* New York: Oxford Univ. Press, 1999.

Sprague, Ken. "Take a First Look at the Hollywood Hills Hotel." *Adirondack Express.* Accessed Jul. 24, 2018. https://www.adirondackexpress.com/take-a-first-look-at-the-hollywood-hills-hotel-by-ken-sprague/.

Spring, George H. "The Annual Indian Pageant at Ticonderoga." *North Country Life* (Summer 1948): 32–39.

Starna, William A. "Mohawk Iroquois Populations: A Revision." *Ethnohistory* 27 (1980): 371–82.

———. "The Oneida Homeland in the Seventeenth Century." In *The Oneida Indian Experience: Two Perspectives,* edited by Jack Campisi and Laurence M. Hauptman, 9–22. Syracuse, NY: Syracuse Univ. Press, 1988.

Starna, William A., and José António Brandão. "From the Mohawk-Mahican War to the Beaver Wars: Questioning the Pattern." *Ethnohistory* 51, no. 4 (Fall 2004): 725–50.

State Commissions of New York and Vermont and of the Central Vermont Delaware & Hudson and Rutland Railroads. "Champlain Tercentenary Celebration July 4–10, 1909." Brochure. Vertical file "Vermont/New York Boundary Lines Records, 1814–1985." VSAR.

Statistics Canada. "Urban Perspectives and Measurements." Modified Nov. 30, 2015. Accessed Jul. 24, 2018. https://www150.statcan.gc.ca/n1/pub/92f0138m/92f0138m2009001-eng.htm.

Stewart, Susan. *On Longing: Narratives of the Miniature, the Gigantic, the Souvenir, the Collection*. Baltimore, MD: Johns Hopkins Univ. Press, 1984.

Stiles, Fred Tracy. *From Then Till Now: History and Tales of the Adirondack Foothills*. Hudson Falls, NY: Washington County Historical Society, 1978.

Stockbridge-Munsee Community, Band of Mohican Indians (community website). Accessed Jul. 26, 2012. http://mohican-nsn.gov.

Stoddard, Seneca Ray. *The Adirondacks: Illustrated*. Albany, NY: Weed, Parsons and Co., 1874.

———. *The Adirondacks Illustrated 38th Year*. Glens Falls, NY: Published by the author, 1912.

———. *Lake George (Illustrated): A Book of To-Day*. Glens Falls, NY: published by the author; Albany, NY: Van Benthuysen and Sons, 1879.

———. "Sagamore Dock." 1906. Photograph #1112. AM-BML.

Stone, William L. *Reminiscences of Saratoga and Ballston*. New York: R. Worthington, 1880.

Strauss, David. "Toward a Consumer Culture: 'Adirondack Murray' and the Wilderness Vacation." *American Quarterly* 39, no. 2 (Summer 1987): 270–83.

Street, Alfred Billings. *The Indian Pass*. New York: Kurd and Houghton, 1869. Accessed May 4, 2013. https://archive.org/details/indianpassoostrerich.

———. *Woods and Waters; or, The Saranacs and Racket*. New York: M. Doolady, 1860.

Strong-Boag, Veronica, and Carole Gerson. *Paddling Her Own Canoe: The Times and Texts of E. Pauline Johnson Tekahionwake*. Toronto: Univ. of Toronto Press, 2000.

Stuckey, Mary E., and John M. Murphy. "By Any Other Name: Rhetorical Colonialism in North America." *American Indian Culture and Research Journal* 25, no. 4 (2001): 73–98.

Sulavik, Stephen B. *Adirondack: Of Indians and Mountains, 1535–1838*. Fleischmanns, NY: Purple Mountain Press, and Blue Mt. Lake, NY: Adirondack Museum, 2005.

Surtees, Robert J. "The Iroquois in Canada." In *The History and Culture of Iroquois Diplomacy: An Interdisciplinary Guide to the Treaties of the Six Nations and Their League*, edited by Francis Jennings et al., 67–83. Syracuse, NY: Syracuse Univ. Press, 1985.

Sylvester, Nathaniel Bartlett. *Historical Sketches of Northern New York and the Adirondack Wilderness: Including Traditions of the Indians, Early Explorers, Pioneer Settlers, Hermit Hunters, &c*. Harrison, NY: Harbor Hill Books, 1973. First published in 1877.

———. *The Historic Muse on Mount MacGregor, One of the Adirondacks near Saratoga*. Troy, NY: N. B. Sylvester, 1885.

———. *History of Saratoga County, New York with Historical Notes on Its Various Towns: Together with Biographical Sketches of Its Prominent Men and Leading Citizens*. Chicago: Gresham Publishing Co., 1893.

Taintor Brothers & Co. *Saratoga Illustrated: The Visitor's Guide of Saratoga Springs*. NY: Taintor Brothers, 1889.

Tanner, W. S. "W. S. Tanner, Lawrence, Kansas, Gives Exclusive Sale to One Merchant in a City of his St. Regis Indian Fancy Baskets." Photograph c. 1894. LC-USZ62-132279, Library of Congress Prints and Photographs Division. Accessed Jan. 21, 2012. http://www.loc.gov/pictures/resource/cph.3c32279/.

Taylor, Alan. "Captain Hendrick Aupaumut: The Dilemmas of an Intercultural Broker." *Ethnohistory* 43, no. 3 (Summer 1996): 431–57.

———. *The Civil War of 1812: American Citizens, British Subjects, Irish Rebels, and Indian Allies*. New York: Vintage Books, 2011.

———. *The Divided Ground: Indians, Settlers, and the Northern Borderland of the American Revolution*. New York: Vintage Books, 2006.

———. *William Cooper's Town: Power and Persuasion on the Frontier of the Early American Republic*. New York: A.A. Knopf: Distributed by Random House, 1995.

Terrie, Philip G. *Contested Terrain: A New History of Nature and People in the Adirondacks*. Syracuse, NY: Syracuse Univ. Press, 1997.

———. *Forever Wild: Environmental Aesthetics and the Adirondack Forest Preserve*. Philadelphia: Temple Univ. Press, 1985.

————. *Wildlife and Wilderness: A History of Adirondack Mammals*. Fleischmanns, NY: Purple Mountain Press, 1993.

Thieret, John W. "Bryophytes as Economic Plants." *Economic Botany* 10, no. 1 (Jan.–Mar. 1956): 75–91.

Thom, Brian. "The Paradox of Boundaries in Coast Salish Territories." *Cultural Geographies* 16, no. 2 (Apr. 2009): 179–205.

Thomas, Lester St. John, assisted by Evelyn Cirino Donohue and Anita Beaudette Ranado. *Timber, Tannery and Tourists*. Lake Luzerne, NY, Committee on Publication of Local History, 1979.

Thompson, Adele S. "Sacandaga: Coney Island of the North." *Adirondack Life* (Spring 1976): 14–17.

Thoreau, Henry David. *The Maine Woods*, with introduction by Edward Hoagland. New York: Penguin Books, 1988. First published in Boston: Ticknor and Fields: 1864.

Timms, Ruth. *Raquette Lake: A Time to Remember*. Utica, NY: North Country Books, 1989.

Tiro, Karim M. *The People of the Standing Stone: The Oneida Nation from the Revolution through the Era of Removal*. Amherst: Univ. of Massachusetts Press, 2011.

Todd, Rev. John. *Long Lake*. Fleishmanns, NY: Purple Mountain Press, 1997. First published in 1845.

————. *Summer Gleanings; or, Sketches and Incidents of a Pastor's Vacation*. Collected and arranged by his daughter. Northampton: Hopkins, Bridgman, and Co. 1852.

Tooker, Elisabeth. "The League of the Iroquois: Its History, Politics, and Ritual." In *Handbook of the North American Indian, Northeast*, vol. 15, edited by Bruce G. Trigger, 418–41. Washington, DC: Smithsonian Institution, 1978.

Tough, Frank. *"As Their Natural Resources Fail": Native Peoples and the Economic History of Northern Manitoba, 1870–1930*. Vancouver: Univ. of British Columbia Press, 1996.

Trautsch, Jasper M. "'Mr. Madison's War' or the Dynamic of Early American Nationalism." *Early American Studies* (Fall 2012): 630–70.

Travelers Steamboat & RR Guide to the Hudson River, Describing the Cities, Towns & Places of Interest along the Route with Maps & Engravings. New York: Phelps and Watson, 1857.

Trent University. Indigenous Studies PhD. "Program Objectives." Accessed Apr. 26, 2012. http://www.trentu.ca/indigenousstudiesphd/program objectives.php.

Trigger, Bruce G. "Early Iroquoian Contacts with Europeans." *Handbook of North American Indians: Northeast,* vol. 15, edited by Bruce G. Trigger, 344–56. Washington, DC: Smithsonian Institution, 1978.

———. *The Children of Aateaentsic: A History of the Huron People to 1660.* Montreal: McGill-Queens Univ. Press, 1976.

Trigger, Bruce G., ed. *Handbook of the North American Indians: Northeast,* vol. 15. Washington, DC: Smithsonian Institution, 1978.

Turner, Frederick Jackson. *The Significance of the Frontier in American History.* Indianapolis: Bobbs-Merrill, 1894. Accessed May 8, 2012. http://xroads.virginia.edu/~hyper/turner/home.html.

Turner, Victor. *From Ritual to Theater: The Human Seriousness of Play.* New York: PAJ Publications, 2001.

University of Iowa. "Archaic Period." *Office of the State Archaeologist, Educational Series 2.* Teacher's pamphlet. Accessed Jan. 18, 2013. http://www.uiowa.edu/~osa/learn/teachers/pamphlets/Archaic-8.pdf.

Urry, John. *The Tourist Gaze.* 2nd ed. London: Sage Publications, 2002.

US Constitution, Amendment XV, §1. Ratified 1870. Accessed at "Fifteenth Amendment to the Constitution: Primary Documents of American History," Library of Congress, Oct. 3, 2012. http://memory.loc.gov/cgi-bin/ampage?collId=llsl&fileName=015/llslo15.db&recNum=379.

US Congress. *Indian Removal Act of 1830,* Stat. 1 (May 28, 1830), 21st Cong., session 1, chap. 148.

———. *Tariff of 1890.* HR 9416. Oct. 1, 1890.

US Department of Health and Human Services, "Defining the Rural Population." Accessed Feb. 10, 2015. http://www.hrsa.gov/ruralhealth/policy/definition_of_rural.html.

US Statutes at Large 43 (1924). Also known as the Indian Citizenship Act.

Usner, Daniel H., Jr. *Indian Work: Language and Livelihood in Native American History.* Cambridge, MA: Harvard Univ. Press, 2009.

Van Kirk, Sylvia. *Many Tender Ties: Women in Fur-Trade Society, 1670–1870.* Winnipeg: Watson and Dwyer, 1999. First published in 1980.

Van Zandt, Cynthia J. *Brothers among Nations: The Pursuit of Intercultural Alliances in Early America, 1580–1660.* Oxford: Oxford Univ. Press, 2008.

Vaughn, Karen I. "John Locke and the Labor Theory of Value." *Journal of Libertarian Studies* 2, no. 4 (1978): 311–26.

Venables, Robert W. "The Clearings and the Woods: The Haudenosaunee (Iroquois) Landscape, Gendered *and* Balanced." In *Archaeology and Preservation of Gendered Landscapes,* edited by Sherene Baugher and Suzanne M. Spencer-Wood, 21–55. New York and London: Springer Books, 2010.

Verhovek, Sam Howe. "Standoff Ends, but Not Mohawk Defiance." *New York Times,* Apr. 14, 1990, 26. Accessed Mar. 25, 2016. http://www.nytimes.com/1990/04/14/nyregion/standoff-ends-but-not-mohawk-defiance.html.

Vibert, Elizabeth. "Real Men Hunt Buffalo: Masculinity, Race, and Class in British Fur Traders' Narratives." In *Cultures of Empire: Colonizers in Britain and the Empire of the Nineteenth and Twentieth Centuries,* edited by Catherine Hall, 281–97. New York: Routledge, 2000.

Vila, Bob. "Great Camp Sagamore," *YouTube* (video). Accessed Jul. 19, 2018. https://www.youtube.com/watch?v=OI6PtZ4s7kg.

Vizenor, Gerald. "Constitution of the White Earth Nation: Definitions of Selected Words." *Anishinaabeg Today,* Sep. 2, 2009, 19.

Wall, Sharon. *The Nurture of Nature: Childhood, Antimodernism, and Ontario Summer Camps, 1920–55.* Vancouver: Univ. of British Columbia Press, 2009.

Wallace, E. R. *Descriptive Guide to the Adirondacks, and Handbook of Travel,* 10th ed. Syracuse, NY: Watson Gill, 1882.

Waller, George. *Saratoga: Saga of an Impious Age.* Englewood Cliffs, NJ: Prentice-Hall, 1966.

Warren, Louis. *The Hunter's Game: Poachers and Conservationists in Twentieth-Century America.* New Haven, CT: Yale Univ. Press, 1997.

———. "The Nature of Conquest: Indians, Americans, and Environmental History." In *A Companion to American Indian History,* edited by Philip J. Deloria and Neal Salisbury, 287–306. Malden, MA: Blackwell Publishing, 2004.

Warrick, Gary. *A Population History of the Huron-Petun, A.D. 500–1650.* Cambridge: Cambridge Univ. Press, 2008.

Watson, Winslow C. *Pioneer History of the Champlain Valley: Being an Account of the Settlement of the Town of Willsborough by William Gilliland, Together with His Journal and Other Papers: And a Memoir, and Historical and Illustrative Notes.* [Albany, NY?]: J. Munsell, 1863.

Webb, Nina H. *Footsteps through the Adirondacks: The Verplanck Colvin Story.* Utica, NY: North Country Books, 1996.

Webber, Charles Wilkins. *The Hunter-Naturalist: Romance of Sporting; or Wild Scenes and Wild Hunters.* Philadelphia: J. B. Lippincott, 1867.

Wessels, William L. "The Abenaki Indians, Early Adirondack Settlers: Architects of the Birch Bark Canoe and the Pack Basket." *Warrensburg News*, Jun. 19, 1969.

———. *Adirondack Profiles.* Lake George, NY: Adirondack Resorts Press, 1961.

Westcott, Lorraine. "Indian Tales Fascinate Historian," Strands of Time, unknown publication. Feb. 1988, 1c. CSSH.

Whisnant, David. *All that Is Native and Fine: The Politics of Culture in an American Region.* Chapel Hill: Univ. of North Carolina Press, 1983.

White, Richard. *The Middle Ground: Indians, Empires and Republics in the Great Lakes Region, 1650–1815.* New York: Cambridge Press, 1991.

Williams, Carol J. *Framing the West: Race, Gender, and the Photographic Frontier in the Pacific Northwest.* Oxford: Oxford Univ. Press, 2003.

Williams, Robert, Jr. *Linking Arms Together: American Indian Treaty Visions of Law and Peace, 1600–1800.* New York: Routledge, 1999.

"Window Display for 'Dr Morse's Indian Root Pills' Colour lithographs, 19th century." Welcome Collection. Accessed Feb. 1, 2013. https://wellcomecollection.org/works/usbmwuxp?query=Window%20Display%20for%20%27Dr%20Morse%27s%20Indian%20Root%20Pills%27&page=1.

Wisecup, Kelly. "Medicine, Communication, and Authority in Samson Occom's Herbal." *Early American Studies* (Fall 2012): 540–65.

Wiseman, Frederick Matthew. *The Voice of the Dawn: An Autohistory of the Abenaki Nation.* Hanover, NH: Univ. Press of New England, 2001.

Wolfe, Patrick. "Settler Colonialism and the Elimination of the Native." *Journal of Genocide Research* 84, no. 4 (2006): 387–409.

———. "The Settler Complex: An Introduction." *American Indian Culture and Research Journal* 37, no. 2 (2013): 1–17.

Woodard, Genevieve. "American Indians in Washington County, New York." Vertical file "Indians of North America." WCHSRL.

Woods, Lynn. "A History in Fragments: Following the Forgotten Trail of Native Adirondack Cultures." *Adirondack Life* 25, no. 7 (Nov.–Dec. 1994): 30–37, 61, 68–72, 78–79.

Yellow Bird, Michael. "What We Want to Be Called: Indigenous Peoples' Perspectives on Racial and Ethnic Identity Labels." *American Indian Quarterly* 23, no. 2 (Spring 1999): 1–21.

Index

Italic page numbers denote illustrations.

Onondaga, 10, 17–18, 21, 61, 64–65,
73–74, 161, 164
Oswegatchie community (La Présen-
tation or La Galette), 10, 18,
64–65, 73–74, 266
Oswegatchie River, 47–48, 62
Oteatohatongwan (Colonel Louis
[Lewis] Cook), 18
Otondosonne, Watso. *See* Watso,
Louis
Otter Creek, NY (Lewis County), 93
Owens, Martha-Lee Edmonds
(unknown Native ancestry), 224.
See also Edmonds, Florence

pack-basket, 39, 128, 142. *See also*
basketmaker/basketmaking
pageants, 207–10, 213. *See also* Indi-
anness; playing Indian
Pakikan, Mary (Marie Anne). *See*
Traversey, Mary (Marie Anne)
Pakikan
Palmertown (Palmerton) Indians, 60,
66, 286n15
Palmertown (Palmerton) Mountains,
60, 66
Panadis, Ana (Abenaki), 212
Panadis, Joseph (Abenaki), 80
Panadis, Lazare. *See* Benedict, Louis
Elijah
Panadis, Xavier. *See* Benedict, Sabael
Parishville, NY (St. Lawrence
County), 67, 82, 122
Parker, Arthur C. (Seneca), 164,
316n46
Paul, Anthony (reverend) (Wampa-
noag), 125–26, 152–53
Paul, Benoni (probably Wampanoag
and Mohegan or Stockbridge), 63

Paul, Christiana Occom (Mohegan),
126, 153
Paul, Christina. *See* Jaqua, Christina
Paul
Paul, James (probably Wampanoag
and Mohegan or Stockbridge), 93
Paul, John (probably Wampanoag and
Mohegan or Stockbridge), 63
Paul, Moses (probably Wampanoag
and Mohegan or Stockbridge), 63
Paul, Samson (probably Wampanoag
and Mohegan or Stockbridge), 64,
75–76
Paul Smiths Hotel, 117, 154
Pezeeko (Mohawk), 75
performance, 25, 176–77, 178–82,
193; marketing strategy, 187–90
Petty, Clarence, 186–87
photographs, 193–96
Picketville, NY (St. Lawrence
County), 67
Piseco Lake (Hamilton County), 41,
45, 52, 75
place of labor and resources, 38–50,
60–61
place of refuge, 6–7, 56, 58–59, 65–70,
72–77. *See also* zone of refuge
plant gathering, 40, 46–47
playing Indian, 135, 203–5, 207–10
Plumley, John, 122, 134
Podunk Indians, 42, 66, 266
politics of culture, 108–9
population, difficult to define, 5–6
Porter, Tom (Sagogweniongwass)
(Mohawk), 37, 178, 220, 223
Port Leyden, NY, 93
Powlus (Mohawk), 94
primitivism, 107, 146. *See also* antimodernism; wilderness tourism
Puffer Pond, 66, 83

Melissa Otis grew up in a small town in the Adirondacks of northeastern New York State. She received her doctorate from the University of Toronto and completed a postdoctoral fellowship at Carleton University in Ottawa. Her scholarship focuses on the history of Iroquoian and Algonquian peoples during the nineteenth and twentieth centuries, a period that is deficient in regional and national narratives. She employs ethnohistorical methodology and is especially interested in the use of material culture as historical primary sources. Otis explores history as a narrative that focuses on sites of encounter, where Indigenous and non-Indigenous peoples interacted and negotiated boundaries of various types over time. She believes an accurate history of the Indigenous peoples of the Western Hemisphere from precontact to the present should be included in social studies and history curricula. This inclusion would represent an embryonic effort to decolonize and reconcile the relationship between Indigenous peoples and settler society who share these lands, albeit unequally. Otis views her scholarship as a way to contribute to this endeavor.

CPSIA information can be obtained
at www.ICGtesting.com
Printed in the USA
LVHW110614021220
673142LV00005B/454